THE SCIENCE
IN SCIENCE FICTION

General Editor Peter Nicholls
Contributors David Langford Brian Stableford

CRESCENT BOOKS
NEW YORK

This 1987 edition published by Crescent Books,
distributed by Crown Publishers, Inc., 225 Park
Avenue South, New York, New York 10003

Editor: Carolyn Eardley
Design: Elizabeth Palmer
Picture Research: Janet Croall and Peter Nicholls
Typesetting: York House Typographic
Reproduction by F. E. Burman Limited, London

Made by Roxby Science Fiction Limited
A division of Roxby Press Ltd.

Library of Congress Cataloging-in-Publication Data

The science in science fiction.

Reprint. Originally published: London: Book Club
Associates, 1982.
Bibliography: p.
Includes index.
1. Science – Popular works.   2. Science fiction.
I. Nicholls, Peter, 1939-   II. Langford, David.
III. Stableford, Brian M.
Q162. S4127   1987   500   87-15542
ISBN 0-517-65335-4

h g f e d c b a

Contents

Introduction 7

CHAPTER 1 Journey into space
Starships: the problem of distance 8
Starships: propulsion methods 10
The ramscoop starship 14
The generation starship 16
Where are the space arks? 18
Space habitats 19
Sports in space 22
Mining the Moon and the asteroids 23
Colonizing other planets 26
Terraforming 28

CHAPTER 2 The secret is energy
Where has all the power gone? 30
Nuclear fission 32
Energy doubling and waste heat 34
Nuclear fusion 37
Renewable energy sources 39
Solar power from satellites 42
Far-future energy 44

CHAPTER 3 Aliens
Are we alone? 46
Alien intelligences on Earth 49
First contact 51
Alien body chemistry 52
Alien appearances 56
Alien life-styles 58
Alien societies 62

CHAPTER 4 The limits of the possible
Imaginary science in science fiction 66
Faster than light and relativity 68
Hyperspace 72
Instantaneous communication 74
The beginning of the universe 76
Antimatter 78
Gravity and antigravity 80
Stars, neutron stars and black holes 82
Entropy and the end of the universe 86

CHAPTER 5 Time travel and other universes
What is time? 88
Time travel in science fiction 90
Time as scientists see it 92
Time travel in physics 94
Alternative universes in science fiction 97
Alternative universes in physics 98

CHAPTER 6 Holocaust and catastrophe
Warfare in science fiction 102
Future weaponry 104
CBW: chemical and biological warfare 107
Nuclear holocaust 109
Natural disasters 112

A new Ice Age or a drowned world? 114
Plague, pollution, overpopulation and famine 116
Reconstruction scenarios 118

CHAPTER 7 Intelligent machines
Mechanical brains 120
Automation and industrial robots 122
Data networks 125
Artificial intelligence 127
Robots 130
Cybernetics and information technology 132
Matter transmission 135

CHAPTER 8 Men and supermen
Better brains 136
How mutations work 138
New organs for old 140
Cyborgs 142
Ageing and immortality 144
Cryonics 147
Genetic engineering 148
Clones 150
Biological engineering: other methods 152
Androids 153
Pantropy: new men for new worlds 154

CHAPTER 9 Dreams and nightmares of the future
Machines and the leisure society 156
Technological tyranny 159
Conditioning and brainwashing 161
Psychotropic drugs 163
Crime and punishment 165

CHAPTER 10 Powers of the mind
The fringes of mental science 168
Psionics 170
Telepathy and the information talents 172
Telekinesis and the brute-force talents 174

CHAPTER 11 Mysteries of the past and present
Flying saucers 176
Ancient astronauts? 180
Vanished civilizations? 184
Children of the wild? 188

CHAPTER 12 Where science fiction gets it wrong
Wrong science in science fiction 190
The hollow Earth 193
Very big and very small 194
Elementary errors in physics 196
Invisibility 198
Force fields and force shields 199
Famous bad predictions 200

Bibliography 202
Acknowledgements 206
Index 207

Introduction

Today, more than ever before, we are aware of the future. The images of science fiction are being thrown at us from all sides, whether we are enthusiasts or not. We can only guess at how accurate these images of the future will turn out to be. They cannot all be correct, because they contradict one another. In one scenario humanity is reaching for the stars in shimmering silver ships; in another we live in a nightmare of computerized surveillance systems; in a third, mankind is reduced to a handful of demoralized, tribal savages, scrabbling for a living among the ruins of a once great civilization. We do not know which of these and hundreds of other alternatives will turn out to be right, but we can ask, 'Could this scenario happen?' In other words, are these images of the future grounded in real science?

Science fiction is seldom, however, intended as direct prediction. More commonly, it asks the question, 'What if . . .?' Although few science fiction writers will admit to being in the prophecy business, many of their predictions have come true: from the water bed to the atom bomb, from H.G. Wells's tanks to Aldous Huxley's euphoria drugs, from artificial satellites (first predicted in 1869) to the most spectacular of all — mankind's first steps on the surface of the Moon.

There is no miracle involved when science fiction writers make good predictions. The good ones keep abreast of scientific and technological developments. Jules Verne, to take an early example, did not himself invent the submarine. But he knew of developments in submarine engineering of which his readership did not, and was able to extrapolate from these. The same applies to nuclear power. Ever since the discovery of radioactivity in the last century, scientists have theorized about the energy locked up in the atom. It is not therefore surprising that numerous writers predicted the atom bomb many years before the first such weapon was actually built.

It can even be argued that science fiction helps to create the very futures it describes, by preparing people's minds for them. Take the example of space travel. The space race was set off by the launching of the first Russian *Sputnik*. Obviously, in terms of improved surveillance techniques and possible advances in weaponry, the Russians had much to gain by entering space. But it is surely more than coincidence that Konstantin Tsiolkovsky, the first scientist to work out the theory of astronautics and rocketry, the father of space flight, was also a science fiction writer. His visionary works were enormously popular in Russia, and his widely publicized dreams encouraged the Russian people to desire the reality. Similarly, the American response to *Sputnik* went beyond the practical — orbital satellites — to the deeply romantic — a landing on the Moon. Why did the hard-headed American government grant NASA such a huge budget for a project with not much chance — it seemed initially — of a practical payoff? Surely the attempt to regain international prestige is not the whole story; many of the senators and congressmen who voted money for the conquest of the Moon must have shared, in a sense, a childhood dream: the reaching of the Moon was the central, passionate symbol of the science fiction they had grown up with.

There are many different kinds of science in science fiction. The best known variety consists of imaginary future technologies that are extrapolated (like Jules Verne's submarine) from what we already know. Some of these developments will almost certainly take place in the near future: cloning, for example, and the creation of machine intelligences. Others, such as ramscoop starships, may still be rather a long way off. More than half of this book is about speculative science of this kind.

Another important kind of science in science fiction is 'imaginary' science, which tends to be much more speculative and often much sillier than the first sort. Most forms of imaginary science used to be regarded merely as useful plot devices, exploited by writers who did not seriously believe that they could ever exist in reality. Three of the commonest examples are time machines, hyperspace travelling, and the idea of alternate universes. Yet modern physics now gives some warrant for ideas as strange as these and even stranger. We can no longer afford to dismiss 'imaginary' science quite as contemptuously or patronizingly as was recently the case. Chapters 4 and 5 of this book are largely devoted to the imaginary science in science fiction.

Then there is the controversial science: those areas of speculation that are rejected by a majority of the scientific community, but pursued by an extremely well publicized minority. We look at some of these in Chapters 10 and 11, and ask such questions as: 'Are there really flying saucers?', 'Does telepathy exist?', 'Did Uri Geller really bend forks?', 'Was there an Atlantis?'.

Not all science fiction is about science. Much of it is thinly disguised fantasy, or frontier-style adventure stories in a new, exotic setting; some of the rest is based on sociological speculation rather than hard science. But this book focuses on the area of science fiction that actually contains science proper. This does not mean that we have confined ourselves to 'intellectual' science fiction. There is plenty of science at the more popular end of the science fiction spectrum, too,

though it is not always good science. We have as much to say about the antimatter drive of *Star Trek* and the space battles of *Star Wars* as we do about the clones imagined in Aldous Huxley's more literary classic, *Brave New World*.

Science fiction is about as old as modern science; it dates back to the industrial revolution. Its changing nature throughout the nineteenth and twentieth centuries has been, among other things, a reflection of the changing nature of science itself, where the old, mechanistic certainties have been lost, to be replaced by a much more complex, tenuous and uncertain pattern of nature's workings. But science fiction, along with public understanding generally, has often lagged behind. Long after the atom was known by physicists to be made up of a complex, uncertainly shifting pattern of protons, neutrons and electrons, science fiction writers were still producing stories about incredible shrinking men who discover that atoms are solid little worlds with tiny people — including princesses — living on their surface. Things are on the whole more plausible now, at least in science fiction in its written form. But science fiction in comics, in illustrations, in the cinema and on our television screens still commits a great many howlers.

There has always been some science fiction that was plausible and responsible. Wells, Huxley and quite a few others had fine, trained, scientific minds. Perhaps too much emphasis has been placed in histories of science fiction on what we might call the 'American' line of development: the gaudy, pulp-magazine adventure stories in the tradition of Edgar Rice Burroughs and his 'Barsoom' and 'Tarzan' books. In Britain, during the 1920s and 1930s, science fiction was not typecast to nearly the same extent as in America as a vulgar

literature, aimed at immature and credulous minds, and completely isolated from the mainstream. Yet, since then, America has produced more good science fiction writers than any other country.

It was not until the 1950s that much science fiction, especially in the USA, reached the comparative respectability of book publication. But the pulp magazines had already improved miraculously, so far as scientific plausibility went, by the beginning of the 1940s. This was because a new generation of writers who really knew and cared about science had arrived on the scene. Many of their names are remembered well, and some of them are still writing — Robert Heinlein and Isaac Asimov were among them. Their stories were still very often written in the crude, racy, hard-bitten dialect of the pulps, but their ideas were fresh and hypnotically interesting. Most of our book is devoted to this generation of writers, and to the increasingly sophisticated writers who have built on their foundations. But today's writers are not immune to ignorance and foolishness. We have thus included a final chapter on the 'wrong' science in science fiction — the often repeated howlers of then and now.

Chapters 1, 2 and 5 and part of 7 are by Peter Nicholls; Chapters 3, part of 7, 8, 9 and 11 are by Brian Stableford; Chapters 4, 6, 10 and 12 are by David Langford. At the end of the book we have included a bibliography with dates and title changes of all the books and stories mentioned in the text, along with suggestions for further reading about the scientific background.

When we use the word 'billion' in this book, we use it in the American sense, that is, 1000 million.

Chapter 1
JOURNEY INTO SPACE

Man has landed on the Moon, and unmanned probes have visited Mercury, Venus, Mars, Jupiter and Saturn. But how likely is it that mankind will ever reach the stars? This, for many years, has been the dominant theme of science fiction.

Starships: the problem of distance

Man has done well in his conquering of the Solar System. In half a century we have progressed from flimsy biplanes to the landing of men on the Moon. We are still a long way from landing men on the other planets, but we have taken the first steps. Space probes have landed on Mars and Venus, and have photographed Mercury, Jupiter and Saturn at close range.

But visiting the stars means travel on an almost unimaginable scale. Today *Apollo* craft take 3 days to reach the Moon, approximately 375,000 km away. In 1973 it took *Pioneer 10* 21 months, achieving a speed of 14 km per second, to reach Jupiter. It will leave the Solar System in 1987, and if it were pointed at one of the nearest stars, Alpha Centauri (which it is not), it would take over 80,000 years to arrive — and there may be little point in visiting Alpha Centauri. For a long time it was thought that the nearest star with any likelihood of possessing a planetary system for possible colonization was Barnard's Star, which is nearly half as far again as Alpha Centauri. But very recent work has cast doubt even on this.

We have now aimed four probes out of the Solar System — *Pioneer 10* and *11* and *Voyager 1* and *2* — but it may be a million years before any of them passes close to a star, although they bear messages for any alien race they may encounter.

We usually measure interstellar distances in light-years, the distance travelled by light, at 300,000 km

per second, in 1 year. It takes light from the Sun about 8 minutes to reach us, and 5½ hours to reach the outermost planet of our Solar System, Pluto. It takes 4.3 years to reach Alpha Centauri.

So far, we have talked only about the closest star. Our Galaxy alone contains around 100 billion stars, and it is 100,000 light-years across. There are only two strategies for overcoming the problem of distance. Our starship must either go very fast, or support its crew for a very long time. The 'slow' strategy is perhaps the easier, though less attractive, since only

our remote descendants will ever know if we were successful. There are two ways of carrying out the 'slow' strategy: one is to launch a generation starship, in which the crew completing the mission consists of the many-times-great-grandchildren of the crew that set out; the other is to put the crew members into suspended animation. If they could 'sleep' for thousands of years, the slow strategy would be more feasible.

What about the other strategy? How do we make a starship go very fast? It is possible, but there are practical problems.

Right: the velocity necessary to reach even the nearest star within one person's lifetime seems incredible to us today. But flight velocities have already achieved an increase of more than 400,000% since 1905. The diagram shows a hypothetical race from London to Paris. The spacecraft *Helios 3*, launched in 1976 and now in orbit round the Sun, is the fastest man-made object in existence today.

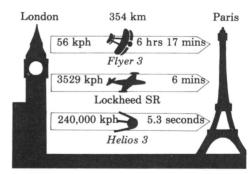

London 354 km Paris

56 kph — *Flyer 3* — 6 hrs 17 mins

3529 kph — *Lockheed SR* — 6 mins

240,000 kph — *Helios 3* — 5.3 seconds

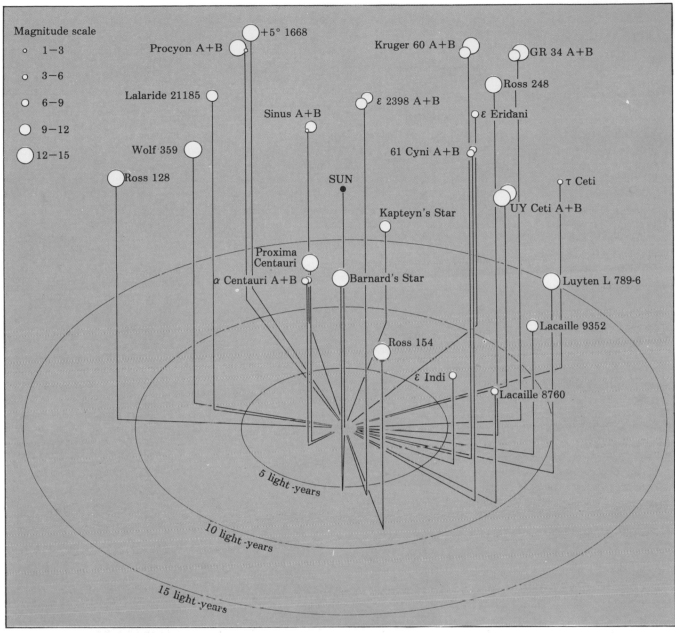

Magnitude scale
○ 1—3
○ 3—6
○ 6—9
○ 9—12
○ 12—15

+5° 1668
Procyon A+B
Kruger 60 A+B
GR 34 A+B
Lalaride 21185
Ross 248
ε 2398 A+B
Sinus A+B
ε Eridani
Wolf 359
61 Cyni A+B
Ross 128
SUN
τ Ceti
Kapteyn's Star
UY Ceti A+B
Proxima Centauri
α Centauri A+B
Barnard's Star
Luyten L 789-6
Lacaille 9352
Ross 154
ε Indi
Lacaille 8760

5 light-years
10 light-years
15 light-years

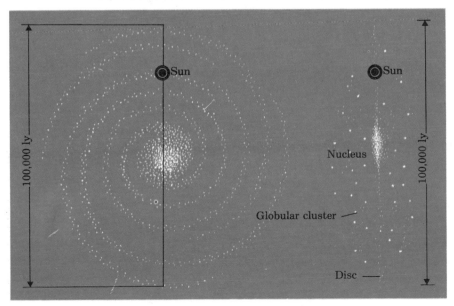

Sun
Sun
100,000 ly
100,000 ly
Nucleus
Globular cluster
Disc

Far left: because we live within the Milky Way, though towards its outer reaches, we do not see it as a disc or spiral; but towards the centre of the Galaxy we do see a broad band of stars in very large numbers; a section is shown here. **Left**: our Galaxy shown schematically from two perspectives: from 'above', showing the spiral structure, with two arms at the centre and four arms in the outer regions; and 'edge on', showing the disc shape. The globular star clusters are mostly outside the central disc. The position of our Sun is shown. **Above**: this three-dimensional representation shows the relative positions in space and magnitudes of the 23 star systems closest to the Sun. Most of the stars are bigger than our Sun. The many double-star systems are unlikely to have planets.

Starships: propulsion methods

The ideal propulsion method would give the starship a continuous acceleration equal to the force of the Earth's gravity. This would quickly build up velocity, as well as giving a comfortable ride for the passengers. But is it possible?

We know two ways, basically, of propelling a starship. Either we push it, as by using the pressure of a laser beam, or it pushes itself. Our present-day rockets push themselves by ejecting mass at high speed. Newton's Third Law of motion, that every action has an equal and opposite reaction, operates here. As the mass, the propellant, is pushed backwards, the rocket is accelerated forwards. There are only two factors that can be varied: the mass of the propellant and the velocity of ejection. The easiest way, of course, is to use a lot of mass, but this is the method with the greatest practical problems, although our present-day Moon-rockets use exactly this technique. The trouble is that the heavier the rocket, the more propellant is needed to push it. Liquid chemical propellant is itself heavy. Thus, most of the propellant of our modern Moon-rockets is in effect 'wasted' by being used to push the mass of the propellant which will be used later. An analogy would be to think of a Moon-rocket as being like a car consisting of 99% fuel tank and 1% room for the driver. Most of the fuel would be used up in driving the fuel tank along. The problem is made easier by using multi-stage rockets. As the propellant in each stage is used, the heavy casing is dropped off. But this is only a partial solution.

Human passengers can only withstand so much acceleration. A very fit man can withstand the pressure of an acceleration equal to around 15 times the force of Earth gravity for only a few moments. Our present Moon-rockets accelerate powerfully for a few minutes, and then coast the rest of the way at a constant velocity, with the occupants feeling the discomfort of weightlessness, or free fall. (Initially, free fall often leads to

nausea; then for a while it is fun; after periods of a week or more it leads to muscular weakness and a leaching of calcium from the astronaut's bones.)

It is generally agreed that a superior method of rocket propulsion, especially once the ship has left Earth's 'gravity well' (for which a powerful acceleration up to a velocity of about 11 km per second is required), would be a long, slow acceleration. Starships of the future

will probably not leave from Earth: they will be constructed in space. If they used a method of propulsion giving an acceleration exactly equal to the force of Earth's gravity, and if this acceleration were continuous, to the occupants of the ship it would be indistinguishable from true gravity. The back of the ship would seem to be 'down', and there would be none of the physical inconveniences associated with free fall. Other forms of imitation gravity are

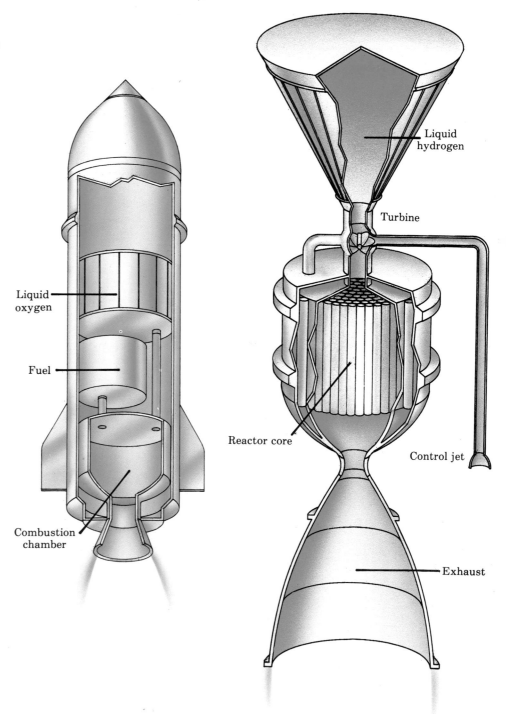

Liquid oxygen

Fuel

Combustion chamber

Liquid hydrogen

Turbine

Reactor core

Control jet

Exhaust

quite possible. The simplest is to have a starship shaped like a wheel, which spins. The centrifugal force would seem like gravity, and the edge of the wheel would appear to be 'down'. With this system, the closer to the centre of the wheel, the lower the 'gravity'; at the hub, there could be a free-fall sports centre!

The velocity of a starship undergoing a continuous acceleration of 1g (1 Earth gravity) would mount up surprisingly swiftly. The

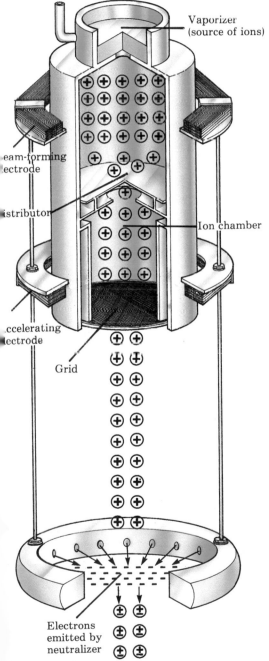

Vaporizer (source of ions)

eam-forming lectrode

istributor

Ion chamber

ccelerating lectrode

Grid

Electrons emitted by neutralizer

ship would travel half a light-year in just under a year of continuous acceleration. But how could this be achieved? Could any ship carry the propellant for such continuous acceleration? And what about slowing down at the end of the trip? There is no perfect answer yet; but Man's ingenuity has, at least on paper, carried him part of the way.

A rocket which used a nuclear fission reactor as a drive would achieve a much higher velocity than one using our present-day liquid or solid chemical propellant, since the power would be so much greater than that given by ordinary combustion. But even the most efficient of nuclear engines — and with shielding they would be rather heavy — is unlikely to give more than 10 times the efficiency of a chemical rocket. Such an engine could plausibly accelerate a starship to 1125 km per second before running out of propellant, but even then it would take around 1000 years to reach the nearest star.

The British Interplanetary Society has come up with a carefully designed variant of the atomic drive. Called Project Daedalus, it consists of an unmanned rocket in two stages

From left to right: (i) The present-day chemical rocket burns a fuel in a chamber with an oxidant, usually liquid oxygen. The high-velocity exhaust gases resulting from this combustion provide the thrust. (ii) In the simplest form of nuclear-thermal rocket (the first model was tested in 1969) liquid hydrogen is pumped through the very hot core of a nuclear reactor. The expanding gases of the heated propellant provide the thrust. Nuclear engines are still too massive to be used economically in space travel. (iii) The ion-drive rocket works on the same principle as present-day particle accelerators. Charged particles are greatly accelerated by an electric field. The existing model shown here concentrates mercury or caesium ions with one electromagnetic coil and accelerates them with a second coil. A third apparatus at the rear of the engine replaces the electrons already stripped from the ions, in order to neutralize them as they are propelled from the ship. If this were not done the spaceship itself would quickly develop a high negative charge, and the mutual repulsion of the ions, all carrying the same positive charge, would decrease the efficiency of the thrust.

designed to fly past Barnard's Star and send back information, the trip there taking around 50 years. After accelerating to 13% of the speed of light in about 4 years, the spaceship would 'coast' the rest of the way. Project Daedalus relies heavily on technologies not yet available to us, but the basic principle is generally regarded as sound. Small pellets of thermonuclear propellant (deuterium and helium-3) are projected into the reaction chamber and bombarded by high-powered electron beams. Nuclear fusion (not fission) results, and the exploding plasma, unimaginably hot and energetic, is swept out of the ship. The electron beams are powered by energy removed from the hot plasma by an induction coil as it leaves the ship.

In other words, the drive consists of a series of very small pulsed H-bomb explosions, at the rate (perhaps optimistically high) of 250 a second. The particular propellant chosen results in reaction products which are all charged particles. The designers did not want any neutrons resulting from the explosion, because, as neutrons are not charged, they cannot be channelled by magnetic fields, and heavy shielding would be required. Unfortunately, helium-3 is extremely rare. The designers believe we should need to extract it from the atmosphere of the planet Jupiter, where it is much more common. This is not a project for the near future.

Some scientists believe that a much more workable system of propulsion would be the ion drive, or electric drive, as it is sometimes known. Such drives, on a small scale, have already been used for orbital adjustments to satellites. An ion is a charged particle, such as an electron or a proton. It carries an electric charge, and can therefore be bent in its course, or accelerated, by a magnetic field. Any atom can be ionized by stripping it of electrons (which carry a negative charge), leaving it positively charged. The heavier the atom used in the ion-drive propellant, the greater the thrust. Mercury is a conveniently heavy but not very expensive element, readily ionized, and is the likeliest propellant. Considerable power will be needed to create the massive magnetic fields required to accelerate these ions to very high speeds (the faster they go, the greater the thrust). This power could be obtained on a small scale by solar batteries, but on a larger scale a nuclear fission plant would probably be needed. Dr Leonard Jaffe of Jet Propulsion Laboratories in California believes that the nuclear ion-drive combination represents a more workable propulsion system than Project Daedalus, one that might be completed by the year 2000.

Project Daedalus and the conventional ion drive have an important factor in common. In both cases the amount of mass per second ejected from the ship is quite small;

the work is achieved by the immense velocities of ejection. The acceleration would also be small — well below 1g — because of the tiny masses involved (even using heavy substances like mercury). But because the rate of ejection is low, the propellant can be conserved for a long time, and the acceleration can be continued for years if necessary.

Project Daedalus would achieve greater velocities than the conventional ion drive, but presents far larger technical difficulties. Both, however, are realistic schemes in terms of present-day technology. If technology advances at its present rate of progress, then this sort of

engineering should be quite possible in the twenty-first century.

It can be seen that most starship schemes try to evade the difficult requirement of carrying a lot of heavy propellant by using high velocities of ejection. But perhaps there is another way of meeting the problem. Is it necessary to carry fuel at all? Dr Robert L. Forward of Hughes Research Labs in California has proposed using the pressure of light itself as a propulsion device. An array of laser beams would be built in space close to the Sun, forming a circle of 250 km in diameter. They need not be remarkably powerful; Dr Forward

suggests the figure of 35 megawatts. The lasers would be beamed in unison at the starship, which would carry a huge, thin, rigid sail of metal. The pressure of the lasers on the sail would accelerate the ship up to velocities where relativistic effects (see pages 68-71) would begin to become perceptible. Slowing the ship down at the other end would be technically complex. Briefly, the ship would swing round the target star and be decelerated by the same lasers on the way back.

The difficulties of building a working starship are great. One problem is that kinetic energy increases according to the square of velocity, so that to get 10 times the speed 100 times the work is needed. Another is that according to Einstein the mass of the ship itself increases as it approaches the speed of light (see pages 68-71), and thus a correspondingly greater amount of propellant would be needed. But there may even be a way round this (see the ramscoop starship discussion on the next page).

There is a simple, cheering, final point about starships. For most purposes, space is a vacuum. Conventional streamlining is not needed because there is no air resistance. So a starship can be literally any shape — a cluster of spheres, a delicate, nautilus-like spiral, or a tiny cockleshell carrying a great silver sail many kilometres wide. Engineering and aesthetics can finally marry, the consummation no longer prevented by such Earth-bound difficulties as gravity and friction. Starships could be unutterably beautiful. There have already been inspired designs by science fiction illustrators, and there is no reason why the great, iron-clad space-hulks of *Star Wars* and *The Black Hole* should not give way, both in films and in reality, to starships of a fragile and airy filigree, like snowdrops, or feathers, or thistledown.

An impression of three starships, each one using a drive that may become possible, from an engineering point of view, within 150 years. **Left:** an ion driven space wheel. The rear engine is well separated from the living quarters around the rim of the slowly revolving wheel. **Upper right:** this starship, thrust forward by the pressure of light itself, has a huge but very thin circular sail, several kilometres in diameter. The drive is provided by a battery of laser beams built near our Sun, and directed in a tight, coherent beam along the line of flight. **Right:** although this starship, named Project Daedalus, will be unmanned, it is designed to carry a payload of 50 tons at the forward end. The spherical tanks in a belt around the waist carry the propellant. Pulsed fusion-bomb explosions take place in the engine bay towards the rear.

The ramscoop starship

One of the most popular kinds of starship in science fiction is the Bussard ramscoop. The design for this spacecraft was suggested by the American physicist Robert Bussard in 1960. The beauty of Bussard's system is that it avoids the problem of carrying massive amounts of fuel by undertaking continuous refuelling while actually in space.

Space, even that between the stars, is not completely empty. By far the commonest element in space is hydrogen, which is the basis of most nuclear fusion reactions. If a spacecraft could somehow collect enough hydrogen from space as it travelled, this could be used to fuel a fusion drive. But, by Earthly standards, interstellar space is close to an absolute vacuum. There are only one or two atoms of hydrogen per cubic centimetre in interstellar space, a gas density only 10^{-24} of that at the Earth's surface.

This is not much, but consider what would happen if, using a conventional ion drive, we accelerated a spaceship to around 1% of the speed of light. At this velocity the spacecraft would be travelling so enormously fast, through such a huge volume of space every second, that the almost vacuum through which it travelled would appear to be relatively dense with hydrogen, in the same way that a plane meets greater air resistance the faster it goes. At this velocity it is believed that the spaceship would meet with enough hydrogen to start collecting it as fuel.

Even then, however, the hydrogen would still be so tenuous that the hydrogen scoop would need to be gigantic. The invisible, funnel-shaped scoop would consist of a vast electromagnetic field projected from great, superconducting coils. This would ionize the hydrogen atoms (give them a positive electric charge) and magnetically funnel them back into the fusion engine. Even a comparatively small starship weighing 100,000 tons would need a collecting field with a radius across the funnel of 34,100 km — more than five times the radius of Earth!

The rewards for this gigantic engineering project would be great. All the fuel and energy necessary for voyages to even the farthest stars would be provided from space itself.

There would be another bonus, too. One of the discoveries made by Einstein and described mathematically in his Special Theory of Relativity (discussed in greater detail on pages 68-71) is that, as an object approaches the speed of light, its subjective time runs more slowly than time is running at its starting point on, say, Earth. 'Ship time', for the crew of a Bussard ramscoop starship, would pass more slowly the faster the ship went (though nobody would be aware of this, except intellectually). The effect would only become important at about 10% of the speed of light, and would increase dramatically as the ship continued to accelerate.

At the constant acceleration of 1g (1 Earth gravity) provided by a ramscoop, these 'relativistic' velocities would be reached quite quickly. At this acceleration, the spaceship could reach the centre of our Galaxy in 20 years (ship time), and any point in the entire universe within one lifetime! During the 20 years taken to reach the Galaxy centre, hundreds of thousands of years would have passed on Earth. But for the crew, it would be a genuine 20 years. No trickery is involved; it is a physical law, not a piece of self-hypnosis.

All of this sounds wonderful. It seems that not very long from now, the Galaxy may be ours for the taking! Recently, however, the concept of the Bussard ramscoop has been sternly criticized by theoreticians of space flight. There are many problems, none of which could be solved with our present knowledge.

First, the superconducting magnets required to set up an electromagnetic field of the required vast size would be so big, and carry

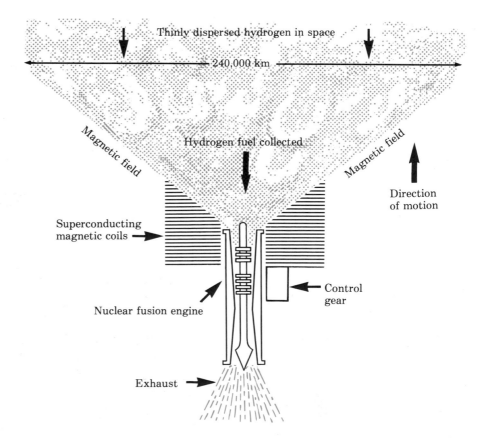

Thinly dispersed hydrogen in space

← 240,000 km →

Magnetic field

Magnetic field

Hydrogen fuel collected

Direction of motion

Superconducting magnetic coils →

Nuclear fusion engine

← Control gear

Exhaust →

Above: a diagram of the workings of a Bussard ramscoop starship, obviously not drawn to scale, based on a sketch in Adrian Berry's *The Iron Sun*. **Right:** an artist's impression of a ramscoop starship in flight. The vanes at the rear are for efficiently dissipating waste heat.

such vast currents, that they would tear themselves apart.

Secondly, the fusion motors need deuterium, a rare isotope of hydrogen (see pages 37-8). Only one hydrogen atom in 6700 is deuterium. Even if some ordinary hydrogen atoms are also persuaded to fuse (as they do in the Sun), it seems that, at best, only 1% of the interstellar gas could be used as fuel. The rest would pile up in front of the spaceship. Much of the energy provided by the 'ramjet' would then be used in ploughing through material that the ramscoop itself had accumulated!

Thirdly, the deuterium fusion process creates neutrons as one of its products. Neutrons, being electrically neutral, cannot be directed by magnetic fields. They whizz off in all directions with very high energy, and are impossible to absorb safely without massive shielding. Either the crew would be fried by neutron radiation, or the ship would be made impossibly heavy because of the necessary shielding. (This is why the Project Daedalus starship does not use the deuterium reaction.)

Fourthly, as the spaceship increases velocity to relativistic speeds, the 'empty' space in front of it would more and more come to resemble a solid wall. If the ship met with more hydrogen than it was able to use, its impact with the hydrogen left over would create radiation 100,000 times greater than the radiation we all get from sunlight. The crew would be instantly fried (again).

Other, more technical criticisms have also been made. The nuclear physicist Tom Heppenheimer believes that more energy would be required to compress the fuel sufficiently than would be gained from the consequent fusion reactions, even if a ramscoop of half-a-light-year diameter was used. In fact, Heppenheimer has suggested rather cruelly that the ramscoop would *dissipate* energy so successfully that it would make an excellent brake for a spaceship with a conventional drive!

Unless these massive theoretical problems can be overcome, it seems that the ramscoop is merely a science fictional dream. It will never propel starships, though it may, one day, be used to slow them down. Science fiction is full of dashed hopes. With the demise of the ramscoop concept, some of the most thrilling science fiction stories ever written are reduced to the status of mere fantasy. The most notable of these is Poul Anderson's *Tau Zero*, in which a ramscoop ship achieves such huge velocities that shipboard time is reduced to an almost unimaginable crawl. In fact, its passengers are able to witness the death of the universe — billions of years in the future for us, but only a few years of travelling for them.

The Bussard ramscoop represents the ultimate in 'fast' strategies for reaching the stars, along with the antimatter/photon drive beloved of *Star Trek* fans. This latter fanciful device has so many theoretical drawbacks (see pages 78-9) that we do not discuss it here. But what of the 'slow' strategies?

The generation starship

The two slow strategies for reaching the stars are the suspended-animation starship and the 'generation' starship.

Suspended animation is a favourite with science fiction writers and film-makers. The films *2001: a Space Odyssey, Dark Star* and *Alien* all contain scenes showing crew members in frozen sleep, literally kept on ice, snoozing the years away until they are needed. (In real life it would be centuries rather than years.)

We discuss cryonics more fully on page 147. It is enough to say here that nobody has yet managed to 'suspend' the life of an animal in this way, so the prospects for cryonic travelling are not too good. Artificial hibernation, in which bodily processes are slowed down without being actually stopped, is a much more promising possibility.

But the most romantic form of 'slow' travelling takes place on a generation starship, sometimes called a 'space ark'. The philosophy of this form of travel is 'What's the hurry?' If life on the ship is pleasant enough, why should it not be thought of as an actual world, where whole generations of crew members live and die just as they would have done back on Earth? A 1000-year voyage to new worlds orbiting other stars would come to seem quite realistic in these circumstances.

One essential for a world is comfortable gravity. Muscles weaken rapidly, and many tasks are much more difficult to perform, in zero gravity. It is believed that long periods spent in these conditions might cause irreversible deterioration, so that when starship colonists actually reached a new world, they might not have the strength to walk upon its surface.

Gravity might be provided by a continuous 1g or ½g thrust from the engine, in which case the rear of the starship would appear to be 'down'. But since the ship would probably

use a fission- or fusion-powered ion drive, the likely thrust would be much lower than this. The simplest answer is to build the ship in the shape of a wheel or a cylinder, and spin it. The centrifugal force would feel just like gravity to the crew. The inner surface of the rim would seem to be 'down', and there would be a free-fall zero-gravity area at the hub of the wheel or the axis of the cylinder.

If the ship is to function as a 'world' for many generations, then it must be big enough to support a population of, say, 1000 in comfort, along with animals and hydroponic farms to provide food, and the vast warehouses of material (very likely including frozen human embryos —

unlike fully developed mammals, embryos even today can be frozen) that will be needed when another world is eventually reached.

The idea of generation starships was first popularized in science fiction in 1941, in the famous story 'Universe' by Robert Heinlein. The idea is much older than that, however, and seems to have been invented by the great Russian pioneer of space flight, Konstantin Tsiolkovsky, who argued for space-going 'Noah's arks' in an essay published in 1928. Nearly all science fiction writers imagine generation starships as very big indeed. The scientific theoreticians are inclined to agree, although they foresee certain natural limitations on the

size of hollow spacecraft. If the starship had a diameter of around 16 km, centrifugal forces in the spinning ship would reach a strength liable to tear it apart. Similarly, a cylinder more than 50 km long might damage itself by building up a 'whipping' motion.

The other technical problem would be the conservation of all materials necessary for life. The Scots writer Duncan Lunan has pointed out that if only one-tenth of a gram of air and other volatiles (a tiny amount) seeped out of the ship every 10 seconds, 3000 tons would be lost over a 1000-year voyage. Air and water would need to be continuously recycled, as would all organic materials.

Left: the vast, spacefaring cities envisaged by modern science fiction illustrators would be far too massive for acceleration to near-light speeds. This striking creation by Tim White is probably

a generation starship. **Above:** space arks appeared on pulp-magazine covers even before they became popular in the stories themselves. This 'modern' version of Noah's Ark, with its military overtones,

appeared on a cover in 1939 while in the real world Germany had occupied Poland and the USSR was invading Finland. The idea of escaping this deluge of events must have seemed attractive.

The scale of such an epic voyage beggars the imagination. It would be as if the ship were manned in the first instance by Anglo-Saxons, and the voyage were completed by contemporary, twentieth-century, people. A thousand years is a long time – long enough for the ship to evolve and continuously develop its own culture. This is the aspect of the generation starship that has most captured the imagination of science fiction writers. Would such a crew be mentally capable of colonizing a planet when they reached it, when their culture insisted that the ship was the whole world? This was the question asked by Robert Heinlein in 'Universe', and later by Brian Aldiss in *Non-Stop* and Harry Harrison in *Captive Universe*. All three writers imagine situations where the purpose of the voyage has long been forgotten, and its communities have devolved into rather primitive, village societies. Samuel Delany also imagines a degeneration into a ballad-composing tribal culture in *The Ballad of Beta-2*. Brian Stableford, too, examines the likely social structure of a generation starship in his novel *Promised Land* (1974). It seemed to him that the purpose of the flight would be remembered but become so obsessive a symbol that it would take on dangerous religious overtones; he calls this the 'promised land' syndrome.

All sorts of writers have been gripped by the symbolic force of the generation starship. The Swedish Nobel-Prize-winning poet Harry Martinson even wrote an epic poem, *Aniara*, on the theme which in turn became an opera with music composed by Blomdahl – one of the better known modern operas.

In life, however, societies seem on the whole to evolve upwards rather than downwards. Life improves, although slowly and with many setbacks, over the generations. It seems not impossible that, with clever social engineering and planning, the crew of such a ship would remain stable and fulfilled, and perhaps very creative. Science fiction writers may have emphasized the pessimistic viewpoint only because it seemed to offer greater opportunities for dramatic conflict. The utopian life is too serene for successful fiction.

At this point we can desert the far future, and come back to the possibilities of the next 50 years. The idea of a generation starship set off some very interesting thoughts in post-war scientists (who had been reared, very often, on just such fictions as Heinlein and Aldiss have written). In the past decade there has been a very significant change of emphasis — see opposite page.

Where are the space arks?

At the end of the 1970s, a change took place in the published papers of scientists writing about the possibilities of extraterrestrial life. It had previously been assumed (see pages 46-8) that the chances of life elsewhere in our Galaxy were very high — an idea popularized by the astronomers Carl Sagan and Frank Drake, and many others.

Suddenly a lot of scientists were not so sure, and the reason for their doubts is directly connected with generation starships. As scientist Robert Sheaffer puts it, 'In an environment where life is abundant, nothing is more rare than an unclaimed resource. ... Are we to believe that, in a galaxy teeming with advanced civilizations, our own rich, lush, warm Earth would remain an unclaimed resource?'

Computer studies on colonization procedures suggest that a spacefaring civilization, situated in the centre of the Galaxy where the stars are older, would (if they had the technology to build space arks that travelled at only 1% of the speed of light) proceed outwards at an average rate of 0.91 light-years per century. At this rate, allowing for a great many 1000-year stops for colonizing new planets, the whole Galaxy would be colonized in 5½ million years — a mere blink of the eye compared with the age of the Galaxy. If ETI (extraterrestrial intelligence) exists, where is it? It should be here, on Earth, already.

Flying-saucer buffs would argue that the aliens are indeed here already (see pages 176-9), but not one case of a flying-saucer visit has been validated. None of the many celebrated scientists at the 'Where are They?' conference in Maryland in 1979 saw any evidence whatever that we are now being visited, or have ever been visited, by aliens.

The mathematician Frank Tipler, of the University of California, believes that self-replicating, uncrewed space probes are an even more likely way of exploring the Galaxy than generation starships. These are sometimes called Von Neumann probes, named after the cyberneticist John von Neumann, who first analysed the concept of machines that can duplicate themselves. They would be equipped with blueprints, enabling them to mine metals and construct copies of themselves, whenever they reached a new planet, moon or asteroid.

Suppose that these probes had no more advanced a propulsion system than the probes we ourselves could build with existing rocket technology. They would average 10,000 years to move from star to star. Even at this snail's pace, it would still take only 300 million years to explore the entire Galaxy, which is 10,000 million years old — only 3% of the Galaxy's lifetime.

Where are they? Why have no alien probes arrived?

Many scientists now believe that the absence of such alien colonizing expeditions points strongly towards the possibility that we ourselves are the only intelligent life in our Galaxy, and that life itself may be more of a cosmic accident than we have recently been inclined to think. The alternative, perhaps rather more cheering idea is that advanced races might not think, as we do, in terms of colonization and conquest. Perhaps these warlike imperatives are the sign of an immature culture. The aliens may still be out there, comfortably living on their own planets, with stable populations and a stable use of energy resources.

For immature mankind, however, the message is clear. It seems very likely that the Galaxy, not yet colonized by others, is open to us.

Space habitats

Of all the ideas about generation starships, the most celebrated intellectual leap forward was that of Gerard K. O'Neill, a high-energy physicist based at Princeton University. If a generation starship can be thought of as a world, he reasoned, then why does it need a destination? Why need we send it to the stars? As O'Neill puts it, 'space itself can be the destination rather than just a corridor'.

His ideas, publicized in *The High Frontier*, have generated an amazing amount of discussion, even though they are not wholly new. Again, Konstantin Tsiolkovsky seems to have been the first to make the suggestion, in his propagandizing novel *Beyond the Planet Earth*. Arthur C. Clarke's *Islands in the Sky*, a children's novel about life in an orbital space station, prefigures several of O'Neill's ideas.

An orbital space station, such as Skylab, is of course a kind of space habitat in itself, but at present such stations are envisaged as space laboratories, or staging points for launching and building spacecraft, rather than ends in themselves.

Behind O'Neill's reasoning, fairly obviously, is a pleasantly romantic notion that space itself would be a good, challenging place in which to live. The very title of his book has a subliminal reference to the old frontier of the American West, the arena of high adventure in the past.

There are good social reasons, too, for colonizing space. O'Neill believes, with many others, that our world is in a poor state. What we need is low-cost energy, new resources, and living space for all. Why not in space itself?, asks O'Neill. Science fiction writers had not really paid this particular idea much attention previously, probably because of what Isaac Asimov has called 'planetary chauvinism' — a kind of lack of imagination.

O'Neill is not much attracted to the idea of colonizing our other planets, such as Mars and Venus. They are not, at the moment, capable of supporting life (but see the discussion of terraforming on pages 28-9), and they exist at the bottom of 'gravity wells', like Earth's own, which means that travel *away* from their gravitational pull will always be very expensive in terms of energy. Another strong reason for building space habitats is that we could move some polluting industry away from Earth's atmosphere and safely out into the vacuum of space. Some industries would be wholly new. It will be possible to make new alloys, for example, in space. It is often difficult to alloy two metals on Earth, since the heavier of the two tends to sink to the bottom. It would be no problem at all in zero gravity.

There is no night-time in space. The sun's radiation is available 24 hours a day for use by solar batteries. Energy is cheap. What would not be cheap, however, would be the actual construction of the space habitats, especially if the raw materials had to be rocketed up from deep down in Earth's gravity well. But why use raw materials from Earth? Why not mine the Moon, or even change the orbit of asteroids so that all their mineral wealth could be exploited from conveniently close at hand? The techniques with which these miracles would be produced are described on pages 23-5.

Where would the space habitats be located? One obvious choice would be to site them in high Earth orbit, but another choice, very popular with science fiction writers, would be to locate them at the five stable Lagrange points. These are areas in space where the gravity from surrounding masses (in this case the Earth, Moon and Sun) is precisely balanced. An object set to rest at a Lagrange point (now more accurately called a Lagrange region, since the point itself performs a slow

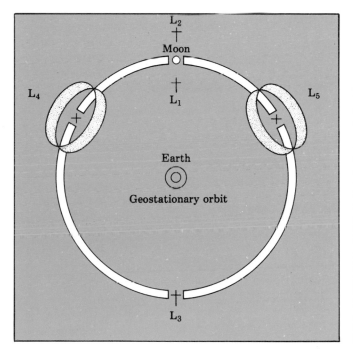

Left: the positions of the five gravitationally stable Lagrange points relative to the Earth (centre) and the Moon. A space city docked at one of these points would stay there. Points L4 and L5 describe slow, 89-day orbits in the regions shown in diagram. Below: this chart shows details of four proposed cities on the cylindrical model. Note the RPM maintaining simulation of Earth gravity, and the dramatic increase in population size with increased diameter.

PROPOSED SPACE COLONIES				
	LENGTH miles (km)	DIAM. miles (km)	RPM	POP. (Max) '000s
MODEL 1	0.62 (1)	0.12 (0.2)	2.85	10
MODEL 2	2.0 (3.2)	0.4 (0.64)	1.67	200
MODEL 3	6.2 (10)	1.2 (2)	0.95	2000
MODEL 4	20 (32)	4 (6.4)	0.53	20,000

orbit in space) would stay there indefinitely. The points, known as L1 to L5 (see diagram, page 19) are all related to the Moon. One lies ahead of the Moon in its orbit, one behind in its orbit, one on the near side of the Moon, one on the far side, and one directly opposite the Moon, at the same distance on the other side of Earth.

Many science fiction writers, John Varley, Robert Silverberg and Mack Reynolds among them, have envisaged the Lagrange areas as crazy utopias. Varley's idea (put forward in his novel *Wizard* and elsewhere) is that minority groups would set out to build their own space habitats. Communists, fundamentalist Christians, radical feminists, homosexuals, or any other groups, could each construct their own worlds, free of the social pressures they deplore back on Earth. Each Lagrange region might contain hundreds of self-contained habitats, some tropical, some arctic, some conventionally built, others like architectural fantasias from an Escher drawing. In a sense, it is the logical end of the whole small-is-beautiful movement. Away with

centralized authority, and back to a system of anarchically linked villages! So popular has the idea been in science fiction that in only five years or so, wildly assorted Lagrange civilizations have already become a cliché.

O'Neill's account of what the habitats would look like is comparatively sober, though surely romantic enough for most tastes. The first, Island One, would have a population of a mere 10,000, living on the inside surface of a sphere perhaps 500 metres in diameter. Each family of five people would have an apartment and garden space of around 300 square metres (much more than many of us have now). The spinning sphere would produce the effect of Earth gravity around its equator. As an occupant strolled north or south towards the poles, gravity would fall off, to one half Earth gravity at the 45° latitudes, and zero gravity at the poles. Windows would let in sunlight, and could be masked to provide an artificial night. Looking straight up, one would see one's distant neighbours apparently suspended from the sky 500 metres above.

Non-rotating docking module

Right: this painting by official NASA artist Don Davis envisages the interior of Gerard O'Neill's projected Island 3 — a cylinder 32 km long with 1300 square km of living space. The artist has assumed a climate on the North Californian model, and has even included a replica of San Francisco's Golden Gate bridge, but other climates could easily be designed. The specifications are similar to those of Model 4 in the chart on page 19.

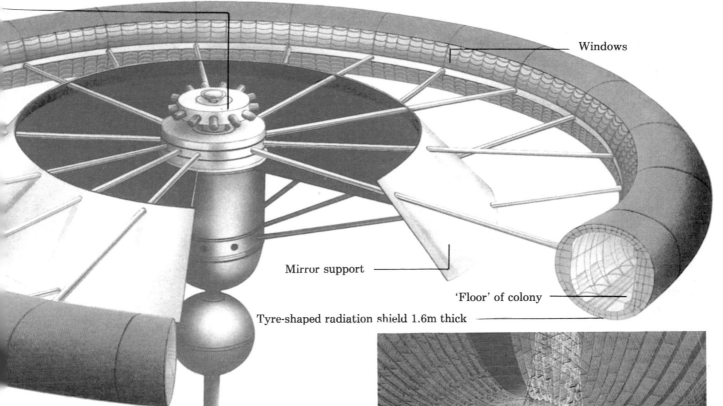

Windows

Mirror support

'Floor' of colony

Tyre-shaped radiation shield 1.6m thick

Above: this torus (doughnut)-shaped habitat was designed in 1979 by British engineer Dr David Sheppard, using as a basis the Stanford Torus designed in 1975. The most important modification is the use of prestressed concrete, made from lunar rock, reinforced by steel cables, for the basic construction material. The structure is nearly 2 km in diameter and has a mass of over 10 million tons. The central axis, where visiting ships would dock, is non-rotating, but the wheel spins. A difficulty is the vast mass of air necessary; we can find oxygen in Moon rocks, but nitrogen may have to be ferried from Earth. **Right:** an artist's impression of the Stanford Torus interior. The windows 'above' correspond to the inward-looking windows in the Sheppard Torus above. The 'floor' which in the upper picture is seen edge-on would feel downwards to the senses because of the wheel's spin.

The curious perspectives of a space habitat have been vividly described in Bob Shaw's story of a childhood day in space, 'Small World'. This story is set in a slightly larger habitat, of cylindrical form, with three inhabited valleys running the length of the cylinder's inner surface, separated by farmland and window strips. O'Neill's Island Two remains spherical, but would be around 1800 metres in diameter, and could support, in comfort, a population of 140,000. Many other designs including the Stanford Torus — see schematic drawing above — have been calculated. A number of them are planned to direct sunlight to the best places at the best times by computer-operated mirrors. Four projected cylindrical habitats are described in the diagram on page 19.

Naturally, O'Neill's ideas have been subjected to a great deal of criticism, especially from those who see them as a form of unrealistic escapism. The economic viability of O'Neill's ideas is, at best, distinctly speculative, and a lot of very optimistic projections are incorporated into them — the fundamental one being that we on Earth would be psychologically prepared to make such a heavy investment. Back in the real world, with the early 1980s being a time of massive budgetary cuts for space and energy programmes, O'Neill's brand of utopianism is not favoured at present. This at least could change. The American government, the world's richest, has already made one massive investment in a utopian project — the exploration of the Moon. It is always possible that they will do something similar again. The rewards (which could well include cheap energy beamed down from space in the form of microwaves — see pages 42-3) may yet prove attractive.

Sports in space

There will be no shortage of recreational facilities in a space habitat. Zero-gravity and low-gravity environments have many possibilities. One of the most popular may turn out to be man-powered flight. Towards the axis of rotation of any Lagrange habitat, the apparent gravity will fall off. Escape velocity, as one travelled towards the zero-gravity region, would become progressively lower. Sportsmen and sportswomen, equipped with wings, could launch themselves into the central space of the habitat and realize one of mankind's ancient dreams — to fly like a bird. At the poles of a Lagrange sphere, no great strength would be required to do this. Pedal flyers operating from the poles may be available even for the elderly, much like the 'pedalos' of today's seaside resorts.

Outside the habitats, more challenging sports will be possible. One of the most interesting will be solar sailing. Our Sun radiates not only light and heat in the form of photons, but also particles: electrons, protons and so on. This constant invisible wind of particles permeates space as it radiates outwards from the Sun. It is this wind that causes the tails of comets to point away from the Sun. The wind fluctuates. Sunspots, for example, cause magnetic 'storms'. Light spacecraft, aluminium shells with great sails made of very thin metallic film, could use this solar wind just as ordinary yachts use Earth's wind, which is made up of moving molecules of oxygen and nitrogen. Even light itself — sunlight in this case — exerts enough pressure to add to the push on the sails. The solar wind is very much more tenuous than an Earthly wind, but, to compensate for this, the gossamer sails could be very much bigger. There are no constraints of gravity to pull at these sails, and their material could be only fractions of a millimetre thick — hardly thicker than that of a soap bubble. A sail may be 600 metres across, or much larger.

As in ordinary sailing, it may be possible to change direction by tacking — a point missed, strangely enough, by some science writers, several of whom imagine that, because the solar wind always blows in much the same direction, solar yachts will be doomed to one-way travel. This is not true. It will even be possible, though difficult, to tack across the solar wind, or at an angle towards it. Though there would be no 'water pressure' against which to turn the space yachts, there would be gravitational 'pressure' from the Sun, the Moon and Earth to utilize.

Arthur C. Clarke was one of the first science fiction writers to imagine solar sailing, as in his story 'Sunjammer' (1964). Since that time, some writers have romantically, if implausibly, imagined great sailing-ships travelling even between the stars, though the pressure of light would indeed be extremely small in the vast empty spaces outside our Solar System. Gene Wolfe, in his continuing saga *The Book of the New Sun*, imagines such a form of travel.

The British Interplanetary Society began plans in 1981 to set up a sponsored solar-sailing race from Earth to the Moon. Launch would be from a satellite, and the tiny remote-controlled 'yachts' would, of course, be unmanned.

Left: most of the theoretical work on solar sailing has been done at the Jet Propulsion Laboratory at the California Institute of Technology. Artist Ken Hodges here envisages a JPL prototype with a sail 30 metres square made from aluminium-coated Mylar .006 mm thick, about one-twenty-fourth the thickness of a human hair. This remote-controlled, unmanned craft was one of several designs to be launched in 1982 and used for a rendezvous with Halley's Comet. NASA cancelled the project.

Mining the Moon and the asteroids

The building of O'Neill-type space habitats would be ruinously expensive if the raw materials had to be ferried up from Earth. Earth, being relatively massive (compared with, say, the Moon or the asteroids), exists at the bottom of a fairly deep gravity well. To overcome Earth's gravity and launch materials into space uses a great deal of power. The Moon has only one-fifth of the surface gravity of Earth; therefore the escape velocity is only one-fifth. The power expended in overcoming gravity to reach this escape velocity is also less. The end result is that objects can be launched from the Moon using 97% less power than objects of the same mass would require if launched from Earth. The difference was graphically illustrated during

the *Apollo* Moon programme for all to see: the rockets that left Earth were vast; the rockets that returned from the Moon were comparatively tiny. The Moon, then, would be a much cheaper source of raw materials than Earth.

Soil samples taken by the crew of *Apollo 14* show that the chemical make-ups of the Moon and Earth are quite similar. Substances that would be readily available from the Moon include steel, aluminium, magnesium, titanium, glass, ceramics and cements. These, as it happens, are just the substances that might be most useful for the construction of space habitats, whether built from steel, aluminium or even concrete. All mining and other processes would be largely carried out by automatic machinery.

Gerard O'Neill has suggested that the most efficient method of launching these materials from the Moon into space — towards, say, the space habitats being built at Lagrange point L2 on the far side of the Moon — would not in fact be

rockets. Why not *throw* the materials into space, where they could be scooped up by construction crews? It might even be simpler to do the chemical processing in space itself, and simply throw up lumps of rock as raw material. The idea is not completely new. The endlessly inventive writer Robert Heinlein suggested something rather similar in his novel *The Moon is a Harsh Mistress*, and Arthur C. Clarke wrote an article on the subject in 1950: 'Electromagnetic Launching as a Major Contribution to Space Flight'.

'Electromagnetic' is the key word also in O'Neill's concept, which he has named the 'mass driver'. This is an electromagnetic catapult, very similar in its working to the magnetic levitation devices that already propel some experimental trains in Japan, hovering above the track. The mass driver is in essence a conveyor belt. It consists of a long, tubular track made up of 'drive' coils, through which an electric current is passed. The current is powered by solar cells, and creates strong magnetic pulses inside the coils. Floating up the centre of the coiled track are magnetic buckets, made up of a container surrounded by one or two coiled superconducting magnets. Like ordinary buckets, they can be filled with whatever you like. As the buckets pass through the drive coils, they are continuously accelerated by the magnetic pulses until they reach lunar escape velocity of 2.4 km per second. Then, as the bucket is suddenly decelerated, its contents fly out into space at just the right velocity and in the right direction to send them into the stable gravitational area of a Lagrange point, where they are captured. The buckets go back to the starting point along a return track that gently curves through 180°, to be removed and reloaded. The relatively expensive buckets are re-used for an indefinite period, and the vacuum on the Moon's surface means that there are practically no problems of friction to diminish efficiency and cause wear and tear.

The mass driver is not a science fiction device — not since 1977 when a test model was built extremely cheaply by enthusiasts at the Massachusetts Institute of

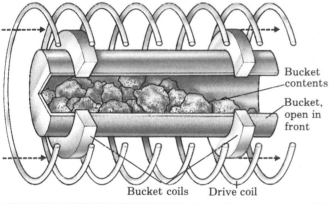

Bucket contents

Bucket, open in front

Bucket coils   Drive coil

Left: the mass driver in schematic form. A pulsed current in the drive coils creates magnetic fields that push on the currents in the superconducting coils attached to the bucket, giving more acceleration with every pulse. **Below**: the 1977 MIT test model.

Technology. It accelerated a one-pound bucket to 100 mph in only 6 feet! This represents an acceleration of 35g. Because the track was traversed in only one-tenth of a second, which is less than the retention time of the human retina, the bucket seemed to disappear at one end and re-materialize at the other. The Moon model would be just over 1 km long, and generate an acceleration of around 130g.

Once the concept of the mass driver had been developed, many new possibilities opened up. Why restrict the mass driver to propelling substances up from the Moon? It would work equally well as a primitive but effective rocket device, providing it had something to throw. It would therefore be ideal for shifting large, partially expendable masses — asteroids, for example. Imagine a mass driver attached to an asteroid. It need not be a very big mass driver, because the escape velocity needed to launch something from an asteroid is quite low; in fact

you could jump off a small asteroid into space with your own muscular power. According to Newton's Third Law, every action has an equal and opposite reaction. The mass driver throws bits of asteroid backwards, and the asteroid moves forwards — very slowly at first, because the bucketfuls of ejected material would be tiny in mass compared with the total mass of the asteroid. Slowly, however, the velocity would build up.

Asteroids are chunks of rock, often very rich in metals, especially iron and nickel, and containing generous components of rare metals such as platinum. This information is gained partly from spectroscopic analysis, and partly by the physical examination of meteorites, which are only mini-asteroids that have collided with Earth. Asteroids range in size from grains of dust to 1000 km across. There are an estimated 3100 asteroids more than ½ km across, and maybe 100,000 smaller but respectably sized rocks with a diameter of 100 metres or more.

Most of them are in orbit around the Sun between the orbits of Mars and Jupiter, and therefore a long way from Earth, but quite a few have eccentric orbits that bring them relatively close to Earth. Amor, for example, has a diameter of 16 km and passes as close as 16 million km to Earth every 8 years. There are probably quite a number of very small captured asteroids already in residence at the five Lagrange points, pulled in and balanced there by the combined gravity systems of Earth and Moon.

For many years one of the most popular themes of science fiction has been the mining of the asteroids, which were envisaged in a number of stories of the 1930s as constituting together a kind of super-Klondyke to which miners would rush to make their fortunes. Stories include Clifford D. Simak's 'The Asteroid of Gold' and Malcolm Jameson's 'Prospectors of Space'. More recently Poul Anderson's episodic novel *Tales of the Flying Mountains*

and a number of Larry Niven's short stories about the 'belters' (inhabitants of the asteroid belt) have developed the same theme, exploring the possibilities of a new human culture built up on the asteroids.

What few of these stories ever considered was the prospect of actually steering asteroids back to an Earth orbit, or to one of the Lagrange points. Yet the development of the mass driver makes the transport of asteroids a near-future, economic possibility. The metal content of these asteroids, even the relatively small ones, makes them highly desirable, and possibly worth the major capital investment necessary to get it.

(Much of the iron and nickel is already in metallic form — pre-smelted, as it were.) A group of enthusiasts in the UK, the Space Settlers Society, is collecting money towards this capital investment (extremely slowly), by charging a membership fee of £5 and a continuing subscription of £1 a month!

American optimists using some highly speculative economic suppositions reckon that a 3-km-thick asteroid could be towed Earthwards for between $100 billion and $200 billion. As much as two-thirds of its contents would have been used as propellant by the mass driver, but the remaining one-third would still yield profits from mining; it has also

been suggested that the asteroid could be used for growing food in space for Earth's hungry millions. (The escape velocity from such an asteroid would be low enough to make it quite simple to deliver parcels of ore and food to Earth, though great care would have to be taken to aim them accurately, and it is not yet clear how expensive it would be to build the necessary metal-foam re-entry containers to prevent the contents from burning up as they entered the atmosphere.) It is quite likely that the metal from asteroids would be more useful for construction work in space than it would be down here on Earth.

A study conducted by NASA was less ambitious. NASA reported that the towing of a 100-metre-thick asteroid back to Earth might well be possible using current technology.

Asteroids come in three main varieties: rocky, metal-rich and carbonaceous. The carbonaceous asteroids contain some water and a fair amount of hydrocarbons as well as minerals. The minerals include oxygen in the form of oxides, and also sulphur. Carbonaceous asteroids may even yield a substance very like oil. They would also be the best bet for settlement, since they would be the simplest to farm.

This raises yet another prospect. If large asteroids can be hollowed out and settled and farmed; if they contain the necessities of life such as oxygen, water and minerals; why bother to bring them back to Earth? They would make very big, very adequate transport devices. We have come back full circle to the idea of the generation starship. Communities living in asteroids could slowly and peacefully make their way to the stars, propelling themselves with mass drivers using solar power at first, and changing to nuclear fission or fusion as they entered the dark interstellar spaces. It is a romantic thought, though when the sums are worked out of how much energy such a trip might require, it begins to look rather difficult. However, though asteroids are big, and therefore expensive to propel, they also have no shortage of conveniently available reaction mass. All the rubble from the hollowed-out centre could be ejected. Hollow asteroids may be the most popular spaceships of the far future.

Left: an artist's impression of a mass driver in position on the Moon's surface, ready to launch construction materials into space. Lunar mountains are in the background. **Above:** the battery of solar cells above powers the mass driver attached to the asteroid. By ejecting asteroid material at high velocity, the mass driver is propelling the asteroid towards Earth. Operations will soon begin on the second asteroid, at left.

Colonizing other planets

There has been a lot of ambitious talk about sending spaceships to the stars, but which stars should we send them to? While there are thought to be 100 billion stars in our Galaxy there are only 60 or so within 16 light-years of us. A chart of some of the closer stars appears on page 9.

Science fiction writers have always assumed that when we reach the stars we shall be seeking Earth-type planets, capable of sustaining human life, in orbit around them. They are probably right; these are what we would need for colonizing. The question is, where would we expect to find them? We need to know the most likely locations before we set out, in order to point our spaceship in the most promising direction.

We can begin by thinking about the different types of stars. Is there any reason to believe that some kinds of stars are more likely to have planets than others?

Stars are divided up by astronomers according to their magnitude and their spectral type. The spectrum of a star, obtained by analysing its light with a spectroscope, tells us its temperature. The bluer a star is, the hotter; the redder it is, the cooler. Stars are currently classified into spectral types O, B, A, F, G, K and M, the hottest (O) stars being blue and the coolest (M) stars being red. The Sun is a yellowish-white type G.

Stars are often plotted on a Hertzsprung-Russell diagram, which plots their absolute magnitudes against their spectral class. Most stars on these diagrams tend to cluster in a band running from upper left (big and hot) down to lower right (small and relatively cool). This is called 'the main sequence'; red giants and supergiants, and white dwarfs, all lie outside it.

Both red giants and blue giants are thought to be too big to possess Earth-type planets, and too short-lived for oxygen-producing life forms to have evolved on any planets that do exist. (The more massive a star is, the faster it burns

its hydrogen fuel.) The dim red dwarfs, the commonest and most long-lived of all stars, are not especially promising either. (One of them, Barnard's Star, the second closest star to the Sun, was thought for some years to give evidence of having a planetary system, but that evidence has recently looked extremely shaky.) A planet circling a red dwarf would have to be very close to it, to be warm enough to support life. But planets orbiting very close to their parent star are believed to rotate very slowly (like Mercury, whose 'day' is 176 Earth-days long), making one side very hot and the other cold for long periods. This may create difficulties for our colonists. We would prefer our planet to have a temperature between the freezing and boiling points of water — a very narrow temperature range that may not readily be found in the vicinity of red dwarfs.

All the theorists believe that life-supporting planets are most likely to exist in orbit around stars rather like our own Sun. Spectral classes G and K are the most popular choice. (White dwarfs are a

possible second best, but here there are even more uncertainties.) There is however a problem with Sun-type stars. We now know that more than half of them form part of a binary or multiple star system — that is, systems with two or more stars in orbit around one another. Theories about the formation of such systems are rather conjectural, but it is likely that the gas clouds from which Sun-type stars evolve tend to produce either multiple star systems, or planetary systems, but not both. Although planets could, in theory, form stable orbits around one of the two stars in a binary system (a very common scenario in science fiction — Brian Aldiss's *Helliconia Spring* is a distinguished recent example), it seems that such systems may not evolve planets in the first place. To be on the safe side, we should send our spaceship to a type G or K star that is not a member of a binary system. (The astronomer S.H. Dole disagrees. He believes that Alpha Centauri, a member of a multiple system, is the best bet. His second and third choices, however, fall into our suggested category. They are

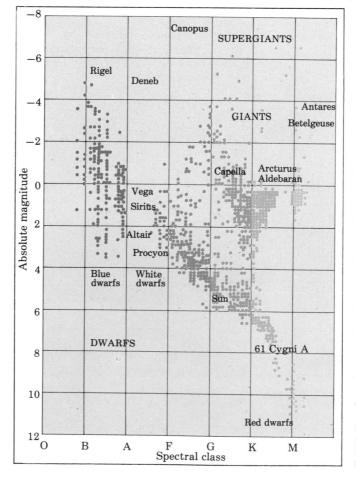

Left: This Hertzsprung-Russell diagram plots the absolute magnitude of stars on the vertical axis, and their spectral class on the horizontal axis. Each dot represents a star. The so-called 'main sequence' to which most stars belong runs from the upper left to the lower right of the diagram. Stars with planets capable of supporting life are most likely to be spectral class G or K along the main sequence.

Left: NASA's space telescope, to be launched in the mid-1980s, may be powerful enough to enable us to see planets circling nearby stars.

1. **2.4-metre primary mirror**
2. **Secondary mirror**
3. **Ridged inside cover** to prevent stray light reaching the telescope
4. **Central baffle** against stray light
5. **Fine guiding sensors** which observe a star and hold telescope pointing in correct direction
6. **Solar panel** for power supply
7. **Scientific instrument module**
8. **Radio antenna** for communication with Earth

Epsilon Eridani at 10.8 light-years and Tau Ceti at 11.8 light-years.)

The next step in our planet search is to aim telescopes at the most likely candidate stars. Today's telescopes are not of much use, but a new generation of more powerful telescopes is being designed. There will be great difficulties in seeing a planet directly through a telescope, because of its dimness in comparison with its parent star, to which it would appear very, very close. The problem becomes simpler, though, if we measure infra-red rather than visible light. Although a planet the size of Jupiter would appear 10,000 times dimmer than its parent star by infra-red, it would be 2.5 billion times dimmer by visible light!

Interferometers may help us, by splitting the light of the star in two, away from the telescope lens. This would allow the reflected light of the planet, which travels a slightly different distance, to be separated out. Direct masking of the star's light may also be possible. These technologies are already being developed.

We may more easily be able to detect planets indirectly, by measuring the tiny perturbation or wobble of the parent star caused by their gravity. (That was how Dr Peter van de Kamp thought he had discovered a planet circling Barnard's Star.) These perturbations would be very small indeed, and extremely difficult to measure accurately, but astrometric (star-measuring) photometers being constructed now may be able to do this.

Another promising development for finding planets is NASA's proposed Space Telescope, which is being built now, and is due to be launched by the Space Shuttle in the mid-1980s. The great advantage of siting a telescope in space is its freedom from all the visual distortions caused by Earth's atmosphere. It is believed that the 2.4-metre lens of the telescope will make viewing 10 times better than the best telescopes on Earth. It will also see further towards the ultra-violet and infra-red ends of the spectrum than we can from Earth. Although the designers did not

intend that the space telescope should be used for planet detection, several astronomers think that it may quite possibly do the job.

We are unlikely to set out for the stars for another 50 years. Within the next 15 years, on the other hand, it will probably be possible to locate those stars within 40 light-years of us that contain planets. By the time we have designed our starships, we shall probably know where to send them.

The actual colonization of the planets will be difficult. Robert Heinlein was one of the pioneers of the enormously popular conquering-other-worlds story, and the blood, sweat and tears that he envisages are no doubt correct in essence, even if he proves to have got the details wrong. We may find Earth-sized planets, with Earth-type gravity and temperature, but it is likely that certain essentials — such as plentiful oxygen for breathing — will be missing. If we develop the technology to reach the stars, however, then making the planets that we find there habitable should also be possible.

Terraforming

The chance of locating other planets that are completely comfortable for human life is low. There are many necessary conditions. These include suitable gravity, temperature range, air pressure and atmospheric constituents (oxygen is necessary); the presence of land masses and oceans; winds and tides of manageable proportions; an absence of harmful radiation; a period of rotation (and therefore a day) neither too long nor too short; geological stability and the absence of lethal micro-organisms.

There are only two general strategies for colonizing worlds that are only partly Earthlike. We could alter ourselves to fit the planet (this is often called 'pantropy' — see pages 154-5), or we could alter the planet to fit ourselves. This is called 'terraforming'.

Terraforming as a theme of science fiction is not new. In *Last and First Men* (1930), Olaf Stapledon imagined the colonizing of Venus. He saw three problems: Venus is too hot (correct); it has no free oxygen in its atmosphere (correct); it is almost entirely covered with oceans (wrong). Stapledon's solution was 'to split up some of the ocean of the planet into hydrogen and oxygen by a vast process of electrolysis. The oxygen . . .would mix with the atmosphere. The hydrogen would . . .be ejected beyond the limits of the atmosphere at so great a speed that it would never return.'

Stapledon's method, as it happens, is irrelevant as well as probably unworkable; but the principle of altering the atmosphere is a good one, and it is true that we need not voyage to other planetary systems to find terraforming opportunities. Our own Solar System has several: Mars and Venus have a surface gravity not too far removed from our own. Our Moon, and several of Jupiter's moons, are other possibilities. Ganymede, the largest of Jupiter's moons, has been a popular 'frontier' colony in science fiction since Robert Heinlein's *Farmer in the Sky* (1950), though we now know that another Jovian moon, Io, has a greater surface gravity. The terraforming of

Ganymede is also the theme of two other novels, Poul Anderson's *The Snows of Ganymede* and Gregory Benford's *Jupiter Project*.

Earth itself has not always been suitable for human life. Three billion years ago our atmosphere consisted largely of carbon dioxide, methane and ammonia. Algae living in the oceans metabolized the carbon dioxide, liberating oxygen into the atmosphere, which in turn broke down the methane and ammonia. All this may have taken a billion years. Scientists believe that substantial quantities of oxygen in any planetary atmosphere would indicate the presence of life.

The constituents of atmosphere have a great effect on surface temperature, because of the so-called 'greenhouse effect' (see pages 34 and 114-15), by which some gases help to retain more of the Sun's heat than does our own atmosphere. Venus, a hell planet with a surface temperature around 470°C, is thought to be suffering from a runaway greenhouse effect; its closeness to the Sun is not enough to explain the high temperatures. The dense, cloudy atmosphere is largely carbon dioxide, and when it rains it probably rains sulphuric acid. The atmosphere extends as high as 60 km from the surface, and the surface pressure is 90 times that on Earth. A man who landed on its surface would first be crushed, then eaten by acid and slowly burned to a crisp.

The astronomer Carl Sagan has suggested terraforming Venus by seeding its atmosphere with 1000 rocket-loads of blue-green algae, which would release oxygen from the carbon dioxide. Everything depends on how fast these algae would multiply in the upper atmosphere before sinking to be destroyed by the heat below. Algae are extremely hardy, and several species live in boiling hot springs. Laboratory experiments show that algae in a carbon dioxide atmosphere proliferate, and also release oxygen, at a satisfying rate. An oxygen-rich atmosphere on Venus might be created in hundreds rather than millions of years if the initial colonies of algae were many and large. As the process continued, Venus would become cooler as the greenhouse effect lessened; the small

amount of water vapour that we know to exist in its atmosphere would fall as rain, and finally shallow lakes would form on the flat Venusian deserts.

Mars is a much more difficult prospect for terraforming. The biological alteration of the atmosphere would not be possible at first, because Mars has very little atmosphere to work with. This is partly due to its lower surface gravity — less than half of Earth's — which is less efficient than ours at preventing atmospheric molecules from dispersing into space.

We would begin work on Mars by warming it up from its present average temperature of −40°C. This could be partly achieved by sprinkling it with dark dust (perhaps mined from its moons) which by absorbing heat better than the present rather reflective surface would increase the planetary temperature. Giant, orbiting mirrors could reflect more sunlight on to the frozen carbon dioxide 'ice-caps', to melt them. (Terraforming Mars by a similar method is one of the themes of Ian Watson's novel *The Martian Inca*.) Mass drivers could be used to steer asteroids (some of them may usefully be made of ice and would provide a water source) into collision courses with Mars, creating craters kilometres deep in which the atmosphere would be denser.

At present the atmospheric pressure on the Martian surface is less than 1% of that on Earth, but with the addition of carbon dioxide and water vapour, it may rise to a density sufficient for the biological conversion of carbon dioxide to oxygen to take place, as we have planned to do with Venus.

These elaborate plans are a long way in the future, for they depend on cheap energy sources which we have not yet developed; but they are perfectly possible in theory. The tools of the terraformer will range from nuclear bombs and mass drivers down to micro-organisms specially tailored for particular environments by genetic engineering. Particularly useful would be the creation of plants, like those imagined by Arthur C. Clarke in *The Sands of Mars*, that break down oxides in rock and soil and release free oxygen.

Not all the temperature-control

of planets will be achieved with greenhouse effects. Dust clouds could be created around Venus-type planets to help reflect the Sun's heat outward. Giant space mirrors could direct extra sunlight towards or away from planetary surfaces, depending on how they were positioned. The ultimate aim of terraforming will be to set up a self sustaining ecology. Terraformed planets and moons will not only need people; they will need animals, fish, trees, grains and especially bacteria: all the necessary ingredients of a viable food chain.

We should not be too ready to reject terraforming as a wild dream. We need to remember how successfully we have unconsciously terraformed our own planet already, seldom for the better. We have noticeably increased the amount of carbon dioxide in our atmosphere in only 100 years, thus possibly altering Earth's climatic balance; in many areas we have reduced the water table, producing heavy ground subsidence; we have destroyed the ecosystems of many inland waters; we have deforested much of Earth; our deserts are advancing — the Sahara by 40 km a year.

This is a tragedy and also a challenge. Like charity, perhaps terraforming should begin at home. If we can succeed in restoring a life-sustaining environment on our own crowded planet, it may be comparatively simple to create such environments on other, emptier worlds.

Above: Artist David Hardy pictures volcanoes on Venus; the dense clouds above allow only a gloomy half-light to reach the surface. (A 1975 radar survey suggests some volcanoes stand in a largely flat land-scape.) A balloon monitor floats in the corrosive atmosphere that creates a real challenge for terraformers. **Right:** cells of cylindrospermum; blue-green algae like these could transform Venus.

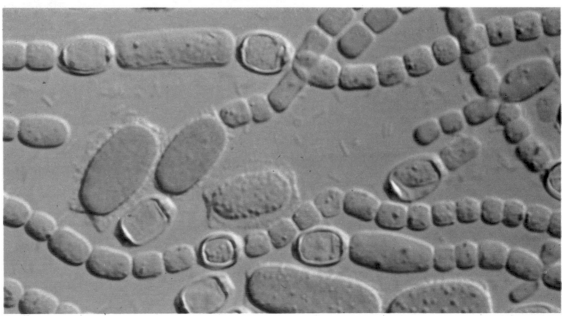

Chapter 2
THE SECRET IS ENERGY

We are told that energy sources in the real world are running out. Are science fiction's high-technology futures therefore an impossible dream? Will the next 100 years see us as a handful of demoralized peasants, or might we still reach the stars?

Where has all the power gone?

Power sources used to be easily come by in science fiction. E.E. 'Doc' Smith's novel *The Skylark of Space*, first published in 1928 and still selling well today, opens with an experiment in a copper bathtub on '"X", the unknown metal'. To the experimenter's surprise, the bathtub whizzes out of the window and straight off into the stratosphere at unbelievable velocity. An 'infra-atomic' energy source has been discovered.

Pulp science fiction in those days was full of miraculous energy sources, used for anything from propelling spaceships to obliterating planets. It was not as crazy as it sounds. Scientists in the real world, too, were bubbling with optimism. It was not until the 1950s that a small number of scientific Jeremiahs began to make themselves heard with gloomy predictions that the energy resources of our planet may not be limitless; it was not until the 1960s that the world really began to listen; and it was not until the 1970s that we all began to feel the pinch, as the price of oil suddenly rocketed.

Now we are thinking about energy more carefully than ever before. This is reflected in science fiction, where today's writers usually make very sure that a plausible energy source is specified before sending spaceships to the stars, or turning Mars into a paradisal garden. Without energy, the technological miracles of science fiction will remain escapist fantasy; with energy they might just become reality.

Not all the world's problems can be solved with an ample supply of energy, but it would help a great deal. With energy we could make the deserts flower, feed the starving millions of the still-developing Third World, seek out raw materials that are at present inaccessible, and bring a better life to the more remote areas of the globe. As to the threat of warfare—full bellies and happy children are a great incentive to peace.

Without energy our already cumbersome social and political institutions will grind to a halt; our cars and aircraft will be discarded, and bicycles will become a luxury item hotly competed for. There will be a social revolution greater than any in the past, as all the machinery set up to develop those twin obsessions of the modern world—growth and progress—simply collapses.

The idea has a certain primitive appeal. In a grey and bureaucratic world the idea of self-reliance, of existing through our own wits and our own strength, has a romantic, individualistic ring to it. Science fiction writers have been satisfying our appetite for stories of the collapse of civilization for almost a century now, with novels from Richard Jefferies' *After London* in 1885, through Walter Miller's *A Canticle for Leibowitz* in 1960, to television series like the British *Survivors* in 1975-7, and many more books and films.

Dreams are one thing. The reality would be misery, carnage, depopulation, and back-breaking labour for the survivors — much bleaker than the empty, anonymous lives in high-rise flats that many of us experience now.

Science fiction's images of a

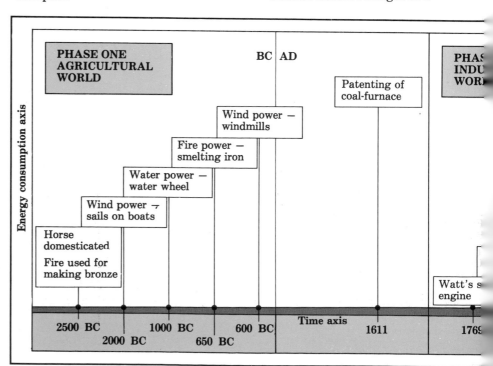

low-technology future may be romantic, but they are also realistic. The fossil fuels really are running out. If the world's energy consumption keeps doubling every decade, as it has been (see pages 34-6), even the least accessible coal-fields will be worked out, and even the oil locked up in shale deposits will be extracted, remarkably soon. Long before then, energy will have come to seem a luxury rather than our birthright. At the moment, we are expending more and more power on obtaining the fuel that will give us more and more power. We are all familiar with the effects of this vicious circle. Easily reachable reserves of petroleum and natural gas will, at the present rate of consumption, be used up by the year 2000; easily reachable coal reserves will be used up by the year 2300.

It is as difficult for us to imagine the past accurately as it is to imagine the future. It is hard to realize just how recently it was that we came to take cheap energy for granted. The stages of the process are shown in the diagram below. We can divide the history of mankind into three phases: agricultural, industrial and technological. The first phase lasted more than 12,000 years; its energy resources were pretty well restricted to muscle-power, water, wind, and wood fires. The industrial phase, powered

largely by steam, lasted less than 150 years. The technological phase, marked by electric power, rapid transport systems and a communications explosion, has lasted less than a century and is already wavering and losing momentum.

The optimists predict a super-technological phase to follow. The small-is-beautiful advocates, along with the pessimists, predict that the very idea of progress will collapse. Another group simply wants to see us stabilize energy consumption at its present level, neither advancing nor retreating.

If we wish to choose the first or even the third of these scenarios, then alternative energy resources must be found. But many of the power sources predicted in science fiction are of no use at all here and now. For example, the mutual annihilation of matter and anti-matter (see pages 78-9) would give vast amounts of energy. But the world's only antimatter is being made (at CERN in Geneva and one or two other places) in submicro-scopic amounts, and the energy being used to make it is vaster, by several orders of magnitude, than the energy that could be extracted from it. A more modest energy source is the solar wind that could propel spaceships to other planets (see page 22), but first the space-craft would have to be raised out of Earth's gravity well—again, very

expensively.

Mass and energy are the basic commodities of the physical universe. Most of the energy comes from stars; our Sun is one of them. Locating energy is easy; exploiting it is the hard part. But we live in an age when fiction must become fact if progress is to continue. In one respect, science fiction has already come true.

Nuclear power, predicted in science fiction since the beginning of the century, is the only present-day technology that is directly competitive with fossil fuels in terms of the cost of production. This is why most Western governments, of whatever political persuasion, and some Asian governments too, are going ahead with plans to build nuclear reactors, despite the massive, well organized and in some ways justified public outcry against them.

Below: the diagram — not to scale — shows turning points in Man's use of energy. Consumption was minimal during the long agricultural phase. In Phase Two, with the Industrial Revolution, coal consumption rose steeply, followed by consumption of gas and then oil at the end of the period. The technological era of high energy use began around 1900, with consumption almost doubling every decade since. How much energy will we need in the coming Phase Four?

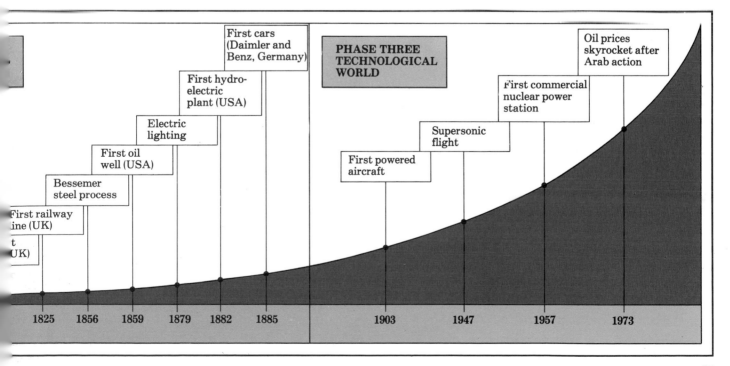

First railway line (UK)

t (UK)

Bessemer steel process

First oil well (USA)

Electric lighting

First hydro-electric plant (USA)

First cars (Daimler and Benz, Germany)

PHASE THREE TECHNOLOGICAL WORLD

First powered aircraft

Supersonic flight

First commercial nuclear power station

Oil prices skyrocket after Arab action

| 1825 | 1856 | 1859 | 1879 | 1882 | 1885 | 1903 | 1947 | 1957 | 1973 |

Nuclear fission

Long before the destruction of Nagasaki and Hiroshima in 1945, atomic power was a concept known to ordinary people. It was one of the most successful and best publicized predictions of science fiction writers. Ever since the discovery by Rutherford and Soddy in 1902 of the radioactive disintegration of uranium, it has been known that power was locked in the atom. Einstein provided the equation in 1905, when in a famous paper he showed the relationship between mass and energy: $E=mc^2$ (the energy locked up in matter equals the mass multiplied by the square of the speed of light). In other words, the disintegration of a tiny mass leads to a relatively vast emission of energy.

Science fiction writers were very quick to take the hint. In fact, one almost forgotten writer, Robert Cromie, got there through some extraordinary leap of the imagination even before the discovery of radioactivity by Antoine Henri Becquerel in 1896. In 1895, Cromie wrote of the power locked in the atom in his novel *The Crack of Doom*, in which a mad scientist utilizes this principle to build a bomb, and holds the world to ransom.

Atom bombs developed a rapid popularity in science fiction after Rutherford's work (see also pages 109-11). George Griffith wrote of atomic missiles in *The Lord of Labour* (1911), and H.G. Wells envisaged the effects of the atom bomb in *The World Set Free* (1914). It is eerie to realize that the weapon which put an end to World War II had in fact been imagined before World War I.

It took science fiction writers a while to consider that atomic energy might be controlled and put to creative purposes. Yet this too had become a familiar theme of science fiction stories by the beginning of the 1940s, before the bomb itself. 'Nerves', by Lester Del Rey, published in 1942, was about an accident in a nuclear power station. Del Rey's description of the public anxieties aroused by the generation of nuclear power turned out to be far-sighted indeed, though some of the present-day fear of nuclear power stations that he so accurately predicted is ill informed. We have been conditioned to think of atomic power in the form of massive explosions, but a full-scale nuclear explosion is one of the least likely scenarios facing nuclear power stations in the real world.

A far more likely scenario is that presented in the 1979 film *The China Syndrome*, which had the financial good fortune to be released just after an accident at the Three Mile Island nuclear power plant near Harrisburg, Pennsylvania. The film is based on the idea that, if the

Left: Blue Cerenkov radiation glows brilliantly and perilously from the core of the Bulk Shielding Reactor, one of four 'swimming pool' reactors at Oak Ridge National Laboratory in the USA. **Right:** this flow plan shows where the cooling-system pump broke down in the no. 2 reactor at the Three Mile Island nuclear power plant in the USA in 1979. Although some back-up safety procedures failed to work, 'meltdown' was averted in the rapidly heating core of the reactor. The accident gave the campaign against nuclear-power generation a great boost.

cooling system of a nuclear reactor broke down in some way, an uncontrolled though not explosive reaction, a 'meltdown', could take place within the core. This would create such high temperatures that fiercely incandescent materials could melt their way right down into the earth (and 'through to China', as one colourful though inaccurate phrase had it—hence the 'China Syndrome'). Dangerous radioactive materials would at the same time be released into the atmosphere.

Although the accident at Three Mile Island did not, in fact, lead to a meltdown, the public concern at the time was not unjustified. The cooling system did break down, the emergency procedures did not work properly, and a small amount of radioactive material was released into the atmosphere. It was only enough, however, according to the US Department of Health, Education and Welfare to cause one additional death from cancer among

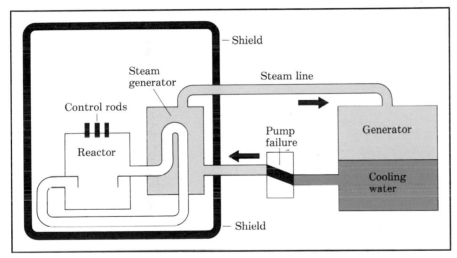

the 2 million people who lived within 50 miles of the accident site. (There have been many other accidents, most of them allegedly minor. However, according to CIA surveillance sources, there have been 14 major accidents in the USSR. Sparse details have been released about two of them. If the CIA is not exaggerating for reasons of its own, thousands of people died at Khystym, in the Urals, in 1958. In 1961 there was a second, 'even more terrifying' accident.)

Nuclear power is quite recent; the first nuclear power plant in the world went into service in the USA in 1957. But now it is so much with us that stories about it would no

longer be classified as science fiction by most readers; they are seen as present-day thrillers. A typical such scenario involves the theft of plutonium from a power station, or from a train or truck, by a terrorist group—and this could indeed happen. Plutonium is formed in nuclear reactors; it can be used to make atomic weapons, and is itself a deadly poison. The exact toxicity of plutonium is in dispute, but scientists believe that even one-ten-millionth of a gram may be a lethal dose, enough to cause cancer. The perils of plutonium are regarded by many as the strongest argument against the construction of nuclear power stations.

The other major problem is the disposal of radioactive waste products. Radioactivity cannot be destroyed, and radioactive wastes will retain some of their potency even after 25,000 years. These wastes are not, however, produced in large quantities. The total

amount of radioactive waste produced by the year 2000 would cover 1 square km to a depth of less than 5 metres. This is a tiny amount, when balanced against the massive pollution already resulting from the burning of fossil fuels. For every 1000 megawatts produced by a coal-fuelled electricity-generating plant, there is an annual release into the atmosphere of approximately 150,000 tons of sulphur dioxide (which is extremely corrosive), 9 million tons of carbon dioxide (which causes the 'greenhouse effect') and many other pollutants. This is the output of only one large, modern plant. The USA alone produces more than 300 times this

amount annually.

By contrast, a 1000-megawatt, fast-breeder nuclear plant produces a quarter of a cubic metre of radio-active waste products a year; but this waste is vastly more lethal than carbon dioxide.

Although there is no hard evidence (the Russian cases mentioned above are only rumours) that one single member of the public has ever been injured in any way by radioactive pollution from a nuclear power plant, some researchers believe that the increase of cancer victims may be due as much to increased radiation in the environment as to smoking. Workers in nuclear power plants seem to be very safe in comparison with, say, workers in the coal industry, where the death rate is more than 100 times as high. In neither industry, however, is it easy to tell if a particular illness, which may only show itself years later, has been directly caused by the conditions of work. In general, though, popular fears about nuclear power seem to be based not so much on what has happened as on what could happen.

Without Earth's naturally occurring background radiation (from cosmic rays and from such radioactive substances as uranium in the Earth's crust), higher forms of organic life would almost certainly have failed to evolve. This includes us. Evolution uses as its working material the natural varia-tions brought about by mutation, which in turn is largely caused by radioactivity.

This is no reason for complacency. We already have plenty of radiation to cause mutations; we need not voluntarily subject ourselves to more. Official figures show that the radiation released into the atmosphere by the use of nuclear reactors is negligible (so far at least) compared with the substantial amounts already there. But cynics might argue that officialdom has a vested interest in nuclear power and might mis-represent the facts. Government controls on the emission of radiation are extremely tight. We are unlikely to give up our nuclear reactors in the near future. We can only hope that these controls are efficiently and honestly applied.

Energy doubling and waste heat

Nuclear power plants, and the burning of fossil fuels, release heat into the biosphere that was not there before. Worries about heat pollution are comparatively recent, and were at first focused on water. Many rivers and lakes used for cooling, in all kinds of power plants, are heated up so much that the delicate balance of life within their waters is destroyed. Now scientists are beginning to worry about the extra heat released directly into the atmosphere. This is not yet a major problem. The total waste heat released by the year 2000 will be no more than one-thousandth of the heat already reaching us from the Sun. But in another 100 years there may be a noticeable rise in world temperature.

The burning of fossil fuels, however, may indirectly bring about a rise in world temperature much faster than this. The temperature of the atmosphere may not be much raised by waste heat (although large industrial cities tend to be warmer than the surrounding countryside), but it may be affected by pollutants in such a way as to trap a larger proportion of the Sun's heat. This is the so-called 'greenhouse effect' (see pages 114-15). Many scientists believe that, as the amount of carbon dioxide released into the atmosphere from burning fuels goes up, more of the Sun's heat will be retained. The carbon dioxide content of the atmosphere has increased by 10% already in the twentieth century, and will have increased by as much as 35% by the year 2000. Earth may get much hotter.

Accurate predictions of the future are notoriously difficult to make. It is true that the disaster scenarios of science fiction—John Brunner's novel *The Sheep Look Up* is an outstandingly depressing example—often take the worst possible interpretation of existing statistics and trends. But these statistics do exist, and we cannot make them go away by ignoring them. The increasing generation and consumption of energy provide some of the most frightening statistics of all.

At the moment the energy consumption of the world is approximately doubling every 10 years. The total consumption of petroleum from its first exploitation in 1859 right through to 1959, for example, was around the same as the consumption in only the following decade, from 1959 to 1969.

The world cannot go on doubling its energy consumption every 10 years for very much longer, and could not do so even if our energy resources were virtually infinite. We would, surprisingly soon, reach a stage where we were pumping more heat into our atmosphere than could ever be radiated back into space. That would be true, at least, if the extra energy we used were taken from sources such as fossil fuels and nuclear reactors where the energy was previously locked up.

If we double our energy requirements every 10 years, then in only 100 years from now we shall be using 1024 times as much energy as we are using now. (This would mean, speaking approximately, that every square metre of Earth's land space would be required to radiate as much additional heat outwards as already falls on it from the Sun.) By the year 2100 Earth would be a hot and uncomfortable place. The melting ice-caps would long since have submerged New York and London.

Nature demands a balance. For the temperature of Earth to remain the same as now, just as much heat must be radiated out into space as we collect from all sources. Most of the heat we collect comes from sunshine; some comes from geo-thermal sources such as volcanoes; and we create more ourselves with every passing year. If we put more heat into the system, then, unless we radiate more out again, the temperature will go up. As the science fiction writer Frederik Pohl once wittily suggested, we could paint Texas white. That would increase the radiation outwards, but it might not be a very popular move with the Texans. To make matters worse, our most efficient outward radiators at present are the polar ice-caps. If the temperature goes up, they will not be here much longer to do the job.

We cannot use energy without creating waste heat; the inexorable law of what the physicists call 'entropy' (see page 86) will not allow it. Because of entropy, no energy generator can run at 100% efficiency. There is always a heat loss. Energy in high forms (low entropy) can readily be degraded into energy in lower forms, but these lower forms (such as the chemical energy locked up in fossil fuels) cannot be converted into higher forms (such as electricity) without heat loss. A familiar example of the waste heat produced in such processes is given by the ordinary electric light bulb. It is quite inefficient in converting electricity into light, which is a relatively 'high' form of energy. Much of the power used goes into waste heat—which is why light bulbs are hot to the touch.

In the face of these energy-

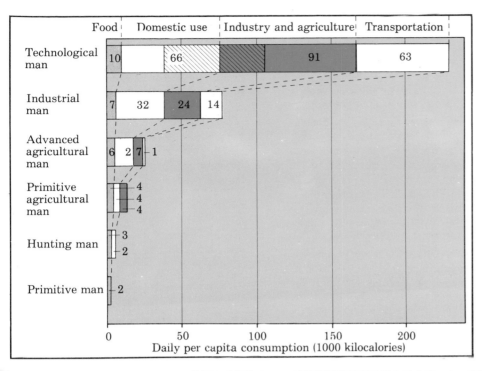

	Food	Domestic use	Industry and agriculture	Transportation
Technological man	10	66		91	63
Industrial man	7	32	24	14
Advanced agricultural man	6	2	7	1
Primitive agricultural man		4	4	4
Hunting man		3	2	
Primitive man	2			

Daily per capita consumption (1000 kilocalories)

doubling statistics, we must ask if our high-technology society, with its high energy consumption, is already doomed. Will it collapse under the strain of its own greed, suffocated by its own hot waste products? Things are not quite as bleak as this yet, and there are at least two routes out of the energy-doubling impasse.

The first is that common sense and a variety of social pressures will force us to slow down our energy consumption—not necessarily to reverse it, but to slow down the rate of increase. For one thing, world population will not continue to grow at the rate by which it was increasing quite recently. Population growth has already slowed down substantially. (The most recent United Nations figures show a population of around 4.5 billion now, and predict a population of 6 billion

Top: the American geographer Earl Cook has worked out the daily consumption of energy for six stages of human development. By 1970 in the USA, technological man was consuming 230,000 kilo-calories per day, much of it in the form of electricity (hatched area). Food includes what is fed to domestic animals. The industrial society is that of England in 1875. Overall energy use is increasing even faster than this shows, since the figures are per head, and now there are many more heads than there were.
Left: a thermal line-scan image of a power station releasing hot effluent into the River Trent in England. Where the water is hot it appears white. More heat is being added to the atmosphere by the steam from the cooling towers. Are we making Earth too hot?

35

by the year 2000, levelling off at 11 billion in the following century—see also page 116.) Sooner or later, the growth had to slow down. If the population kept on increasing at the old rate, there would not be enough space for us all to stand in after a surprisingly few centuries had passed. As world population stabilizes, so will energy consumption.

The second possible way out of the impasse is to seek energy sources that do not pollute the atmosphere with carbon dioxide, which causes the 'greenhouse effect', and with waste heat. The fossil fuels do both, but they are in any case running out. Nuclear power does not produce carbon dioxide, but it does produce a great deal of waste heat, and has a fearsome potential for radioactive pollution. Furthermore, nuclear-fission power stations are not exempt from energy-doubling problems. The rare isotope uranium-235, which is used to fuel nuclear reactors, will not last indefinitely. Much of our readily accessible uranium will be used up by the end of this century. Uranium-235 can be replaced by the artifical element plutonium-239, which is manufactured in fast-breeder reactors. (These get their name from the fact that while producing power they produce plutonium fuel as well.) Our uranium reserves can in this way be eked out to last for at least 1000 years, and probably much longer. But good news usually comes at a cost. ('There ain't no such thing as a free lunch', as the science fiction writer Robert Heinlein has sagely observed in several of his novels.) Fast-breeder reactors necessarily operate at a much higher temperature than ordinary nuclear reactors, and the dangers of a 'meltdown' in the case of an accident are correspondingly greater. And their main product, plutonium, is a deadly, toxic material from which atom bombs can easily be made, even by comparatively backward nations. (Hence the political fuss about the great powers' giving nuclear-reactor technology to such nations as Iraq and Pakistan. Where the reactor is built, the bomb can follow soon after.) The first fast-breeder reactor was built at Dounreay on the North Scottish coast. It came into service

in 1959.

Nuclear power is not the only answer, however. There are many energy systems on Earth (and outside it) which are already powered by heat from the Sun. There is sunshine itself; there is the energy potential of living plants (from which we can get alcohol); there are wind, waves and currents. There is also the naturally occurring heat from geothermal energy— volcanoes and hot springs. The heat from all these sources already exists. If we use it, we are not creating new heat to pump into our atmosphere. To preserve our biosphere, we may have to learn how to make economic use of these systems—or move our heavy

industries out into space.

There is an increasing public demand for the exploitation of these so-called 'invariant energy systems'. (We analyse the most important of them on pages 39-41). But the biggest 'free lunch' of all is nuclear fusion (see pages 37-8), which offers such huge rewards that governments yearn to use it, despite the waste-heat problems it would inevitably bring in its wake.

Cities are hotter than rural areas, partly because of the amount of waste heat created in them, and partly because of the heat absorbed and re-radiated by concrete and asphalt. This infra-red satellite picture, in which hot areas appear darker, clearly shows several cities, including London and Paris.

Nuclear fusion

In science fiction, by far the most popular technique for producing energy is nuclear fusion. There are two reasons for this. One is extremely romantic, the other extremely practical.

The romantic reason is that the process of nuclear fusion comes close to duplicating what happens in the Sun. We lived in caves not so long ago. There could be no more romantic a symbol of our evolution than the harnessing of those same energies that light up our sky by day (the Sun) and by night (the stars).

The practical reason is that nuclear fusion is (theoretically) cheap. It releases more energy than nuclear fission and it uses cheaper materials. This is why fusion power is not just a dream of science fiction writers; it is the subject of millions of dollars' worth of research every year. (But if we are to have fusion by the year 2000, which a number of fusion scientists believe to be possible, the sum set aside for research will have to be measured in billions, not millions.)

What is nuclear fusion? Like nuclear fission, it relies on the fact that mass can be converted into energy. In fission, the nuclei of the unstable atoms of rare, heavy elements are broken down into the nuclei of lighter elements, releasing energy in the process. Fusion is rather more elegant; it takes place with much lighter and more abundant elements, and is a putting together rather than a tearing apart.

The process works by squeezing the nuclei of hydrogen atoms together, fusing them into helium atoms, plus an emission of energy. Hydrogen is by far the most common element in the universe; even on Earth it is extremely common, being one of the two constitutents of water (the other is oxygen). However, ordinary hydrogen is of no use for fusion under Earthly conditions: it is too stable. But hydrogen exists in two other forms (isotopes), both of which can be used in fusion processes.

Ordinary hydrogen is the simplest of all elements. Its atom consists of a nucleus containing one proton, around which a single electron orbits. Heavy hydrogen, known as deuterium, has a nucleus consisting of one proton and one neutron. It is relatively uncommon; for every 6700 atoms of ordinary hydrogen there is only 1 atom of deuterium; but given the vast size of our oceans, even 1 part in 6700 represents a colossal total mass. The cost of separating out the deuterium from ordinary sea water would be negligible in relation to the energy that would result from deuterium fusion reactions.

An even more useful isotope of hydrogen is tritium, a kind of super-heavy hydrogen. The tritium atom has a nucleus consisting of one proton and two neutrons. Unfortunately, tritium is very rare in nature; but it is comparatively simple to make artificially. This is done by bombarding a rather more common element, lithium, with neutrons.

There are complications to the fusion process. Energy can be gained by squeezing deuterium nuclei together (see diagram); half

the nuclei take part in the first of the two reactions and half in the second. Energy can also be gained by squeezing deuterium together with tritium nuclei (see diagram). This last reaction gives the most energy immediately, but since tritium is one product of the first two reactions, it is the deuterium-deuterium fusion process that gives the most energy in the long run. This would seem the best process to use, then, especially as it utilizes a relatively abundant isotope. (The energy locked up in the deuterium of 1 cubic metre of water is equal to that produced by burning 300 tons of coal.) The bad news is that both kinds of fusion are extremely difficult to bring about, and the better of the two, deuterium-deuterium, needs an even higher operating temperature than the other. Present-day research, therefore, concentrates on the deuterium-tritium reaction.

The temperature gives us the problem. It is very difficult to force the nuclei of two atoms to fuse together because, containing protons as they do, they are both positively charged. Everybody knows how difficult it is to push the positive poles of two magnets together; they repel each other powerfully. The atomic nuclei have to be thrown together so vigorously that the electric repulsion is overcome. This, as it happens, requires a great deal of force. The nuclei have to be given an extremely high kinetic energy before they are moving fast enough to fuse. In everyday language, that means that they must be very hot—hotter, in fact, than the Sun. (The Sun, being very dense, can pull off the trick more easily; the force of gravity comes into play in helping to squeeze the nuclei together.) We can already do it: the result is the hydrogen bomb. But the real question is, how do we control the process? This is the problem on which so much research is being carried out today.

To make fusion work by the Tokamak method (see illustration), we need to create, for a fraction of a second, a thin plasma of ionized deuterium and tritium at a temperature of around 100 million degrees centigrade. This cannot be done in an ordinary container. What

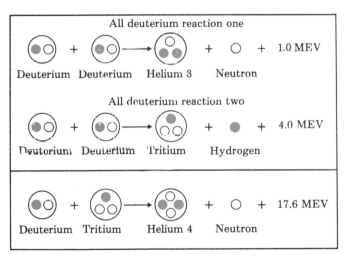

All deuterium reaction one

Deuterium + Deuterium → Helium 3 + Neutron + 1.0 MEV

All deuterium reaction two

Deuterium + Deuterium → Tritium + Hydrogen + 4.0 MEV

Deuterium + Tritium → Helium 4 + Neutron + 17.6 MEV

The upper two reactions take place when deuterium atoms are fused at huge temperatures; half the atoms fuse in the first process and half in the second. The lower equation shows deuterium-tritium fusion. The dark dots are protons, the light ones are neutrons. The figures show the energy that is emitted.

is being attempted is the creation of a container that does not consist of matter at all, but of a magnetic field that will keep the protons within it. This is sometimes known as a 'magnetic bottle'.

Despite the difficulties, fusion has already been attained on a small scale in laboratories, but only for a fraction of a second. We need a continuous process, where all the excess energy (beyond that required to keep the plasma hot enough to carry on fusing) could be used to heat, say, a fast-flowing stream of potassium. This heat would then be used to generate electricity. Research has not yet reached the break-even stage at which the amount of energy taken out of the system is as great as the amount of energy required to cause the fusion in the first place.

Another promising line of research is directed towards the bombardment from all sides of tiny, frozen pellets of deuterium and tritium by a battery of laser beams (see diagram), each one operating within a billionth of a second of all the others. The highly energetic laser beams would force the pellet to implode (to explode inwards). This also creates the necessary conditions for fusion.

It is easy to see why the idea of fusion power is so attractive: it uses a cheap fuel, found in sea water, that should last us for the foreseeable future; it gives a higher energy yield than nuclear fission; there is less risk of environmental pollution (though the high-energy neutrons produced will create some radioactivity); and, best of all, it is a process which cannot by its very nature get out of control. Any explosion, even the beginning of one, causes the process to stop automatically. Fusion can only take place under conditions of extreme compression.

It may happen. It probably will, though the technological problems of creating and sustaining the unimaginably high temperature are formidable. Nuclear fusion is not quite perfect, however, for use on Earth (though it may turn out to be the best method of powering a starship—see pages 10-13). We are back to the old problem of putting more heat into the biosphere with no easy way of getting rid of it.

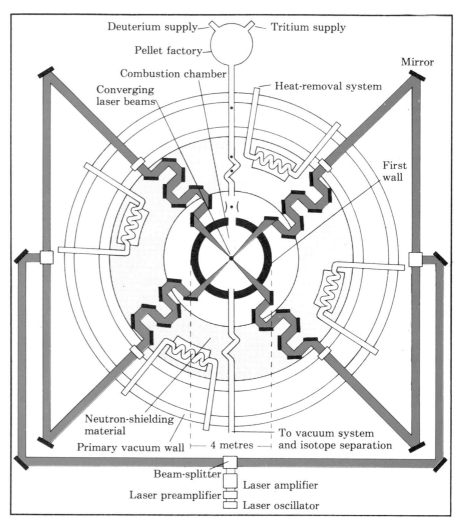

Above: this is how a laser-fusion power plant might operate. Liquid pellets of tritium and deuterium about 1 mm in diameter are guided electro- statically in a zigzag to the central combustion chamber, where they are imploded by converging laser beams, and the heat removed.

Below: most fusion research is carried out in tokamaks (Russian acronym for toroidal magnetic chamber) like this one, the Large Torus at Princeton University. The very hot fusion materials are confined in a vacuum vessel by magnetic fields generated by massive coils.

Renewable energy sources

How much 'free' energy does the whole world receive every day? If we can convert this 'free' energy into usable forms (electricity, for example) we are not drawing on the bank, and we are not emitting waste heat that was not already circulating to begin with. There are basically three sources of 'free' energy—renewable energy sources, or 'invariant energy systems', as they are sometimes called.

The smallest of these is the power locked up in the ocean tides. This power comes from the combined kinetic and potential energy of the Earth-Moon-Sun system, and is ultimately derived from gravity. Tidal energy is less

than 0.002% of the total energy we receive on Earth.

The second is geothermal energy, which is the heat conducted up from Earth's hot interior. Some of this is in the form of hot springs and volcanoes, and most of it, less spectacularly, is quietly moving up through the soil. Geothermal energy is a little less than 0.02% of the total energy we receive on Earth.

The third renewable energy source is radiation from the Sun. The total solar radiation intercepted by Earth is 1.73×10^{17} watts: more than 99.98% of the total energy we receive on Earth. About 30% of the solar energy we receive is re-radiated straight back into space as short-wavelength radiation. About 47% is absorbed by the oceans, the land and the atmosphere, and converted straight into the heat that maintains Earth at a fairly constant

temperature. Most of the rest is used to evaporate water which eventually falls again as rain, in the hydrologic cycle; it also ultimately provides the energy to drive the winds, the waves and ocean currents. Finally, a tiny fraction is used by plants for photosynthesis, and converted into chemical energy. When the plants die and rot, this energy is released again, except for those tiny amounts of vegetation that become trapped in conditions where free rotting cannot take place. These form coal, oil and pockets of natural gas. They are our rapidly diminishing fossil fuels which took many millions of years to form and only a few hundred to use up.

It does not take an arithmetical genius to see that solar power is the most generous of the above sources. Tidal power and geothermal power may be useful in some, highly localized areas; but they cannot conceivably provide us with all our energy requirements, even today.

The turbines of a tidal power plant are turned by the weight of the water trapped at high tide behind floodgates. It has been estimated that if all the suitable bays and estuaries in the USA were dammed for the generation of tidal power, the total output would be around 100 gigawatts (100,000 megawatts). This sounds impressive, until we learn that the electricity consumption of the USA was already three times that amount by 1970. Tidal power around the world will at best be a useful back-up system. It will also create enormous damage to the ecological systems (which include tourists) of many pleasant bays and harbours throughout the world, if put into operation on a large scale.

Geothermal power is already generated at various places around the world. The plant at Lardarello, in Italy, was built in 1904, and now

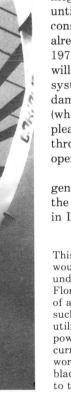

This giant turbine would be moored underwater off the Florida coast, one of a chain of 230 such generators utilizing the most powerful ocean current in the world to turn the blades, according to the designers Bill Mouton and Peter Lissaman. This imaginary prototype is *Coriolis One*. The Gulf Stream flows through the 168-metre diameter duct at 2.5 metres per second. Its output is around 43 megawatts.

generates 370 megawatts; it uses naturally occurring steam. However, the areas where Earth's internal heat rises to the surface at the necessary high temperatures are comparatively few, though we can drill down towards the heat ourselves (see diagram). Dormant volcanoes are not a good risk, since the plant would be wiped out in an eruption. There are pollution problems with geothermal power. Water from underground sources often has a high mineral content, leading to problems of corrosion. It has been estimated that geothermal plants could generate 100 gigawatts by the end of this century; but, though useful, this would cater for only a fraction of our estimated needs by that time.

The most attractive renewable energy source is solar power. It exists in many forms, some of them far from obvious. For example, the Sun heats up the surface water of oceans, and the difference in temperature between the surface water and the water beneath can be used to generate power. Such a station, still in the experimental stage, exists near Hawaii. Solar power drives the ocean currents, too. It has been suggested that we could tap the mighty power of the Gulf Stream with gigantic, underwater, rotating blades (see picture on page 39).

It is solar power that evaporates the water from the oceans that falls again as rain, and creates rivers. Thus all hydroelectric power, which is generated by descending river or lake water, is ultimately solar power. Solar power also creates winds. Wind-power, one of the most ancient power sources on Earth, has proved especially attractive to many of the ecologically conscious pressure groups: it has such a clean feeling to it. There is no pollution, and not much is needed in the way of heavy machinery. Unfortunately, except in those rare areas of the world that have consistent high winds, it is remarkably inefficient. In order to build enough windmills to generate electric power on a really useful scale we would have to cover the landscape with them. The ecologists might not be so keen, then, on the visual pollution that would result.

Solar power can even be used to

replace fossil fuels directly. After all, it is solar power that grows plants! Alcohol, a good fuel for automobiles, can readily be distilled from a great variety of plants. (This technique for generating chemical energy is often referred to as the 'biomass system'.) It would take a great many plants to replace the amount of petroleum used today, but in some countries this might just be possible. Unfortunately, every hectare of productive ground used for growing plants for fuel is a hectare less for growing plants for food.

It makes more sense to take solar power from unproductive land, such as deserts or the ice-caps. Deserts are better; they receive a great deal more direct sunlight. The 'solar constant' is an important figure here. This is the amount of radiation from the Sun that is intercepted by the Earth. It works out at about 1.4 kilowatts per square metre, but much of this is absorbed by the atmosphere, especially in cloudy areas. Also, in southern and northern latitudes, where the Sun's rays strike Earth at a more acute angle, the amount of

radiation is obviously less for every square metre. Solar power, then, is best exploited in cloudless desert or semi-desert areas not too far north or south. (The equator might seem to be an ideal site, until we remember how often equatorial conditions are cloudy. Also, at the moment, few nations situated on or near the equator have the economic resources to build solar power generators on a large scale. Nevertheless, the best sites are within 30° of the equator.)

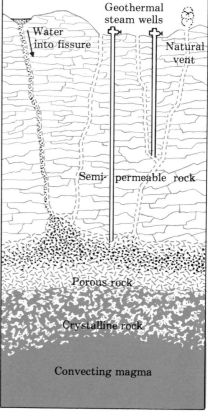

Right: The diagram shows how hot water, of maybe 260°C, trapped in the porous rock layer under great pressure can be tapped by wells driven through the relatively impermeable cap rock that holds the water in, unless it escapes as steam through natural vents. **Below**: steel pipes carry high-pressure steam at the geothermal power station at Wairakei in New Zealand. Corrosion is a problem.

In fact, the *average* amount of the Sun's energy actually reaching a square metre of Earth's surface is only 730 watts, during the hours of daylight. The sums are quite simple. To convert sunlight into power on a large scale, we would have to cover quite a lot of desert. This is especially true at the moment, when we do not convert sunlight to electricity at an efficiency of more than around 14%. Technological advances may drive that figure up to 25%, but probably no further. For a 1000-megawatt plant, a land area of between 20 and 70 square km would be needed, according to the method of energy conversion used. (One optimistic estimate gives 12 square km as a future possibility.) To supply the near-future needs of the USA, for example, 40,000 square km of desert (probably in Nevada or Arizona) may need to be covered. This is not quite such a huge area as it sounds at first; it is, roughly, 13.5% of the area of Arizona.

The two most popular methods of converting sunlight to electric power are by solar cell, in which the conversion (by way of semi-conductor chips) is direct, and by steam turbine. The first method is considerably more expensive, at the moment, to install; but because solar cells have no moving parts,

they are extraordinarily durable and reliable. The second method is to construct an array of pivoting, concave mirrors; these mirrors focus the sunlight they receive on to a central heat collector, which gets very hot. (Everybody knows that you can make fire with a small magnifying glass; it is easy to imagine the temperatures attainable when the sunlight from thousands of square metres is focused on a single point.)

Because sunlight turns off at night, large-scale schemes must have carefully designed energy storage systems to smooth out the daily variation. (Similar problems arise with wind, wave and tidal power.)

Most of the solar power exploited today is used domestically, where it often does not need to be converted to electricity: it is mostly used for space and water heating, and (using heat pumps) for refrigeration. The US government is at present spending vast-sounding sums on solar power research ($470 million in 1979), but in fact they represent less than 3% of the overall energy budget. Businessmen prefer nuclear power (which has bigger profits because the energy source is not freely available), and so, at the moment, do politicians. But all this may change. Solar technology is already making a great deal of

money at the domestic level.

Given the obvious advantages, why has the world — especially those areas, like North Africa, Australia and the USA, that possess their own deserts — not yet turned to solar power? (Cloudy countries such as the UK would have to import solar-generated electricity from their warmer neighbours.) Solar power should please even the devotees of nuclear fusion, since it utilizes a vast nuclear-fusion energy generator — the Sun — at a comfortably safe distance of 150 million km away. The reason for our not yet having turned to solar power on a large scale is one of finance. Estimates differ, but at the moment it seems that to build solar plants will be about half as expensive again as to build nuclear power plants. There are many uncertainties. The fact that solar plants are likely to last much longer might bring the price down, when future running costs are calculated into the sum, but governments have seldom been good at taking the long view.

However, this 50% cost margin is not very large. As fossil fuels and uranium become scarcer and more expensive, and as safety precautions with nuclear plants also get more expensive, then solar power might very well come, in the near future, to be an economic bargain.

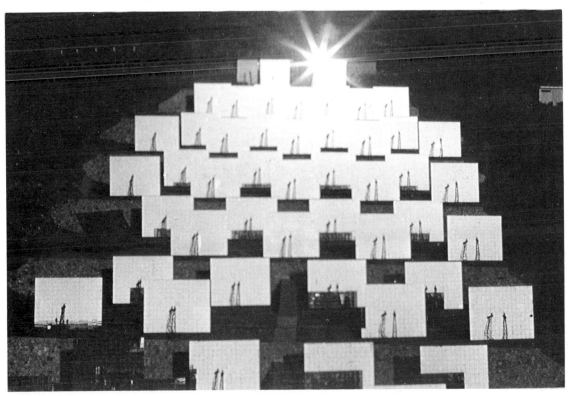

This experimental solar power station in the French Pyrenees does not generate a great deal of electricity, but it points towards a promising future. The mirrors in this array can be tracked to follow the Sun; they focus its light on to a giant parabolic mirror, which focuses an intensely hot beam on a single point. However, conversion of sunlight into electricity cannot yet compete with nuclear power or fossil fuels in terms of cheapness.

Solar power from satellites

Solar power plants on Earth take up a lot of room. A simple exercise in lateral thinking has produced a possible answer to the problem. Why not put the solar collectors out in space, where they would not get in anybody's way? This would have its advantages. There would be no night-time shut-off. Also, the Sun's radiation at sea-level has already been partly dissipated by the atmosphere, but outside the atmosphere it would be collected at full strength.

Many systems have been proposed for satellite solar power. All envisage large satellites in geo-synchronous orbit; that is to say, in orbit at precisely the right height (36,000 km) to maintain the satellite's position exactly above a given point on Earth. Huge, light-weight panels of solar cells would be spread out like giant wings on each side of the central living capsule; wings perhaps 5 km wide and 10 km long. In free fall, metal is not subject to gravitational stresses, and gigantic engineering projects that would collapse under their own weight on Earth become quite plausible in space.

The power (now in the form of electricity) collected by the satellite would then, according to the currently most popular theory, be converted into microwave radiation, the same as the radiation in micro-wave ovens, a kind of high-energy, very-short-wave radio. The micro-waves would be broadcast in a very tight beam to collecting antennae on Earth. (Over the 36,000 km, the beam would not spread very widely, but the collecting antennae would still cover an area of 10 km×13 km — more than twice the size of Manhattan.) Here the microwaves would be converted back into electricity at an efficiency of more than 80%. There would be very little absorption of energy by the atmo-sphere. One such satellite power station would have an output of 5000 megawatts — about five times the power of most existing large generators on Earth.

This concept was first proposed in 1968 by Dr Peter Glaser of

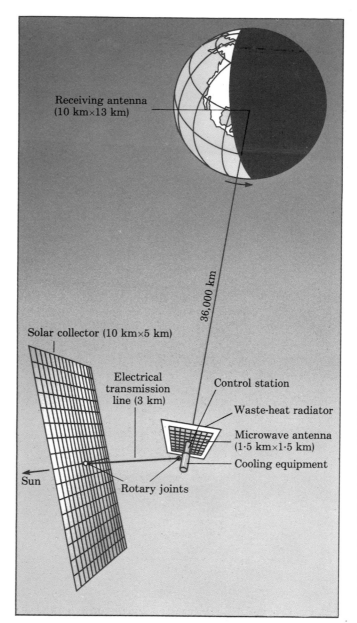

Receiving antenna (10 km×13 km)

36,000 km

Solar collector (10 km×5 km)

Electrical transmission line (3 km)

Control station

Waste-heat radiator

Microwave antenna (1·5 km×1·5 km)

Cooling equipment

Sun

Rotary joints

Left: The huge collecting panel of a solar satellite would intercept sunlight, convert it into electricity, and then beam the power to Earth in the form of micro-waves. Each satellite would be in geosynchronous orbit above the equator, and thus stationary with respect to the collecting antennae on Earth below. One satellite would weigh 50,000 tons, cost around $27,000 million (£15,000 million) and generate 5 giga-watts of power — about five times as much as the largest generators on Earth. Only a dream? The US government spent over $16 million investigating it. The result — muted optimism. **Below:** Boeing Aerospace's con-ception of a solar power satellite under construction. A space shuttle is docked at the assembly bay, right. A heavy lift cargo vehicle approaches, left.

Massachusetts. Since then the US government has funded a $16 million study of the project, which has been widely publicized.

People who are afraid (naturally enough) of being fried or cancer-ridden if caught in such a beam have resoundingly criticized the project as an example of techno-logical thinking run wild. It seems, however, that the beam would not be so concentrated when it reached Earth as to incinerate passers-by, or even, according to official sources, injure them in any way. (The collecting areas would, of course, be out of bounds, though propagandiz-ing art-work shows cows grazing peacefully in the middle of the collecting-antennae area.) Also, a

more general use, costs will go down. More science-fiction-minded engineers are not too worried about this problem. They suggest we get the raw materials from the Moon; they would be easier to lift into space than they would be from Earth (see pages 23-5).

The possibility of power from solar satellites highlights the continuing debate between science-fiction-minded, technological optimists and more cautious 'realists'. Both groups have a voice in government, but it has to be said that in the early 1980s the optimists' chances of going ahead with such schemes look slim indeed, at least for the next decade. Economists see the solar satellite

megawatts—equal to 200 large nuclear power stations. The enterprising part of the scheme would be the use of glacier ice as the primary construction material for dams and channels. In another scheme, just as ambitious and rather more lunatic, it is proposed to divert the Niger river through the Sahara, under the Mediterranean, over the Alps and into Germany, where useful hot water would result for the Germans. Schemes ranging from the practical to the hare-brained are endless.

The problems of generating power are closely connected to the problems of its distribution. Vast amounts of electricity generated in the Australian desert or in the Gulf

The collecting antennae for a solar power satellite will take up a lot of room — six times as much space as a coal-burning power plant of the same capacity. A possible answer for the UK, for example, would be to build an artificial island in the North Sea, on which the antennae would stand in serried ranks as in this artist's con-ception: an expensive project with an area of 100 km^2 or more.

simple fail safe system could be built to ensure that if, by some accident, the beam failed to lock on to the antennae cluster, it would instantly be harmlessly dissipated. Further research needs to be done, however, on the effects of low-concentration microwaves on organic life (which includes people), and it is understandable that the project should receive a somewhat nervous reception. Some scientists have proposed that lasers, which can be focused even more tightly, should replace microwave beams as the means of transmitting the energy down to Earth.

The technical problems are vast, of course. The capital cost of raising heavy equipment into orbit would at the moment be prohibitive, though as the space shuttle comes into

scheme as laughable. Military strategists will certainly advise the USA or any other nation that to put all their energy eggs in one very vulnerable basket in space, where they could be readily knocked out by enemy missiles, would be stark lunacy. The high-technology futures imagined by utopian visionaries depend on a much greater degree of international peace and co-operation than the world can boast of now.

The construction of solar power satellites is only one of many high-technology power-generating projects that have been suggested for the near future. For example, the annual summer melting of the Greenland ice-cap, at a height of 2000-3000 metres, could provide hydroelectric schemes with an estimated output of 200,000

Stream will not do much to help peasants in Cambodia or even office-workers in London, unless more efficient methods of international power distribution are worked out. Energy can be beamed; it can also be stored and shipped in chemical form. The possibilities are endless, but are a long way from realization on any but an experimental scale. The building of global energy networks will have as much to do with supranational corporations and international banks as with engineers.

The energy schemes discussed so far have all been located on Earth or in its immediate vicinity. Many science fiction writers would regard this near-future emphasis as rather provincial. Should we look further ahead and further out?

Far-future energy

When we look into the far future, and away from Earth, the possibilities for power generation expand by many orders of magnitude. Ever since the days of *Flash Gordon* and before, science fiction writers have been toying with the idea of vast energies capable of vaporizing whole planets at a stroke, but they were usually rather reticent about how these energies would be achieved, and understandably so. In the past 20 years, however, the scientists have been putting their minds to the same question.

One of the first scientists to take the question seriously was the Soviet astronomer Nikolai Kardashev, a prominent member of the group of Russian scientists searching the heavens for traces of extraterrestrial life. In 1964 Kardashev speculated about the kinds of advanced alien society that might exist elsewhere, and decided that the most useful method of classification would be to divide such theoretical societies up according to their energy consumption.

A Phase I society exploits the energy resources of its own planet, including the incident sunlight. A Phase II society exploits all the energy of its own sun, thus increasing its energy exploitation around 100,000 billion times. A Phase III society exploits all the energy resources of its own galaxy, thus further increasing its energy exploitation around 100 billion times. (It would follow from all this, of course, that a Phase III society would be the easiest to detect, since its signals would be strongest.)

Our own Earth is on the way to becoming a Phase I civilization, but it still has a long way to go. Seen from this perspective, all the previous sections of this chapter have been examining the strategies for our reaching a Phase I status.

At this point we need to introduce the theories of Freeman Dyson, the English-born, American physicist who has become a guru for science fiction fans, because of the amazingly wide-ranging nature of his mathematically based speculations on the nature of our universe and the life that may exist in it. Also, Dyson has been prepared to publish his conjectures in sober scientific journals, where they have reached an audience which might have dismissed them out of hand if they had appeared in, say, a science fiction magazine in the first instance.

In 1959, in a short paper published in *Science* entitled 'Search for Artificial Stellar Sources of Infra-Red Radiation', Dyson revolutionized science fiction thinking overnight. His reasoning, a little simplified, went as follows. If societies on other planets orbiting other stars are at all like our own, then they use more energy every year as their society evolves, just as we have done. Even a modest growth rate of 1% annually in the consumption of energy (much lower than our own doubling of energy consumption every decade) would lead to an increase of 10^{12} (1000 billion) in only 3000 years. This is a nice example of a sum familiar to those who have decent bank accounts — compound interest.

Although Dyson was too early to use Kardashev's terminology, he was clearly talking about the transition from a Phase I civilization to a Phase II. Earth could not support a growth even a tiny fraction as large as this. The only way this growth could be sustained would be to use *all* the energy of the Sun, and the only way, said Dyson, to trap all the Sun's radiation would be to build a sphere around it.

Such a giant sphere was originally proposed in 1937 in the science fiction novel *Star Maker* by Olaf Stapledon: 'Every solar system [was] surrounded by a gauze of light traps, which focused the escaping solar energy for intelligent use.' However, these are now called 'Dyson spheres' by all science fiction readers. If such a sphere were built in our own Solar System, it would probably be built so that

Below: in 1964, the Russian astronomer Nikolai Kardashev proposed that growing technological societies passed through three possible phases of energy use. We have not yet achieved Phase One on Earth; our solar and tidal power is still untapped. The culmination of Phase Two is a Dyson sphere.

Three types of future society: after Kardashev

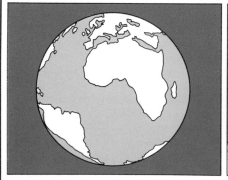

Phase One:
resources of a whole planet utilized

Phase Two:
resources of a whole solar system utilized

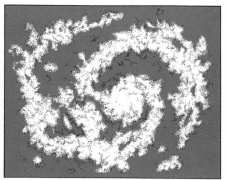

Phase Three:
resources of a whole galaxy utilized

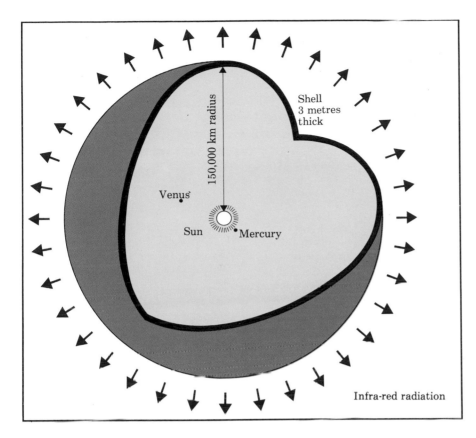

Shell
3 metres
thick

150,000 km radius

Venus

Sun   Mercury

Infra-red radiation

its radius would be the same as the present distance of the Earth from the Sun. We would live on the inside surface of the sphere, facing the Sun. It would always be noon.

There would be drawbacks. There would be no gravity to start with, unless we generated it artificially by spinning the sphere, but that would restrict the comfortably habitable zone to a belt round the sphere's equator. Or perhaps, by then, we shall know how to generate gravity directly.

There would be plenty of room. The surface area of the inside of the sphere would be approximately 1 billion times that of Earth.

It would be difficult to build, but the raw materials are at hand. We might start by using the asteroids, and later on use Mars and then Jupiter. Jupiter alone would give us enough mass to make the shell of the sphere at least 3 metres thick. We can hardly conceive of such a plan in terms of our present-day technology, but we are discussing a high-energy future, with around 1000 billion times as much energy to use as we have now.

In practice the idea of an unbroken sphere would probably not work. Its very rigidity would subject it to tremendous stresses

that would probably tear it apart. But we need not go all the way. A useful compromise might be to build a spherical shell of individual worldlets — perhaps a million of them — each one orbiting independently. A lot of sunlight would leak through the gaps, but we would retain a great deal.

Waste heat, which as on Earth would largely take the form of infra-red radiation, would be pumped out through the shell away from the Sun. It follows—and this was Dyson's point—that, if we are seeking intelligent life elsewhere in the Galaxy, we should keep an eye out for objects radiating in the infra-red. We have observed a number of these already. Who knows? Perhaps some of them are Dyson spheres. From the outside such a sphere would look like a dully luminous, giant red star—a rather sinister sight.

The most celebrated science fiction novel to use the idea of a Dyson sphere is *Ringworld* by Larry Niven, though in fact, as the title suggests, Niven opts for a belt like a cartwheel rather than an entire sphere; he has also written interestingly on Dyson's theories in an article in his collection *A Hole in Space*. (One of the technical draw-

backs of Niven's *Ringworld* is discussed on pages 190-1.) Bob Shaw's novel *Orbitsville* envisages a complete sphere, and is breathtaking in its evocation of sheer size. It is difficult for us even to imagine a living space a billion times greater than our own. These and other science fiction writers should be congratulated for being so quick to pick up Dyson's hint. But it was Dyson himself who made the initial imaginative leap, who first saw the ultimate, logical consequences of an energy budget that suffers from annual inflation.

A Phase III civilization, exploiting the energy resources of a galaxy, does not exist in our own vicinity. If it did, we should already know about it. It would be chewing up stars as casually as we throw another log of wood on to the fire; it would be using gamma ray lasers (see pages 104-5) to cause stars to go nova if the fire died down further; and if its civilization really started feeling the energy pinch, it would manipulate black holes to collide (see page 106). (One scientific paper describes black holes as 'the largest energy storehouse in the universe'.) Science fiction writer and physicist Stanley Schmidt has suggested that the colossal explosions observed at the heart of some galaxies, like M82, may be 'industrial accidents'. It seems probable that black-hole technology will be the basis of all Phase III civilizations.

Energy is where both science and science fiction begin. With only a small supply of energy we shall be rather chilly stay-at-homes. With ample resources we may reach the stars in real life, as well as in our imaginations.

Chapter 3
ALIENS

The majority of scientists — and nearly all science fiction writers — take it for granted that life exists on many other worlds within our Galaxy. We are already trying to make contact with intelligent aliens.

Are we alone?

The American theoretical astronomers Frank Drake and Carl Sagan devised, in 1961, an equation to indicate the number of 'communicative civilizations' in the Galaxy:

$$N = R^* \cdot f_p \cdot n_e \cdot f_l \cdot f_i \cdot f_c \cdot L$$

In the equation, N is the number of communicative civilizations; R^* is the number of stars in the Galaxy; f_p is the fraction of stars which possess planetary systems; n_e is the average number of Earthlike planets per system; f_l is the fraction of Earthlike planets where life actually develops; f_i is the fraction of life-systems which give rise to intelligent life-forms; f_c is the fraction of intelligent species willing and able to communicate with other worlds; and L is the average lifetime of a communicative civilization expressed as a fraction of the lifetime of the Galaxy.

Obviously, the figures which we fill in for each of the symbols are guesses. Even R^* is not known precisely. Different people tend to come up with different 'solutions' to the equation: for instance, the astronomer George Abell thinks that the likeliest figures give an answer for N somewhere between 100 million and 10,000 million. If these figures are anything like correct, there might well be another communicative civilization within a few hundred light-years of the Sun. Abell suggests 300 light-years as a possible figure. (Quite recently, the scientific community has been moving back to a more sceptical attitude to the possibilities of alien life — see 'Where are the space arks?', page 18.)

We've been looking — though not very hard — for signs of these other civilizations for some time. In the jargon of scientists, the task is known as SETI — the Search for Extra-Terrestrial Intelligence. In 1960 Frank Drake set up Project Ozma at the National Radio Astronomy Observatory in Greenbank, West Virginia. This project scanned two nearby sunlike stars, Epsilon Eridani and Tau Ceti (see star chart on page 9), for radio signals at a wavelength of 21 cm. Since 1960 a few hundred nearby stars have been similarly scanned, both by the NRAO and by the Gorky Radiophysical Institute in the Soviet Union. So far, no signal has been picked up.

Project Ozma undertook a task considerably more difficult than searching for a needle in a haystack, but its strategy in selecting that one particular wavelength was basically sound. Only a very small portion of the electromagnetic spectrum is suitable for interstellar communication. This portion consists of those penetrative waves which are neither absorbed by clouds of interstellar gas, nor bounced back off the Earth's atmosphere. Within this narrow range, the wavelength of 21 cm is of particular importance to radio astronomers, because radiation of this wavelength is emitted by hydrogen atoms in interstellar space and is therefore useful in learning about the distribution of hydrogen within the galaxy. Radio astronomers using this frequency as a matter of routine would be likely to pick up a message, and we believe that a communicative civilization would pick that frequency on which to broadcast in order to maximize the likelihood that its message would get through.

There is a problem in 'tuning in' to a message from the stars. This is caused by the very same background radiation that makes the 21-cm wavelength appropriate; but any regular and repetitive series of pulses would not be too difficult to pick out from the background noise.

In 1971 the Ames Research Centre of NASA sponsored a study which produced plans for a listening

device for the more efficient monitoring of nearby stars. The design that resulted was Project Cyclops, which would consist of a vast array of radio antennae, each one over 100 metres in diameter, to be arranged over an area 5 km across. This device would be able to scan every star within 1000 light-years in a few decades. When it was designed its cost was estimated at 10 billion dollars. No plans have yet been made to go ahead with the project.

As well as trying to receive messages we have made attempts to send them. In 1974 the radio-telescope at Arecibo in Puerto Rico was used to transmit a signal toward the globular star cluster in Hercules named M13. As the cluster is 24,000 light-years away, it will be some time before the message is received — if there is anyone there to receive it. This was in fact our second message to the stars; the first was

the engraved plaque carried by the *Pioneer 10* spacecraft launched from Cape Kennedy in 1972. *Pioneer 10* passed close to Jupiter in 1973 (this being the purpose of its mission) and then went on into deep space. This message will take much longer to reach a destination, if it ever does so, than the M13 signal: *Pioneer* will take 80,000 years to travel a mere 4 light-years (which is approximately the same distance as that between the Sun and its nearest neighbouring star). The two *Voyager* spacecraft which in 1981 sent back pictures of Saturn (having earlier transmitted information about Jupiter) carry a rather more sophisticated message in the form of a long-playing record, which encodes both sounds and pictures. Again, the prospect of its being picked up within the next few hundred thousand years is remote.

As all these figures imply, inter-

stellar communication is unlikely to take the form of a dialogue. If our nearest talking neighbours are hundreds of light-years away there is little point in our attempting to ask one another questions to which only our remote descendants would receive the answers. The astronomer Ronald Bracewell has suggested that we might have to take our place in a 'Galactic Club' in which civilizations would pass on any information received from elsewhere by incorporating it into their own transmissions; thus, everyone would benefit from the unselfishness of all. Cynics might suggest that the Galactic Club should rather be thought of as the Galactic Chain-Letter, which might easily fail by virtue of a low rate of participation.

The message which was dispatched in the direction of M13 in 1974 took the form of a long string of blips and spaces: a long binary

The giant array of radio antennae proposed for Project Cyclops. If television stations of about the same power as ours on Earth existed on a planet 50 light-years away, Project Cyclops could receive the pictures.

number, repeated many times. This
is the logical form for interstellar
messages. The actual binary number
is of no importance in itself; what is
vital is the rearrangement of the
blips in a two-dimensional array to
form a diagram. If the total number
of 'bits' (blips and spaces) in the
signal is the product of two prime
numbers there are only two possible
grids in which the blips can be
distributed, and it ought to be
obvious to a receiver which of the
two is the significant one.

The designing of two-dimensional arrays which pack a lot of
information into a limited space has
been a popular game. Science fiction
novels which describe the receiving
of such messages on Earth include
James Gunn's *The Listeners*,
Fred Hoyle and John Elliot's *A for
Andromeda* and *The Cassiopeia
Affair* by Chloe Zerwick and
Harrison Brown. In these novels it
is assumed that the receipt of a
message from the stars would be a
momentous event, whose significance in the course of human

history might be comparable to the
invention of the wheel or (more
modestly) the printing press. The
technological value of any information received is generally regarded
as a minor issue in comparison with
the proof that we are not alone:
knowledge which might transform
our attitude to ourselves and to one
another. Most writers argue that the
change would be for the better: in
both *The Listeners* and Norman
Spinrad's *Song from the Stars* the
most important lesson to be learned
from communication with the stars
is a moral one about communicating
with each other.

Below: the great
radio-telescope at
Arecibo, Puerto
Rico, from which a
message was
broadcast to the
stars in 1974.
Right: the message
itself, decoded
as a picture. It
lists the numbers
1 to 10 in binary

form, gives the
atomic numbers
of five of the
elements basic to
life, and pictures a
DNA helix, and a
human being
standing above
the symbol for
Earth, shown as
the third planet
out from the Sun.

Alien intelligences on Earth

Attempts to communicate with alien intelligences are not entirely restricted to the use of radio-telescopes. The possibility remains that there are other sentient beings here on Earth. The fact that after intensive study and argument this does still rank as a possibility demonstrates some of the difficulties which might be involved in communicating with aliens who differ from us biologically as much as or more than our nearest relatives on Earth. For example, there may be intelligent beings who lack the hands with which to make technological gadgets like radio-telescopes.

The main contenders for the title of being Earth's other intelligent species belong to the mammalian order Cetacea: whales and dolphins. Because these mammals have returned to live in the sea they do not have problems with weight, and thus can develop brains which are large in proportion to their bodies (a large brain, and hence a heavy head, is a liability to any land-living mammal which does not stand upright). Most smaller cetaceans are sociable and co-operative, and many of them make a wide range of sounds which might be part of a complicated system of communication. The most intelligent appear to be various kinds of dolphin and the somewhat larger Orcas (sometimes called 'killer whales'). Various researchers have been trying to communicate with dolphins since the 1950s, when a major project was mounted at the Communications Research Institute in Coral Gables, Florida, which was for some time under the directorship of John Lilly, the most celebrated of early workers in this field. Though this establishment is no longer active, others have taken up the work.

Dolphins in captivity are affectionate, both to one another and to human beings, and apparently take great delight in playing games. Both of these traits are considered (by us) to be very 'human'. Dolphins can be taught to respond in complex ways to various signals, including a few verbal responses which make primitive dialogue between men and dolphins possible. It is actually rather surprising to find that we can get along so well with a species so unlike our own.

The dolphin lives in a 'sensory world' very different from ours. Dolphins can see and hear, and also possess senses of touch and 'smell' (chemosensitivity), but the balance between these senses, and the ways they exploit them, are quite different from the ways we use our sensory capacities. Sight is much less useful under water, and dolphins

A psychologist at the Institute of Primate Studies in Norman, Oklahoma, shows a chimpanzee the word for 'baby' in sign language. Some apes have developed quite large 'vocabularies' after being taught like this.

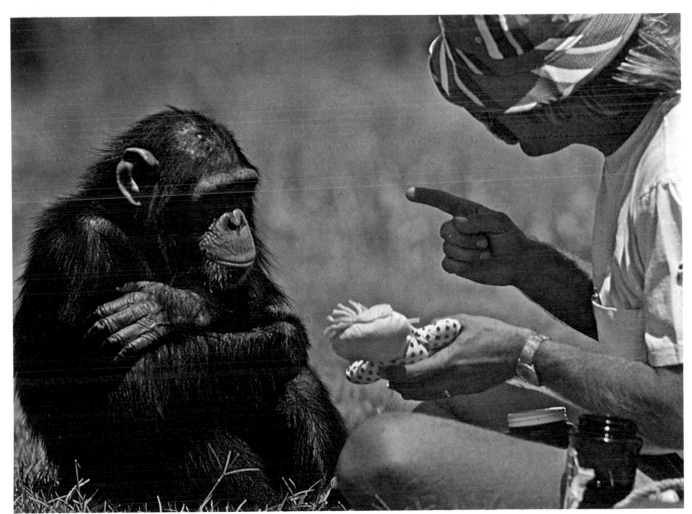

'map out' their environments by means of echo-location.

The sounds which cetaceans transmit can be very complicated. The marine biologist Roger Payne spent a great deal of time in the 1960s recording the 'songs' of humpback whales, some of which last a full half-hour. Many of these, and sometimes the whole repertoire, might be repeated. The number of bits of information contained within these songs is large — of the order of millions — and their information-carrying capacity may be equal to many complex human communications. (Carl Sagan, for instance, estimates that the number of bits of information in a half-hour whale-song is about equal to the number of bits of information in the *Odyssey*.) As to what these songs might say, however, we have no idea.

Many people have drawn a harsh moral from the fact that, while on one hand we recognize that dolphins and whales may be sentient and intelligent, on the other hand we hunt them down in order to supply various industries (including those producing dog meat and cosmetics) with various parts of their bodies. Sometimes they are slaughtered simply because they compete with fishermen for food. It is frequently observed, also, that the US Defense Department took a strong interest in dolphin research: if we could learn to talk with dolphins, then we could perhaps use them in warfare, taking advantage of their good nature in order to persuade them to deliver bombs and spy-devices to appropriate locations. Much of the science fiction about communication with dolphins revolves around this tangled moral issue. In Robert Merle's *The Day of the Dolphin* a group of people try to protect their dolphin friends from

exploitation by the military forces, while in Ian Watson's *The Jonah Kit* scientists find a way to open a sophisticated channel of communication between human beings and cetaceans, with the result that the cetaceans are driven to mass suicide. It seems to be almost universally believed that whales and dolphins are much nicer and more sensitive than we are.

Experiments with chimpanzees and, more recently, gorillas in America have indicated that our nearest relatives might also be capable of more distinguished mental feats than we had previously assumed. Chimps reared in human families have been taught to 'speak' by using the sign language employed by deaf-and-dumb people, and have proved quite talkative. Some of them, it seems, can make up new words by combining signs, and one or two of them have been credited

with constructing sentences, though the evidence of this is disputed. One gorilla, Koko, is said to have a vocabulary of 600 'words'; in a thin disguise she appears as Amy, the 'heroine' of Michael Crichton's interesting science fiction adventure story *Congo*, in which she acts as an interpreter between human beings and wild gorillas.

Though other land animals do not at present seem to qualify as alien intelligences, some science fiction writers have imagined that with a slight artificial boost — perhaps administered by drugs or by genetic engineering — they might actually become so. There have been several stories about dogs with artificially augmented intelligence, the most famous being Olaf Stapledon's *Sirius*. The general opinion of these stories is that such 'artificial aliens' would hold rather low opinions of us.

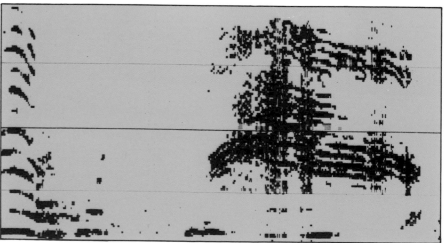

Above right: experiments in communication with dolphins are no longer unusual, but Sea World Marine Parks in the USA have gone one step further in working with killer whales. This one responds to hand signals.
Right: spectrogram of the song of a humpback whale, recorded near Hawaii in 1982, shows clearly the complexity of the whale's vocalizations, which contain many more 'bits' of information per second than human speech.

First contact

If there were in fact a Galactic Club, and we were to join it, we should still be a long way from meeting alien beings face to face. If the nearest communicative civilization is hundreds of light-years away, the difficulties of holding a conversation are surpassed by the difficulties of arranging a rendezvous. Science fiction writers, however, have found the prospect of an actual contact with aliens so interesting that they have been prepared to overlook the problems posed by distance (see pages 8-9).

If we could travel through the vast wilderness of interstellar space quickly enough to establish a social relationship between the human race and one or more alien species, then the problem of communication would take on a new dimension. We should have to figure out a way not merely to exchange information, but actually to get along with them. Science fiction writers have usually assumed that the relationship might be troubled.

One of the clichés of science fiction is the alien invasion story in which — as in H.G. Wells's *War of the Worlds* — monstrous beings descend from the skies with the aim of stealing our world and destroying or enslaving humanity. This version of contact with aliens is not as popular in fiction as it was, but some writers still suppose that our relationships with alien races would need to be competitive, and that we might have to take our place in a Galaxy-wide struggle for existence in which only the fittest would survive. Thus, in Robert Heinlein's *Starship Troopers*, human military forces must fight an all-out war against alien Bugs so different from us in outlook that there is no possibility of reaching a peaceful settlement.

One of the most famous science fiction stories about a meeting between human and alien, Murray Leinster's 'First Contact' (1945), predicts that the mutual suspicion of the two parties will be great enough to cause severe problems. The Russian writer Ivan Yefremov was moved by 'First Contact' to write his own similar story, 'The Heart of the Serpent', in which

human and alien greet one another gladly and without suspicion because both are sufficiently advanced to have achieved communist social organization; but Western writers have never found this argument convincing.

It is fashionable today for science fiction writers to welcome the possibility of a meeting with aliens with a rather earnest enthusiasm. Joe Haldeman's *The Forever War*, for instance, imagines a situation very similar to that envisaged by Heinlein in *Starship Troopers*, but it turns out finally that the war was all a mistake and that there is much that the human race can and must learn from the aliens it has been fighting. Many other writers are hopeful that extraterrestrial aliens will, like dolphins, turn out to be nicer beings than we are. They recognize, though, that many people will not be content with that assumption, and cannot help being a

little anxious about it themselves. In Thomas M. Disch's *The Genocides*, aliens who are never actually seen turn the Earth into a gigantic vegetable patch and gradually eliminate mankind along with all the other minor pests. Stories such as this remind us that, although it may be tempting to imagine that high intelligence leads to scrupulous moral behaviour, the evidence which we ourselves provide suggests otherwise.

If we are no more successful at getting along with aliens than we are at getting along with one another, then it might be better if the Galactic Club were unable and unwilling to hold meetings.

In older science fiction the first contact between man and alien was usually envisaged gloomily. The unfortunate meeting shown here is from a publicity still for the film *This Island Earth* (1954).

Alien body chemistry

Less than 100 years ago it was regarded as highly likely by some astronomers — notably Percival Lowell — that our nearest neighbours in the universe would be found right next door, on the planet Mars. On the evidence available to him, Lowell believed that Mars was a cool and arid world consisting mostly of red deserts, but neverthe-less perfectly capable of sustaining Earthlike life. He believed strongly in the 'canals' reported and mapped by various observers, and con-sidered their existence to be good evidence that Mars had intelligent inhabitants. Unfortunately, the canals turned out to be a combina-tion of optical illusion and wishful thinking, and since the landing of the *Mariner* probes in 1976 the hope that Mars might harbour life has almost died away.

Early science fiction writers had great hopes of Venus as well as Mars. They imagined it to be hot and cloudy, sometimes covered by tropical forest and swamp, and sometimes by a vast ocean. The *Venera* probes of the mid-1960s destroyed these hopes, revealing that the surface of Venus is very hot indeed, and quite unsuitable for Earthly life.

Earthlike life is dependent on two main factors. The first is the presence of water in the liquid state, because water acts as the suspen-sion medium for all the important chemical reactions which sustain living systems. Life on Earth originally developed in the sea, the first living systems evolving in the 'hot organic soup' of the primeval ocean. Land-based organisms carry their watery heritage with them, locked inside their cells. The second factor is the ability of carbon atoms to form long chains, so that a very large number of different com-pounds, with a vast range of possible functions, can be formed from carbon atoms in combination with a few others— mostly hydrogen, oxygen and nitrogen.

Our exploration of space has shown us that there is no other planet in the Solar System where liquid water is present. Venus is too hot and Mars too cold. We can now only hope to find other Earthlike worlds orbiting distant stars.

This does not necessarily mean, however, that there is no life at all elsewhere in the Solar System. It is conceivable that there might be other suspension media capable of supporting complex organic reactions, and even bases for living structures other than chains of carbon atoms. Optimistic astrono-mers now look to Jupiter as the most likely nearest abode of extra-terrestrial life.

Data recovered from the *Pioneer* and *Voyager* probes of the 1970s suggest to us that Jupiter is a gigantic ball of gas and liquid with no solid surface. Its atmosphere accounts for the outermost 1000 km of its 71,000-km radius. The upper atmosphere is very turbulent; the famous Great Red Spot is an enor-mous anticyclone 21,000 km long, and there are many smaller anti-cyclones. The Jovian atmosphere is mostly hydrogen, with some methane (CH_4), ethene (C_2H_2), ethane C_2H_6), ammonia (NH_3), water and phosphine (PH_3). The temperature of the outer atmosphere is about $-110°C$. Clearly, under these conditions one could not expect to find Earthlike life, but the significant point is that two of the common constituents of the atmo-sphere might, in their liquid form, substitute for water as suspension media for organic compounds. Ammonia may be the more likely, in that it will dissolve much the same range of organic compounds as water will. Methane, however, may also be a possibility if lipid molecules (fats, etc.) could take over the roles played by protein molecules in Earthly living systems.

One problem in speculative bio-chemistry which remains if Jupiter is to be considered a possible abode of life is that of temperature. Ammonia and methane are liquid at much lower temperatures than water — at temperatures, in fact, where the kinds of chemical reactions on which Earthly life is based would happen very slowly, if at all. (This is why freezing inhibits organic decay.) It is unlikely that a life-system could thrive at $-110°C$ even if ammonia or methane were liquid at that temperature. Two other factors have, however, to be taken into account: firstly, the fact that Jupiter does generate some internal heat; and secondly, the effects of the pressure of Jupiter's dense atmosphere. If a little imagination is used in building these factors into the situation it becomes possible to imagine environments deep within the Jovian atmosphere that might not be too hostile to life.

Thus, there is some sort of warrant for the kinds of organism which some science fiction writers have recently placed in the Jovian atmosphere. In his story 'A Meeting with Medusa', Arthur C. Clarke imagines giant, jellyfish-like 'medusas' repelling the attacks of

more mobile 'mantas' by means of electrical defence systems. Gregory Benford and Gordon Eklund, in *If the Stars are Gods*, imagine a rather less troubled situation, with giant, silvery gasbags floating serenely through the hydrocarbon snow and the ammonia cirrus clouds.

While so much attention has been focused in the last few years on the colder reaches of the Solar System, few science fiction writers have been tempted to construct imaginary biochemistries appropriate to worlds much hotter than the Earth. The basic features of such a biochemistry would still be the same. First of all, a suspension

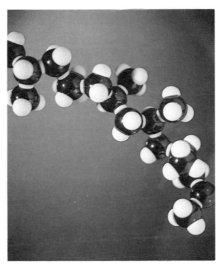

Left: a schematic model of a simple hydrocarbon molecule (polypropylene). The carbon atoms are black and the hydrogen atoms white. The ability of carbon atoms to form long chains with other atoms is basic to the chemistry of life as we know it. **Below:** the atmosphere of the planet Jupiter, as imagined by Arthur C. Clarke in his short story

'A Meeting with Medusa', contains several spectacular life-forms. The giant, mile-wide, aerial-plankton-eating medusas are preyed upon by the smaller, carnivorous mantas, but can defend themselves with electricity (like eels). Several scientists believe that Jupiter's atmosphere could support some kind of life.

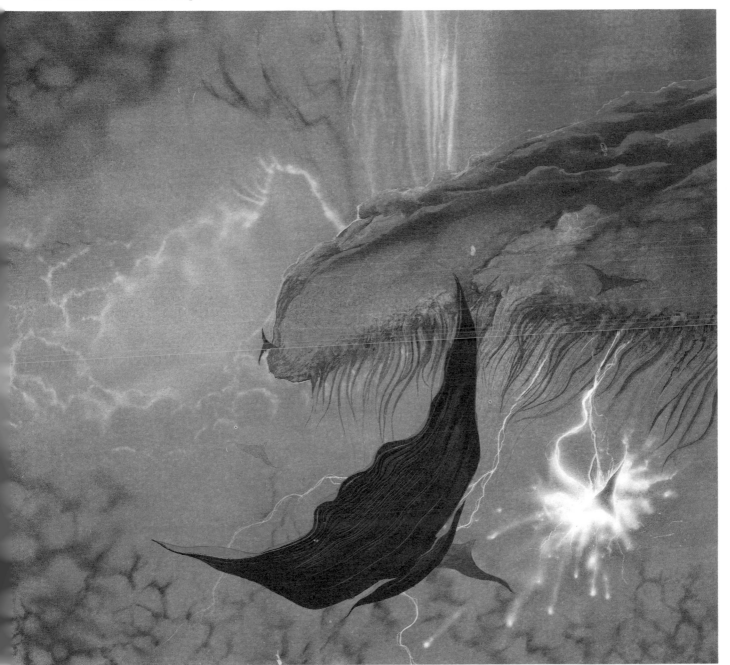

medium would be needed which is liquid at much higher temperatures than water. Sulphur is one possible candidate. An extra problem arises, though, in connection with long-chain carbon molecules whose other main constituents are hydrogen and oxygen. Such molecules would break down at temperatures high enough to liquefy sulphur, and would thus have to be replaced by something more stable. There is a class of carbon-chain molecules called fluorocarbons which might conceivably fit the bill, but by now we are getting very far away from the chemistry of life on Earth.

Biochemical plausibility has never been a serious limitation to the imagination of science fiction writers. A favourite theme has long been the notion of life based on silicon rather than on carbon. Silicon atoms can form long chains, and are particularly versatile when they alternate with oxygen atoms to form a class of compounds called silicones. To fit these molecules into a pattern of energy-economics taxes the imagination heavily, but the possibility of brains made out of naturally grown silicon chips is aesthetically attractive. Unfortunately, because of their rather stony or metallic quality, most silicon-based life-forms in science fiction tend to resemble boulders or television aerials, and are thus more than a little boring. And, as the American chemist Cyril Ponnamperuma says, 'If evolution could have used silicon, it would have made something out of silicon — there's a lot of silicon around' — a strong argument. Few scientists believe in the possibility of life based on silicon, which is almost certainly too stable a substance to form chemical bonds flexible enough to be a basis for life.

Some of the properties of life-systems — a high degree of order and the capacity for growth — are also shown by the crystal lattices formed by many chemical compounds. The simplicity of such lattices does not really permit us to think sensibly of 'crystalline life' but many science fiction writers have been attracted by the analogy and by the prospect of living creatures sculptured out of gemstones. Crystalline life-forms are even more inert than silicon ones, but sometimes they think beautiful thoughts, as in Benford and Eklund's *If the Stars are Gods*. (This novel also toys with the biochemically unlikely notion that stars might be in some quasi-supernatural sense alive and sentient.)

Silicon life-forms are generally imagined to be rather undramatic, but the silicon aliens of the film *The Monolith Monsters* (1957), which landed from a meteorite, are satisfyingly destructive as they chew rocks and then lurch towards a tiny Arizona town.

In much science fiction, 'life' is little more than a word — a mysterious property that can be attributed to more or less any object. Special mention must be made, though, of some exceptionally strange imaginary life-systems which are supported by ingenious arguments on the part of their creators.

In his novel *The Black Cloud* the cosmologist Fred Hoyle imagines life and intelligence evolving within a cloud of interstellar dust, which becomes an 'organism' big enough to surround a sun in order to warm itself. Hoyle thinks that this idea warrants very serious consideration, and in his much later non-fiction book *Lifecloud* (written with N.C. Wickramasinghe) he argues that life may first evolve in space, and that the hot organic soup from which it emerges may be found not in planetary oceans but inside the heads of comets. These arguments are highly controversial, especially when they are extended in *Diseases from Space* to account for epidemics in terms of the bombardment of Earth with bacteria and viruses from the tails of passing comets.

While the idea of viruses evolving in space may seem unlikely, we know that some of the chemicals of life do exist elsewhere — and not just in planets like Jupiter. Since 1968 many of the molecules basic to chemical evolution, such as water, carbon dioxide, ammonia and hydrogen cyanide, have been found spectroscopically in interstellar space. Organic molecules, including amino acids, have also been found in meteorites by Cyril Ponnamperuma and others.

Ponnamperuma believes that all alien life must be organic and carbon-based, but other scientists — mainly physicists, who always seem especially ready to enter the wilder realms of speculation — consider there is warrant for believing that even Hoyle's intelligent black cloud, a completely inorganic entity, could exist. The American physicist Gerald Feinberg has speculated that space itself could hold two life forms, 'plasmodes' and 'radiobes', the former evolving within suns, the latter in interstellar space. Plasmodes develop patterns of organized motion from random collisions of electrons and ions. They are alive in that they are structured, they metabolize (feeding on energy in this case) and they replicate (by converting random into non-random particle clusters magnetically). These are the three basic elements of life: structure, feeding and reproduction.

The physicist Freeman Dyson, inventor of the Dyson sphere (see page 44), also believes that life may exist away from planetary surfaces. He asks, 'Is the basis of consciousness matter or structure? If I could make a copy of my brain with the same structure but using different materials, would the copy think it was me?' He goes on to argue (in *Review of Modern Physics*) that if the answer is structure, then Hoyle's black cloud could exist, 'organizing itself and communicating with itself by means of electromagnetic forces'.

Another very bizarre life-system is that envisaged by Isaac Asimov in *The Gods Themselves*, which features gaseous life-forms existing in a parallel universe (see pages 98-9) where the laws of physics are different. This is one of the very few attempts to describe a biochemistry so different from our own that it requires a different underlying physics to make it plausible. Unusual physical conditions are also featured in *Dragon's Egg*, a novel by the physicist Robert L. Forward which describes the evolution of flat, amoeba-like, intelligent life-forms half a centimetre in diameter on the surface of a neutron star whose surface gravity is 67 billion times that of Earth. These are the most ambitiously peculiar of all the examples of imaginary alien life.

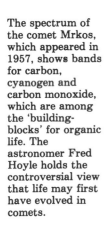

A great boost was given to the idea of life on Mars at the beginning of this century by the work of the astronomer Percival Lowell. He produced detailed maps of what he supposed to be a great, artificial system of canals. It was a sad blow for science fiction readers when these were shown to be an optical illusion.

The spectrum of the comet Mrkos, which appeared in 1957, shows bands for carbon, cyanogen and carbon monoxide, which are among the 'building-blocks' for organic life. The astronomer Fred Hoyle holds the controversial view that life may first have evolved in comets.

Alien appearances

There is, of course, much more to the business of designing alien beings than matters of biochemistry. Most aliens in science fiction are assumed to be very similar to ourselves in their basic biochemistry and are supposed to live on Earth-like worlds. When we move beyond the question of how organisms work to the questions of what they look like and how they interact with one another, we are in the realm of speculative ecology.

Many science fiction writers pay little attention to ecological issues. Edgar Rice Burroughs, for example, thought nothing back in 1912 of populating his imaginary Mars, in *Princess of Mars* and its 10 sequels, with giant predatory *banths* without providing herds of herbivorous animals as prey. Writers of science fiction thrillers and the makers of science fiction films, dedicated to the presentation of horrifying monsters of all shapes and sizes, rarely bother to ask how such monsters fit into a sensible

ecological matrix. Despite this frequent dereliction of duty, though, it is actually easier for science fiction writers without specialized knowledge to undertake exercises in speculative ecology than to do so in speculative biochemistry. It is also more rewarding in dramatic terms. It does not take too much intellectual effort to appreciate that organisms must be adapted both to their physical environment and to their relationships with other organisms, and there is abundant room here for ingenious invention.

Life on Earth is governed by several kinds of physical constraint, and it has been simple enough for science fiction writers to alter one or more of these constraints in order to consider the effects on life-forms. The most obvious constraint is that of gravity, which places crucial limitations on the mechanical design of bodies. One implication of this is that, where the force of gravity is less, organisms either might grow larger or, alternatively, might be more delicately constructed. The reverse is also true, and it would be

extremely difficult for human beings to function adequately where the force of gravity was significantly greater: our bones and muscles would have to be much stronger.

The most famous science fiction novel in which gravity is the main factor affecting the local life-system is Hal Clement's *Mission of Gravity*. This is set on the planet Mesklin, which rotates on its axis once every 18 minutes, and is in consequence shaped something like an aspirin tablet. Its gravity varies from three times that of Earth at the equator (where centrifugal forces counteract gravity) to 700 times that of Earth at the poles. Clement's Mesklinites are quite small and tend to hug the ground: they resemble giant centipedes with special forelimbs modified for gripping.

Another possible consequence of low gravity is that it might make flight much easier and hence much more common as part of the behavioural repertoire of organisms. The ability to fly, however, depends not only on low weight but also on the presence of a suitably dense atmosphere. As it seems plausible that

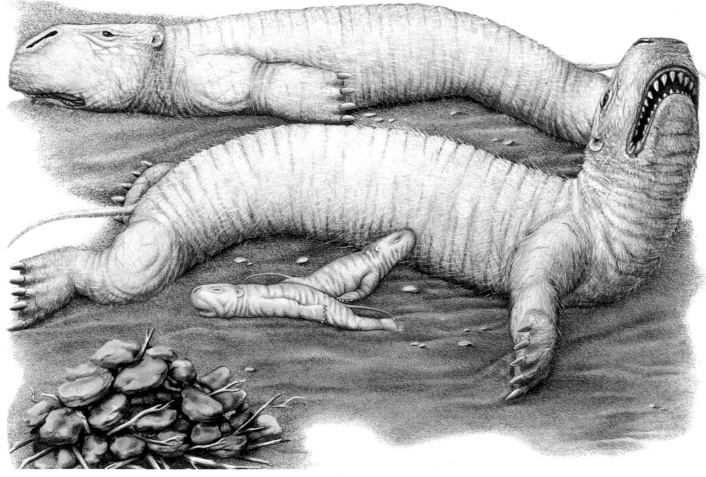

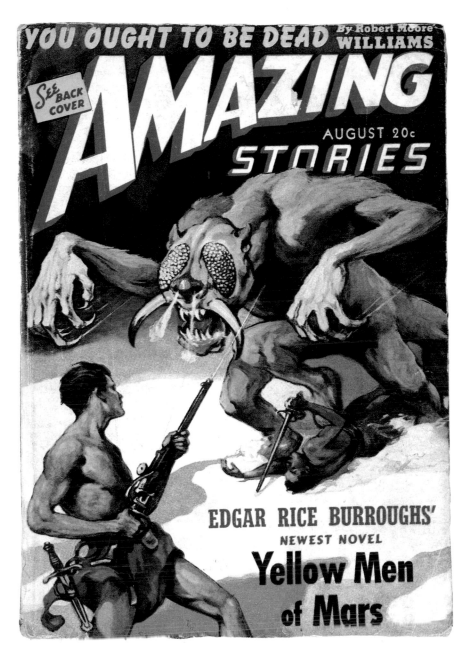

YOU OUGHT TO BE DEAD By Robert Moore Williams

SEE BACK COVER

AMAZING STORIES

AUGUST 20c

EDGAR RICE BURROUGHS'
NEWEST NOVEL
Yellow Men of Mars

winged humanoids realistically — with an adequate wing musculature (see page 194) and convincing metabolism — are featured in several stories by Poul Anderson, most notably *War of the Wing-Men* and *The People of the Wind*. The latter book has feathery aliens, but in general winged aliens are batlike rather than birdlike.

Another important physical constraint in the shaping of planetary life-systems is the relative proportions of land and sea. Science fiction writers have always been intrigued by the notion of watery worlds where life never had the opportunity to leave the sea; the fact that they can no longer make Venus fit the bill has simply driven them further afield. The more endearing aliens designed for such worlds tend to be sleek, furry creatures in which the humanoid form is plausibly modified to become more seal-like or more otter-like. The most intelligent of the Earthly invertebrates — the octopus family, the cephalopods — have also been popular models, and appear in some of the most memorable water-world stories. Jack Vance's story 'The Gift of Gab' deals with the problems faced by human beings trying to establish communication with intelligent cephalopods who can produce no sounds, but use a complex sign language with their tentacles.

Some of the most interesting alien ecological systems designed by science fiction writers are those in which organisms are adapted to extreme cyclical changes in climate — usually because the worlds envisaged are parts of double-star systems. Hal Clement describes the organisms which inhabit such a world in *Cycle of Fire*; a rather more dramatic cycle of climatic changes over much longer periods is the basis of Poul Anderson's *Fire Time*. A complex series of biological changes in response to climatic cycles also takes place in Brian Aldiss's novel *Helliconia Spring* (1982). Earthly examples which provide imaginative aid in such works as these include the lung-fishes which can go into suspended animation when rivers dry up, and desert plants which bloom only briefly at intervals of several years when the rain comes.

Left: the zoologist Dougal Dixon has studied the ways in which animals may evolve on Earth; many of his examples would serve very well as models for alien life. Here Dixon's carnivorous desert sharks, evolved from insectivorous stock, make an interesting comparison with the giant sand-worms of Frank Herbert's novel *Dune*. The sharks are usually submerged in the sand.

Above: Edgar Rice Burroughs' romances set on Mars are exciting but ecologically unsound. For example, he failed to provide his alien carnivores with herbivores to prey upon. This magazine cover from 1941, illustrating one of his very last Mars stories, makes up in spectacular nastiness for what it loses in plausibility. The artist was John Allen St John.

the lower a world's gravity the less atmosphere it would have, and vice versa, problems arise in imagining situations where flight would become very easy. Most science fiction stories which feature extensive airborne ecologies are set on so-called 'gas-giant worlds', like Jupiter, where atmospheric density is great but gravity (because of the large size of the worlds and their low overall density) is moderate.

Earthlike worlds populated by winged humanoids are very common in science fiction, but this owes more to our familiarity with images of angels and the myth of Icarus, and to our envy of the birds, than to ecological or physiological plausibility. Serious attempts to present

Alien life-styles

There is much more scope for the free play of the imagination when it comes to alien ecology — the business of constructing food chains and equipping alien beings with the means to secure their food supplies and to reproduce. Science fiction writers and illustrators have always enjoyed designing cunning and alarming predators to menace Earthly space-travellers; such design is much enlivened by incorporating the monstrous creatures into an exotic but coherent ecological background. One of the first writers to do this with appropriate ingenuity was Stanley G. Weinbaum, and such stories as 'The Mad Moon', 'Parasite Planet' and 'Flight on Titan' (all 1935) are still unsurpassed in the sheer delight which they take in devising weird life-systems, though they are fatally dated in other ways.

The most common variation used by science fiction writers involves attributing intelligence (and hence dominance) to non-human creatures. To imagine that intelligent humanoids might have evolved from cats rather than apes is relatively straightforward, but certain difficulties stand in the way of the ever popular lizard-men who figure so frequently as science fictional villains. Reptiles, having no internal temperature control, are rather limited in the amount of brain activity they can indulge in; the same problem might limit the possibility of intelligence in cephalopods. Science fiction writers occasionally attribute intelligence to viruses or plants, but these exotic creations are clearly implausible without a good deal of apologetic argument to explain what they can have developed to substitute for brains, and how the complexity of their actions is so great as to require intelligent co-ordination.

Even conscientious science fiction writers tend to assume that intelligence would be strongly favoured by natural selection in all possible circumstances. This is not necessarily so: the vast majority of Earthly organisms are highly successful and perfectly well adapted to their circumstances without being conspicuously intelligent

and without having anything obvious to gain from becoming more intelligent. It remains to be seen whether our intelligence will guarantee us a longer evolutionary lifetime than worms, flies, snails or mushrooms, but after studying the form no serious gambler would make us the favourites.

It seems reasonable to argue that intelligence is only advantageous to certain kinds of organisms, and therefore goes hand-in-hand (if the pun may be excused) with such traits as manipulative ability. If human beings did not walk upright, freeing their forelimbs to develop hands instead of paws, they could not have developed the kind of intelligence they have. Similarly, intelligent beings must be sociable, because intelligence also arises out of the need to communicate. The fact that most mammals and birds show a degree of intelligence not seen in reptiles is connected with the fact that they generally have more complicated social relationships, especially in connection with the rearing of young. The more

sociable animals are, and the more able they are to interfere with and transform their own environment, the more intelligent they are likely to become. The same principle must be applied to alien beings: their intelligence must fit in with the logic of their situation.

The association of intelligence with communication has led science fiction writers to imagine a range of peculiar and ingenious communication systems (leaving aside 'occult' means like telepathy). Systems of 'sign-language' are most popular — for instance, the Asadi in Michael Bishop's novel *Transfigurations* communicate by means of rapid colour changes in the irises of their eyes, and their 'books' are plastic discs with central lenses which flash out long colour sequences. Even when they do use sound-waves for

The octopus, a cephalopod, is the most highly developed of invertebrates. Octopoid aliens, once a cliché of horror stories, are sometimes seen now as clever and sensitive! But could cold-blooded creatures be intelligent?

communication, alien 'languages' are sometimes very different from human ones — communication by means of musical chords, as in the film *Close Encounters of the Third Kind* (1977), is a familiar variation.

The design of alien life-forms —

especially when it comes to fitting them into food chains and describing methods of reproduction — relies heavily on forms found within the Earthly life-systems. The great changes undergone by insects as they pass through larval and pupal forms to adulthood has been a constant source of inspiration. Aliens which undergo a whole series of metamorphoses are featured in many stories, notably James Blish's *A Case of Conscience*, in which the inhabitants of the planet Lithia recapitulate their evolutionary history as they develop from egg to adult.

The planet Lithia is also notable for being a well thought-out example of the popular science fiction idea of the 'big planet'. This is a planet without heavy metals. Being less dense than our own metal-heavy Earth, such a

planet — if it had Earthly gravity and therefore Earthly mass — would have to be big, maybe twice the diameter of our own. Jack Vance's novel *Big Planet* is set on one of the more celebrated examples. However, if our own Solar System is as representative of planetary evolution throughout the Galaxy as some scientists believe, such planets may be rare or non-existent. Alien life on these planets would tend towards the primitive (by our standards), as technology would be difficult to establish without metals, though Blish's Lithians do very well with ceramic materials.

The design of complicated alien reproductive systems is perhaps best exemplified in the work of Philip José Farmer, who has shown a consistent interest in alien sexual relations. His story 'Mother' features a remarkable encounter

Left: the Chulpex are intelligent, insect-derived aliens, invented by Avram Davidson in his novel *Masters of the Maze*. On Earth some insects use tools, practise agriculture and build dwellings, so perhaps such a life-form may not be absurd. The Chulpex have inflexible minds, rather like real insects, whose actions appear to result from reflexes rather than thought.

Below: 'Mother', the invention of writer Philip José Farmer, is a female alien who disguises herself as a rock. She lures small animals to her by emitting attractive sexual odours, and then traps them in her womb-like interior where they first stimulate her to self-fertilization by their efforts to escape, and then are eaten. This is no more bizarre than some life-cycles that actually exist on Earth.

between a human being and an immobile female alien which relies upon trapping other creatures to stimulate self-fertilization in much the same way that many Earthly flowers depend on attracting insects. The alien mother in Farmer's story then rears her active young in her uterus-like interior. The human protagonist, after initial resistance, settles down to a comfortable lifetime — literally 'back to the womb'.

A life-cycle which is often borrowed by science fiction writers is that of the ichneumon fly, which lays its eggs in live caterpillars so that when the larvae hatch they enjoy an abundant supply of fresh meat. The idea of aliens which can use human beings in this fashion is a wonderfully horrific one, and cinematic special effects allow it to be displayed gruesomely in the film *Alien* (1979). Even at a more elementary level the notion of alien parasites which might infest human beings is ready-made for melodrama, and analogies with the myth of

vampirism and the idea of demonic possession are frequently invoked. In Robert Heinlein's novel *The Puppet Masters*, loathsome, slug-like creatures attach themselves to people, feeding on their bodies and taking control of their minds.

Though such stories are exciting they are biologically suspect. Most parasites are, in fact, rather choosy about the hosts which they attack; parasites and their hosts tend to evolve together and are co-adapted. Also, from an ecological point of view, the most successful parasite is likely to be the most 'prudent' — the one which inflicts least harm or, where destruction of the host is necessary, behaves like a sensible conservationist in maintaining its resources. Arguably, the really well adapted parasite is one that does not harm its host at all, but actually provides some return for hospitality. This kind of relationship, symbiosis, is a notion which has fascinated science fiction writers just as much as the notion of monstrous alien parasites.

On Earth there seem to be very few mutually beneficial relationships between animals (most of the real examples are of plant/animal symbiosis), but science fiction writers have been relatively generous in scattering such relationships around on other worlds. Inevitably, science fiction writers have been drawn to the prospect of symbiotic relationships between human beings and aliens, though these are biologically suspect for exactly the same reasons that human/alien parasitism is suspect. Particularly ingenious are a few stories which suggest that we are already living unknowingly in parasitic or symbiotic relationships with alien beings. In Eric Frank Russell's *Sinister Barrier*, people discover that we are maintained like cattle by invisible alien 'vampires' which feed upon the energy of our nasty emotions; while the heroes of Clifford Simak's *Time and Again* and Bob Shaw's *Palace of Eternity* make the much more comforting discovery that we live in symbiotic

Left: an ichneumon grub emerges from the dying body of its host, a caterpillar of the African monarch butterfly. The idea of a living but paralysed creature used to supply a continuing banquet of fresh meat for young carnivorous aliens has provided a popular scenario in science fiction of the more horrific kind since 1939, when A.E. van Vogt published his story 'Discord in Scarlet'. This story's plot of a carnivore loose in a spaceship is notably similar to that of the recent film *Alien*.

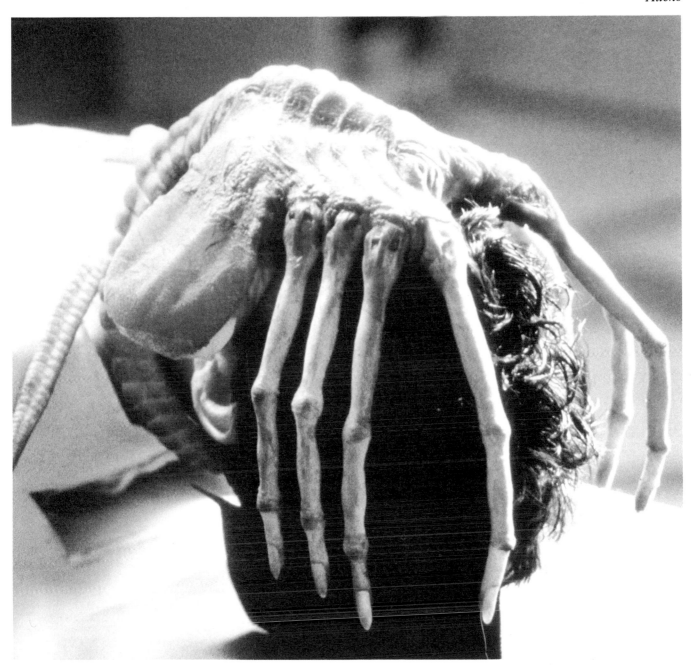

Above: the complicated and unpleasant life-cycle of the creature in the film *Alien* is here shown at an early stage. The hand-like creature has inserted a tube into its victim's throat and deposited an embryo within his lungs, from which it will later burst in a memorable shower of blood. The idea is loosely based on the life-cycle of the ichneumon fly.

harmony with equally undetectable energy-beings that provide a secular substitute for souls.

It is understandable that science fiction writers have mainly concentrated, for dramatic purposes, on one or two species of intelligent aliens at a time. There are few attempts in science fiction to describe whole life-systems with all their complex profusion. Science fiction has not produced — and almost certainly cannot produce — anything as wonderfully diverse and complex as Earth's life-system: the task is impossibly great and would yield little in the way of dramatic rewards. There are, however, some notable attempts to offer visions of exotic life-systems which are, by implication, as complex as the one that produced us. A most impressive biological phantasmagoria is presented in Brian Aldiss's *Hothouse*, though this is actually a far-future Earth, much changed by evolution, rather than an alien world. Nothing quite as rich has been credited to an alien world, but such writers as Poul Anderson and Hal Clement are always adventurous and conscientious in suggesting complexity and diversity. It is not infrequent for writers trying to construct whole life-systems to get carried away. They may impute a mystical harmony to the whole complex of ecological relationships, as in Piers Anthony's *Omnivore* or the several stories in which whole life-systems are imagined as single organisms, including the world-spanning network of plant life in Ursula Le Guin's 'Vaster Than Empires and More Slow' and the living planet in Stanislaw Lem's *Solaris*.

Alien societies

Alien sociology must grow out of
alien ecology. Biology acts as a
constraint upon the kinds of society
which are possible. A society of
flying fruit-eaters is likely to be
very different in its customs from a
society of land-bound meat-eaters.
In those many stories where science
fiction writers have been unwilling
to pay attention to such matters,
aliens tend to be no more, effectively, than human beings in funny
costumes, and alien society a
travesty of our own.

In trying to construct believable
alien societies, writers have drawn
on two main sources of inspiration:
the reports of anthropologists about
the beliefs and customs of primitive
human societies, and the one out-
standing example of an alternative
mode of social organization provided
by nature — the hive-organization of
the social insects. Of these, the
second has been far more important.

An insect hive is organized
around a single reproductive
individual: the queen. A few males
(drones) are maintained in order to
fertilize the queen's eggs, but the
vast majority of the population are
sterile females whose function is to
support and secure the reproductive
activity of the queen. Most of these
sterile females are 'workers', but in
some insects there are other specialized kinds — notably the 'soldiers'
employed by several species of ant.
The popular terminology implies
that the queen is the favoured
individual and all the rest merely
her slaves; but sociobiological
analysis of the genetics of hive-
societies has shown that it is in the
interest of the genes carried by the
workers to invest in the production
of sisters rather than daughters, and
hence it might be more appropriate
to see the queen as the slave of the
workers, forced by them to mass-
produce young on their behalf.

The image of the ant-hive has
always been available to science
fiction writers as a cardinal example
of a hyper-organized society in
which individual identity is entirely
subservient to the interests of the
group; to most writers this has
seemed horrifying. In H.G. Wells's
The First Men in the Moon, the
scientist Cavor, stranded on the

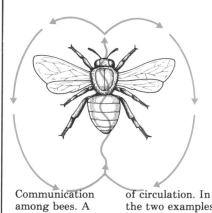

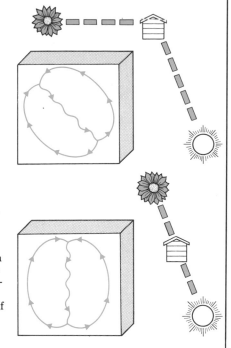

Communication
among bees. A
honey-bee signals
the direction of a
pollen source it
has discovered by
returning to the
hive and perform-
ing a carefully
oriented, figure-of-
eight-shaped
dance. The arrows
show the direction
of circulation. In
the two examples
here, the axis and
direction of circu-
lation of the
waggle dance
show the direction
of the pollen-bear-
ing flowers in rela-
tion to the hive
and the position of
the Sun.

Moon, sends messages to Earth
describing the hive-society of the
Selenites, stressing the remarkable
efficiency of its division of labour
and the inapplicability of such
concepts as 'freedom' or 'self' to its
members. This image recurs again
and again throughout the history of
science fiction, which has created
numerous hive-societies whose
members are almost human. One
of the most famous is described in
L. Sprague de Camp's *Rogue Queen*.

One reason for the popularity of
the theme is that Western writers
tend to see the communist world,
simplistically, as suppressing
individualism. Hive-society stories
in science fiction are often intended
to have a present-day political
application.

The behaviour of ants and bees
is very complex by insect standards,
and their processes of communication (which involve chemical
'messages' and 'dances' that signal
the direction and distance of food
sources) are relatively sophisticated.
This has led some commentators to
credit hives with a kind of collective
intelligence: a 'hive-mind'.
Fascinating as this notion is, there
is probably very little sense to it,
and it is used in most science fiction
stories in a clearly illegitimate
supernatural fashion.

Interestingly, there seems to
have been a noticeable shift in

Science fiction
writers have not
very often
exploited a
difference of size
between the sexes
of alien species,
although there are
many Earthly
examples. The
female black
widow spider is
much larger than
her mate, and the
courtship shown
here may prove
fatal to the male
partner. In angler
fish also the sexes
are of different
sizes: the picture
shows the larger
female with two
attendant males.

The highly organized structure of the beehive is here shown by bees *(Apis mellifera)* working together on a honeycomb. All are workers, except for the slightly larger queen (marked with an arrow). The hive structure has been used by many writers as a model for alien societies.

recent opinion regarding the horrific nature of hivelike organization. Though the hive-aliens in Robert Heinlein's *Starship Troopers* (1959) were implacable enemies of man, the hive-aliens in Joe Haldeman's *The Forever War* (1974) not only turn out to be quite nice but set an important example which humankind may follow to its considerable benefit. This new sympathy, however, is by no means unanimous.

The use of anthropological data to provide models for the design of alien societies has been much more restricted. Two of the most interesting attempts to use such analogies are *The Word for World is Forest* by Ursula Le Guin and *Transfigurations* by Michael Bishop — two authors much better informed about cultural anthropology than most. Both works (inevitably) involve aliens which are almost human, and represent conscientious attempts to create customs and rituals to fit particular, rather strange, environments and ways of life. Attempts to design social systems for non-humanoid aliens are much rarer because the task is so much more

difficult. One valiant effort is found in John Brunner's *Total Eclipse*, in which a party of humans attempts to discover why a race of crablike aliens has become extinct in spite of its superior technology.

Some of the most exotic images of alien society have arisen out of a consideration of possible modes of reproduction. There have been a few descriptions of alien social relationships which are made more complex by virtue of the fact that the aliens have three sexes instead of two. This is the case with the gaseous aliens of Isaac Asimov's *The Gods Themselves* and with the flippered, water-dwelling Spicans in Piers Anthony's *Cluster*. The most extravagant story along these lines is William Tenn's farce 'Venus and the Seven Sexes'.

Variants of the ichneumon fly's reproductive cycle have been incorporated into two impressive stories of humanoid alien societies where reproductive females are eaten away from within by their developing offspring: Philip José Farmer's *The Lovers* and Gardner Dozois's *Strangers*. Though the idea

is conveniently horrific it does not make much sense in an evolutionary context: it would be more economical for the female to transfer her eggs to the body of the male. (Males are biologically less important than females — a fact amply demonstrated by the female praying mantis, who makes a meal of her mate while copulating.) Biological role-differentiation of the two sexes might be taken to much further extremes, but for some reason this is a chain of reasoning not much exploited by science fiction writers. The Hungarian satirist Frigyes Karinthy, however, used the theme in *Capillária*, in describing a bizarre underwater civilization where the females are humanoid but the males are tiny monstrous creatures kept as domestic animals.

It is perhaps curious that the aspect of alien culture which has received most attention from science fiction writers is alien religion. Especially in recent years, much ingenuity has been brought to bear on the task of integrating types of religious belief with hypothetical biology. In Robert Silverberg's

Aliens

Alien religion could take many forms, some almost unimaginable to us. We cannot be sure, in Gilbert Williams' painting 'Dragon Song', whether the crystals that are being worshipped here are sentient or merely symbolic.

Downward to the Earth, for instance, the alien Nildoror have a mythology of rebirth which turns out to corrrespond to actual processes of metamorphosis in their own life-cycle. In George R.R. Martin's 'A Song for Lya', an alien religious belief in the survival of the personality after death also turns out to be true: when it is time to die the aliens allow their brains to be absorbed into a living, jelly-like mass which preserves their minds. One can detect behind these stories a rather wistful note of wishful thinking. It is commonplace these days for the alien condition to seem a rather more attractive prospect than the human condition in the eyes of many writers; the reason for this is that it does not take much imagination to make it so.

In recent science fiction, webs of ecological relationship on alien planets (and, by implication, on Earth also) are often seen as forming a mystical pattern. Understanding this pattern may be seen as an act of worship. By far the most influential science fiction novel in this respect was Frank Herbert's *Dune*, published in 1965, around the time when it was becoming obvious that we were making a mess of our own ecology on Earth.

Dune is set on a desert planet. Its ingeniously designed ecosystem includes water-obsessed tribesmen, giant sandworms, microscopic sand plankton, immensely valuable spices and the 'water of life', a hallucinogenic drug used by the tribesmen to give a direct, mystical access to an awareness of natural relationship. *Dune* insists that we must learn to understand the harmony of ecological relationships, and flow with them. (Books of this kind are a science fictional analogue to the ideologies of such groups as the Friends of the Earth and the Ecology Party.) Some of *Dune's* details are scientifically problematic, but its influence in encouraging other writers to design plausible ecosystems outweighs its minor flaws.

Although the design of alien ecologies and alien societies as sketched out above may seem to be little more than wild adventures of the imagination, there are in fact many ways in which those adventures can be made responsible in terms of scientific reality and —

more importantly — of the scientific method. We may ask of such fictions that they are coherent in terms of their biochemistry and in their awareness of ecological issues and the logic of natural selection. Whether there are alien life-systems elsewhere in the universe we do not yet know, but what we do know about the nature of life and its possible origins suggests to us that it is not at all unlikely. The attempt to imagine possible forms that intelligent life might take, with attendant problems of communication and co-existence, is by no means a futile exercise, even if

it only serves to remind us how different we ourselves might have been, in body and in mind, had the circumstances of our evolution been different.

It might even be argued that the endeavours of science fiction writers have already had one positive result. The image of the alien being as a monstrous invader of Earth has largely been laid to rest. We have already, to some extent at least, been desensitized to the fear of the alien. If contact with alien life were to be achieved in the near future, we would be less prone to panic and more ready to talk.

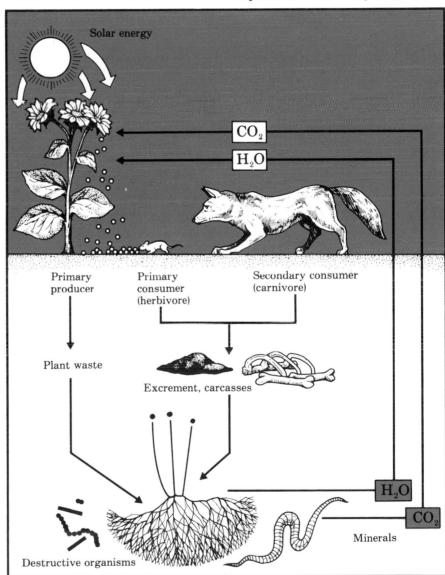

Above: any writer who creates an alien world must design for it a workable ecology, if the story is to carry scientific conviction. The major components of the food chain on Earth are shown here. The final links in the chain are important — the bacteria, fungi etc. that live on decaying organic matter (plant waste, excrement and carcasses) releasing nutrients for plants. Any populated alien planet would necessarily have a series of life-forms broadly parallel to those above. The fine details of the ecology will in turn specify the nature of the alien societies which are part of it.

Chapter 4
THE LIMITS OF THE POSSIBLE

Some of the best loved ideas of science fiction appear to be sternly prohibited, in real life, by nature's laws as we know them. But might there be loopholes?

Imaginary science in science fiction

Most of the marvellous technologies and miraculous new life-forms imagined in science fiction's tomorrows are rooted in the knowledge that we have today. But many science fiction writers resent being pinned down to a drily responsible examination of actual probabilities. The laws of nature give them claustrophobia, seeming as they do to render impossible some of the most dramatic and interesting scenarios in science fiction. If we are not allowed to travel faster than light, how shall we ever colonize the Galaxy, or even travel from one star to another in a single lifetime? If we are not allowed to have time machines, how can we ever visit the past or the future?

The fact that a story or novel has one major element of imaginary science does not mean that the whole story becomes nonsense. Very often the use of imaginary science is a necessity if the writer is to create a situation where he can go ahead with the truly scientific component of his speculations.

H.G. Wells's famous novel *The Time Machine* is an excellent example. The imaginary science here is the idea of the time machine itself. So far as we know (see pages 88-95), a time machine of this sort is a physical impossibility. But, without it, Wells would have been unable to speculate on the future evolution of the human species — his real subject matter — except in a dry and abstract way. The imaginary scientific device gave him the vividness and immediacy that he had to have.

There are thousands of similar examples. James Blish's *Cities in Flight* has faster-than-light travel and antigravity — two kinds of imaginary science — in its epic story of space hoboes looking for work all over the universe. The book is full of inventive and fascinating real science, in areas ranging from anthropology to physics, but it requires the imaginary science for its framework.

There are four kinds of imaginary science that are fundamental to science fiction: faster-than-light travel, antigravity, time travel, and the idea of alternate universes. All of these are ideas that allow writers a freedom of setting. Human beings can be placed, using these ideas, anywhere in time or space, or even in worlds parallel to our own where history has taken a different course.

Until quite recently, few readers and even fewer scientists would have given these four ideas any scientific credence. But there are aspects of theoretical physics that seem to offer some loopholes. Nature's laws cannot be broken, but it may be possible, in certain very bizarre circumstances, to bend them or make a detour around them. Whether or not this is ever likely to happen in real life is another question. The circumstances where

nature's laws start to look fuzzy round the edges are extreme, and very far removed from our present-day capacity to achieve them. These circumstances are discussed in this chapter and the next. This chapter deals mainly with the imaginary science that has a basis in cosmology — the physical nature of our universe. Chapter 5 deals with two special cases: time travel and alternate universes.

What are the laws of nature that govern our universe, and can we be certain that we now understand them? The three basic items that scientists measure to build up their picture of the universe are mass, distance and time. These elements of universal structure are dealt with quite straightforwardly (as invariants) in the old, mechanistic physics that was built up by Sir Isaac Newton and others in the seventeenth century and afterwards.

At the beginning of the twentieth century it became clear (largely due to Einstein's work) that the 'laws' of Newtonian physics, though they were perfectly adequate for all ordinary measurements, broke down in some extreme conditions. The rules of relativistic physics were substituted. We discuss them in the following pages.

But relativistic physics is not the end of the story, and we have already moved beyond Einstein. There is also quantum physics, which Einstein loathed, because it was a theory that introduced an element of uncertainty, even of gambling, into our map of the universe, especially at the subatomic

level. It was quantum mechanics that Einstein attacked with his dismissive remark: 'God does not play dice'.

Each of these three views of the physical world has produced its own 'laws', and all of these laws have been tested by experiment many times over. They work. Newtonian physics works perfectly well on the ordinary scale of things. Motor cars, aeroplanes and even planets obey its laws so closely that it is very difficult to detect any variation from the values predicted by Newtonian physics for their velocity and mass.

Relativistic physics comes into its own at the cosmic level, where great velocities and huge masses are involved. It works pretty well at the subatomic level, too (think of the atom bomb), though the random uncertainties and statistical predictions of the third kind of physics, quantum physics, are also needed in order to explain the behaviour of matter and energy at these tiny levels of existence.

Until recently quantum physics has usually been restricted to the subatomic level, but certain theoretical aspects of the behaviour of 'black holes', for example, seem to call for quantum physics at the macroscopic level too. The idea of quantum mechanics applied to the very big is fairly recent and the reconciliation of quantum physics with relativistic physics is one of the most exciting challenges faced by physicists today.

A science fiction writer is perfectly free to imagine a 'new' physics, but he is not free — unless

he is writing fantasy — to jettison the old physics. Any new physics can do no more than modify the old; it cannot replace it. Modern physics, however, is nothing if not flexible, and we need not fear that the inexorable laws of matter will drain all the excitement out of our future possibilities. Physicists themselves are awestruck at some of the situations they believe to be possible — situations that often go far beyond anything that the average science fiction writer could conceive. Some physicists even believe, charmingly and cheerily, that, if a thing is possible, then somewhere or other it must exist.

The following chapters about modern physics and imaginary science form a continuous narrative, a brisk sightseeing tour of the more bizarre mental landscapes opened up by scientists and philosophers, and colonized zestfully by a lunatic army of writers, always ready to do battle with the unimaginable.

The four most important kinds of imaginary science in science fiction, from left to right:
(i) Alternate universes; the hero of *2001: A Space Odyssey* has travelled through a dimensional gate to see an alternate self, very old, in an aristocratic bedroom.
(ii) Antigravity;

floating boy in film *Earth II*. If it is only zero gravity, why are objects resting on the table?
(iii) Time Travel; Dr Who emerges from his disguised time machine in the television series *Dr Who*.
(iv) Faster Than Light; the starship *Enterprise* in *Star Trek: The Motion Picture*.

Faster than light and relativity

We may not yet have made traffic regulations for space, but already the universe seems to have an unbreakable speed limit. The greatest problem of science fictional space travel is that, as far as we can tell, nothing can move faster than light.

This causes no trouble in daily life since the speed of light is so great — about 300,000 km per second. Travel is more awkward in physicist George Gamow's scientific fable *Mr Tompkins in Wonderland*, where light moves at a sedate 15 kph. Gamow's cyclist can pedal as furiously as he likes without ever quite reaching the natural speed limit; real-life spacecraft would have the same problem as they approached the fatal velocity *c* (the speed of light in vacuum). Einstein's Special Theory of Relativity has advantages as well as disadvantages: by travelling closer and closer to velocity *c* you can make any journey seem as short as you like — though only to yourself!

Special relativity — first formulated by Einstein in 1905 — begins with the astonishing experimental fact that *c* never changes, no matter what moving system you measure it from. A car might travel at 100 kph, and to another car following at 60 kph the apparent (relative) speed of the first car would seem to be only 40 kph. But a ray of light appears to move at exactly the same speed *c* whether measured from either car or by someone standing at the roadside. Leaving out several pages of calculations, the final result of *c*'s invariability is that other natural properties of matter that we consider to be constant must themselves vary as matter approaches the speed of light. Although it seems contrary to the dictates of 'common sense', the mathematics of the situation demands that a spaceship's mass and length, and even the timekeeping of its clocks, will alter as its speed (relative to watchers on Earth) changes.

But why, just because *c* is unvarying, is it a natural speed limit? This follows from the equation for the factor by which mass, length and time are altered — a factor called *tau*, equal to $\sqrt{1-v^2/c^2}$. When *v*, the velocity of the spaceship, is much smaller than *c*, *tau* is only just less than 1 and 'common-sense' physics works as usual. Even at a speed of a million kph, *tau* only drops to about 0.9999996: to someone standing still, the ship's length would seem to have shrunk by this factor while its onboard clocks would run this much more slowly. The ship's mass would be divided by *tau* and would increase, to about 1.0000004 of its 'stationary' value. The peculiarities of relativity are still unnoticeable.

By the time our ship has boosted to 150,000 km per second — half the speed of light — *tau* has fallen to 0.866. Ship time is flowing at less than seven-eighths of the normal rate; the ship's mass has risen by more than 15%. Because the mass is greater, more work must now be done to accelerate the ship; as it travels faster still, the mass rises further. Much of the energy used to push the ship is actually being transformed into mass — in accordance with Einstein's famous equation $E=mc^2$ (energy equals mass multiplied by the square of *c*, so 1 kg of mass equals a monstrous 90 million billion joules of energy). As the velocity *v* comes closer to *c*, *tau* approaches zero and the ship's

---

$\mu \rightarrow e+\nu+\bar{\nu}$
Speed zero: average time for decay 2.2 microseconds

$\mu \longrightarrow e+\nu+\bar{\nu}$
Speed 0.9*c*: average time 5 microseconds

$\mu \longrightarrow \quad e+\nu+\bar{\nu}$
Speed 0.99*c*: average time 15.6 microseconds

$\mu \longrightarrow\longrightarrow \quad e+\nu+\bar{\nu}$
0.999*c*: average time 49 microseconds

$\mu \longrightarrow\longrightarrow\longrightarrow \quad e+\nu+\bar{\nu}$
Speed 0.9999*c*: average time 155 microseconds

Scale of time-lines:
1mm to one microsecond

The muon (μ) is a particle which, on average, decays after about 2.2 microseconds into an electron (e), a neutrino (ν) and an anti-neutrino ($\bar{\nu}$).

When it travels close to the speed of light (*c*), the stretching of time caused by relativity makes it take longer and longer to decay as it

nears *c*. This has been measured experimentally and is an important proof of relativity. Muons created at the top of the atmosphere

by the impact of cosmic rays on air molecules would not exist for long enough to be detected at ground level if it were not for this effect.

We can visualize some of the effects of relativistic distortion if we imagine the speed of light to be a modest 15kph. To the stationary observer the unmoving bicycle on the left would, of course, be undistorted. But the two moving bicycles, both of them approaching the speed of light, would seem unnaturally compressed along the axis in which they are moving. The effect would be the same whether they were approaching him or receding from him, though the Doppler effect would make the approaching cyclist appear blue, and the receding cyclist appear red. A moving cyclist, on the other hand, would see the houses he was passing as extremely tall and thin (see right), but would perceive no change in his own dimensions. Indeed, from his point of view, there is no change. Obviously the moving cyclists are very fit, since the energy with which they are pedalling must be equal to that released in around a million H-bomb explosions. This is because, as they approach the speed of light, they have increased their mass at least tenfold, and the energy to be converted into this mass increase can only come from their pedalling. They would be better off walking.

mass grows towards infinity — meaning that to accelerate all the way to the speed of light, an infinite amount of energy (fuel) is needed. Plainly this is not a practical proposition. Stories of ships accelerating to travel 237 light-years in 48 hours, as in E.E. Smith's *Skylark of Space*, or half a light-year every minute, as in A.E. van Vogt's 'The Storm', simply will not do. Light takes exactly 1 year to travel 1 light-year, and without infinite energy we can never go quite that fast.

But remember that the ship's clock runs more slowly. If we travel 1 light-year at 99.99% of *c*, then from the viewpoint of someone watching the journey from Earth, the time taken will be a year plus about 53 minutes. At this speed, though, *tau* has shrunk to about 0.01414: the ship's clocks are running at only 0.01414 times the rate of Earth clocks, so inside the ship the journey appears to take only 5 days and a few hours. (People in the ship see the relativistic shrinkage of length from the other viewpoint — to them, their flight path and indeed the whole universe seem to have shrunk by the factor 0.01414 along the direction of travel. To them, acceleration does not so much increase their speed as reduce the distance to be covered.) If the ship could turn and fly straight back to Earth at the same speed, it would return just over 2 years after starting . . . but the ship's clock and crew would have noticed the passing of only 10 days or so. Remember, though, that fantastic amounts of energy are needed — the ship's mass would have increased about 71 times, soaking up energy at a ruinous rate of exchange. The conversion of less than 1 gm of mass provided all the energy of the Hiroshima bomb. The amount of energy that would be needed to convert into the mass of 70 starships is almost unimaginable.

With longer flights at speeds still closer to *c*, decades or centuries might pass on Earth during what seems a short interstellar hop to the travellers. Ursula Le Guin, in *Rocannon's World*, compares this with legends of enchanted hills where you spend one night with the Little Folk while years pass outside — Le Guin's 'goblins' give her unsuspecting heroine a ride on a relativistic ship with much the same effect. Dozens of novels feature unnaturally youthful star travellers returning to a changed future world, examples being George Turner's *Beloved Son* and Robert Heinlein's *Time for the Stars*, where the hero cheerfully marries his great-great-niece.

These incredible effects have been checked by experiment. Muons ('heavy electrons') normally break down quickly into other particles — but at relativistic speeds their 'clocks' are slowed and the breakdown is delayed. (If breakdown were not delayed, they would not get as far as the detection chambers.) Beams of electrons have been accelerated close to c — and sure enough, they become more and more massive while never actually reaching the velocity c.

One theoretical way round the problem of ever increasing mass is to cancel out our spaceship's mass — somehow. E.E. Smith does this in his 'Lensman' books, where massless ships routinely travel at speeds far greater than c. Unfortunately, mass is not so easily jettisoned: it is a basic property of the particles making up solid matter. No mass presumably means no matter, and thus no ship. Other particles, like photons, are said to have zero 'rest mass', which is misleading, since a photon cannot actually be brought to rest without destroying it. All the massless particles can exist only while travelling exactly at the speed of light. In his story 'The Billiard Ball', Isaac Asimov suggests that if some ordinary object's mass *could* be reduced to zero, it would shoot off with velocity c (punching neat holes in bystanders en route).

What happens to *tau* if we travel faster than light (FTL)? Ignoring the practical problem of how to reach FTL speeds without the speedometer first registering that forbidden value c, let us look at the mathematics. We can try making the velocity v bigger than c in the *tau* equation. If, say, v is about 1.4 times c then v^2 is twice c^2 and *tau* equals the square root of -1 ($\sqrt{-1}$). Any velocity above c makes *tau* a multiple of this imaginary number, so called because there is no real number which gives -1 when multiplied by itself. The FTL spaceship's altered mass, length and timeflow *have become imaginary numbers.*

There are two ways of looking at this alarming result. The first is to take it as nonsensical — a proof that FTL travel is mathematically silly.

The second is to find a way of interpreting the 'unreal' figures: imaginary numbers are often used in mathematical short cuts that lead to real answers. A possible answer here is that the imaginary figures are real in another universe which is, so to speak, on the other side of the light barrier. Everything in this universe would move faster than light, and it would be impossible to slow a mass all the way down to velocity c — since in the FTL universe you would have to put energy into a spaceship to slow it down, energy which would grow to infinity as the speed *dropped* to c.

Although all this is just a bare mathematical possibility, FTL particles have been given the name 'tachyons' — as distinct from the slower-than-light 'tardyons' of our universe (e.g. protons, electrons) and the massless 'luxons', which travel only at velocity c (photons, gravitons). Writers have unabashedly borrowed the name: Bob Shaw's *The Palace of Eternity* features such delights as a million-ton tachyonic spaceship travelling at 30,000 times the speed of light.

There are several objections. First, there is no experimental evidence for the existence of tachyons. Secondly, that infinite, unclimbable 'light barrier' still stands between us and hopes of tachyonic travel. Thirdly, there is a mathematical symmetry which suggests that from the viewpoint of a tachyon universe, it is *our* universe where FTL travel is possible — meaning that there are no travel advantages, wherever you are. And lastly, as will be discussed in the next chapter, tachyons are likely to behave as though they travel backwards in time — breaking the law of causality.

Causality (see also pages 90-1) is an empirical law, one which has never been proved but which lies at the roots of science. It says, simply, that effects happen after causes. A bullet cannot hit its target until after the trigger is pulled; a man cannot die without having been born. This sounds trite, but when it is coupled with Einstein's work the result is that not only tachyonic travel but all other FTL journeys are forbidden.

Einstein's great discovery is that any viewpoint is as good as any other. We must rely on what our eyes tell us about space and time: there is no absolute master clock for the universe, for example, since any such clock would seem to run at different rates depending on how quickly we moved relative to it. A fast spaceship travels 1 light-year in just over a year, as measured from Earth — or in just over 5 days, as measured by someone aboard. Both measurements are equally 'correct', and both comply with the law of causality. Before it can arrive 1 light-year from Earth, the ship must be seen to leave Earth: people on and off the ship differ about the time between these events but not about the order in which they happen.

But suppose the ship travels faster than light. Someone waiting for it, 1 light-year out, would first see the ship arrive on his doorstep; the image of the ship's launch would follow later, since light travels only at velocity c. From this fellow's viewpoint, *which is just as valid as any other,* the ship has arrived before it set out — and bang goes causality.

An FTL ship could flit about as in Piers Anthony's eccentric novel *Macroscope* (1969), overtaking light in its journey through space and seeing first a man's death, then his old age, backwards through time until his birth — again in defiance of causality. Either there is something wrong with Einstein's theory (which has been thoroughly tested) or causality (which though never proven is a cornerstone of physics) — or FTL journeys of any kind are impossible.

Still, *might* there be exceptions to the rule of causality? What, after all, caused the beginning of the universe and of time itself? On the fringes of physics, in the quantum theory of subatomic particles or the unknowable space inside a black hole, there are hints that causality *may* not be a universal rule.

This astronaut has returned to Earth after a 5-year trip to the stars at near light-speed. Fifty years have passed on Earth and his identical twin brother who has come to the spaceport to meet him is now 75. The reunion is a strange one for both twins — in effect, one is seeing himself as he was, the other sees himself as he will be.

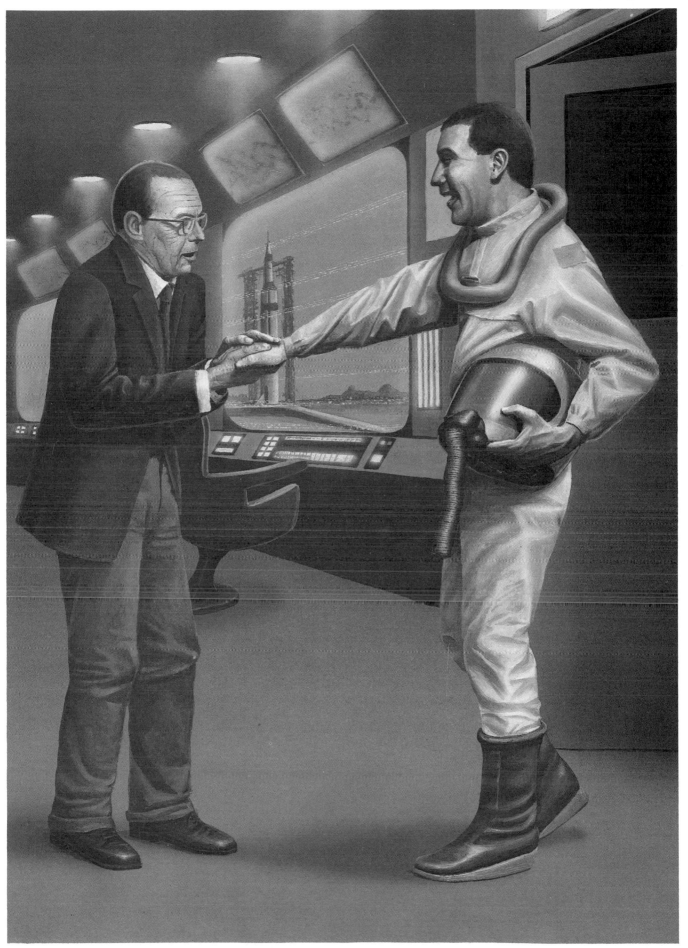

Hyperspace

If we cannot move faster than light in this universe, perhaps we can take a short cut. Might there be a way to slip out of ordinary space, travel along secret back alleys of space/time, and return to our own universe at some point far from where we started?

Hyperspace is the science fictional name for the 'other space' used in such short cuts. The word was invented by John W. Campbell for his short story 'The Mightiest Machine' (1934), and unashamedly stolen by hundreds of writers since. Today, hyperspace is part of science fiction's standard furniture — solving all those awkward problems of travel to the stars.

Although it *sounds* different from travelling faster than light while staying in this universe, taking a hyperspatial short cut leads to exactly the same clash with relativity and causality. The simple fact of having got from A to B in less time than a ray of light could travel between those points is enough to violate causality. But we shall ignore that problem for now, and look at what hyperspace might actually be.

One view of hyperspace is as a higher-dimensioned space in which our three-dimensional universe is somehow folded and crumpled — in the way that we can crumple a two-dimensional piece of paper into a three-dimensional ball. If the paper were an astronomical map, two stars a long way apart on the map could be brought close together when the map is folded so that different parts of it touch. An insect on this map need not crawl the full map distance from one star to the other: it could hop across at the point where crumpling has brought those stars close in three-dimensional (though not in two-dimensional) space. In Robert Heinlein's *Starman Jones* spaceships take this kind of short cut, leaping from one point in our space to another, 'far-off' one which has been brought close by the (invisible to us) crumpling of three-dimensional space through four-dimensional hyperspace. How, then, do we escape from our own space to take such short cuts? Apparently we would have to move in a direction at right angles to every possible direction in our space, which is about as likely as is a two-dimensional figure on a cinema screen which suddenly steps out into the room.

A more common view of hyperspace is as a 'universe next door' much smaller than our own, with every point in hyperspace corresponding to one in this universe. Mathematicians call this a 'one-to-one' mapping. So hyperspace behaves like a little map of our own universe, a map which can be visited — as though we could step from London to the point marked 'London' on the map, walk a short distance to the point marked 'New York', and step out of the map into the real New York. Again, the difficulty is getting into the map — into hyperspace — in the first place.

This model features in Frederik Pohl's story 'The Mapmakers', in which (logically enough) an error in positioning of 1 cm on the 'map' can bring a ship back to normal space millions of light-years from its planned destination. There is no reason why hyperspace travel should be even this simple. In Bob Shaw's *Night Walk* the hyperspace universe has a fiendishly complicated shape, like a mathematician's nightmare — the odds are that inexperienced travellers will end up at completely random points in our space, and will never get home again.

Still more depressing is George R.R. Martin's story 'FTA', where people break into hyperspace and find that it is not a short cut after all. Why, apart from wishful thinking, should it be? In this story, to go via hyperspace takes longer.

All these ideas are fiction — but there are scientific theories that go much further than the idea of short cuts through another universe. In today's quantum physics, the building blocks of the universe are no more than ripples in a universal something called the quantum field. Protons, neutrons, electrons . . . all are fluctuations of 'empty space', and what we call 'matter' is a stable pattern of such ripples. If enough energy is available, matter can be created out of 'nothing': under the right conditions a high-energy gamma ray can become an electron and a positron (antielectron).

On the microscopic scale, then, it seems that empty space may not be the nice smooth something, or nothing, that science has always supposed. What looks like vacuum is 'really' foaming and vibrating with energy fluctuations, so that a single cubic cm of empty space can be said to be packed with energy equivalent to a mass of around 10^{91} kg. (Remember that the conversion of only 1 kg releases more energy than a 20-megaton hydrogen bomb!) One result of this foamlike structure of space is the likely existence of countless 'wormholes' connecting different parts of space, like little tubes, centimetres long, that run

Hyperspace is usually considered in science fiction to be a kind of fourth dimension. The question is, if scientist Robert Lansing has to enter the fourth dimension every time he walks through a wall in the film *4D Man* (1959), how can we see him? To make matters worse, every time he walks through people they die of old age and he gets younger. This is an effect unknown to science.

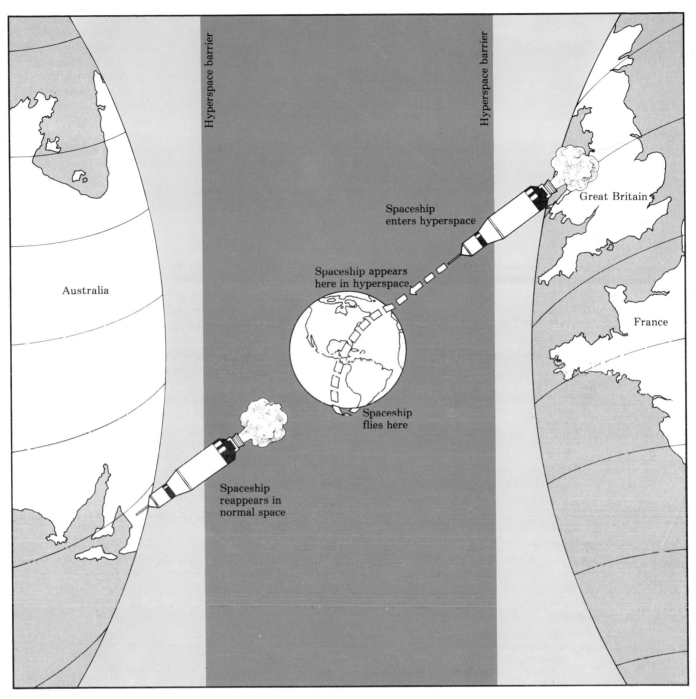

Hyperspace barrier

Hyperspace barrier

Australia

Spaceship
enters hyperspace

Spaceship appears
here in hyperspace

Great Britain

France

Spaceship
flies here

Spaceship
reappears in
normal space

outside space and back again at
some distant point. John A. Wheeler,
the scientist mainly responsible for
this view, describes the wormholes as
running through 'superspace', which
sounds very like what science fiction
calls 'hyperspace'. The theory of
superspace goes further, though,
since it appears that tiny 'quantum'
wormholes must connect every part
of space to every other part! (The
word 'wormhole' is sometimes used,
in a rather different sense, to
describe a possible zone of transition
at the centre of a rotating black hole
— see pages 94-6.)

Oddly enough, the rules of relativity and causality have no objection
to these wormholes. The short cut is
free to exist, provided that we do
not defy causality by travelling
along it — and since superspace
wormholes are of submicroscopic
width, it does not seem very likely
that mighty spaceships will be
zooming through them as in *Star
Trek — the Motion Picture* (1980).
Even an electron is about 100 billion
billion times too large to squeeze
through. But perhaps we can send
messages through wormholes and at
least have an instantaneous
telephone line to anywhere in the
universe: read on!

One popular view
of hyperspace is
that every point in
it corresponds to
one point in our
universe — this is
called one-to-one
mapping — but
that it is much
smaller. The
rocket flying from
England to
Australia in our
diagram enters
hyperspace,
circumnavigates
the hyperspace
Earth in next to
no time, and
emerges at its

destination.
However there is
nothing to say
that equivalent
points in hyper-
space would be
arranged *in the
same order*, in
which case they
would have to be
carefully surveyed
by explorers. If
hyperspace is
really going to
resemble an
abstract painting
by Jackson
Pollock, we might
be better off
without it.

Instantaneous communication

Instantaneous communicators in science fiction are supposed to evade reality by transmitting nothing material, but just pure information. One suggested FTL communicator is outrageously simple. It consists of a perfectly rigid rod, as many light-years long as required. Since the rod is rigid, its whole length will move when we push the near end, and instantaneous messages can be sent to the stars in suitably coded pushes and pulls. This, of course, is nonsense. There is no such thing as a perfectly rigid rod, and the energy of each push would travel along the rod, like a sound wave along a pipe, at much less than light-speed.

Another suggestion: take two of these light-years-long rods, hanging side by side in space. Near Earth the rods touch; they are at a very small angle to each other, so that their far ends are centimetres apart. If one rod is moved sideways it will slide over the other until, after a short time, the Earth ends of the rods are a few centimetres apart while the far ends are touching. In that short time, without any mass or energy being sent faster than light, *something* has travelled light-years along the rods: the point at which they touch has moved all the way from Earth to the far end. Could this be used to transmit information? In fact the answer is 'no'. The more subtle radio-wave version of this trick, which appears as the 'ultrawave communicator' in several stories by James Blish, would not work either. The flaw is that the entire length of the sideways-moving rod must already be moving before the rods' point of contact can travel faster than light; those at the far end would already know that the 'signal' was coming and would receive absolutely no more information from it. Physicists call this a 'non-meaningful super-light signal'. We can aim a laser at the Moon and swivel it so that a bright spot moves across the Moon's surface with FTL speed — but the spot carries no information from one part of the Moon to another.

It is impossible to avoid relativity and causality by sending only information faster than light. The difficulty is the same: any FTL message will seem, to some observers, to arrive before it is sent — and our view of the universe cannot tolerate this.

Science fiction contains two instantaneous communicators that are infernally plausible — Ursula Le Guin's 'ansible' and James Blish's 'Dirac communicator'. The ansible appears in several Le Guin books, and its inventor is the hero of her *The Dispossessed*. It is supposed to be based on a theory which supersedes Einstein's, but includes Einstein's as a special case (just as Newton's laws of motion are a special case of Einstein's, perfectly usable where speeds are much less than that of light). The problem of causality is avoided by talk of 'simultaneity' — messages do not actually travel from one ansible to another, they only seem to!

James Blish, in *The Quincunx of Time*, takes a different line. His Dirac transmitter — named after the real-life physicist Paul Dirac — sends messages that can be picked up by any Dirac receiver, past, present or future. This eliminates the paradox of events happening before their causes, since in Blish's world the future is unchangeable, like the past. Determinism is the rule of the day: if the bullet *must* reach the target and the finger *must* pull the trigger, it no longer makes sense to talk about whether one of these events is the cause of the other. Instead, in a deterministic universe, all events are fixed like atoms in a rigid crystal and can be looked at in any order.

Happily, the whole trend of modern quantum physics is against determinism. Determinism says that any decision we make is powerless to change anything — it would have happened anyway. In quantum physics it can be said that the whole universe is the creation of decisions we make. The basic idea is that no event is 'real' unless it can be observed in one way or another — and if we observe it we change it, according to how we decide to observe it. To observe something we must light it up, bounce photons off it — and the impacts of the photons themselves will change the movement of the object. When it is large, like a football, the change is unnoticeable; when it is small, like an electron, collision with a single photon can alter its course hugely. This leads to the physicist Heisenberg's Uncertainty Principle of 1927: we can measure the position of

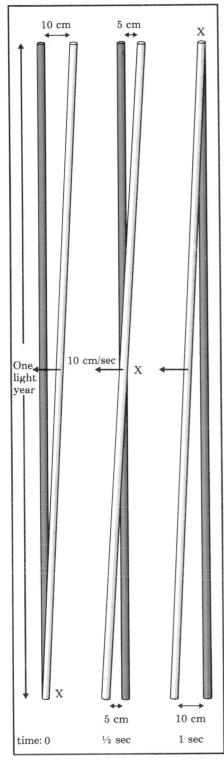

10 cm   5 cm   X

10 cm/sec   X

One
light
year

X

5 cm   10 cm

time: 0   ½ sec   1 sec

an electron at a given moment by hitting it with a photon and making its new velocity uncertain, or we can measure its velocity at the expense of certainty about its position.

In the end it seems that particles have no real, definite position or velocity until one or the other is measured (we cannot measure both at the same time). Particles spread out through space as fuzzy 'probability functions' which predict where they are *likely* to be; when we take a measurement this probability wave collapses for a moment into something behaving like a solid particle. How does this connect with FTL communication? It seems possible to design experiments dealing with the combined probability function of *two* particles produced at the same time but travelling in opposite directions. By making measurements on one particle we can deduce things about the other; there is a subtle possibility that because of the way quantum physics works, we can instantaneously affect the far-away particle by choosing which measure-

ment we make on the near one.

Such an experiment was first performed in 1972 (see diagram), and the results were confirmed in Paris in 1981. If the results can be accepted, then there is a faster-than-light connection between each pair of particles, perhaps even through quantum 'wormholes'. Relativity, of course, predicts that no useful information can be sent along such a route. Quantum physicists, however, sometimes adopt a more cavalier attitude towards questions of cause and effect. In his paper 'Are Super-luminal Connections Necessary?' (1977), the American physicist Henry Stapp wrote: 'Quantum phenomena provide prima facie evidence that information gets around in ways that do not conform to classical ideas. Thus the idea that information is transferred super-luminally (faster than light) is, a priori, not unreasonable.'

Experiments and theory of this kind imply fascinating possibilities. They may even imply the possibility of alternate universes (see pages 98-101).

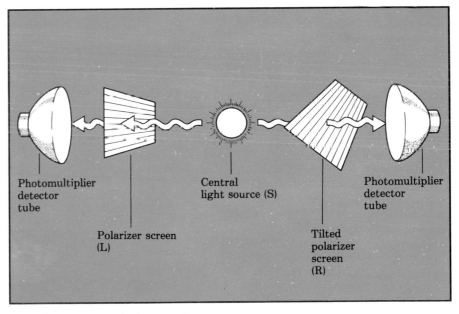

Photomultiplier detector tube

Polarizer screen (L)

Central light source (S)

Tilted polarizer screen (R)

Photomultiplier detector tube

Left: an artist's impression of the screen of a Dirac receiver, the instantaneous communicator of James Blish's *The Quincunx of Time*. **Above:** an imaginary FTL communicator, made of two rods, each 1 light-year long. The dark rod

remains still; the other is moved sideways 10 cm. They touch at point X. Point X moves 1 light-year in 1 second. **Right:** The physicists John Clauser and Stuart Freedman did this experiment in 1972. (A very much more

sophisticated version was carried out by Alain Aspect in Paris in 1981, confirming the results.) Photons are emitted in pairs from source S, in opposite directions. They have to pass through polarizers, which filter out

photons whose waves are not aligned to them. A correlation between what happens on both sides would be expected when the polarizers are parallel, but here one is tilted obliquely to the other. Einsteinian theory said

correlation would fall off to a greater extent than quantum theory predicts. Quantum theory wins. The experiment shows that a decision about the angle of the polarizer on side R affects the polarization of the photons on the

left hand side L. This is measured by correlating the number of clicks in the two detectors. The big problem is not yet solved. How do the photons on side L get the information about what is happening to the photons on side R?

The beginning of the universe

The beginning of our universe is one of the most fascinating problems of science, with timescales measured in billions of years. Strangely, such a stupendous event has been neglected in science fiction. But what is there to say about a time when, according to modern theory, the universe was so full of hellish energy that not even atoms could survive? A ringside view of creation does appear in Poul Anderson's novel *Tau Zero*, where (see pages 190-1) he bends the facts a little to make his story work. He introduces a spaceship which orbits *outside* the monobloc containing all the mass and energy of the universe-to-be . . . but today's physics says there will be no outside.

The favourite view of cosmologists, the Big Bang theory, says that the universe is expanding from the impetus of some original explosion. Observations of distant galaxies show that they are all moving away from us (because the light they give out is shifted towards the red end of the spectrum, in the same way that the note of a train's whistle sounds lower when the train is moving away). But there is no reason to suppose that the perfectly average part of space where we live is a central slum from which everything else is moving away. On the contrary; there is good reason to believe that each of those distant galaxies would see itself in the same position, with all the others moving away from it. The universe is expanding, all *space* is getting bigger, and everything is getting further from everything else.

To understand this, think of the universe as the skin of a balloon with all the galaxies painted on it. If the balloon is inflated a little more, the area of the skin increases, and so do all the distances between galaxies. Of course the universe is not being inflated by pumping something into it: perhaps it can be thought of as the outer shockwave of the original explosion, a surface which gets bigger thanks to its own outward momentum. Even if the universe is infinite it still means

something to say that it expands, since there is a steady change of scale which carries its parts further away from one another.

Once we know the rate at which the universe expands, and the rate at which that expansion is slowing down (since, though flying apart, the galaxies are being attracted together by gravity), we can work back towards the beginning of the universe. It seems that this happened between 10 and 20 billion years ago. Near the very beginning it is as though the surface of our imaginary 'balloon' were completely and thickly covered in 'paint'. As the balloon expands this paint breaks into flakes. The separating flakes correspond to galaxies, or rather to protogalaxies — the hot gas clouds from which galaxies will condense. So, near the beginning there is no unpainted part of the balloon's surface — no free space anywhere in the universe. The primordial monobloc *is* the universe.

In his book *The First Three Minutes* (1977), the physicist Steven Weinberg traces the early moments of creation as calculated by science.

At zero time the temperature of the universe would be enormous, perhaps infinite. For the first hundredth of a second of expansion the picture is made insanely complex by the presence of high-energy mesons and perhaps even free quarks (the subnuclear particles which, according to many theories, make up 'fundamental' particles like

protons and neutrons). After a hundredth of a second the temperature is about 100 billion °C, too little to break up protons and neutrons, which now become stable. The universe is packed tight with lighter particles (electrons, positrons) and, above all, radiation. Its density is billions of times that of water: 1 cubic cm of the plasma filling the universe would weigh thousands of tons. Some believe the universe is infinite now and would have been infinite then; others estimate that today's universe is finite, with a circumference of about 125 billion light-years, in which case its circumference a hundredth of a second from the beginning would have been about 4 light-years. But, as with an insect crawling on our imaginary balloon, no amount of travel can bring us to the edge. The circumference is a measure of the distance you must travel, in what seems a straight line, to return through curved space to the same spot.

After about 14 seconds the temperature has fallen to only 3 billion degrees or so, too low for

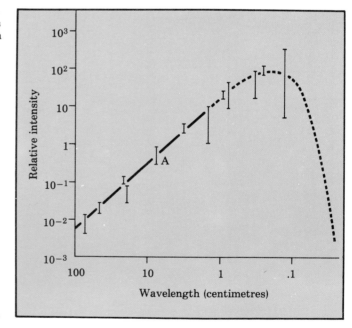

In 1965 the physicists Arno Penzias and Robert Wilson detected an unexpected radiation in the radio-wave band at a wavelength (A) of 7 cm, to which their apparatus was accidentally tuned. Further experiments showed that the radiation could be graphed as shown here. The curve suggests a background radiation of 3° above absolute zero — a ghostly message from the original Big Bang.

more electrons and positrons to be created spontaneously from energy: the electrons and positrons annihilate each other and mostly vanish. After a little over 3 minutes the temperature is so low (under a billion degrees) that the relatively tiny number of neutrons and protons created in that first hundredth of a second can join into nuclei without

The further into the universe we look, the further back into the past we see, since light from distant objects was emitted a long time ago. The redshift of light corresponds to the velocity with which the object emitting the light is receding from us. Thus the oldest objects in the universe, which are moving away from us with the greatest speed, have the largest redshifts. By peering far into the universe, astronomers can partially reconstruct its history. This chart gives a timescale of events in our universe since the Big Bang. It indicates when some of the universe's major features were formed. The cosmic background radiation detected by Penzias and Wilson in 1965 dates from less than 1 million years after the Big Bang — a mere blink of the eye on a cosmic timescale.

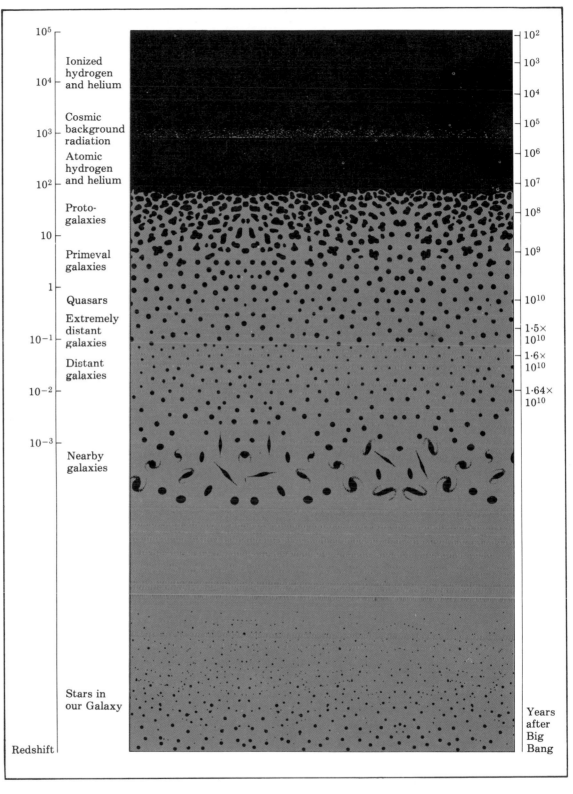

Redshift		Years after Big Bang
	Ionized hydrogen and helium	
	Cosmic background radiation	
	Atomic hydrogen and helium	
	Proto-galaxies	
	Primeval galaxies	
	Quasars	
	Extremely distant galaxies	
	Distant galaxies	
	Nearby galaxies	
	Stars in our Galaxy	

being blasted apart again by the high-energy radiation. But atoms are not formed for another 700,000 years, when the temperature has fallen to the point at which electrons are no longer stripped away from nuclei by the radiation which still fills the universe. Later, after gravity has condensed these atoms successively into protogalaxies, galaxies, protostars and stars, heavier elements are 'cooked up' in stars and hurled out via nova explosions.

One famous piece of evidence for this theory comes from the radiation originally filling space. The fall of temperature was caused by 'stretching' of short, high-energy wavelengths into longer, lower-energy ones as space expanded. The original radiation is still around us, though very stretched indeed — and in the 1960s this 'fossil' radiation was detected, now corresponding to a temperature only 3° above absolute zero.

So will the universe now expand for ever? We shall come back to that.

Antimatter

When the universe was formed, antimatter was just as likely to be created as matter. Ordinary matter has negatively charged electrons circling positively charged nuclei; antimatter would have positively charged antielectrons – positrons – and nuclei with a negative charge.

All nuclei are built from protons (positive electric charge) and neutrons (no charge): antinuclei would contain antiprotons (negative charge) and antineutrons. Though they have no charge, antineutrons differ from neutrons in having opposite 'spin' and 'baryon number', two important quantities in the bookkeeping of particle physics: all heavy particles, like protons or neutrons, are called baryons. A firm rule is that the total baryon number of a system cannot change, though this apparently fails inside black holes. A neutron (baryon number +1) can become a proton (baryon number +1) and an electron (baryon number 0 since an electron is not a baryon but a light particle, or lepton). The total electric charge stays at zero and the total baryon number at +1. But a proton cannot simply be annihilated.

A proton and an antiproton (baryon number −1) *can* join together in a 'suicide pact'. The two heavy particles meet in a flare of energy and vanish, their mass converted to high-energy radiation while their opposite charges and baryon numbers cancel out. We can make antiprotons in the laboratory by turning this process round, using a particle accelerator to smash protons together at such enormous energies that the energy of collision is more than twice the mass/energy of a proton. The resulting reaction is written: $p+p \rightarrow p+p+p+\bar{p}$. Two protons (p) become three plus an antiproton ($\bar{p}$); the total baryon number before is $1+1=2$, and after the collision it is $1+1+1-1...$ still 2.

Antiprotons are routinely created like this at research establishments such as CERN in Geneva, for use in further experiments. (The world's first collisions between high-energy beams of protons and antiprotons were observed at CERN early in 1981.) If an antiproton teams up with a positron, the result is an atom of neutral antihydrogen; by building bigger nuclei from antiprotons and antineutrons, and providing them with orbital positrons, we could theoretically make a complete range of antimatter elements which would react with each other exactly as ordinary elements do. Two atoms of antihydrogen and one of antioxygen would become a molecule of antiwater, and so on. But if we could make up a litre of antiwater (something which at present rates of CERN antiproton production – less than one trillionth of a gram produced so far – would take longer than the universe may have to run), what on earth would we keep it in?

As antimatter touches matter, they annihilate each other. The total combined mass is released in a spectacular blast of energy. In a fission bomb a maximum of 0.1% of the plutonium mass can become energy; for a fusion bomb the maximum figure is about 0.5%; the figure for antimatter could approach 100%. We could call it 200%, since the explosion releases the energy of our 1 kg of antimatter *plus* that of the 1 kg of matter with which it reacts. Electrons and positrons, baryons and antibaryons come together and vanish into high-energy gamma rays (plus a certain number of harmless neutrinos, which pass through whole planets without effect). Hitting ordinary matter, our 1 kg of antimatter explodes with the force of up to 43 million tons of TNT – as though several thousand Hiroshima bombs were detonated at once. In *Star Trek*, the starship *Enterprise* is propelled by a controlled version of such explosions, but the television series never explained how the antimatter was created or stored.

Earlier science fiction writers often made two mistakes about antimatter. Some thought it had negative *mass*, and would thus feel gravity as a push rather than a pull – an example is E.E. Smith's 'negasphere' in *Gray Lensman*. If this were so, the antiproton's negative mass/energy would cancel the proton's when they met, and nothing would remain; in reality, two extremely high-energy gamma photons are produced. (Why two? To balance momentum: an explosion cannot explode in one direction only.) Today's theories of the universe say that there is no such thing as negative mass. The second

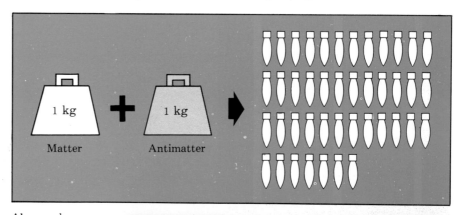

Above: when matter meets antimatter the annihilation is complete. 1 kg of matter combined with 1 kg of antimatter would release the energy of 43 exploding 1-megaton H-bombs. This process is said to propel the starship *Enterprise* in TV's *Star Trek*. No wonder Scotty, the engineer, always looks worried.

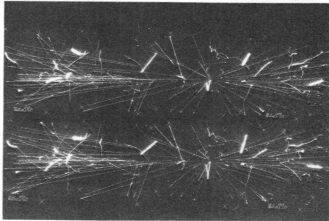

and more subtle mistake is the idea that antiwater would only annihilate with ordinary water, and could safely be kept in (say) an iron container. Not so: it is the subatomic particles that react so destructively, and their arrangement makes no difference.

So how can antimatter be stored? Space seems the only place, both for storage and for large-scale production. On Earth, gravity will sooner or later pull any lump of antimatter into disastrous contact with matter. One exception to this rule appears at CERN, where fast-moving antiprotons can be held in a 'storage ring' around which they constantly move, accelerated — and kept away from the walls of the vacuum chamber — by magnetic fields. This only works for charged particles, however; it does not work for antineutrons, for example.

Jack Williamson's *Seetee Ship* and *Seetee Shock* deal with antimatter, 'seetee' or 'CT' meaning 'contraterrene', the old science fictional term for antimatter. One suggested weapon is a bomb made from a hollow magnet, inside which an antimatter magnet is suspended in vacuum by weak magnetic repulsion. Drop the bomb and the shock makes the inner magnet hit the outer one. How could we make this device using tools of normal matter? Williamson's books rely on manipulation by artificial gravity fields — another unlikely idea.

Though antimatter can be manufactured, slowly, natural antimatter has never been found. In theory we should expect equal amounts of matter and antimatter to be formed at the beginning of the universe — perhaps some distant galaxies are made of antimatter that somehow became separated from matter long ago? In that case we might one day find a wandering antimatter planet from another galaxy, as in Larry Niven's story 'Flatlander'; but the cosmic rays that reach Earth from far-off parts are often made up of protons or even nuclei, never of antiprotons or antinuclei. There may be no natural antimatter anywhere.

In that case, what happened to it? The most obvious answer is that, as predicted by theory, all the matter and antimatter underwent mutual annihilation in the first seconds of creation; but why, then, do we still have matter? Although it seems unlikely that more matter than antimatter should be formed, perhaps only such a universe can ever contain matter, stars and intelligent life. The physicist Steven Weinberg calculates that the number of particles just after the moment of creation, in the more-matter-than-antimatter scenario, would have exceeded the number of antiparticles by only one part in 1000 million. After the mutual annihilation, the universe we know was built up from that tiny residue of one 1000 millionth.

An alternative theory, produced by the physicist M. Goldhaber in 1956, is that the universe divided into two parts immediately after its formation — the universe of matter that we live in, and an alternate universe of antimatter that cannot be observed by us (see also pages 98-9).

Such questions of astrophysics as 'Where did the antimatter go?' have led to surprisingly little speculation in science fiction. The British writer Ian Watson, however, is typically ready to step in where angels fear to tread, and his novel *The Jonah Kit* (1975) ingeniously proposes that the antimatter disappeared inside mini black holes, where distinctions between matter and antimatter would become meaningless.

Left: the giant antiproton accumulator built by CERN. Here antimatter in the form of antiprotons is concentrated, the momentum-spread is compressed, and the antimatter is 'stacked' in a vacuum tube (left). The next step is to aim beams of protons and antiprotons at one another in a synchrotron, and to photograph the tracks of colliding particles, using a new technique: image intensifiers with a gain of 2000. **Far left:** a stereo view showing the first collisions between antiproton and proton beams in 1981 at CERN.

Gravity and antigravity

In the beginning, gravity was the least important of forces, and even now it is the weakest force in nature. But the universe has been dominated by gravity for billions of years and will be so until the very end.

The secret of gravity is that, unlike the fantastically powerful force that holds atomic nuclei together, it can operate at long range; unlike the moderately powerful electromagnetic force, it always attracts and never repels. A concentration of electric charge big enough to exert useful force will fly apart, thanks to its own electric repulsion; but mass naturally collects together in great lumps such as stars, producing large gravitational forces. A gravity field, though, is not simply an invisible elastic which pulls objects together. Gravity is bound up with the shape of space itself.

According to Einstein's General Theory of Relativity, published in 1915, space is curved by the presence of mass: a gravitational field is a curving of space. We cannot step out of space to make sure it curves, but, as the ancients deduced Earth's curvature from indirect measurements, we can do this for space. On any flat map of Earth, the shortest distance between two points will generally be shown as a curve: only a globe makes complete sense. And in space, where the shortest distance between two points is defined by the path of light, scientists find that starlight is distinctly curved in the strong gravitational field near our Sun. (Normally the Sun's light drowns that of stars near it in the sky — the bending of starlight was first measured during the total eclipse of 1919.)

One rough model of Einstein's universe is a thin rubber sheet whose two dimensions represent the three of space. Each bit of mass in the universe rests on this sheet and makes a dent in it: the larger the mass, the deeper the dent. The Sun rests in the huge pit of its own gravity — a pit shaped like a trumpet-mouth, sloping more and more steeply towards the bottom. (The steepness of the slope corresponds to the strength of the gravitational field.) Some way up this slope, Earth rolls round the pit like a roulette ball — accompanied by its own smaller pit of gravity, with the Moon rolling round that pit.

Every part of the rubber sheet (space) is curved to some extent by the masses on it; near the Sun the curvature is strong enough to make a measurable difference to a 'straight line' passing close by — a straight line or geodesic in this model being the shortest distance *along the surface of the sheet* between points, just as a great circle is the shortest distance along the surface of the Earth. Gravity and geometry are the same in Einstein's model, and the straight-line path of light depends on the shape of space.

If a new mass were dropped on to this rubber-sheet model, or if an existing mass were accelerated sharply, tremors would expand out across the sheet — gravity waves. In the real universe we cannot create mass (or destroy it completely, which would have the same effect), but the acceleration of mass does indeed produce gravity waves, just as the acceleration of charged electrons in a circuit produces electromagnetic waves. A 'packet' of gravity radiation is called a graviton, corresponding to the electromagnetic photon. The

Above: the actor Peter Ustinov with a rubber-sheet model of space, showing warping caused by gravity. Our Sun is represented by a billiard ball. From the BBC's *Einstein's Universe.*
Left: Professor J. Weber with one of his 3-ton, aluminium, gravitational-wave detectors. In theory, such waves would create tiny, measurable distortions in the metal. Weber used a second, identical detector hundreds of kilometres away. If effects occur at the same time, evidence is stronger. Positive results have not been confirmed as definitely gravitational.

gravitons created by an accelerating car or spaceship are feeble and, to us, undetectable — but the superhigh acceleration of large masses falling into black holes would produce powerful gravity waves, as in Jerry Pournelle's 'He Fell Into a Dark Hole'. Like earthquake shocks travelling at lightspeed through empty space, these could distort or even tear apart nearby matter.

Earth is so far from powerful sources of gravity waves that they can only be detected by ultrasensitive apparatus — measuring atom-sized distortions in large masses of metal. Also detected are traffic noises and scientists' heavy breathing. A second, far-off detector is needed: fast-moving gravity waves will trigger both detectors almost simultaneously, while anything recorded by one alone must be spurious. Effects have certainly been recorded by the detectors, but their source is uncertain, and not all scientists believe that they are unequivocally due to gravity waves.

Science fiction writers have used our crude, rubber, general-relativistic model to justify favourite gimmicks of artificial gravity and antigravity. Could we bend space artificially and

create our own gravity fields? One fictional supervillain planned to do this between the Earth and the Sun in such a way that sunlight would be deflected, plunging the Earth into darkness. This requires artificial space-curvature, which must be caused by artificial mass — the existence and acceleration of mass is *all* that shapes space. And artificial mass would need to have all the properties of real mass.

Suppose that we could reduce the effects of gravity by making the rubber sheet stiffer, so that the dents in it would be less deep and the gravity field produced by a given mass would be smaller. Remember that the rubber sheet is only a model: making it stiffer corresponds in the real world to rebuilding the framework of space-time — a daunting task. The unchangeable speed of light would apparently be increased locally, and causality would go down the drain. Effectively we would be making mass vanish without a trace — another improbability. Asimov's story 'The Billiard Ball' suggests that flattening out the curvature of space would make energy appear from nowhere — even more improbable.

Finally, there is antigravity: no work, no effort, we simply fall up to the stars. In *Count-Down*, Charles Eric Maine explained that all that was needed was to bend the rubber sheet of the model 'the other way'. Which way, asked James Blish, is the other way? Just as an artificial gravity field needs an artificial mass indistinguishable from a real one, artificial antigravity demands a negative mass and negative space-curvature. Negative energy is apparently conceivable, though only as a mathematical fiction on the submicroscopic quantum level (and only near a black hole) — but negative mass has never been found. Nor does today's physics even allow for the possibility. So much for anti-gravity.

Below: Christopher Foss's rendition of New York and associated bedrock flying through space, as imagined by James Blish in *Cities in Flight*. This miraculous feat is accomplished with the 'spindizzy', the most celebrated antigravity device in science fiction. This 'gravitron-polarity generator', unfortunately, is a piece of purely imaginary science. It would take more than Blish's doubletalk about electron spin to counteract the force of gravity.

Stars, neutron stars and black holes

Gravity is responsible for the birth of stars; its attraction makes stars condense from clouds of floating gas. And when a star's fire goes out, gravity crushes it into a white dwarf, a neutron star or, strangest of all, a black hole.

The life of a star is a struggle between gravity and nuclear reactions; eventually gravity will always win. The 'temporary' balance (which in our Sun seems set to last for billions of years) comes about because as gravity forces nuclei in a star together, it produces nuclear reactions between them — which is why stars shine. The tremendous heat and outward pressure of radiation from the nuclear fusion in a star's core are enough to balance the immense inward pull of

gravity — until the nuclear fuel (hydrogen) runs low.

When this happens, the core of the star will shrink, though its surface can expand, so an ordinary star can swell to a 'red giant'. As the core falls inwards, gravitational energy is converted to heat: the temperature rises to the point where new and more complex nuclear reactions can take place, for a while restoring the balance of radiation pressure against gravity. Ordinary stars get energy by fusing hydrogen into helium; a giant can re-use this helium in the hotter reaction which fuses helium into carbon; heavier and heavier elements are formed in reactions at still higher temperatures. Sometimes the starting up of a new fusion reaction can tip the balance too far against gravity, so the star blows off mass in a nova explosion — which is how the heavier elements formed in stars find their way back into space.

Many less massive stars (less

than six times heavier than the Sun) may simply blow off their outer layers and settle to a long period of slow contraction, kept hot by gravitational energy set free as they shrink. These are called 'white dwarfs': a typical one might have the size of Earth and 50% more mass than the Sun.

More exciting things happen with bigger stars, as shrinkage increases and core temperature soars. Eventually the cascade of useful nuclear reactions will halt, with most of the core converted to iron (which cannot be fused to heavier elements without putting energy *in* — using iron as nuclear fuel is like trying to burn ice). Finally, the enormous core temperatures produced by gravitational shrinking smash the iron itself back to helium, soaking up incredible quantities of energy — again, as though ice has been thrown on the fire.

The core no longer radiates at

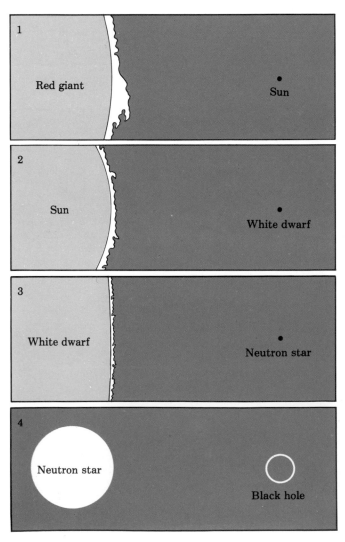

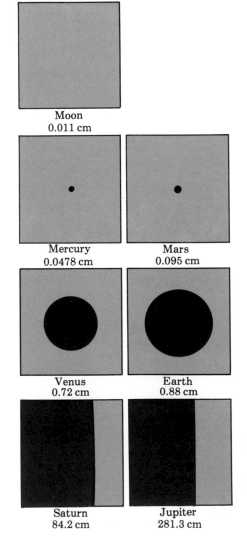

Left: the stars with the largest diameter are red giants, maybe 320 million km across; the smallest are stars that have contracted into black holes. The diagram shows some relative sizes to scale. The astonishing thing is that stellar objects with these relative sizes would have approximately the same mass. The shrinking in size is related to the greater density in each case.
Right: this diagram shows the *actual sizes* of black holes having the same mass as various members of our Solar System. (The planets, of course, could not become black holes; there is not nearly enough gravity.) The Sun is not included; its black-hole radius of 3 km would not fit.

Moon
0.011 cm

Mercury
0.0478 cm

Mars
0.095 cm

Venus
0.72 cm

Earth
0.88 cm

Saturn
84.2 cm

Jupiter
281.3 cm

anything like the intensity needed to balance gravity. It collapses with a tremendous energy flash that blows the star apart in a supernova explosion. For a few days, while this happens, the star shines 1000 billion times brighter. What remains is the core, crushed in that final collapse into something which is not matter as we know it. Electrons have been squashed against protons until the charges cancel and they become neutrons; there are no separate atomic nuclei any more, just a spherical mass of neutrons, like one giant nucleus. This is a neutron star. Millions of times denser than a white dwarf, a neutron star can pack the mass of the Sun into a radius of several kilometres.

Because it is so compact and heavy, a neutron star has a gigantic gravitational field. The one in Larry Niven's story 'Neutron Star' (1.3 solar masses, under 20 km diameter) would exert a force of more than 200 billion Earth gravities at its surface, enough to crush anything there into a thin film of degenerate matter; Earth itself would be drawn in by this gravity and reduced to a layer about 1 cm thick on its surface. Even for a nearby spaceship in free fall, such gravity could cause lethal tidal forces.

Tides on Earth are caused by the variation of Moon gravity with distance: the seas facing the Moon are pulled a little more than Earth's core, while the seas on Earth's other side are pulled a little less, the effect being to hump up the waters on either side. Niven's free-falling spaceship comes close to his neutron star, to somewhat over 11 km from its centre. The ship feels a pull of well over 100 billion gravities, and the fact that the pilot's head is further from the neutron star than his feet means a difference of some 50 million gravities between the pull at his head and his feet. He would presumably be torn apart (though this tidal force is understated for the purposes of the story — Niven obviously wanted the pilot to survive).

Astronomers have detected what seem to be neutron stars — spinning ones whose magnetic fields tangle with surrounding gas plasma to generate a radio beam that sweeps round with the star's spin, as if it were a lighthouse. Each time the

An astronaut falling into a black hole (shown here as a funnel-shaped curve in the structure of space) would be most uncomfortably stretched by tidal forces. The gravity at his feet would be millions of times stronger than at his head, and his feet would fall faster. As he entered the event horizon he would be a long, thin wire, hundreds of kilometres tall.

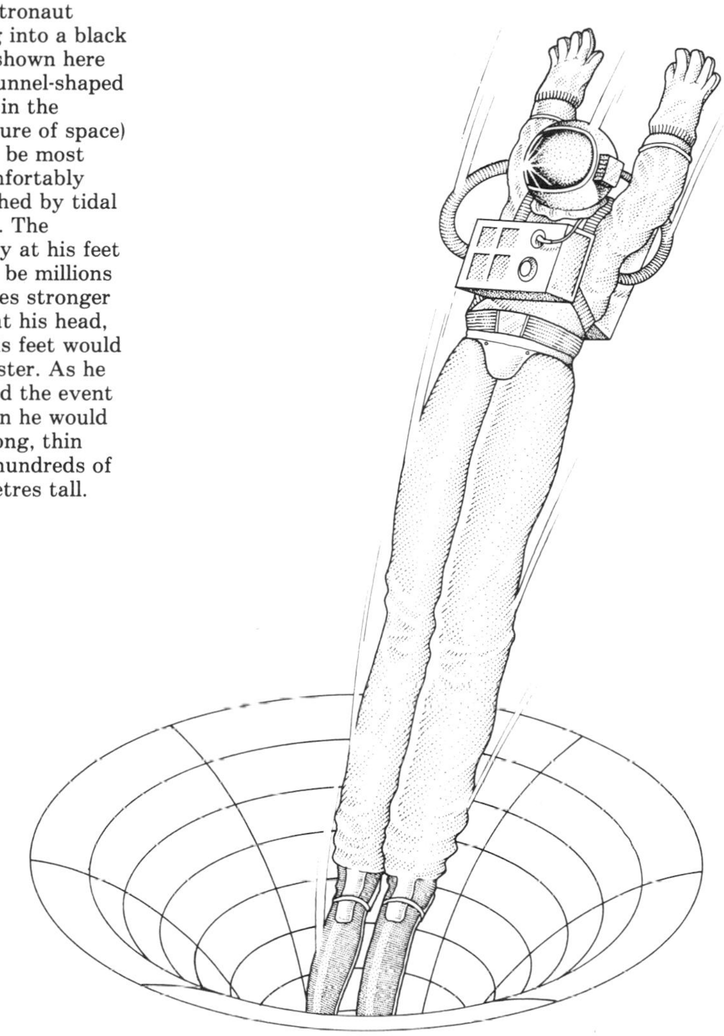

beam points our way — usually once a second or thereabouts — a click of radio noise can be heard on Earth. These neutron-star transmitters are called 'pulsars'.

What use is a neutron star to us? Scientists would certainly love to conduct experiments in those colossal gravity fields. Gregory Benford's novel *The Stars in Shroud* features a fast-orbiting neutron star used as a kind of interstellar motorway junction, with spaceships exploiting its gravity to swing rapidly to new courses, and gaining or losing momentum as desired. The possibilities of such stars are limited, though — especially when compared with their even weirder cousins, black holes.

When a star with a mass of more than about three times the Sun's reaches the point of collapse, it does not stop collapsing when (like a neutron star) it has reached the maximum possible density for matter in this universe. Instead it drops out of the universe altogether,

leaving an empty black hole in space.

This is a prediction of general relativity. Strong gravitational fields slow down time (see pages 94-5), and even the fields of white dwarfs shift their light measurably towards the red end of the spectrum (corresponding to lower frequencies of radiation). For any given mass there is a particular length called the 'Schwarzschild radius', and if that mass can be packed into a sphere with this radius, the surface gravity is so great that the slowing of time becomes infinite. As far as the rest of the universe is concerned, the collapse of a star with sufficient mass takes place more and more slowly as the Schwarzschild radius is approached — and at this radius the collapse seems to halt altogether. At the same time the surface of the star, which has been getting redder and dimmer through the milliseconds of the collapse, goes black and vanishes — at the Schwarzschild radius all light is redshifted out of existence.

This is Einstein's version. An earlier view was to think of an object so massive that the escape velocity — the speed at which you would have to throw a stone from the surface to make sure it never came down — was just greater than the speed of light. This gives the right formula for the Schwarzschild radius (which is proportional to the mass — double the mass and you double the radius) but is otherwise misleading. In a black hole the object itself vanishes. No matter can withstand the frightful gravitational forces, and everything collapses to a mathematical point (a singularity) at the centre of the hole. All that remains is the gravity field. But no light can shine through this emptiness, since any light reaching the 'event horizon' at the Schwarzschild radius is infinitely redshifted and can never get out again.

Matter thrown into a black hole loses all its identity. The only measurable properties of black holes are mass, event-horizon radius, rotation, electric charge and popularity with science fiction writers. A hole with the mass of our Sun would measure about 6 km across the diameter of the event horizon; one star of the Cygnus X-1 binary is thought to be a black hole of similar stellar mass. A black hole with Earth's mass would be less than 2 cm in diameter, and could happily 'eat' the whole Earth to double its size. Tiny, superdense black holes no bigger than a proton can also exist, but their formation would need pressures greater than the greatest available in our universe (those in collapsing stars) — such mini-holes could have been formed in the Big Bang, that first hundredth-second of the universe, but by nothing since.

These tiny 'quantum' black holes were briefly fashionable in 1970s science fiction. Several stories in which they feature can be found in Jerry Pournelle's anthology, *Black Holes*. A small, dense mass could be wobbled electrostatically to generate gravity waves (Larry Niven's 'The Hole Man'), or used as an invisible, unstoppable weapon to eat spaceships (Niven's 'The Borderland of Sol'). Mathematical studies have since shown that black

holes are not quite black — there is a 'quantum leakage' of radiation which increases towards infinity for smaller and smaller holes. Large holes of planetary or greater mass are reasonably stable; any hole weighing less than a billion tons or so (imagine the weight of Everest squeezed to the size of an atomic nucleus) would have radiated all its mass away as energy since its formation at the beginning of the universe. Even more exasperating, holes decay faster as they shrink. By the time one has dropped to a manageable mass of a few thousand tons, its remaining lifetime is only about a second. The conversion of mass to energy would make that last second a multi-million megaton explosion.

Because the black-hole pheno-menon depends not just on density but on total mass, it seems possible that at the other end of the scale a low-density black hole could exist — a huge one. In this case there would not be a singularity at the centre. Such black holes may exist at the centres of galaxies, absorbing stars without first disrupting them. They could contain stars, planets and life inside, while seeming to be a conventional black hole from the outside, like the black galaxy in Barry Malzberg's highly scientific novel *Galaxies*. It has even been seriously suggested that our entire universe is a black hole.

The most fascinating possibility of black holes is their use as short cuts through space. Anyone entering an ordinary high-density black hole must fall inwards and be crushed to

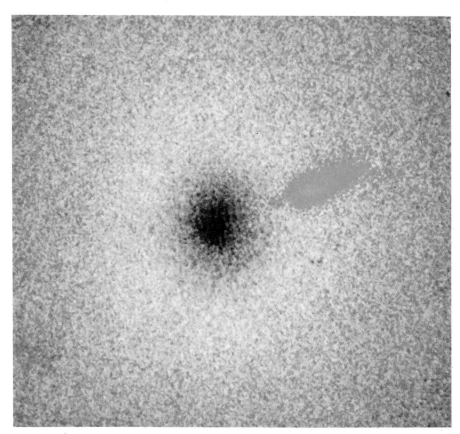

Above: Galaxy M87 in the Virgo cluster is famous for the enormous jet emitted from it, which contains as much material as a million suns. Some astronomers believe that a vast black hole may lie at the heart of M87. If matter falls into spinning black holes, unlike static ones, it seems that part of it may be violently ejected just before reaching the event horizon. If entire globular clusters of stars were falling into such a hole in M87, the ejected, high-energy material could explain the jet. Violent events are not unusual in other galaxies, several of which seem to be exploding.
Right: Angus McKie's painting of a spaceship approaching a black hole is quite accurate scientifically. One can deduce from the diameter of the hole that the ship is at a distance of about 5 Schwarzschild radii from it. Around the perimeter of the black hole light from other stars has been trapped into temporary orbit. The result is an apparent piling up of star images around the event horizon.

a point at the singularity. But the mathematics of a *spinning* black hole (see also pages 94-6) offers the chance of entering and following a twisted path which, in seeming defiance of relativity, lands you somewhere far away outside the hole. Thus Joe Haldeman's *The Forever War* has battleships flying along such paths from hole to hole, and such a hole features as the 'stargate' in Joan Vinge's *The Snow Queen*. But, as always when there seems to be a way round relativity, there are snags.

The obvious one is that wherever the short cut leads, the relativistic halting of time as we reach the event horizon will mean that our universe will age and die before we enter the interior of the hole, let alone leave it. The destina-

tion may be another universe, but there can be no return. Some physicists calculate that anyone travelling along such a path would radiate his entire mass away as gravity waves en route — which sounds unhealthy. It is also likely that a real-life hole, into which more mass is constantly being pulled by gravity, would form another, internal singularity which would close off the short-cut route.

A more practical use for black holes is as high-technology power sources or stores. The death of a tiny hole would release huge power, but such tiny holes can only now be formed by the slow decay of black holes that have the mass of stars — a process which will take from 10^{60} to 10^{70} years! More practically, we could steal energy from matter

falling into holes or tap the rotational energy of a spinning black hole. Two holes could be combined, an event so destructive that we discuss it under 'Holocaust and Catastrophe' (see pages 104-6).

At the singularity within a hole, physics breaks down completely. The whole mass of the hole is concentrated in this point, which has *zero* size. Normally the singularity is covered up by 'cosmic censorship', by the event horizon which prevents our seeing it. But with the death of a hole and the vanishing of the event horizon, a massless singularity might still remain — a point where the rules of space and time fail, where anything at all may (and perhaps eventually must) emerge. Science fiction can imagine nothing stranger.

Entropy and the end of the universe

The gloomy statement that the universe is running down is not just trendy science fictional pessimism. It is an accurate translation of the second law of thermodynamics — the law of increasing entropy.

All transfers of energy in our universe are controlled by the laws of thermodynamics. The first law states that mass/energy cannot be created or destroyed — in gambling terms, 'you can't win'. The second law adds that the disorganization or entropy of the universe increases with every energy transfer — some energy is always degraded to useless, low-level heat (see also pages 34-6). In gambling terms, 'you can't break even, either'. There is a loophole in the second law allowing perfectly efficient energy transfers at a temperature of absolute zero ($-273.15\,°C$): this is neatly plugged by the third law, which rules out the possibility of achieving this temperature. The gambler's equivalent is 'you can't even stay out of the game'.

Another view of entropy is as 'anti-information'. The higher the entropy of a system, the lower is the amount of information contained in it or needed to describe it. This page carries much well written and useful information, and the full specification for reproducing the paper and printing another, identical page would be a sizeable document. But if the page were burnt and reduced to molecular dust, the information content would be a mere list of simple chemicals to be mixed in the right proportion. The loss of information corresponds to the increased entropy of the system.

Where did all the information in the universe come from, if its beginning was as disorganized as the Big Bang? A suggested answer to this awkward question concerns the expansion of the universe, which has outraced its contents and produced unevenness — matter separating and condensing into galaxies rather than becoming a thinner and thinner gas by following the expansion of space. The beginning involved a sizeable jolt of negative entropy, resulting in increased complexity — more information. Only when the contents of the universe catch up with its ever slowing expansion will the law of entropy apply to the universe as a whole, as it now applies to all its separate parts.

Entropy is a potent theme of science fiction — the swollen, dying Sun of H.G. Wells's *The Time Machine*, the intergalactic signals which in J.G. Ballard's story 'The Voices of Time' are counting down to the end of the universe. Though some details of this entropic running down are unclear, there seems no escape from its effects. (The local effects of entropy, both literal and metaphorical, play an important role in the pessimistic 'New Wave' of science fiction; they include rusting, decay, growing old, the accumulation of rubbish in city streets and even the fading away of love affairs as the brightness of their initial spark dies.)

The amount of mass in our universe is probably not enough for gravity ever to overcome the slowing expansion of space. If this is so, then billions of years in the future the dimming stars will go out for lack of fuel, becoming dead hulks: 'black dwarfs', neutron stars or black holes. Multiple collisions between these remnants — in the centres of galaxies, where stars are relatively close together — will form supermassive black holes whose gravity will suck in more and more of the galactic debris. Eventually its further expansion cools the universe to the point where even large black holes pick up less energy than the tiny amount they throw out — they begin to shrink by radiation, as previously described. The time taken for them to dwindle to the point where they are again as bright as stars (though much tinier) is so immense that every rock in the universe will have flowed into spherical shape under the influence of 10^{65} years of its own gravity.

But in the end there will be no matter. The likelihood is that all matter will collect into a number of gigantic black holes whose quantum radiation will convert their mass to energy over still huger stretches of

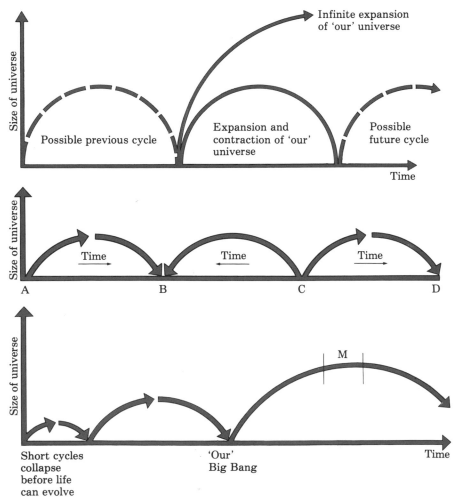

time, eventually leaving nothing but feeble heat energy evenly distributed over the entire universe. There is nothing else. Entropy has reached maximum, and almost the only bit of information left in the universe is the density of its useless energy. This glum state of affairs is called the 'heat death' of the universe.

Science fiction sometimes refuses to let things stop there. Asimov's story 'The Last Question' deals with the problem of setting entropy into reverse: by the time of the heat death humanity has built a computer-god which duly creates another universe. Indeed we or our machines could theoretically carry on long after the death of stars, gathering and fighting over mass for new stars, or hoarding energy in black holes . . . burning our own lights after everything else is dark. The physicist Freeman Dyson has listed a great many highly speculative scientific possibilities along these lines in his paper 'Time Without End: Physics and Biology in an Open Universe' (*Review of Modern Physics*, July 1979). He

reaches the surprising conclusion, supported by mathematics, that 'the total energy required for indefinite survival is finite'.

The alternative is that the universe may reach its maximum expansion and shrink again towards the conditions of the beginning. This could happen if its density is greater than a certain critical value. Not enough mass seems to exist to make up this value: but we suspect that the 'massless' neutrino does after all have a small mass. The countless neutrinos in 'empty space' could tip the balance and start all space on the road to gravitational collapse.

The heat death leaves the universe slowly falling in temperature as photons are 'stretched' by its continuing expansion. If the universe shrinks there will be another kind of heat death, since all the existing radiation will be 'compressed' to higher energies and the overall temperature will rise. The energy of billions of years of radiating stars will have been added to the original Big Bang radiation, making things

hotter still. The inexorable contraction of space would make the galaxies collide; eventually matter and stars would vaporize to superhot plasma. As though a film of the Big Bang were being played in reverse, the universe would shrink through stages of incredible heat and density, to the point (about a hundredth of a second from the End) when baryons and space-time itself break down and its fate becomes unknowable. In the similar scenario envisaged at the end of James Blish's novel *The Triumph of Time*, new universes bounce up from the death of the old, and the heroes of his story, touchingly but implausibly, become each one 'his own monobloc'.

Could a cosmic 'bounce' set a new universe expanding from the ruins of the old? The theory is popular in science fiction, but we may never know. Only through science fiction can we imagine the dizzy viewpoint of the being in Olaf Stapledon's *Star Maker*, who coldly creates universes as works of art and studies them from outside.

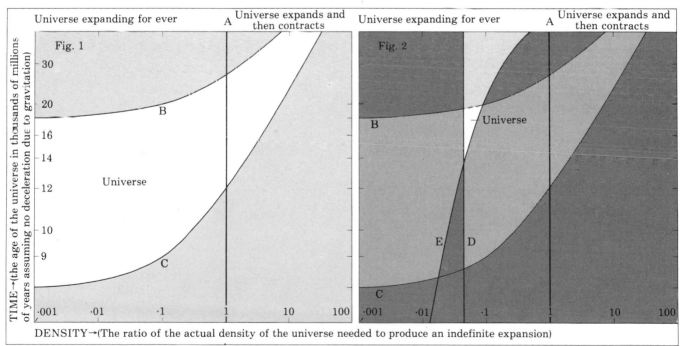

Left: three possible scenarios for evolution of our universe. Size of universe is shown vertically and time is shown horizontally.
(i) here we see the choice between an oscillating universe that con-

tinues to expand and contract in cycles, and a continuously expanding universe.
(ii) Paul Davies' theory that time reverses with each 'cosmic bounce'; as it runs backwards it rejuvenates the universe

back to the monobloc we came from, between B and C, so that AB and CD are identical 'ageing cycles'.
(iii) the Landsberg-Park model of a universe bigger with each successive bounce. Our universe would be

in position M, where it is still expanding. **Above left:** diagram showing the general theory. Variable factors are age of a universe and its density. The white area bounded by lines B and C is

where the two can be theoretically related, and universes could exist. Density must be at least as high as line A before a universe can contract again. **Above right:** the case of our own universe. Lines D and E

show the density limits within which, observations suggest, our universe must exist. Unless we have underestimated the amount of matter in our universe, therefore, it seems it will expand for ever.

Chapter 5
TIME TRAVEL AND OTHER UNIVERSES

Is our common-sense scepticism about time travel and other universes supported by modern science?

What is time?

Time is one of the strangest properties of our universe. We all know about it; our grammar has past and future tenses; we speak of seconds, minutes and hours, of yesterday and tomorrow. Yet few of us could say exactly what time is.

The scientific idea of time used to be quite straightforward: time was a fundamental property of the universe, experienced by every part of the universe at the same rate. (This solid view of time has been completely eroded by twentieth-century physics, especially the Theory of Relativity — see pages 68-71.) While scientists just before the modern period (after Newton but before Einstein) were content to regard time as an objective pheno-menon, however, the philosophers of the same period were considering the interaction of time with people.

We might almost say that there are two kinds of time: 'subjective' time, discussed by the philosophers, which is time as it is perceived by people, and 'scientific' time, a fundamental property of the universe that continues whether people are there or not. The two sorts of time are not necessarily contradictory (though sometimes they are), and both have captured the imagination of science fiction and fantasy writers. We begin by concentrating on the philosophers and their debates on the nature of time, and looking at some of the ways in which these debates have re-emerged in science fiction.

Do newborn babies have a sense of the passage of time? The nineteenth-century philosopher Immanuel Kant thought so. He believed that time was *a priori*, something we experience directly from the beginning. It touches our senses as directly as does the perfume when we smell a rose. Time, for Kant, was something at least as real as the rose. It exists, as a separate thing, outside us. Other philosophers believed that time is a construct of the human mind, a useful abstraction which is not real in the same way that a rose is real. They believed that what we do experience directly is an order of events. Time is a human invention, necessary to make sense of this order of events.

Einstein went further. Time, he said, has no independent existence apart from the order of events by which we measure it. Time in this sense, however, is real enough for the scientist. Scientific time is the interval between events. Scientists are concerned to measure these intervals as accurately as possible in order to formulate laws describing the way nature works. Nowadays they do this by using so-called atomic clocks, which are accurate to a fraction of a millionth of a second.

The idea of subjective time is less scientific, and harder to pin down. It grew out of the debate about time that followed Kant, and was important to the philosopher Henri Bergson, who treats time as something entirely derived from

Left: in the film *Somewhere in Time* (1980) Christopher Reeve dresses up in Edwardian clothes and travels into the past by sheer willpower to meet an actress (Jane Seymour), with whose portrait he had fallen in love. According to one theory of time — 'all time is eternally present' — this is improbable but not impossible. It does, however, defy the principle of causality, for if he had consummated his love, his son would have been old enough to be his father.
Right: are we imprisoned by time only because we believe in the imaginary bars of time's bleak cage?

property of the universe, but only a creation in the minds of people who look at the universe and try to make sense of it. But alas, it seems almost certain that time, or at least an order of events, *does* objectively exist. If it does not, what is it that atomic clocks measure? The maverick French philosopher Jerome Deshusses has sceptically responded to this question by saying that 'everything used to measure time really measures space.'

Even if time itself is an objective phenomenon—and the case continues to be argued by philosophers—the perception of it by human beings is a very subjective matter indeed. Most of us remember nostalgically how long summer holidays seemed to be when we were children. There are many science fiction stories that imagine peculiarly bizarre ways of perceiving time. Two of the best are not really scientific, because they violate the principle of causality (see pages 70 and 90). Brian Aldiss's story 'Man in his Time' deals with a man who perceives time just over 3 minutes ahead of everybody else. In Norman Spinrad's 'The Weed of Time', a boy eats a weed that makes him see his whole lifetime as simultaneously present. Thus, as a baby, he already knows he will eat the weed before (according to our time-limited point of view) he has ever eaten it! It makes a crazy kind of sense, but it would not work. The strangest story of all, curiously enough, is the one that offers the least violation of the laws of physics. In David Masson's classic story 'Traveller's Rest', a war is taking place on the northern frontiers of a land in which everybody's perception of time slows down as they travel south. A soldier on leave goes south, marries, has children, and in middle age receives a message that his leave is cancelled. He travels north, to arrive at his bunker 22 minutes (local time) after he left. Something rather similar would happen, according to physicists, as a spaceship moved progressively closer to a black hole (see pages 94-6).

The oldest and most popular model of time sees it as a river: this is the idea of time that we find in most early science fiction stories that deal with the subject.

subjective experience. The newborn baby would not experience time directly, according to Bergson; he would have to *learn* how to experience it. Interestingly, several experiments conducted more recently by psychologists have supported this view.

Many people would object that having to learn something does not make it any less real. But suppose, as the novelist J.B. Priestley (who wrote several plays about time) supposed, that time exists only because we have been taught to experience it. Could we not unlearn this teaching? Some Australian aborigines died when they were cursed by having a bone pointed at them. They died because they *believed* it would kill them. The belief had been taught to them, powerfully, and imprinted on their minds. The Priestley school of thought considers that time is like this: it imprisons us only because we *believe* we are trapped by it. Some

wonderfully imaginative fantasies have been written on this theme. The hero of *The Time Stream* by John Taine (mathematician Eric Temple Bell), travels in time through 'an involuntary twist of the mind'. The hero of Jack Finney's gripping novel *Time and Again* moves into a nineteenth-century apartment building in New York, and carefully removes from his surroundings all evidence of the twentieth century. By an effort of will he rids himself of his twentieth-century time-imprinting, and when he walks out into a wintry Central Park he is in New York in 1882. Richard Matheson's novel *Bid Time Return*, filmed as *Somewhere in Time* (1980), has a hero who does almost exactly the same thing, but he is propelled back into the present when he finds a modern coin in the lining of the nineteenth-century frock-coat he had hired.

These stories would be plausible if time were not a truly objective

Time travel in science fiction

A kind of time travel already exists. When we look into the night sky at, say, the Andromeda nebula, we are looking at a galaxy 2 million light-years away, and what we see is how it was 2 million years ago: we are gazing directly at the past. However, physicists tell us that personal, as opposed to visual, time travel must remain imaginary, because it violates the principle of causality.

In science fiction, the earliest time-travel stories did not propose any proper explanation or scientific mechanism for getting from one time to another. One of these was Mark Twain's novel *A Connecticut Yankee in King Arthur's Court* (1889), in which a man is displaced back to the Middle Ages after being struck by lightning—but, in effect, this is just a form of magic.

A common time-travel device was the long sleep, often unexplained, from which the sleeper wakes up in the future, like Washington Irving's Rip Van Winkle. A more selective rationale is given by stories of freezing people for long periods, as in the nine-teenth-century novel *10,000 Years in a Block of Ice* (1889) by Louis Boussenard. But these are not genuine time-travel stories, for the traveller travels not *through* time, but only *with* time.

H.G. Wells's famous first novel, *The Time Machine* (1895), was by no means the first time-travel story, but it was the first that imagined a deliberate travelling through time by apparently scientific means, as opposed to fantastic means— although the science is never explained. However, it was an earlier novel, a comic fantasy, that first exploited the paradox in time travel which the scientifically trained Wells ignored—its possible violation of the principle of causality. This novel, by F. Anstey, is *The Time Bargain* (1891), better known as *Tourmalin's Time Cheques*. The hero of the story is given a cheque book, whose cheques, written against a mysterious time bank, give him periods of time in the future. But his future self, able

to witness a future personal disaster, returns to the present and acts on his knowledge, thus *changing* the future. But if the future is changed, how could he have visited it?

Wells in *The Time Machine* seems to have used the simplest of all models of time, in which it is seen as a river. The time traveller goes further and further down-stream into the future, almost to the end of the world, and then returns (with almost no lapse of contemporary time) to his late-Victorian present. None of his actions changes the course of time, and it is as if the time-river has just one, permanent and unchanging course.

'Time, like an ever-rolling stream, bears all its sons away,' wrote the hymn-writer Isaac Watts in his famous version of the 90th Psalm. But, as Richard Matheson comments in *Bid Time Return*, 'Intellectually, this is unsatisfying, because streams have banks. There-fore we are forced to consider what it is that stands still while time is flowing. And where are we? On the banks or in the water?' The idea is depressing in another way, too, for if the course of the river is fixed, then all time already exists, the future is unalterable, even if we have not seen it yet, and all our so-called 'choices' are meaningless: we should not have 'free will'. In philosophy and theology this idea is well known under the name of 'determinism', and it still plays a role in some areas of physics. But even though people often carelessly compare time to a river, few of them, whether scientists or not, seriously believe that the future is fixed.

Suppose Wells's traveller had gone back into the past, instead, and had accidentally murdered his own father before his father had met his mother. Then there could, logic-ally, have been no time traveller at all. His action would have made himself a logical impossibility. What would happen? Would he flicker out of existence? But if he did not exist, how could he have murdered his father? This is the paradox.

The principle of causality, which exists in both physics and philosophy, states that causes must precede effects. If a man goes back in time to murder his father before

he is conceived, then we have an effect (the son) which not only precedes the cause (his own conception), but renders the cause non-existent: we have an effect without a cause.

If a modern time traveller went back and assassinated Hitler in 1938, then returned to the present, what would he find? The world could not possibly be the same, for World War II, if it happened at all, would have taken a different course. But if one simple action could create a whole new world, is not the principle of conservation of energy violated? Could we have so huge a change at so small a cost?

Science fiction writers try to overcome this problem of paradox in a variety of different ways, usually by imagining that each meaningful action the time traveller takes, whether in the future or in the past, creates a new, branching, probabi-lity universe (see pages 97-101).

Violating the principle of

causality may be bad science, but it can be fun. Many time-travel stories go in for very elaborate violations, such as the family Robert Heinlein created in his story ' " — All You Zombies — " ' in which strategic time travel and a sex change allow a man to become his own father and mother, thus creating a perfectly closed loop.

Very recently, modern physics

seems to have found possible loopholes in the principle of causality that might conceivably allow time travel. One is in the theory of faster-than-light particles (tachyons), and the other in a theoretical property of certain kinds of black hole (see pages 94-6).

The time dilation effect that comes into noticeable operation when an object such as a spaceship approaches the speed of light (see pages 68-71) has naturally been exploited many times by science fiction writers. But although an astronaut who has experienced this effect will live further into the future than, say, his stay-at-home brother, he is no more literally travelling *through* time than Rip Van Winkle was when he fell asleep. He is travelling, more rapidly than usual, *with* time. The order of events remains the same for both brothers (though telescoped closer together for the travelling brother), and causality is not violated.

There are various intriguing science fiction notions concerning time that can only call upon very distant support from science. A notable example is A.E. van Vogt's novel *The Weapon Shops of Isher*, in which a man thrown alternately, as if on a seesaw, into increasingly distant pasts and futures, accumulates so much energy (for surely time travel requires energy) that,

when he finally explodes in the distant past, it is the intensity of this release of energy that catalyses the creation of the Sun and the planets. This is one of the ultimate time paradoxes. More soberly, Ian Watson's story 'The Very Slow Time Machine' tells of a future time traveller in a machine which, before it is projected even further into the future, must (like a catapult) first be very slowly pulled back into the past. To baffled present-day observers he seems to be experiencing normal duration, but in reverse. There is a remote sense in which physics supports the relationship between time and energy that these stories rather vaguely suggest. The initial energy of the Big Bang that gave birth to our universe (see pages 76-7) is thought to be directly connected to the nature of time in the universe. We do not know exactly how much energy this was, but we do know that the greater the initial energy,

Far left: the hero of *Altered States* (1981), played by William Hurt, accidentally undertakes a kind of internalized time travel when he reverts to an earlier evolutionary stage after experiments in altered states of consciousness. Left: an alien from the future, a caveman and a contemporary man co-exist in Gordon Dickson's novel *Time Storm*, for which this is a cover illustration. The theory is that violent turbulence in time itself has brought about areas of time slippage on Earth.

the longer time itself will last before the universe reaches its heat-death or collapses back into a monobloc.

One curious and evocative science fiction notion about time travel has no firm scientific basis at all. This is the idea that different historical eras could exist, on Earth, in different localities. In Fred Hoyle's *October the First is Too Late*, it is 1966 in Britain, 1917 in

France and 425 BC in Greece. Brian W. Aldiss in *Frankenstein Unbound* and, later, Gordon R. Dickson in *Time Storm*, both imagine worlds in which there are localized areas of time slippage. Time travel is accomplished by moving from one place to another. (There is a great deal of physics in Hoyle's book, including an argument that the concept of the 'present' has no validity in science. Scientists may believe in an 'arrow of time'—see pages 92-3—but in one of Einstein's last letters, in 1955, he wrote: 'People like us, who believe in physics, know that the distinction between past, present and future is only a stubbornly persistent illusion.')

Science fiction has even invented internalized time travel. An ingenious version of this idea was introduced by Paddy Chayefsky in his recent novel *Altered States*. (The film of the book, with the same title, was released in 1981.) The story argues that our evolutionary past is encoded in our genetic structure. The hero, using psychotropic drugs and sensory deprivation techniques, literally brings his own past into the present. He reverts to being a primitive hominid, and then into a sort of thick, primordial, organic soup! All this makes for exciting viewing in the cinema, but there is more mysticism than science in the idea. It is one thing to argue—quite accurately—that the nature of our consciousness reflects our genetic being, but quite another thing to reverse the argument, and say that by altering our consciousness we can alter our genetic make-up and physically revert to our evolutionary past. It is rather like saying that by fiddling with the controls on our television sets we can alter the nature of reality back at the transmitter.

Science fiction writers have made a lively contribution to philosophical thinking about time, and there are few technical or philosophical books on the subject that do not refer repeatedly to their stories. Although as much imaginary as real science creeps into the genre, the time-travel story remains one of the most colourful and energetic areas of science fiction.

Time as scientists see it

There is much more to time, even in the rigorous view of scientists, than merely the interval between events. The scientific concept of time is itself so rich with possibilities that it gives writers plenty of room to manoeuvre, even without going into the realms of 'imaginary' science.

When scientists refer to time as a dimension, they basically mean something rather obvious. As H.G. Wells's time traveller pointed out, back in 1895, to describe any object it is necessary to say not only *where* it is (using the three dimensions of space—length, breadth and height), but also *when* it is. Any object has a duration of existence, and to specify its position and qualities we need to be exact about time. A man in Sydney in 1967 may be different from the same man in London in 1982. This may seem an easy way of thinking about time, but a little more thought shows its difficulties. Time is, in one vital respect, different from the three dimensions of space. We can move about in any dimension of space—backwards, forwards, and so on. But we can only move forwards in time, and at the moment we can only do this at the rate dictated by time itself for slow-moving objects. (As we approach the speed of light, however, we can increase the rate at which we travel forwards through time—see pages 68-71.)

Einstein showed us that the universe was actually made up of a four-dimensional amalgam of space and time which he termed the 'space-time continuum'. It is hard enough to imagine the emptiness of space as having a structure in the first place, but Einstein went on to show that space-time could stretch, bend and distort almost like a sheet of rubber. Time itself, which in Einstein's theory is a variable and not an absolute, is distorted in the region of large masses.

In Einstein's theory, the very existence of time depends on the presence of space, and it is impossible to think of time as a thing in itself. As a consequence, the whole idea of infinite time, stretching back endlessly into the

past, and forward endlessly into the future, is wrong. If the universe began as a primal monobloc which had no dimensions of space, then we can say that time itself began with the explosion of that monobloc. Therefore time itself will end when the monobloc reappears, with the contraction of the universe back into primal matter at the end of its life, as many cosmologists believe it will (see pages 86-7). The cosmologist Paul Davies and others go further, arguing that 'before' and 'after' our own universe there may have been an infinite number of other universes (see diagram on page 87), some of which may be indistinguishable from ours. If it were possible for a time traveller to cross the timeless gap between universes, he might enter a universe the same as ours, but at a different point in time. This gives a possible scientific

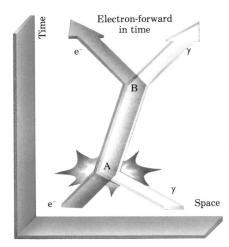

basis for the old idea of time as a great cycle, as the ancient Mayans believed. The idea often emerges in science fiction, as in John Taine's *The Time Stream* and in Michael Moorcock's *The Hollow Lands*, in which the hero and heroine travel to the Paleozoic Age by going forwards in time rather than backwards.

Since it seems obvious to us that time runs forwards, and that causes precede effects, it is a very curious thing that many of the laws of physics as described by scientists would be equally valid whichever way time ran. In other words, the direction of time, sometimes called the 'arrow of time', could be reversed without conflicting with the laws of nature. The only scientific principle that seems to show that time must run in the direction in which we all intuitively perceive

it to run is the so-called Second Law of Thermodynamics (see page 86). This is the principle which says, to put it simply, that as time runs forwards hot things get cooler and energy tends to become evenly distributed in the universe. This is true of our Sun, and of a cup of coffee, in exactly the same way. It is not reversible. Leave a cup of coffee on a table and it will not get hotter. But there is a loophole even here. The Second Law is not of the same kind as most of the laws of nature. It is a statistical principle that works on the probabilities of what billions of atomic and subatomic particles will do. In effect, it says that the cup of coffee will *probably* get cooler (there is a very high degree of probability), but not certainly. Individual particles are not subject to statistics. On a sub-microscopic level, it is quite possible

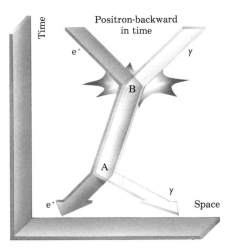

Above left: an electron (e^-) collides with a photon (γ) at point A, absorbs it, changes direction, emits a photon again at B and again changes direction. **Above:** the same particle track can be interpreted as showing a positron (e^+) travelling back in time. **Right:** a tiger, located between time gaps in our universe, prowls through the room in which you are reading this book.

that actual reversals of time do take place, and that individual particles move backwards in time.

The cosmologist Thomas Gold has seriously suggested that the present direction of time is a temporary phenomenon and a consequence of the way our universe is currently expanding. He prophesies that the universe will begin to contract again (a controversial theory), and he believes that time will also literally run backwards at the same time. In such a bizarre scenario even human thoughts would be reversed, and the idea of effects taking place before their causes would seem normal.

A world in which all time runs backwards is hard to imagine, but our perception of what is strange is merely the result of our own every-day experiences. Two science fiction novels imagine such worlds: Brian Aldiss's *An Age*, and Philip K. Dick's *Counter-Clock World*. In Aldiss's book the true, backward direction of time has been concealed by our own faulty perceptions, and memory is actually clairvoyance. In both books life begins when a man arises from the grave, and ends when he slides feet-first into the womb.

There is one scientific idea—it has not yet received much attention in science fiction—that opens up all sorts of possibilities for the 'positioning' of alternate universes (see pages 97-101). This is the 'chronon theory', the idea that time is not continuous, but is made up of tiny particles, jammed together like beads on a string. The shortest interval of time known to scientists is the time taken for a quantum event (such as an electron slipping from an outer to an inner shell of an atom) to take place. Theoretically, such a time interval is not of definite duration, but only has an approximate, fuzzy and unmeasur-able size. In a sense, time intervals as small as this do not exist in our physical universe. The smallest definite time interval is the 'chronon', calculated to be 10^{-24} seconds (one million, million, miilion, millionth of a second)—the time it would take for light to cross the smallest interval of space known to exist. We, of course, have the illusion of seeing time as continuous (just as we see a film as continuous, although in actuality it consists of 24 'frozen' frames per second).

If the chronon theory is true, then between each fundamental interval of time there would be gaps (timeless gaps to us, that we could never perceive or measure) in which the basic units of time belonging to other universes could fit. There might be an infinite series of real, solid universes fitted into the probability gaps between the quantum events of our own. In the very room in which you are reading, a tiger could be prowling through the green shades of an alternate jungle. Time might not be such an obvious phenomenon, after all. We should do well not to take it for granted.

Time travel in physics

There are two areas where modern physics, despite the principle of causality, might allow a kind of time travel. Neither, however, is likely to allow Man himself to undertake time travel in the near future, if ever, and both rely on highly conjectural mathematical theories, supported by no experimental evidence.

Both of these conjectures—one concerning faster-than-light particles and the other concerning black holes—would revolutionize physics if proven. In science, just one incompatible fact is enough to topple an entire, elaborate edifice of theory. The theory that would be toppled, the principle of causality, that causes precede effects, seems obvious in the light of common sense, but it has never been proven. If time-travelling tachyons are discovered, or if black holes are ever used for time travel, then bang goes causality, and the chief theoretical obstacle to time travel of all kinds has been removed. The anarchists among us, those of us who are not

'tardyons', particles that travel more slowly than light. They can get closer and closer to the speed of light, but will never reach it until infinite time has elapsed. Tachyons, faster-than-light particles, which can exist in theory, would need infinite energy and infinite time to slow down to the speed of light. The question is, can tachyons exist in our universe, and if so, how would they appear to us? Suppose we met a spaceship composed entirely of tachyons. We would see it reach us first, and then, subsequently, see it launched; this is because the light image of its launching would take longer to reach us than the faster-than-light spaceship itself. In fact, it would visually appear as travelling away from us, back along its own flight path. In other words, we see a tachyonic object as receding backwards in time! This is not an optical illusion; it is an actual fact readily predictable from the Theory of Relativity. Returning to our relativistic assassin, suppose a tachyonic bullet were fired. We should see the hole in the victim before we saw the trigger pulled. In fact, armed with the information about the bullet hole we could send a tachyonic message to the assassin

primeval chaos; or else, conceivably, they may have become isolated from our own universe of tardyonic particles, and created an alternate universe of their own, forever separated from us by the impassable barrier of the speed of light.

If tachyons continue to be created in our universe, they may be detectable in cosmic ray showers. Some Australian researchers in 1973 thought they had found evidence that advance, faster-than-light warnings of cosmic ray showers were being received on their photographic plates, but this evidence is generally regarded as dubious. Thousands of cloud-chamber records of collisions between fundamental particles have also been scanned by searchers for tachyons. The idea is that, if we found reactions with more mass and energy coming out than went in, we might suspect that tachyonic interactions were donating energy to the system. No such evidence has been found.

There is no theoretical way in which we can convert either ourselves or our spaceships into tachyons, so they will never help us literally to travel through time. However, if we could generate

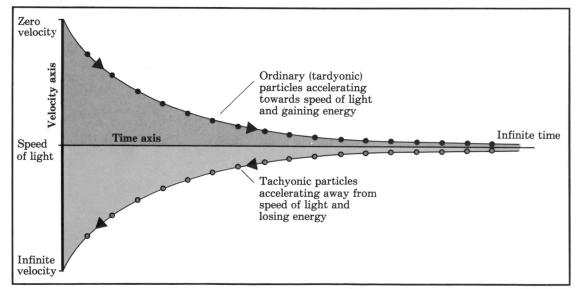

Left: ordinary 'tardyonic' matter can never speed up enough to reach the speed of light. Tachyonic matter can never slow up enough to reach it. A tachyon universe would be a mathematical mirror image of our own, but it is doubtful whether tachyons can exist in our universe. **Right**: embedding diagrams of a black-hole 'wormhole' evolving in time (see page 96).

too alarmed at the thought of a bullet hole through a body causing a gun to be fired, may be delighted. The world as a whole would no doubt be dismayed.

We have already met tachyons in the course of a discussion of faster-than-light travel (see page 71). The universe of mass with which we are familiar, however, is made up of

forbidding him to shoot, thus creating a time paradox.

How would tachyons be detected by scientists? Many tachyons may have been created at the moment of the Big Bang that launched our universe, but they would in a matter of minutes have all plunged backwards in time to the monobloc and been lost again in its

tachyons, beam them, and modulate the beam to transmit information, we could send messages into the past. This is the theme of Gregory Benford's distinguished novel *Timescape*, in which the inhabitants of a polluted and suffering future Earth use tachyonic signals in a desperate attempt to warn us, in the present, about where we are going wrong. Of all science fiction novels, incidentally, this is the one that gives the most vivid account of how physicists think. This is not surprising, for Benford is himself a professor of theoretical physics.

We have discussed the formation of black holes, and some of their theoretical properties (see pages 82-5). We mentioned the curious nature of spinning black holes, and suggested that they could be used as short cuts through space. It also seems that they could be used for short cuts through time. Why? The explanation is too complex mathematically for the layman to understand easily, even when it is spelled out for the length of an entire book. (One of the best books on the subject is *The Cosmic Frontiers of General Relativity* by William J. Kaufman.) We can, however, suggest the sort of reasoning involved in the theory by going back to Einstein's General Theory of Relativity, published in 1915. This was, in most respects, a theory of gravity (see pages 80-1). One prediction of the theory is that gravity causes time to slow down.

The concentrated gravity of a black hole is vast indeed. Time slows down the closer one gets to the event horizon, and at the event horizon time stops altogether so far as any observer (located at a safe distance) is concerned. If we stood outside a black hole and watched someone fall in, we should see him frozen at the event horizon for ever after.

The perception of time by the person falling in would be rather different. He would remain conscious inside the event horizon, and to him the passage of time would feel normal, though if he looked over his shoulder he would see the light from a universe infinitely far in the future, but getting younger very rapidly during the one-ten-thousandth of a second it takes him to reach the singularity in the middle. The explanation is that the time distortion due to gravity has effectively become so strong that time and space have reversed their roles in the region between the event horizon and the singularity. The falling person's trip through space has become a trip through time. If the falling person could use a rocket to escape again

from the black hole before he reached the singularity, he would find himself in another time. But alas, such a re-emergence from a static black hole is mathematically forbidden.

In real life, however, black holes would almost certainly not be static. They would be spinning, for they are formed from the contraction of stars which all, so far as we know, rotate. Our Sun, for example, rotates once every 4 weeks; if it contracted it would rotate faster, just as a twirling skater does when she pulls her arms inwards.

The mathematics of rotating black holes are very complex, and were not solved until 1963, when the Australian mathematician Roy P. Kerr found a complete solution to the relevant field equations. It turned out that there are two important differences between rotating and static black holes. The singularity at the centre of a rotating black hole would be not a point, but a ring. Furthermore, there would be two event horizons, an outer and an inner, which would only merge into one in the case of a black hole which is spinning so fast that its angular momentum equals

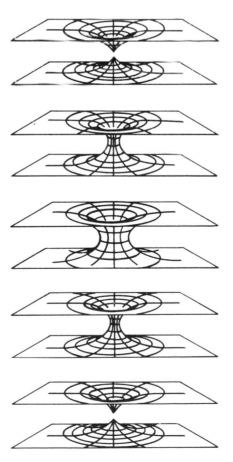

its mass; in practice, this means spinning very rapidly, just as real-life black holes are said to do.

A spaceship entering a rotating black hole at an angle to the equatorial plane would not necessarily be crushed out of existence; it could go through the ring-shaped singularity. But where and when would it emerge? It seems that it would emerge in what, according to some theoreticians, would be another universe of negative space; this is mathematically equivalent to an antigravity universe. Other theoreticians suppose that this other universe may turn out to be our own, but far removed in both space and time from the point of entry into the black hole in the first place.

The spaceship would not even need to go through the singularity. Trips into and then out of the event horizon are mathematically possible in the case of rotating black holes, unlike static ones. Each such trip would also end up in another universe, which is often interpreted to be mathematically equivalent to the past or the future of our own. Thus a rotating black hole is, in theory, a time machine. Curiously, most science fiction on the subject exploits the idea of black holes as gateways to instantaneous space travel rather than time travel, though the mathematics suggests that you cannot have one without the other. This may be because the time-travel implications of black holes have been less well publicized.

Furthermore, there is not just one alternate universe available to the traveller through spinning black holes, but an infinite series of them. (This is unlike the situation with a static black hole, where there is just one alternate universe, on the far side of the singularity, and it cannot be reached.) Which other universe the spaceship would end up in would depend on its angle of approach and its own rotation relative to the rotation of the black hole. Only one thing is certain. The spaceship could never return to its starting point, either in time or in space. Our black-hole time-travellers would never be able to return home. It is questionable, therefore, how useful such a form of travel would turn out to be. Science fiction writers have tended to ignore this

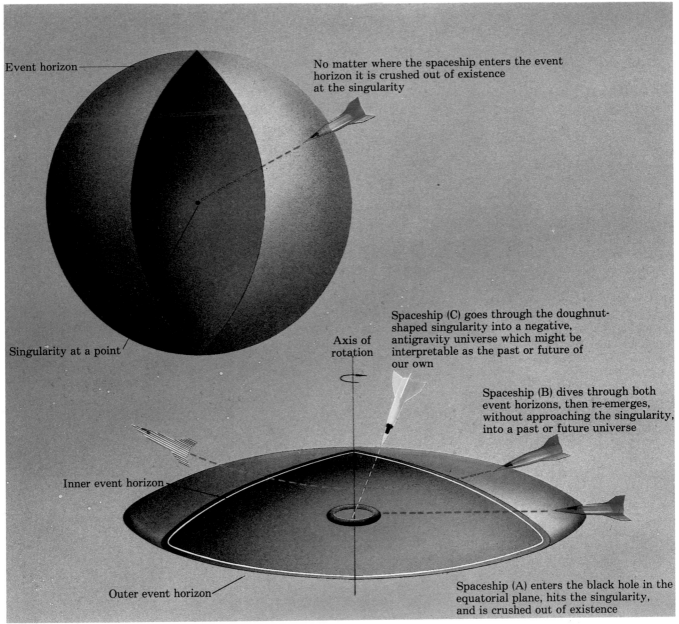

Event horizon

No matter where the spaceship enters the event horizon it is crushed out of existence at the singularity

Singularity at a point

Axis of rotation

Spaceship (C) goes through the doughnut-shaped singularity into a negative, antigravity universe which might be interpretable as the past or future of our own

Spaceship (B) dives through both event horizons, then re-emerges, without approaching the singularity, into a past or future universe

Inner event horizon

Outer event horizon

Spaceship (A) enters the black hole in the equatorial plane, hits the singularity, and is crushed out of existence

uncomfortable fact, and the scientific basis of such novels as Joan D. Vinge's *The Snow Queen*, which envisages black holes as rapid-transit systems, is very suspect and almost certainly wrong.

In talking about gravity (see pages 80-1), we referred to the rubber-sheet model of space-time, where indentations on the sheet correspond to the presence of mass. These models of space-time are sometimes called 'embedding diagrams'. If we draw the universes on opposite sides of a static black-hole singularity in a series of embedding diagrams (starting earlier in time and finishing later in time—see illustration on page 95), we see that as the black hole evolves they link up. Such an

evolution is over in less than one-ten-thousandth of a second for a static black hole with the same mass as that of our Sun; but the 'bridge' is more stable for a rotating black hole. This bridge is another way of envisaging the gate through which black-hole travellers would pass, and it is often, rather confusingly, called a 'wormhole'. A black-hole wormhole is a tunnel through time and space, and is a little different from, and much bigger than, the quantum wormholes discussed earlier (see page 73).

All these possibilities of black holes seem amazing, but it must be emphasized that there is a great deal of controversy among theorists about whether the geometry involved (about which there is much

The diagram shows the fate of spaceships entering either a static (spherical) black hole or a rotating (lens-shaped) black hole. All spaceships in the first case are destroyed. In the second case, it is theorized that only spaceships entering the

double event horizon in the equatorial plane will be crushed at the singularity. Other spaceships may avoid the singularity altogether, or even pass through it, in both cases entering another universe, perhaps the past or future of our own.

agreement) can be properly interpreted to give these results. Many scientists think not. If a black hole is a time-gate, then the once rock-solid principle of causality is badly shaken, if not destroyed. This may be why some physicists are unhappy about the possibility.

Alternative universes in science fiction

It is convenient to divide the alternative universes of science fiction into two groups: parallel universes and alternate universes. An alternate universe (it usually takes the form of an alternate Earth) is a universe as it might be as a consequence of some hypothetical alteration of history. Parallel universes are ones which somehow exist alongside our own, but in some other dimension. Often a whole series are imagined, lying as close together as the pages in a book, but each page dimensionally dislocated from every other page. Clifford D. Simak's *Ring Around the Sun* imagines a series of parallel Earths available for us to colonize once we have learned the trick of crossing the dimensions. A series of novels by Keith Laumer, beginning with *Worlds of the Imperium*, imagines an infinite series of parallel Earths, each one very like its neighbour, but with tiny historical changes that build up into major differences as the traveller moves further and further from his home world. A still more sophisticated version appears in Roger Zelazny's series of 'Amber' romances, in which the shifts in reality from parallel world to parallel world can be manipulated by certain travellers. This can be linked with the idea of participatory reality (see pages 98-101).

Science fiction that locates parallel universes in higher-dimensional locations can never really be tested against scientific reality. The existence of such universes is easy to postulate, but how would we reach them? Most of the means proposed for entering these dimensions are scientific doubletalk (as in David Duncan's *Occam's Razor*, in which the other world is reached through an oddity in the topological structure of soap films stretched on wire frames), or outright mysticism (as in A. Merritt's deeply romantic tale *The Ship of Ishtar*, in which the power of love transcends all dimensional limitations). Nevertheless, mathematical speculation about the nature

of higher-dimensional space is perfectly legitimate, even though this space may have no existence outside the world of thought. The best modern example is *White Light*, a surrealist science fiction novel, by the mathematician Rudy Rucker, that is largely set in universes based on the mathematics of infinite series.

One reason that science fiction writers invented alternate universes was that in this way they would

avoid trapping themselves in time paradoxes when they wrote time-travel stories. If a time traveller enters the past and changes history —there are more than 400 such stories and novels—from that moment two futures exist: the one the time traveller came from, and the one he has just created in potentiality. One of the classic treatments, *Bring the Jubilee* by Ward Moore, concerns an America where the South won the Civil War; a time-travelling historian changes the course of the Battle of Gettysburg, history branches, and the new world that ensues is the one we all know.

Alternate-world stories need not contain time travel at all. A fine example is Keith Roberts' *Pavane*, which is set in a Catholic England

of the present day, the Protestant movement having been badly set back by the assassination of Elizabeth I in the sixteenth century. Philip K. Dick's *The Man in the High Castle* is set on the west coast of an America that lost the Second World War; this area is governed now by the Japanese. Similarly, Kevin Brownlow's film *It Happened Here* (1963) shows the results of a successful Nazi invasion of Britain. Nearly all of Michael Moorcock's

This painting by Patrick Woodroffe illustrates *The War Lord of the Air* by Michael Moorcock. The novel is set in an alternate universe in which the British Empire, supported by an air force of great dirigibles, is still the world's strongest power in 1973! The bewildered hero is about to be rescued here from a ruined city in the Himalayas.

work involves what he calls the 'multiverse', an infinite series of alternate and parallel universes, many of them depending on minor variations in history. In his amusingly patriotic *The War Lord of the Air*, Moorcock describes an alternate 1973 in which the world remains at peace under a Pax Britannica imposed by a mighty British Empire. There has been no war since the Boer War; the British air force and its colonial offshoots are justifiably proud of their huge, graceful, helium-filled airships.

It was not until after science fiction writers had invented the alternate universe that theoretical physicists came along and gave the whole idea a possible scientific rationale.

97

Alternative universes in physics

Three kinds of 'other' universes for which science seems to give some warrant have been considered already: the antimatter universe that may have formed immediately after the 'Big Bang' (see page 79); the tachyonic universe that may have formed immediately after the 'Big Bang' (see pages 71 and 94); and time-displaced universes existing in the interstices between our own fundamental time units (see page 93).

The very phrase 'alternative universe', however, creates a philosophical problem. Is not our own universe, by definition, all that there is? We cannot hope to locate other universes by searching either in space or in time, because these dimensions are properties of our own universe, and anything existing in space-time is by definition not another universe but part of our own. Space-time does not exist outside our universe. In fact, there is no 'outside'. 'Where', then, could another universe be located?

The answer that might be given with a shrug of the shoulders is 'somewhere else that is neither part of our space nor part of our time'. This is theoretically acceptable though not helpful; there is no philosophical problem in theorizing about other universes with their own space and their own time; there is, however, a major problem when we consider such another universe (antimatter, say, or tachyonic) impinging on our own, because it is then, by definition, not 'other'. If another universe interacts with our own — even, for example, by our visiting it, which would constitute a transfer of energy — then, again, it is not truly 'other'.

The theoretical interface between our universe and another is almost unimaginable because of its enormous potentiality for philosophical paradox. This has not prevented science fiction writers from imagining it. In *A Wreath of Stars* by Bob Shaw, the space occupied by the solar system of an anti-neutrino universe is somehow the 'same'

space as is occupied by our own Solar System. There is even an anti-neutrino planet literally 'within' Earth. It was ingenious of Shaw to choose anti-neutrinos, for the neutrino (and presumably the anti-neutrino as well) hardly interacts with anything at all, so the problems are minimized. Nevertheless, some problems remain; for example, the occupants of the other universe are able to see the light emitted from ours, but the light transfer mechanism is never really explained.

Similar problems arise with Isaac Asimov's novel *The Gods Themselves*, which deals with an energy interchange, mutually beneficial, between two parallel universes. Asimov amusingly recognizes the problem himself: 'I won't bother with the mathematics, but . . . the natural laws of the two universes are being mixed.' (Our own natural laws are thought to result directly from the physical conditions at the moment of the Big Bang; the force of gravity, for example, might be quite different in another universe—see the discussion of physical constants below.)

Mechanisms for mass/energy transfer between universes may turn out to exist, but science has not yet come up with one, other than the conditions inside a black hole where to some degree our universe's laws of nature are suspended. The inside of a black hole is already, in one sense, 'outside' our universe.

It is in some of the more bizarre possibilities suggested by quantum physics that we can find a rationale for alternate universes splitting off with every historical decision, as described in science fiction.

Part of the novelty of quantum physics lies in its inclusion of the observer as part of the experiment. Before we examine what this means at the subatomic level, it is worth considering what it could mean at the macroscopic level—at the level of our universe itself. It can be argued, though it looks unbelievably arrogant, that the universe would not be here if we (or some other intelligent life-form) were not here to observe it.

If the physical constants of our universe had differed by only a few per cent, life could not have come into being. The very atoms of which our bodies are made were cooked up

in supernovae. If the so-called 'weak nuclear force' (see page 199) had been a little weaker, or a little stronger, the process of nuclear fusion by which stars burn could not have taken place, and atoms heavier than hydrogen (including most atoms necessary for life) could never have been formed. There are many other such accidents of the physics of our universe that have fitted it to the narrow constraints within which life can exist, but are they accidents?

The physicist Freeman Dyson observes, quite conservatively, that 'the universe is an unexpectedly hospitable place for living creatures to make their home in'. The physicist John Wheeler goes very much further in the same direction. He asks, 'May the universe in some strange sense be "brought into being" by the participation of those who participate? "Participation" is the incontrovertible new concept given by quantum mechanics. It strikes down the "observer" of classical theory, the man who stands safely behind the thick glass wall and watches what goes on without taking part.' Ian Watson, a science fiction writer, points to the obvious problem with this extreme view: 'How can the initial value data of our universe, which later will make life possible, conceivably be determined by something which only arises billions of years later— namely life?' He gives an answer by suggesting that those billions of years may be delusory, and that from the universe's point of view, time is 'simultaneously and permanently present to itself'. It is very clear that questions of this kind go well beyond what we think of as physics, and enter the realm of philosophy, or even theology.

The status of the observer came to be fundamental to quantum physics, but the starting point of this paradoxical science was the dual nature of light, which can be considered both as a wave phenomenon (as shown by Thomas Young in 1803) and as a beam of separate particles, or quanta. These particles of light, whose existence was shown by Einstein in 1905 as necessary to explain the photo-electric effect, are called photons. (Einstein won the Nobel Prize in 1921 for this work, rather than for his Theory of Relativity.)

Thomas Young's experiment showing that light acts as if made up of waves is shown in the diagram. If a light source is set up in front of a screen with two slits, with a second screen behind it, we get an interference pattern on the second screen, consisting of alternate bands of dark and light. (Interference patterns can take place with all wave phenomena. We can see them by throwing two pebbles into a pool and observing the intersecting patterns of the ripples.)

The experiment is quite straightforward if considered in terms of waves. But we should think about it again, this time imagining light as a series of separate photons. With the second slit closed, we get a single splash of light on the rear screen; in exactly

photons. Electrons, however, have mass; they are matter, unlike light, which is energy—or so everyone once thought. But the result is the same! There are interference patterns. Electrons also, therefore, have some qualities of waves, and some qualities of particles. We could call them 'wavicles'.

What followed from all of this was a mathematical treatment of probability. We cannot predict exactly where an individual photon in the double-slit experiment will land, but we can predict what percentage of probability there is that it will land in one area rather than another. Quantum mechanics is the technique that is used to predict the mathematical probability of this and all other subatomic events occurring. It works on statistical averages; for individual events

see by—they would actually be gamma rays in this case—add energy to the system.) It all boils down to this: we cannot observe any subatomic event without altering it. The atom, by 1927, could no longer be imagined as a crisp, clear, tiny 'object'. It became fuzzy and cloudy, just as much an idea as an actual thing. The sub-microscopic world is ghostly and indeterminate, only sharpening into focus when it is observed, and only a partial focus even then.

The physicist Erwin Schrödinger, one of the scientific giants of the period, was one of those who developed a way of thinking about the subatomic world that put together the idea of probability waves and the idea of the participant observer. He once illustrated some of the results in a

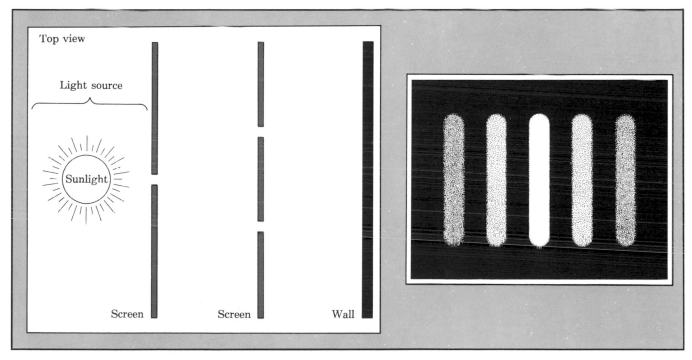

the same area, we get a band of darkness when both slits are open. This is very difficult to explain if we think of light as made up of particles, for consider an individual photon going through the first slit when the second slit is closed. It will land where the band of darkness would be if the second slit were open. The great mystery is, how did the photon going through the first slit *know* that the second slit was closed, and change its course accordingly?

We can do the same sort of experiment with electrons instead of

cannot be predicted. In order to work out these probabilities, quantum mechanics has to treat even particles as if they were wave functions.

The next step, brought about by the physicist Werner Heisenberg's 'uncertainty principle' of 1927, was to bring the observer into the picture. Heisenberg showed that we cannot determine both the position and the momentum of a subatomic particle. (If, for example, we observe the position of a particle, the very act of observation will change its momentum, for the light waves we

Above left: Thomas Young's famous experiment in 1803 showing that light is made up of waves. The light source was sunlight passing through a hole in a screen. The beam of light passed through a second screen with two vertical slits. Young found that when both slits were open, alternate bands of darkness and

light resulted (**above**). The bands of light at the sides were dimmer. This result shows that light waves are 'interfering'; waves reinforce one another in some areas and cancel each other out in others. Strangely, a similar result is found with beams of electrons, which were once thought of as 'solid' particles.

famous parable about a cat –a kind of 'thought experiment'.

Suppose that a cat is placed in a sealed room, in which is standing a flask of prussic acid. Suspended above the flask by a string is a hammer. The string will be automatically released if a geiger counter in the next room registers any radioactivity. Next to the geiger counter is a mildly radioactive substance which has precisely one chance in two of emitting detectable radiation in one hour. (We know from quantum mechanics that the chance of a quantum of radiation being emitted can be described by a probability wave function.) What is the situation at the end of the hour, just before a scientist comes to look?

According to common sense, there is a 50-50 chance that the room will contain a dead cat. According to Schrödinger, the contents of the room can be described by an equation, which represents a complex wave-packet, mathematically equivalent to a half-dead, half-live cat. The wave-probability packet does not collapse until somebody comes to look. Then, and only then, does one possibility become actual and the other vanish. The fate of the cat is not determined until an observer looks.

The conventional 'Copenhagen Interpretation' of quantum mechanics, however, sees all this as useful mathematical formalism, rather than a literal reality.

Many quantum physicists,

however, see it as a literal truth, and they are supported by the Clauser-Freedman experiment and its later, more accurate, repetitions (see page 75) which suggest that whether or not a photon lands in a given area literally depends on how the observer chooses to measure it. The probability wave-function for the photon does not collapse into one or another actuality until somebody looks at it. Similarly, the cat is neither dead nor alive until somebody looks at it.

Many quantum theorists go further. According to the Superdeterminist Interpretation of quantum mechanics, the fate of the

cat has been determined since the beginning of time, and nothing the scientist-observer does makes any difference, since he, too, was fated to do it.

According to one form of Nonobjectivist Interpretation of quantum mechanics, which holds that the universe has no reality outside observation, the fate of the cat is determined by the expectations of the observer. If he is a pessimist the cat will be dead; if he is an optimist the cat will be alive.

According to the Many-Worlds Interpretation of quantum mechanics, as proposed by Hugh

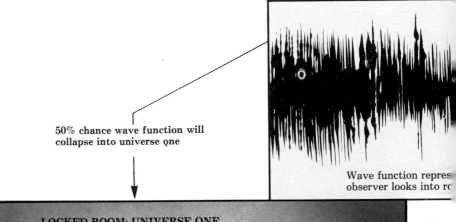

50% chance wave function will collapse into universe one

Wave function repres[...]
observer looks into r[...]

LOCKED ROOM: UNIVERSE ONE

Hammer suspended by string

Flask of prussic acid

Live cat

The famous paradox of Schrödinger's cat: is it no more than a mathematician's game, or does it refer to an actual 'reality'? The cat is locked in a room for 1 hour with a flask of prussic acid, above which a hammer is suspended. If a geiger counter detects radiation in that period, the hammer will fall. The picture shows the two common-sense possibilities that may result.

But what is in the room before an observer looks? Since the fate of the cat is linked to the emission of radiation — a 50% chance — quantum theory suggests that, as with the radiation, the cat must be represented by a wave equation. Until someone comes to look, and the wave function collapses into one or the other probability, the room must contain a wave-form of a half-dead, half-live cat!

Everett, John Wheeler and Neill Graham, at the moment the scientist comes to look the world splits into two branches, in one of which a cheerful scientist finds his cat alive, in the other of which a morose scientist is faced with a dead pet. This is not a joke: it is a serious scientific conclusion. (One of the clearest accounts of the theory is given by Bryce S. DeWitt in *Physics Today*, September 1970, in a paper entitled 'Quantum Mechanics and Reality: Could the Solution to the Dilemma of Indeterminism be a Universe in Which All Possible Outcomes of an Experiment Actually Occur?')

It is the Many-Worlds Interpretation that gives a warrant for the alternate universes of science fiction writers, though few of them ever refer to it. But the theory goes further—far beyond the wildest dreams of most writers. New universes do not only result from, say, a British failure to defeat the Spanish Armada, as in John Brunner's *Times Without Number*. It is *all* choices that lead to a new universe splitting off. At a fundamental level, this includes every quantum event. Every time an electron either moves or fails to move to a new energy level, for example, a new universe is created.

Theories such as these are among the most intellectually staggering in science, though not all quantum theorists would agree that ideas which are useful on the sub-microscopic level tell us anything useful about reality on our level.

Quantum theory is sufficiently outrageous to clash disturbingly with relativistic physics, which, for example, forbids the transfer of information at speeds faster than light (see pages 74-5). This is in direct conflict with one of the theorems of quantum mechanics, Bell's Theorem, which states that any two particles that have once been in contact continue to influence each other no matter how far apart they move, until one of them interacts or is observed — ultimately the same thing. This would mean, in practice, that the entire universe is multiply connected by faster-than-light signals. (The interaction has been described as 'cosmic glue'.)

A Nobel Prize certainly awaits the first scientist who successfully reconciles quantum and relativity physics. The British physicist Stephen Hawking is generally believed to have got the closest, so far, with his mathematical work on black holes.

A few of the more intellectually daring science fiction writers have dipped their toes in quantum theory. The idea of observers creating their own reality, and of branching probability universes, is central to the complex action of Ian Watson's *The Jonah Kit*, which even devotes a page or two to Schrödinger's unfortunate cat. There is also, of course, the 'Schrödinger's Cat' trilogy by Robert Anton Wilson. This is a crazed fantasia set in intersecting alternative universes whose absurdities and strange events are designed to knock the stuffing out of a great many sacred cows, political and sexual, even including the theory of relativity. Wilson comes close to proposing quantum physics as a new religion for what we call, appropriately enough, the 'alternative culture'. He may have been aware of a remark once made by the Nobel Prize-winning physicist Niels Bohr: 'Those who are not shocked when they first come across quantum theory cannot possibly have understood it.'

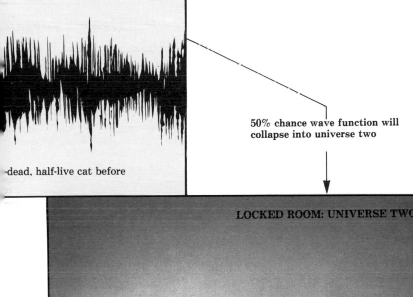

-dead, half-live cat before

50% chance wave function will collapse into universe two

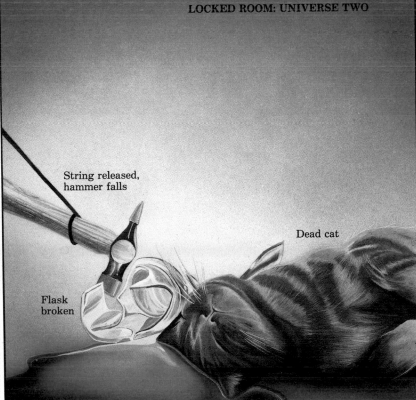

LOCKED ROOM: UNIVERSE TWO

String released, hammer falls

Flask broken

Dead cat

Chapter 6
HOLOCAUST AND CATASTROPHE

There is something in most of us that loves the thought of huge destruction, the grandeur of disasters and warfare. Only in science fiction can we take these dangerous dreams to their ultimate without actually destroying the world.

Warfare in science fiction

Science fiction writers find it hard to outdo the horrors of twentieth-century warfare. Doomsday weapons and planet-smashers have looked a little pale and unconvincing since the development of nuclear weapons in real life. Warfare remains a popular subject, however, with science fictional battles expanded in three main directions. The fighting can extend immensely through space; it can stretch over enormous lengths of time; and it can make use of fantastic weapons.

The film *Star Wars* (1977), drawing on countless science fictional sources for its imagery, deals with war raging through a galaxy. Vast distances are covered without effort; gigantic battle-wagons like the planet-sized Death Star have firepower to shatter whole worlds. We are not meant to take this as scientific gospel — but it is

worth considering why the mighty battles of *Star Wars* (and books like E.E.Smith's 'Lensman' series) are not convincing to the scientist.

The problems of battles stretching across light-years begin with the difficulties of starship travel (see Chapter 1). Any 'fast' starship possible in the near future would be a frail thing, all surplus mass trimmed away to increase the efficiency of acceleration. This does not sound like the armoured, space-going dreadnoughts of *Star Wars*; and such a stripped-down speedster would still be limited to (almost) the speed of light, taking 10,000 years to cross our Galaxy. *Star Wars* villain Darth Vader might be getting a little elderly by the time we caught up with him.

In *The Forever War*, however, Joe Haldeman describes such a situation. His soldiers flit about space between battles, each journey taking many years but (thanks to the effects of relativity — see pages 68-71) seeming very quick to the travellers, who fight a war endlessly stretched through time. This asks

for a rather unlikely persistence back at headquarters, where hundreds of years are passing.

Are galaxy-spanning and planet-smashing battles nonsense, then? Not necessarily: but much new technology is needed. High-speed travel through hyperspace — or something similar — would only be the beginning. There would also be the question of finding an opponent, since space is so huge that anyone choosing not to fight would always be able to hide. New energy sources would be necessary if we wanted to indulge in planet-smashing — something which at present seems insanely wasteful, for to break Earth to rubble would need an energy blast equivalent to the simultaneous dropping of 10 million billion 1-megaton hydrogen bombs, each releasing the explosive energy of a million tons of TNT. More plausibly, and millions of times more economically, the whole surface of Earth could be blasted with nuclear weapons and sterilized, as in Poul Anderson's novel *After Doomsday*. It would be pleasant to

Super-technological weaponry dominated the cover illustration of the 1930s pulp magazines. The first two are by Frank R. Paul and the third is by H.W. Wesso — two famous science fiction artists of the period. The flying buzz saw is a bizarrely short-sighted extrapolation, but the death rays of the other two pictures anticipate the lasers of today.

Futuristic warfare is one of the oldest themes in science fiction. Here 1920s London is laid waste by bombs dropped from airships, the work of a romantic rebel against wicked capitalism. The illustration by Fred T. Jane (founder of a famous series of books about warships and aeroplanes) dates from 1893, long before aerial warfare became a reality. The book is *Hartmann the Anarchist* by E. Douglas Fawcett.

think that if we had such power at our command, we would also have the maturity to give up war and spend our time converting barren planets into liveable ones.

But science fiction also provides new enemies to fight. Robert Heinlein's *Starship Troopers*, which suggests that war is a good thing because it makes a man of you, contains typically nasty aliens, called Bugs. The Bugs are insanely evil and can be slaughtered without any pangs of conscience. Even more faceless and evil are killer machines, like the 'Berserkers' from Fred Saberhagen's series of that name: spacegoing robots programmed to destroy all life. Would another, alien race create such machines, or fight us directly? Some scientists have argued that any warlike race would destroy itself before developing the ability to leave its own home planet, which is not an encouraging prospect for mankind. Others, including many science fiction writers, have imagined terrible wars caused not by ill-will but by failure

to communicate with alien minds.

Some interesting scenarios for warfare concern the early days of future space colonization. If huge solar-energy collectors are placed in orbit to beam power to Earth (see pages 42-3), if complete spacegoing colonies are built at Lagrange points L4 and L5 (see pages 19-21), if the Moon is colonized and mined . . . then there are endless possibilities for blackmail and warfare. Those microwave power beams from the solar-energy collectors could be focused and aimed at cities rather than at the receivers. Robert Heinlein's *The Moon is a Harsh Mistress* deals with a Moon colony's war of independence, featuring such technology as an electromagnetic cannon to boost raw materials from the Moon into space and back towards Earth. This device (now called the 'mass driver' — see pages 23-5) has already been designed for space-colony building, since it is cheaper to boost materials from the Moon than from the Earth's greater

gravity. A 'bucket' of cargo is accelerated by a series of electromagnetic rings and hurled at high speed into space. Heinlein's revolutionaries throw rocks in this way, angling them to fall on Earthly targets. The final impact speed is around 40,000 km per hour, gained during the long fall into Earth's gravity; the energy released when a 1-ton rock strikes would be equivalent to the explosion of about 15 tons of TNT.

Science fiction used to regard a planet as a heavily armed and impregnable base. But the high ground has always been the advantageous place in war, and space colonies or spacecraft would be, in effect, on top of a gravity hill thousands of miles high. A missile from below has to struggle up against gravity; a lump of rock dropped from above will simply fall, and (if massive enough not to burn up in the atmosphere) strike with appalling force. We may see some interesting strategies in the first war of near space.

Future weaponry

Science fiction has never lacked impressive and deadly weaponry, with a range from hand-held 'blasters' to gadgets which sterilize whole solar systems by making their suns explode as novae. More and more of these nightmares are now becoming scientifically possible.

The death ray, the energy gun and the blaster were all hackneyed science fictional props by the 1950s. Though intelligently used in such books as Arthur C. Clarke's *Earthlight*, energy weapons seemed about to be laughed away like the traditional 'blunt instrument' of detective fiction. But in 1960 the first laser was demonstrated, and death rays became 'respectable', though scientists refused at that time to believe that lasers could ever put out death-dealing power.

The acronym 'Laser' stands for 'Light Amplification by Stimulated Emission of Radiation': the key word is 'stimulated'. All lasers operate by 'pumping' energy into some material so that large numbers of its electrons are precariously balanced at a high energy level, eager to drop back to the normal or ground state. As each electron drops back, it gives up its excess energy by throwing out a packet of radiation — a photon.

Each laser material — ruby, for example — has its own characteristic energy gap between the upper ('balanced') and the ground energy

states, each size of gap giving a particular frequency to the photon radiation emitted. If radiation with this particular frequency now falls on an energized atom, it *stimulates* it into emitting its own photon — in the same way that a gong vibrates when its note is struck on the piano. Each new photon can stimulate more energized atoms, on and on in a chain reaction. A surge of light builds up in the laser, and is reflected back and forth between precisely spaced mirrors to give a parallel beam, which forms a standing wave of light, like the standing sound waves in an organ pipe. If one mirror is partly transparent, an intense output beam can escape.

The laser arms race is producing more and more destructive beams. Many means of pumping in energy have been tried: light flashes, electrical discharges, neutron flux from a nuclear reactor, high-energy gas flows in the carbon dioxide gas-dynamic laser and violent chemical reactions in the hydrogen/fluorine laser. The last two are the most powerful. Carbon dioxide lasers with outputs in the megawatt range now lead the field in laser weaponry. These emit invisible infra-red radiation — though the beam is visible when fired through the air, since its tremendous energy breaks down the air molecules in a row of sparks like tiny lightning bolts.

Such lasers work better in

Above: the USAF has mounted a laser weapon on a conventional Boeing airliner for high-atmosphere tests.
Left: the great power of a 2000-joule laser beam, itself invisible, ionizes the air during its 20-microsecond pulse, leaving a trail of sparks. The further that lasers are beamed (in air), the weaker they are when they reach their target — a grave limitation to their use as weapons on Earth.

vacuum than in air, which soaks up the power and scatters the beam. Yet tests have shown that a large laser can destroy a small anti-tank missile at a range of 1 km. In other top secret experiments, lasers have been fired at planes or in orbit. The first trials against planes seemed unpromising; but a British study in 1981 predicted that ground-based anti-aircraft lasers would be in routine use by 1995. Even a hand-held laser weapon has been patented, though it looks too cumbersome for practical use.

In space there is no air, and the laser-armed killer satellite seems a real possibility. This could have great nuisance value in war, sniping at reconnaissance satellites or even

disabling long-range nuclear missiles, which leave the atmosphere at the peaks of their flight paths. But enormous shoals of laser satellites would be needed to destroy a full attack wave of missiles. Moreover, a swarm of killer satellites would provide targets for similar ones sent up by the enemy. The orbital fighting might be a stalemate of satellites battling against each other. It seems unlikely that satellite-based lasers will be used against targets on the ground: the beam would be scattered as it came down through the atmosphere.

Ever since George O. Smith's heroes in his *Venus Equilateral* (1947) fought with a realistically

described electron-beam weapon, there has been much scientific interest in such particle beams. Less subtle in their physics than lasers, these devices accelerate electrons or protons to huge speeds, electro-magnetically, and discharge them as a beam. This is less effective in air than a laser; even in orbit there are problems, such as beam spread (since the charged particles repel each other) and bending of the beam in Earth's magnetic field. And particle-beam satellites would be larger — better targets — than laser satellites. There are still such possibilities as ground-based particle beams which use power from nuclear explosions to punch through the atmosphere — but for

A BBC 'Horizon' television programme in 1981 considered the likelihood of laser weaponry mounted on satellites, and concluded that it would be an expensive and inefficient way to wage war. In this BBC mock-up the laser beam is seen as blue, for clarity, but such beams would actually be invisible in the vacuum of space.

now the big money is on the lasers.

In theory, lasers need not be restricted to low-energy radiation such as infra-red or visible light. These involve energy shifts of electrons in atoms. But it might be possible to tap the much larger energy shifts within the atomic nucleus itself, to produce a gamma-ray laser, or graser. Gamma-ray photons are millions of times more energetic than the infra-red photons produced by today's biggest lasers. But though an X-ray laser pumped by a nuclear explosion has been tested — X-rays have more energy than visible light — our technology lacks the controlled power to pump a graser. It would be a true death ray, horrifyingly powerful. A few billion megawatts of graser power might blow up a sun — make it go nova — at many light-years' range. Oddly enough, this is proposed as a peaceful project, to mine rare elements from the cores of suns, or to increase local hydrogen density for use as fuel by ramscoop starships (see page 14); but there are also unfriendly possibilities.

Moving away from present-day science, we can imagine that other peaceful devices could be converted to weapons. A starship moving at relativistic speeds — close to that of light — is itself a horrifying weapon thanks to its tremendous kinetic energy. Ten tons would be a very modest 'rest' mass for a starship, but at 99.99% of lightspeed its mass would be more than 70 times greater: should it hit something, such as a planet, the extra mass would be converted to energy in a 22-million-megaton explosion. Continents could be smashed and portions of Earth's atmosphere stripped away. Defensive measures against this weapon are almost impossible, since it would follow so hard on the heels of light itself: the alert from an early warning station as far out as Pluto would take nearly 5 hours to reach Earth, and the doomsday machine would arrive about a fifth of a second later.

What power could drive a ship to such speeds? Many writers, including the scriptwriters of TV's *Star Trek*, have toyed with the idea of antimatter power sources. These would almost totally convert a combination of matter and anti-matter to energy. However, large

chunks of antimatter (see pages 78-9) may not exist in nature; and to manufacture even tiny amounts is incredibly expensive. If the stuff could be found floating in space, then there would be no need to convert it to a starship's driving energy: it would be much simpler to send this antimatter asteroid or meteoroid falling towards the enemy down on Earth or wherever he may be. (It can be 'pushed' by squirting gas at it: the annihilation reaction between gas molecules and anti-matter will act like a rocket motor to drive the antimatter through space.) If our 10-ton starship were made of antimatter it could strike the Earth and react with 10 tons of ordinary matter — soil — in an explosion of more than 400,000 megatons, without having to move fast at all.

The relativistic bomb and the antimatter meteor fall into the small-arms category when compared with the ultimate weapon — the energy flash produced by black holes that have been manipulated to collide. Science fictional black-hole weapons tend to be minor (Larry Niven's story 'The Borderland of Sol' features a tiny black hole which is manipulated to 'eat' spacecraft), or unbelievable, as in Colin Kapp's *The Chaos Weapon*. This weapon is fed by an ammo belt of suns and focused by 10 black holes — but Kapp's hero nevertheless survives a direct hit!

The possibilities of colliding black holes seem to follow from sober physics. In theory, although no energy can normally be extracted from a single large black hole, two identical holes could be combined in such a way that up to 29% of their combined mass would be thrown out as radiation, elementary particles and antiparticles. The remaining mass would form a single larger black hole. This sounds undramatic — but if the colliding holes were each about 6 km across (the diameter of a black hole with the same mass as our Sun), the explosion as they met would equal the detonation of more than 10^{31} megatons of TNT. This is many times more energy than the Sun itself will emit over the millions of years of its lifetime, from birth to death. Solar systems would be erased by such an ultimate explosion, and planets sterilized at a range of many light-years. The black hole collision could not be called a tactical weapon!

Weapons need not use brute force. Gregory Benford devises an interesting psychological weapon in *The Stars in Shroud*, in which the alien Quarn use direct sensory input to release — rather implausibly — primeval human fears of being crowded. An entire human population is destroyed by mass psychosis as its members all desperately avoid one another and crawl into holes in the ground.

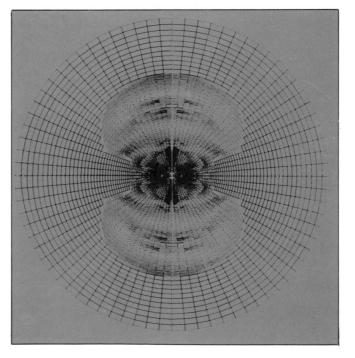

Two physicists at Princeton University produced this computer simulation (left) of the gravity waves resulting from the collision of two black holes. Almost one-third of their mass would be converted into a raging blast of radiation, and one-thousandth directly converted into a fierce torrent of gravity waves.

CBW: chemical and biological warfare

Artificial plagues and poisons are the most economical of present-day weapons. They are also the most difficult to control once released.

The principles of biological warfare are simple. Micro-organisms are carefully bred, or modified by genetic engineering, to create deadly new strains of disease. Old diseases can be deliberately resurrected — smallpox, for example, is now extinct outside the laboratory, and there will soon be practically no one immune to this disease. These biological weapons are two-edged, since they can all too swiftly spread back to the user nation — carried by birds, insects or people — perhaps too fast for vaccination measures to be effective. Why use such danger-ously unreliable weapons? In *Time of the Fourth Horseman*, Chelsea Quinn Yarbro suggests a conspiracy of doctors who spread plague to end the world's overpopulation. For whatever reasons, in real life a number of nations are known to be conducting research into biological warfare — officially so that they can be ready to defend themselves against it. Winston Churchill is alleged to have considered using the anthrax bacillus as a weapon in World War II.

Genetically tailored diseases offer other nasty possibilities. A virus might be designed to attack only people of a certain racial heritage, just as sickle cell anaemia is mainly confined to blacks — and as the racist handguns of Robert Heinlein's *Sixth Column* would kill only the slant-eyed villains.

Biowar need not be waged only against people. The effectiveness of Dutch Elm disease gives extra plausibility to the film *No Blade of Grass* (from John Christopher's book *The Death of Grass*), where grass and all cereal crops are killed off by a virus. This, again, would be a weapon as deadly to the aggressor as to the victim. But suppose the target country had just one major crop — for example, turnips. The attacker need only design a turnip-destroying virus, set it loose, and watch his enemy starve.

Going still further, biowar could be turned against inanimate substances. An episode of the BBC's TV series *Doomwatch* (later a book — *Mutant 59: The Plastic Eater* by Kit Pedler and Gerry Davis) suggested a micro-organism adapted to feed on plastics — instant biodegradability. We might go further and design one which would infect people harmlessly, making them 'carriers'; the micro-organism itself would be tailored to eat chemical explosives. As

Left: Farmers in Desio, Italy, examine sheep which died in 1980 after grazing on land chemically polluted by Dioxin four years earlier. This substance is very close in chemical structure to the nerve gases currently stock-piled in the USA.

Above: A rebel Afghan soldier in 1981 displays chemical-warfare protection equipment captured from Russian soldiers. The presence of the equipment suggests that stories of the Russians' use of toxic chemicals against the Afghans may be true.

Defoliant chemicals used by the Americans during the Vietnam war had a dramatic effect. A massive strip of jungle has been destroyed to create a buffer zone. Enemy soldiers would be exposed if they tried to cross it.

assembly-line workers breathed on them, the explosive triggers of nuclear weapons would quietly rot away.

Chemical warfare is less easy to wage, since chemicals do not breed and spread like micro-organisms. Defoliants withered great areas of Vietnam jungle, but the plants simply grew again. 250 tons of today's VX gas, the principal nerve gas stockpiled in the USA, released over a large city, could cause as many deaths as a 5-megaton H-bomb: only a tiny amount is needed to kill a man, but to spray a city would mean enormous wastage.

In today's world chemical warfare is already a big (and profitable) business. It is estimated that the USA will spend 8 billion dollars on

nerve gases between 1982 and 1986. The favoured device of the 1980s is the 'binary' nerve gas — two chemicals relatively harmless in themselves that become lethal in quantities as small as a microgram when mixed — 50 times more deadly than cyanide. NATO wargames have for some time made the assumption that chemical weapons will be used in a future war.

Nerve gases can be absorbed into the body through the skin or mouth, and once inside they attack the central nervous system. A lethal dose kills in minutes: sweating, vomiting and filling of the lungs with mucus are followed rapidly by respiratory failure and paralysis. A smaller dose can lead to prolonged agony and permanent damage.

Less is known about Soviet Russian capabilities for waging chemical warfare, though there have been many reports of the use of chemical weapons by the Soviets in Afghanistan, Laos and Kampuchea. The Soviets are thought to prefer the so-called 'yellow rain', allegedly made from mycotoxins (poisons derived from fungi). These poisons, which have been researched by the military in America and Russia for 30 years, cause immediate fatal bleeding from all bodily orifices.

The fact that such weapons already exist in large quantities may explain why they seldom appear in science fiction. They belong to the realm of present-day science fact. Many science fiction writers — along with some military theorists — prefer the possibilities of psychedelic drugs which could disorient the victims without permanently disabling them. Brian Aldiss's *Barefoot in the Head* takes place after the 'Acid Head War', which has left people on permanent LSD trips. (The addition of LSD to the water supply was a feature of alleged hippy conspiracies in the late 1960s. Fortunately or unfortunately — according to point of view — LSD is highly degradable in water, and would rapidly lose its effectiveness.) Robert Silverberg's 'How It Was When The Past Went Away' features memory-erasing drugs in the water supply. But memory drugs do not yet exist, and the military establishment would surely never allow Aldiss's LSD aerosols: people might start enjoying war.

Nuclear holocaust

The nuclear fireball and mushroom cloud are the dominant images of near-future warfare both in science fiction and in real life. After decades as a prediction (see pages 32-3) and then a possibility, the nuclear holocaust is a tired cliché of science fiction, but one that persists.

Atomic bombs were the subject of several famous predictions in science fiction. In 1914 H.G. Wells's *The World Set Free* dealt not only with the bomb but with radioactive contamination — enthusiasts usually forgive Wells for such details as having the bombs thrown by hand from open-cockpit aeroplanes. And in 1944 Cleve Cartmill's short story 'Deadline' provoked the wrath of the FBI by featuring an atomic weapon

which used lithium deuteride, a material under investigation in the secret weapons research field, though not usable until the fusion bombs of the 1950s.

In theory, nuclear weapons are simple devices; in practice they are very difficult to build. A fission bomb — as was dropped on Hiroshima and Nagasaki — depends on putting together a 'supercritical mass' of uranium-235 or plutonium-239: that achieved, the explosion follows at once. The first problem is that U-235 is rare (more than 99% of natural uranium is a different isotope, U-238), while Pu-239 is almost non-existent in nature and must be made artificially in nuclear reactors. A second problem is that unless a critical mass is put together with incredible speed, the U-235 (or Pu-239) will

simply melt and flow away!

U-235 is an unstable radioactive isotope. Though the nuclei of U-235 atoms have an average lifetime of hundreds of millions of years, some will always be undergoing spontaneous fission in any lump of uranium metal, breaking up into lighter and more stable elements, and also throwing out radiation and free neutrons. Some of these neutrons hit other U-235 nuclei and cause them in turn to undergo fission. A shower of neutrons builds

The sinister fireball above Bikini Atoll after the first H-bomb tests in 1956 has become the visual symbol of nuclear holocaust for people all over the world.

109

up, but will escape quickly from a small lump of U-235. With a larger lump, the neutrons are more likely to cause fissions before escaping; the overall level of fissions rises as the lump is made larger still, and so does the heating produced by fission. When 'critical mass' is reached the U-235 behaves like a nuclear reactor, producing neutrons exactly as fast as they can escape: with the addition of a little more uranium it beomes slightly super-critical, power and temperature rising rapidly until at last the metal melts and flows away. For an explosion it is necessary to assemble a highly supercritical mass, smashing smaller pieces of U-235 together with precisely timed conventional explosives. Then at last there is a runaway chain reaction: tremendous energy is generated before the mass can fly apart; when it does, a nuclear blast takes place.

Fusion bombs — H-bombs — work by forcing together light atomic nuclei like those of deuterium (heavy hydrogen). Heavier elements are formed and vast energy is released. This can only happen at colossal pressures

and temperatures — in fact we need a fission bomb to touch off the fusion bomb. So, although fusion is relatively 'clean', not producing long-lived radioactive fallout, there is contamination from the 'dirty' fission bomb used as the trigger. There are various ways of making H-bombs bigger and better — up to 100 megatons in some Soviet tests — and they all make the explosion dirtier than ever.

One lesson of nuclear research was that it is impossible to keep the laws of nature secret. Details of the fission and fusion bombs leaked out, leading to the duplication of American research in other countries and the nuclear stalemate predicted in Robert Heinlein's short story 'Solution Unsatisfactory', written in 1941.

If the stalemate breaks, what then? The jargon of World War III is well known, with ICBMs (inter-continental ballistic missiles) rising from their silos in East and West, boosting into space high over the North Pole before plunging back to release their MIRVs (multiple independently retargetable vehicles) — a sheaf of smaller missiles which spread and scatter to their targets.

Below, the ABM (anti-ballistic missile) interceptors rise to defend military installations, each inter-ceptor a tiny nuclear missile — all futile against the potential might of the 'second strike' of more ICBMs, plus SRAMs (short range attack missiles) carried by bombers, and SLBMs (submarine-launched ballistic missiles). It adds up to a picture of MAD, the reason nobody wants to fight a nuclear war: Mutual Assured Destruction.

This holocaust has passed out of the realm of science fiction. We have fictional documentary films like *The War Game* (1965), showing the shattering effect of a quite small nuclear attack. We have figures for the likely death toll in a 'total' World War III fought with several thousand strategic nuclear weapons on either side: about 50% of the population of the USA and USSR could die in the attacks, rising towards 90% as injuries, radiation sickness, disease and fallout took effect.

The new weapons of nuclear war are supposed to reduce the chance of this holocaust either by being less destructive, like the neutron bomb, or by being more difficult to make a

The charred corpse of a victim of the atom bomb dropped on Nagasaki by the Americans in August 1945. Had the body been closer to the blast centre, it would simply have been evaporated.

An artist's conception of an MX missile-carrying transport device. The missiles would be moved randomly about a huge network of underground tunnels in the American West. Not knowing where the missiles were at a given moment, an enemy would not (in theory) be able to destroy them. The vast budget necessary to construct the system means that the original plan may never be put into practice.

preventive attack against. If one superpower could eliminate enough of another's nuclear weapons in a sneak attack, there might be a temptation to do so in the hope of 'winning' the resulting war. One weapon designed to prevent this was the MX missile system in its original planned version: ICBMs move along gigantic underground railways and can burst out anywhere from their hidden tunnels. Until then, the enemy is not supposed to know where to aim. More cheaply, short-range cruise missiles can be stockpiled in enormous numbers, too many to be eliminated by a first strike. They can be launched from planes, ships or submarines, or even kept moving in closed trucks, ready to fire from anywhere on the road. The cruise missile's secret is its microcomputer 'brain', which follows the programmed land-map at such low altitude that many defences cannot be brought to bear. Eventually it explodes within metres of the chosen target. Though less brainy than the bomb in the 1974 film *Dark Star* (which invented religion for itself and exploded on the words 'Let there be light'), these missiles are in the great science fictional tradition of almost intelligent machines.

As for the neutron bomb, it is essentially a small H-bomb. By careful engineering the fission-bomb trigger is made smaller and the physical explosion reduced, leaving the flash of neutrons and other hard radiation as the chief killing agent. Though less destructive than strategic H-bombs, it is still a moderately 'dirty' bomb. Some military theorists have tried to class it as a minor tactical weapon whose use need not lead to further nuclear war, but others disagree. Neutron bombs are in the kiloton — 1000 tons of TNT — explosive range; blasts equivalent to as little as 100 tons of TNT have been tested, but they grow less cost-effective below the multi-kiloton range. Such delights as the nuclear bazooka shells of Kingsley Amis's *The Anti-Death League* or the hand-held atomic pistols in such books as A.E. van Vogt's *Slan* are still definitely science fiction.

What could provoke the use of the world's nuclear arsenals? NATO theorists often imagine a USSR invasion of Europe as leading to a last-ditch use of short-range tactical weapons (as the German joke goes, a tactical nuclear weapon is one which lands on Germany). Others fear that superpowers will be drawn into an escalating war beginning in the Middle East or another contentious zone. Science fiction, with its liking for melodrama, tends to imagine vast events as being set in motion by individuals. Thus in the film *Twilight's Last Gleaming*

(1976) a renegade US general takes over a missile base and blackmails the government with his threat of starting a nuclear war. The classic film is *Dr Strangelove* (1963), in which a lunatic US general went further and actually launched a nuclear attack. Such 'accidental' routes to World War III became more convincing after many recent false alarms on the American defence computers were reported. We can only hope that if a large meteor or comet ever falls destructively (see page 112), the people in charge will allow for the chance of its *not* being a nuclear attack.

Dr Strangelove also features the ultimate nuclear weapon. Such pastimes as planet-smashing are impossible with today's weapons: very large bombs blow themselves apart before all the nuclear material can explode, and in the higher megatonne ranges the explosive efficiency becomes ever lower. But a sufficient number of particularly dirty explosions might add up to the Doomsday Bomb of *Dr Strangelove*, which uses fallout as its chief killing agent and spreads contamination round the world. The high wind-streams that carried dust from Krakatoa's eruption, which coloured sunsets all over the Earth, would carry fallout just as effectively. If somebody hated life enough, it might be possible.

Natural disasters

Impressive though the firepower of our nuclear weapons may seem, natural disasters put them to shame. H-bombs release several megatons; the Siberian meteorite that struck near Tunguska in 1908 may have had an impact energy of 30 megatons — its devastation remains clearly visible today — while the 1883 volcanic eruption at Krakatoa was measurable in hundreds of megatons and the largest earthquakes in thousands.

Fortunately, both volcanoes and earthquakes spend most of their energy harmlessly. Krakatoa blasted into the air some 6 cubic km of earth and rock, harmless except to those it fell on; major earthquakes cause small movements of very large masses of rock and spend their energy that way, setting the whole Earth ringing on a note far below the range of hearing. John

Christopher's novel *A Wrinkle in the Skin* described massive earthquakes all over the world, but this is an unlikely situation. Large quakes and volcanoes confine themselves to zones where the plates of the Earth's crust grind against each other, like the 'Ring of Fire' round most of the Pacific. We would have to visit other, stranger worlds to find such problems as are described in Colin Kapp's story 'The Railways up on Cannis': Cannis-4 is a thin-crusted imaginary world where to stick a spade into the ground is to risk an instant volcano.

The danger of falling meteors, asteroids or comets is less easily dismissed. Our Solar System contains uncounted billions of rocks, from dust-motes to planetoids: the orbit of each is continuously influenced by the combined gravity-pulls of everything else in the system (particularly the Sun and Jupiter), and their paths change as though in some silent pinball

machine. Thousands of tons of material from space fall towards Earth each year, virtually all of it burning up before reaching the ground. But occasionally something arrives which is big enough to lose only its outer surface on the way through our atmosphere.

Some very large objects do come alarmingly close. The asteroid Eros has come within 22 million km of Earth, a very small distance on the cosmic scale. Another, Icarus, came within 6.5 million km in 1968; a third, Hermes, was expected to come within a few hundred thousand km (closer than the Moon) but failed to turn up. Presumably it was diverted by, say, the influence of Jupiter — but what if it had been diverted a little the other way, to hit the Earth?

Ignoring atmospheric friction and the orbital speed of Earth and the asteroid, we can calculate a rough impact energy based on a final velocity of about 40,000 kph

Opposite: the fear that Earth would be destroyed in a great holocaust is much older than science fiction, and is often connected with religion. The apocalypse preceding Judgement Day is here depicted by the nineteenth-century artist John Martin.
Left: the devastation wrought by the Tunguska meteorite in Siberia in 1908 remains visible. Many thousands of dead trees lie there still, their trunks pointing away from the point of blast.

(the speed reached by a body falling to Earth from infinity — or a few million km, the same for practical purposes). Icarus, smallest of those mentioned, is about 1 km across and would hit with a 75,000 megaton explosion — dwarfing the total megatonnage of the world's nuclear stockpiles. Hermes, about 2 km in diameter, weighs in at a 220,000 megaton explosion, and Eros at 75 million megatons.

The atmosphere is small protection against such monsters: they will flash through it in seconds, producing a hot, explosive shockwave which scorches and blasts for perhaps hundreds of km about the point of impact. A grain of hope is that — although in films like *Meteor* (1979) the impact area tends to be a city, generally New York — for a land-strike the odds favour a wilderness where, as with earthquakes, much of the tremendous energy would be soaked up in the Earth itself.

But 71% of Earth's surface is ocean: there is a 71% chance that any falling body will hit the sea, erasing coastlines with tidal waves. A well worked-out treatment is *Lucifer's Hammer* by Larry Niven and Jerry Pournelle, in which the Hammer is a comet — a mass of ice-welded rocks. The energy of a major

impact in the sea instantly boils vast quantities of water: thick clouds and torrential rains appear, and also, less convincingly, a new Ice Age, as sunlight is blocked from the Earth. (Another theory is that all the water vapour in the atmosphere will make the Earth warmer by increasing the 'greenhouse effect' — see page 114.)

We need worry less about some calamities. The film *The Day The Earth Caught Fire* (1961) has Earth falling into the Sun, knocked from its orbit by nuclear tests. In real life, only a collision with a really large asteroid like Ceres (12,000 billion megatons impact energy) could shift our orbit significantly, and the collision itself would sterilize the Earth. Another film, *When Worlds Collide* (1951), features a wandering star whose gravity produces giant tides and earthquakes — disastrous, as usual, to New York, which vanishes under a tidal wave. But a passing star is fantastically unlikely, and something we would see coming for centuries before its arrival. Matters are different in Fritz Leiber's *The Wanderer*, where a spacefaring planet comes flitting through hyperspace to wreak gravitational destruction on Earth. This is hardly a natural disaster, but some dark

body — a planet with low reflectivity or a black hole — could indeed approach the Solar System without our knowledge. Only bright objects can be seen in telescopes.

In another traditional disaster the Sun goes nova, flaring up in a millionfold increase of brightness and heat to burn all Earthly life and perhaps vaporize the planet. However, ours is a young Sun which we hope will go on burning for thousands of millions of years. Certainly it is too small to blow apart completely as a supernova, a much more impressive event: the remnants of a supernova observed as a great light in the sky in AD 1054 are still visible as the Crab Nebula.

Though safe from this, we may not be safe from other supernovae far away — whose effects are hard to predict. In Ian Watson's story 'The Roentgen Refugees' the supernova is Sirius, 9 light-years away; massive radiation kills everything not protected by deep shelters, leaving a sterile Earth. *The Twilight of Briareus* by Richard Cowper features an equally convincing supernova 150 light-years distant, whose blast of high-energy radiation shocks our weather system into a new Ice Age — an all too familiar scenario.

A new Ice Age or a drowned world

We think of Ice Ages as slow, creeping things — not the dramatic stuff of which science fiction is made. But some scientists believe that surprisingly quick climatic changes are possible, especially if human tampering should disturb the balance of the world's climate.

It is some 10,000 years since the end of the Pleistocene era which began about 2,500,000 years earlier and included the four great Ice Ages. If the ice returns, we doubt that it will be quite as swift as in Arthur C. Clarke's short story 'The Forgotten Enemy', where the last man on Earth wakes up one morning to find the glaciers knocking at his door. More convincing is the grim realism of John Christopher's *The World in Winter*, in which a bitter winter simply fails to lift: the balance has somehow been tipped and the ice is returning. Some such rapid 'climatic flip' might explain the famous Siberian frozen mammoths, which were so well preserved (some even having fresh grass in their stomachs) that it seems they may have been buried in a snowfall which never gave way to a thaw.

Once an Ice Age has begun, it can continue growing by a process of positive feedback. More snow and ice increase the albedo of the Earth (the proportion of sunlight it reflects back into space); thus the climate cools further; and thus there is yet more snow and ice, on and on in a vicious circle. Glaciers grow southward from the Arctic because their ice fails to melt as quickly as when the world was warmer — and again the albedo increases. There are some ingenious theories to account for why an Ice Age should ever stop. One is that the Arctic Ocean acts as a safety valve: when it finally freezes it can no longer supply moisture to the north wind by evaporation, and so *less* snow falls.

The initial tipping of the balance could take place in many ways. There could be an 'Act of God' from space, such as the shock of supernova radiation or an ocean-vaporizing meteor strike as discussed on pages 112-13. (Such events might also tip the balance the other way towards a drowned world: it is uncertain.) The dust-veil raised by volcanic eruptions may also increase the albedo — British climatologist Hubert Lamb has found that many of the coldest, wettest summers have occurred in 'volcanic dust years'. Or we may raise the albedo too far ourselves — by building too many roads and cities which tend to reflect more sunlight than ordinary countryside; by discharging smog and dust particles which add to our cloud cover (clouds being the largest single factor in raising albedo); even passively by letting the deserts grow, increasing their huge areas of sun-reflecting sand. Once the process has gone far enough to reduce Earth's average annual temperature by a few degrees centigrade, then — according to the estimates — the glaciers grow.

Ice at least provides a beautiful

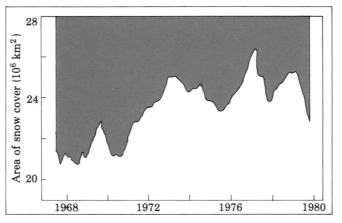

Left: fears that the 'greenhouse effect' will create a 'drowned world' are now more fashionable than fears of a new Ice Age. But as this diagram shows, the snow cover over the Northern Hemisphere has increased in recent years. The more snow, the greater the albedo, with consequent heat loss.

Right: the drowned world scenario has always been popular in science fiction. The 1933 film *Deluge* shown here was based on a best-selling novel of the same title by S. Fowler Wright. Great earthquakes are followed by tidal waves and a subsidence of many of Earth's landmasses. The scenario is just as popular today, though now the flooding is seen as due to the melting of the ice-caps because the 'greenhouse effect' has warmed the atmosphere.

and romantic landscape. Coleridge's fantastic poem *The Rime of the Ancient Mariner,* written in 1798, is lyrical about the Antarctic, which at the time was the stuff of science fiction. The strange film *Quintet* (1979) is set in an impressively icebound city; the chill grinding of glaciers fills the background of Anna Kavan's Ice-Age novel *Ice* (1967); many other works of science fiction use the ice landscape to great effect. The Ice-Age novel with the strongest and most interesting scientific basis is probably *The Sixth Winter* (1979) by Douglas Orgill and John Gribbin.

Unfortunately, the probabilities are in the other direction, where the feedback process works in reverse. The result is a drowned world. The ice retreats, the albedo drops, the temperature goes up, more ice melts. A rise of only a few degrees in Earth's average annual temperature means that the glaciers of Greenland and Antarctica will melt. At the height of an Ice Age the seas would be hundreds of metres lower than today, with the water locked up on land as ice; if Antarctica and Greenland were melted back to rock and soil, the seas would be about 60 metres higher. Most of the world's major cities, which are on or near coasts, would be submerged.

This is the situation of J.G. Ballard's bizarre novel *The Drowned World,* where all the Earth has become tropical and most of our civilization is under water. Ballard suggested instabilities in the Sun as the cause, but grimmer and more convincing explanations can be found closer to home.

Our civilization burns great quantities of coal and oil (see pages 34-6), adding to the carbon dioxide in the air, and thus to the 'greenhouse effect'. In a greenhouse, infra-red (heat) radiation from the Sun warms the contents, and when warm they emit infra-red of their own — but different, longer wavelengths of infra-red which cannot escape through the greenhouse glass. Carbon dioxide, like glass, is a good absorber of infra-red, and by pumping it into the atmosphere we are sealing ourselves under thicker layers of 'greenhouse glass'. Plants consume this gas even as we make it (and breathe it out), but we are constantly cutting down forests and thus cutting down on the total amount of carbon dioxide used up — leaving more free carbon dioxide in the atmosphere. When we burn the wood, or anything else (including nuclear fuel), the waste heat makes our greenhouse temperature rise.

So far it seems that all the factors working towards a man-made Ice Age are being balanced by the greenhouse effect and the trend towards a man-made 'drowned world'. Long may the balance continue.

Science fiction writers, ingeniously destructive people that they are, have devoted much thought to means of tilting the balance and drowning the Earth. The implacable undersea aliens in John Wyndham's *The Kraken Wakes* spend much effort in directing atomically heated water at frozen northern seas from below — a rather wasteful-sounding process. More economically, the villains of Gerald Kersh's *The Great Wash* plan to reshape the ocean floor with gigantic nuclear weapons and thus divert the Gulf Stream's warm currents to the polar ice — with no particular motive beyond a general luxuriation in villainy, it would seem. And in Karel Capek's 1936 classic *War with the Newts,* the water-dwelling Newt creatures try the approach direct: rather than raise the level of the sea, they equip themselves with high explosives and patiently set about lowering the land.

Meanwhile, though, the balance seems to continue.

Left: in Robert Altman's 1979 film *Quintet* the world is in the grip of a new Ice Age, and human relationships are frozen too — except for Paul Newman's, of course. His girlfriend, played by Brigitte Fossey, is pregnant, to the amazement of the city people they meet later. She dies, however, as will everybody else eventually. Would we survive a new Ice Age in real life?

Plague, pollution, overpopulation and famine

Are these four linked threats science fiction? Already the world suffers epidemics, though usually mild ones; it stews in pollution, it bulges at the seams with people, and even today whole countries are starving. Environmentalists and science fiction writers follow the trends further.

Overpopulation is the most fundamental of these evils, since it leads to the using up of resources and the spoiling of the environment. Large, crowded populations make the perfect 'culture dish' in which new plagues can grow and spread.

Science fiction has many gloomy — or blackly comic — versions of overpopulation. J.G. Ballard's story 'Billennium' allows each person four square metres of living space, which later drops to three. In *The Space Merchants* by Frederik Pohl and Cyril Kornbluth, individual steps in public staircases are rented as sleeping spaces. Robert Silverberg's *The World Inside* features thousand-storey tower blocks each housing close on a million people. And in *A Torrent of Faces* by James Blish and Norman L. Knight, world population is pushed about as far as

it can go — a total of 1000 billion people (today's world population is about 4.5 billion) are crammed into cities of 10 million people apiece — 100,000 cities. To quote Blish and Knight, 'And so they lived happily ever after — but it wasn't easy.' The gloomy reality seems to be that without enormous changes in our society (*A Torrent of Faces* relies heavily on total co-operation from *everyone*), civilization is likely to fall apart before such figures can be reached.

The two traditional science fiction answers to overpopulation are not cheering. The first is to send millions of people into space as colonists. In reality, this would be like the story of the marching Chinese whose numbers increase too fast for them ever to finish walking past a given spot. No plausible technology can move people off

Earth faster than they breed. The other solution is worse: a disaster which cuts down the population to manageable size.

Excess population can bring its own disaster. Caged and overcrowded animals tend to have an enormously increased death rate through stress, suffering sudden 'population crash' to much lower numbers as they spend their time aggressively competing for space rather than breeding. (John Brunner's *Stand on Zanzibar* features some harrowing looks at such stresses in an overcrowded world.) Brian Aldiss's *Greybeard* can be taken as a parable of such behaviour; in it, our aggression — nuclear testing — leads to a dramatic population crash as mankind becomes sterile. Undramatic measures like birth control are less popular in science fiction, a not

WORLD POPULATION INCREASE IN THE CHRISTIAN ERA

Year (A.D.)	World population (Billions)	Doubling time in years
1	0.25 (?)	1650 (?)
1650	0.50	200
1850	1.1	80
1930	2.0	45
1975	4.0	?

Above: the most notable feature of this population chart is the ever decreasing period in which population has doubled. The rate of increase is now falling, but growth remains spectacular: 4.5 billion in 1982, a projected 6 billion in 2000, possibly stabilizing at 11 billion within 125 years, according to recent UN predictions.
Right: pollution is now a world-wide problem. The picture shows dead fish in the heavily polluted Seine, with Paris in the background.

untypical treatment being Patrick Wyatt's *Irish Rose*: here the white races sterilize themselves by the use of an 'improved' Pill, leaving everyone else to inherit the Earth. In many of science fiction's futures, the bearing of children has become a criminal activity (see pages 165-7).

The famine resulting from overpopulation plays its part in the grimness of Harry Harrison's *Make Room! Make Room!* (filmed as *Soylent Green*) — water is rationed; the hero lives on margarine-smeared biscuits; meat has vanished from the menu. Indeed a meat diet is absurdly expensive to produce, relative to grains and crops — but that is not likely to stop us encouraging further famine by gobbling more and more meat.

Death by pollution became a popular theme of science fiction in the 1970s, most grippingly in John Brunner's *The Sheep Look Up*, a survey of human folly as depressing as any non-fiction tract. It gives a detailed catalogue of American pollution of earth, air and water, and holds out no hope: at the end of the book, all America is burning. Besides fouling the air and contaminating our food as waste chemicals build up in mammals, fish and plants, pollution can also have larger-scale effects like the climatic disasters mentioned in the last section. Perhaps a race which allows

cars to pump lead into the atmosphere — legal in the UK though not the USA — and inexorably damage the intelligence of children does not deserve to have a future.

As forests die off or are cut down, erosion makes the waste spaces into deserts and speeds the death of more vegetation, perhaps until we reach the situation of Bob Shaw's *Shadow of Heaven*, where herbicides have killed all wild greenery, dust-bowls stretch across continents and humanity eats a universal diet of seafood and synthetics. In that world plants are preserved in special environmental museums like the spacegoing greenhouses of the film *Silent Running*; in real life, it is possible that no one would bother.

We have seen three of the four horsemen of the modernized Apocalypse: Famine with the traditional scales to measure out insufficient food, Overpopulation with a ruler to allot insufficient space, and Pollution armed with an exhaust pipe. There is still Plague, which thanks to modern medicine seems less threatening — but is it?

Some science fiction writers, and some scientists, have imagined plagues from space: Michael Crichton's *The Andromeda Strain* (book and film) is a notable example written by a doctor of medicine, while Fred Hoyle's 'non-fictional'

Diseases from Space attempts to blame many real-life epidemics on viruses which float between worlds. The consensus among other scientists is that a disease from space is extremely unlikely, since there is almost no chance that something from 'out there' would be evolutionarily adapted to prey on *us* — a likelihood recognized in Harry Harrison's *Plague from Space*, in which an apparently natural plague proves to have been tailored to us by sinister aliens.

Plagues from Earth are the chief worry. Our development of antibiotics against dangerous bacteria is itself dangerous: their use removes from the biosphere those bacteria which antibiotics kill (originally the vast majority) and favours the few which can survive our medicines. Micro-organisms reproduce in hours, rather than months or years. They mutate with equal speed, and the continued use of any antibiotic drug guarantees huge populations of microbes immune to it. Every so often such 'new' diseases get out of hand, as with the frequent new strains of influenza. One day we may expect something more deadly, like the world-killing plague of George R. Stewart's *Earth Abides*. Such plague germs can be regarded as a planetary antibiotic, to cure Earth of its infection of people, leaving just a few who are immune.

Overpopulation brings with it an increasing pressure for living space in the cities. Japan, inventive as always, has come up with one bizarre solution — the 'capsule hotel'. Each reinforced fibre 'room' is a tiny cell with radio, mini-television, fire sprinkler system and telephone, all in a few cubic metres.

Reconstruction scenarios

When civilization crumbles at the impact of plague, nuclear war, energy shortage or natural disaster — is that the end? Almost certainly there will be attempts to pick up the pieces and start afresh.

There is a whole branch of science fiction dealing with life after the holocaust, the life-style depending closely on the nature of the holocaust. Nuclear war leads to cancer, radiation sickness from fallout, and the danger of 'hot' contaminated areas: traditionally, in science fiction, the radiation will cause strangely mutated people and animals, as in John Wyndham's *The Chrysalids* or Roger Zelazny's *This Immortal*. (In practice, evolution involves minor mutations over many, many generations: major mutations are overwhelmingly likely to cripple or kill.) Plague might seem a tidier end to civilization; few writers gave much thought to the heaps of rotting bodies until Stephen King's *The Stand*.

Afterwards, people *may* revert to savagery — even cannibalism, as in *The Long Loud Silence* by Wilson Tucker. Primitive tribesmen or feudal warriors prowl the ruined cities or stare at the half-buried Statue of Liberty (the trademark of post-holocaust science fiction, used on many magazine covers and later in the film *Planet of the Apes*, 1968). Perhaps they will die out, or at least abandon civilization like the young folk of George R. Stewart's *Earth Abides* — but it is much more likely that in real life people would hang on to the last shreds of the old world, as they do in *The Stand*.

One possibility is that, after nuclear war, humanity will turn

Right: this haunting image by artist Bob Layzell encapsulates the typical mood of science fiction set in a post-holocaust period. There is a certain beauty in the unused nuclear missiles and the radar scanners, but their outlines are already blurred with greenery as Nature reasserts herself.

away in disgust from the evils of technology. Examples from science fiction are Edmund Cooper's *The Cloud Walker*, where the Luddite Church does unpleasant things to anyone who re-invents machines, and Norman Spinrad's *Songs from the Stars*, in which the good people are hippies and the bad ones 'Black Scientists'. But in both books, science comes creeping back — the moral of *The Cloud Walker* being that the enlightened man with technology can firebomb those without. Perhaps with this in mind, the hero of Heinlein's *Farnham's Freehold* equips his fallout shelter for a

single-handed reconstruction of high technology, armed with a rifle, the Boy Scout manual and the *Encyclopaedia Britannica*. Many American 'survivalists' in real life already seem to look forward to a time when, with their hoarded stockpiles of survival equipment, they can start running the post-holocaust world.

The final word on hatred of technology came from Kurt Vonnegut in his *Player Piano*, in which revolutionaries happily smash the evil machines, but are later found in the ruins, putting the machines together again with equal enthusiasm — which seems to

say something fundamental about human nature.

The aim of reconstruction is doubtless a safe and happy civilization, a wiser society which has learnt from all our mistakes and will not repeat them. But 'the only thing we learn from history is that we learn nothing from history'. The rebuilding comes full circle in Walter M. Miller's fine novel *A Canticle for Leibowitz*, in which monks preserve knowledge through the new Dark Ages after World War III, eventually rebuilding civilization to the point where, again, it culminates in nuclear war.

Two noble-looking savages on a raft gaze placidly at the Statue of Liberty, now a relic of a bygone age. Judging from the size of the trees at its base, civilization faded some time back. Such images, never better rendered than here, on the cover of a 1941 *Astounding Science Fiction* magazine, became the trademark of post-holocaust scenarios.

When civilization crumbles, tribal cruelties follow rapidly, according to science fiction. These riders, seemingly a blend of Hell's Angels and Vikings, are out to get food and women from a small band of survivors in the film *No Blade of Grass* (1970). World-wide famine was the catastrophe in this future scenario, and reconstruction seems a long way off.

119

Chapter 7
INTELLIGENT MACHINES

Will computers develop real intelligence? And will each of us one day be plugged into a worldwide data network? A revolution is taking place, and the result may well be a cybernetic society.

Mechanical brains

In 1946, American scientists completed the construction of the world's first functional electronic computer, ENIAC. It weighed 30 tons, had 18,000 vacuum tubes, and kept breaking down. When working, it could make 5000 calculations per second. To mass-produce such machines would have been astronomically expensive, and nobody even tried.

Today, we can buy a desk computer that plugs into a television set for about the same price as dinner for two at a good restaurant. Instead of vacuum tubes, it has thousands of micro-miniaturized transistors engraved on a few chips of silicon. The heart of such desk computers is a single microprocessor of a kind devised by M.E. Hoff in 1969, which works in harness with two 'memory chips' — one to move data into the micro-processor and one to move data out. These three chips effectively constitute a whole general-purpose computer. Each of Hoff's first chips measured about 4 mm×3 mm, carried 2250 transistors and could handle 100,000 calculations per second. On recent chips 3 million transistors have been fitted on to 6.25 square cm.

Since the Intel Corporation of Santa Clara, California, began manufacturing microcomputers in 1971 they have been adapted for use in — among other things — calculators, watches, video games, industrial robots, weapon-guidance systems, blood-chemistry analysers, taxi-meters, postal scales, washing machines, microwave ovens and cash-registers. They are beginning

to have multiple effects in such fields as television, telephonics, printing and photocopying.

This rapid expansion of computer technology in a mere 35 years represents an advance in technique that is quite astonishing. The probable effects of the new technology are so wide-ranging that people quite confidently speak of a Post-Industrial Revolution. Micro-processors promise dramatic changes in places of work, in the home, in education and in medicine. Their use will have an effect on all areas of our lives, not in the distant future but within the next few decades. The possibilities for change

in the way we live are so numerous, and the potential patterns of change so complicated, that it is very difficult indeed to come up with a realistic picture of what life in 50 years' time might be like.

This is one area of technological change where science has leapt ahead of the imaginative reach of science fiction writers, who are only now beginning to accommodate themselves to the new horizons of possibility. 'Mechanical brains' have featured widely in science fiction for some considerable time. The earliest ones date back to the nineteenth century, which is not entirely surprising when one recalls that

using X-ray etching techniques it is possible to cut channels 0.1 microns wide: not quite down to atomic size, but only about 1000 times bigger. A small particle of radioactivity, at this scale, might flip a tiny transistor from the 'off' to the 'on' configuration. Although error-correcting circuits can be built, a point of diminishing returns will be reached if we carry miniaturization too far.

X-rays are used in the technology of extreme miniaturization for a startling reason. At this scale the photo-etching techniques used to engrave chips cannot use visible light. With wavelengths around half a micron, visible light is too 'clumsy' a tool! X-rays, with their much smaller wavelengths, become necessary.

Not all future computers may be made from silicon chips. Some present-day computing structures, for example, have been 'grown' from branching nodules of ferrous sulphate. Many computer theorists have conjectured that the 'biochip' — made of protein molecules sandwiched between glass and metal — might be the basic unit of tomorrow's computers. Some companies (see page 143) are already carrying out developmental work on these 'organic' computers.

Most science fiction stories about the use of computers in future society imagine a centralization of computer-power analogous to the centralization of political power in modern states. Stories such as Ira Levin's *This Perfect Day* and Isaac Asimov's 'The Life and Times of MULTIVAC' foresee the development of a vast, single computer which will effectively run the world. But what we are at present seeing is something rather different from this collection of all our computational eggs into one basket. In 1975 — 30 years after ENIAC — there were about 200,000 digital computers in the world. By 1985 there are likely to be 20,000,000. In the developed countries computers may soon out-number people. It may, however, become possible to link large numbers of these computers with various networks, so that they can work together — an easier task to accomplish with machines than with human beings.

Left: the move from the thermionic valve to the microchip took less than 25 years to accomplish, and the result is one of the most spectacular of all technological revolutions. The tiny dark square in the central circuit is a silicon chip containing perhaps 100,000 transistors, each one doing a job that used to be done by one valve. The factor of miniaturization is around 20 million to one, and still growing.
Above: this enlargement of a chip made by Rockwell, real size inset, shows the microcircuits.

Charles Babbage attempted to build an 'analytical engine' in the 1830s. He failed only because the machine-tool industry was inadequate to the task of shaping parts to his precise specifications. After ENIAC, it was easy enough for writers to imagine better and more capable calculating machines, but they tended to take it for granted that better must mean bigger. Clifford Simak's 'Limiting Factor', published in 1949, imagines a computer, so huge that it covers an entire world, which is then abandoned by its creators because it is still not big enough. Even as late as 1966, D.F. Jones called his ultimate computer *Colossus*, in the novel of that name.

Meanwhile, in the real world, computer scientists are trying to develop a new generation of micro-microchips which will be shrunk by another order of magnitude. Computers with an information-carrying capacity akin to that of the human brain can already be packaged in a similar volume. Although the pattern of connections within mechanical brains are less complex than those within biological ones, the mechanical brains do work very much faster.

Is there a lower limit, beyond which we cannot make the micro-microchip any smaller? Yes: some experimental circuits are now engraved with such tiny lines that quantum fluctuations are possibly interfering with their reliability. By

121

Automation and industrial robots

As the capability of calculating machines advances, people are not wholly reassured by their reduction in size to an apparently manageable scale. The fear that computers might 'take over' first our jobs, then our economic and political institutions, is increasing rather than decreasing. A highly ironic novel commenting on this anxiety is *The Great Computer* by Olof Johannesson (the pseudonym of Nobel Prize-winning astronomer Hannes Alfven). He imagines a distant future when intelligent machines look back over their evolutionary history, from the time that they first outstripped their now extinct creators.

Automatic machinery began taking over jobs previously done by men in the early days of the Industrial Revolution. In England,

the Luddites lodged their famous objection to the process before the battle of Waterloo. The computer revolution has accelerated this process dramatically by widening the capabilities of machines to take in a whole new range of tasks.

Industrial robots are specialized machines which go through a series of programmed motions in order to carry out a particular task. They are extremely useful in performing routine, repetitive tasks, because they keep going indefinitely and never get bored or careless. Much of the work on production-lines is of this type, because the whole essence of a production-line is that it breaks down a complicated task into a series of simple ones. Robots are widely used for paint-spraying and other kinds of coating processes, for welding (especially spot-welding), for pressing and die-casting, and in injection-moulding.

It is Japanese industry that has invested most heavily in the automation of its factories. By the end

of 1980 there were reported to be 60,000 sophisticated robots in Japan, as opposed to 3000 in the USA and a mere 105 in Britain. By the end of 1981 Japan had 77,000 industrial robots — around 70% of the rapidly growing world population of such machines. Such robots are very different from the robots of science fiction. These tend to be humanoid, although there is an interesting pair of stories by Anthony Boucher, 'Q.U.R.' and 'Robinc', written in the 1940s to champion 'usuform robots' — their form fits their function — against humanoid ones. However, factory automation has usually been regarded as a rather mundane issue by science fiction writers, although *Player Piano* by Kurt Vonnegut interestingly examines the possible social consequences of general automation.

In recent years there has been a significant advance in robot evolution due to the incorporation of microprocessors. Before 1970,

Left: factory automation has not progressed as far in the UK as in the USA or Japan. But the British Steel finishing mill at Newport in Wales has a factory floor almost empty of people. The automated processes are monitored in the control room in the foreground.

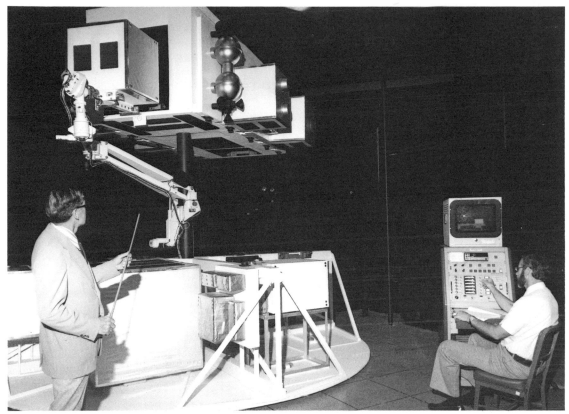

Left: this NASA maintenance robot, which will be used to repair satellites in orbit, is being tested at the Marshall Space Flight Center in Alabama. At this point of the test the robot is being controlled from the console at right, but in space it will be capable of limited autonomous movement controlled by a computer program. Robot machines are capable now of an astonishing versatility, but they can only manipulate parts of a standard design.

progress in robotics was mainly a matter of devising more efficient joints and steering mechanisms to make the 'mechanical hands' more dexterous. The actual behaviour of the machines was quite straightforward, consisting of a series of precisely repeated motions. Robots were used for such tasks as assembling components into a more complex structure, but only if all the parts were delivered to precise points in order to be picked up. Now, a machine can be equipped with visual sensors which allow it to search for and recognize appropriate parts, guiding itself to them and altering its pick-up manoeuvre to suit the circumstances. Such machines can complete half-finished assemblies, or dismantle them, if they have been assembled incorrectly, and rectify the error. These robots are so flexible in their behaviour that they are performing tasks which, if performed by a human being, would require intelligence (this is one definition of 'artificial intelligence'). Automata of this kind are still mainly experimental, but the impact that they will have on industry is obvious: they represent a new generation of industrial robots which are no longer restricted to stereotyped

movements on the production-line.

Remote-controlled robots have been popular in science fiction for a long time, and recent developments in robot sensors will soon allow science fiction's dreams to become reality. Microsurgery, for example, becomes a real possibility with machines that are in part an extension of the surgeon's hands, in part a close-up visual system enlarging microscopic parts to visible size.

True robots, with a degree of autonomy, will probably be used in dangerous tasks such as underwater repair, working in deep mines or in those contaminated with gas, and in factories using corrosive or poisonous materials. The development of such remote-control systems has been accelerated by the space programme, where a number of robot systems are already in use.

The ultimate level of automation is that satirized by John Sladek in his novel *The Reproductive System*. This is the self-reproducing machine. In Sladek's story these machines come close to taking over the world. The idea is not peculiar to Sladek: one of its earliest appearances was in the machine society of Samuel Butler's *Erewhon* (1872). In a popular fictional version of the idea warfare is carried out by self-

replicating fighting machines, even after the people who built the machines have been wiped out. The classic story of this type is Philip K. Dick's 'Second Variety', which tells the sad tale of the last human survivors in such a war.

Are such machines possible? In theory, yes. They were first described mathematically in 1948 by one of the earliest and greatest of cybernetic theorists, John von Neumann. He showed that any self-replicating machine needed four components: A is an automatic factory; B is a duplicator which takes an instruction and copies it; C is a controller hooked up to A and B. When C is given an instruction it first passes it to B for duplication, then to A for action, and finally supplies the copied instructions to the parts that A produces. Component D is a written instruction containing the complete specifications that allow A to manufacture the entire system: A plus B plus C. These four components, both necessary and sufficient to do the job, are reflected in living cells, which reproduce using four interlocking systems parallel to those theorized by Von Neumann, although he could not have known this at the time he formulated his theory.

Von Neumann's ideas have been used as a basis for a proposed factory on the Moon which would produce other factories. Similarly the proposed self-replicating space probes (see page 18) are referred to as Von Neumann probes. Nothing in the real world yet approaches the dramatic simplicity of Von Neumann's scheme. But Fujitsu Fanuc Ltd in Japan has built a factory, entirely staffed with robots, which manufactures robots at the rate of 100 a month. Only the final assembly is carried out by human beings. It is interesting to note that, although the use of industrial robots is feared as a likely cause of unemployment, Japan, which has more automation than any other country, has only 2% unemployment, the lowest of any industrial nation in the world.

It is not only in factories that the computer revolution is making itself felt. Microprocessors hold out the prospect of a dramatic transformation in office work. We are all well aware of the fact that many companies have computerized their financial records. Computers prepare our bank statements, send us bills and write us letters offering services. We all know, too, how difficult it is to conduct a dialogue with these computers if some kind of error occurs — or even if we simply want them to stop pestering us. There is a horribly plausible science fiction story by Gordon R. Dickson, 'Computers Don't Argue', in which a man's dispute with a book club involves him in computerized litigation, which eventually — owing to a slight hitch — leads to his being executed.

Computer-held records are much easier to deal with than conventional filing-systems (so much easier that people are becoming justifiably concerned with the confidentiality of various kinds of records, which is now much easier to breach). The work put into preparing and editing documentary material can also, now, be made very much easier by the use of 'word processors'. Instead of typing on to a page, a typist can type into a computer-memory which can display its contents on a screen. The system allows the production of as many identical copies of the final text as are required, in whatever format is required.

The word-processing and storage aspects of the microcomputer revolution may yet transform society more radically than the industrial aspects. Computers are excellent for storing, manipulating and transmitting data. The resulting data networks that are even now being built up, especially in the industrially developed nations, have implications for us all. Such networks may completely change our lifestyles, both at work and at leisure, within a decade.

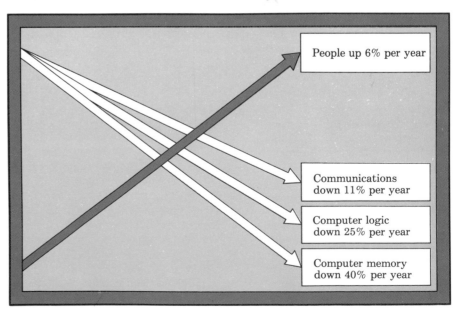

People up 6% per year

Communications down 11% per year

Computer logic down 25% per year

Computer memory down 40% per year

Above: brisk action at the annual Micromouse competition in Europe. Robot hobbyists build mechanical 'mice' which have to traverse a maze. The winner is the one that reaches the centre fastest. This good fun has a serious side: advances in robot design can result from games like this.

Right: the economics of automation at a glance. People are costing more while computer equipment is costing less. Computer 'memory' is falling in price even faster than the built-in, pre-programmed circuits that perform logical operations.

Data networks

When we can communicate with one another via electronic machinery as sophisticated as that made possible by new technology, there may be no need to gather people together into a central location. If one adds to the benefits of word processing such new developments as the establishment of an electronic mailing system, whereby a message is transmitted from one display-screen to another, becoming an actual document only at the delivery point (if at all), then the probable transformation of office work becomes profound. It is now reasonable to imagine the abolition of offices as places where people actually assemble. Office work can be done in a home suitably equipped with computer terminals and display-screens.

However, recent studies conducted by experts in the psychology of work suggest that people value the friendships and social contacts of office life, and may be reluctant to retreat to a kind of work-cocoon at home. It is by no means certain that the days of the office are numbered.

Over the last 50 years there has been a steady reduction in the percentage of the work force employed in manufacturing processes, and a corresponding increase in the fraction employed on the bureaucratic side of industry, and, of course, of government. It is interesting to separate out the so-called 'information industries' from the other service industries. The information industries are those involved in the manufacture of information equipment, such as computers, televisions and telephones, and in the processing of information (bureaucrats both public and private are included here). By separating out these industries we can see just how radically Western societies have already been transformed into information-processing societies over the past few decades. But the bureaucracies themselves are now at risk, for computers can replace human beings in most information-processing tasks.

Recent advances in telecommunications, especially communication-satellite networks and the use of optical fibres for radically increasing the volume of

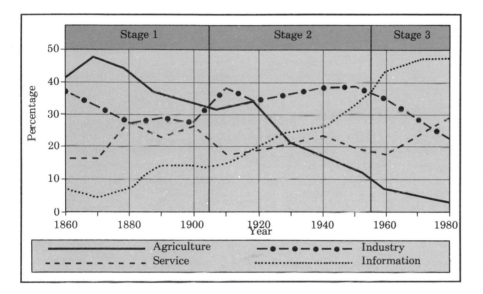

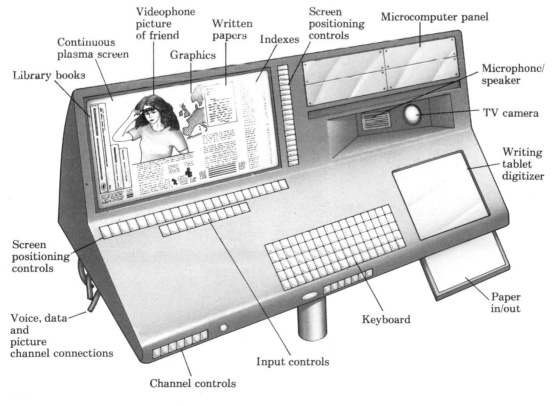

Above: the changing composition of the US workforce from 1860 to 1980. The three stages are the agricultural, industrial and information economies. The story is much the same throughout the developed world.
Left: an information console of the kind that may be used widely within 15 years (based on an illustration in *Wireless World*, July 1978). Will such communication devices reduce face-to-face relationships between people?

information that can be transmitted by cable, have been spectacular. When the effects of this technology are added to the effects of computer technology, we see the beginnings of a global data network. Some of the results will be trivial and some far-reaching. Electronic transfer of funds, instant shopping at the push of a button, access to major reference libraries via the television screen: these facets of the future are already available, in a somewhat rudimentary form, to subscribers to the British Prestel videotext system, for example, which at the moment is the largest such system in the world. More sophisticated systems will be developed soon. The use of printers hooked up to computerized television receivers will bring about the advent of the electronic newspaper. The contents will be selected by ourselves and printed in the privacy of the home. Miniaturization will bring the portable communicator/computer worn on the wrist, so that the wearer can remain plugged into the global data network even while skiing or driving a car. These futuristic miracles are quite likely to happen soon, since the economics of the information industry — unlike almost all other industries — suggest that its products are becoming cheaper all the time.

Many of these advances seem trivial until their implications are considered. If, from the point of view of productivity, it no longer matters where you live (since office work can be carried out at home, and factories supervised and even fields ploughed by remote control), then the traditional function of cities and towns has gone. Until now the pressures have been all the other way. The world's major cities, especially in the Third World, have been growing enormously. In 10 years' time, however, this trend may have been reversed.

The global data network has its nightmare aspects, too. We may increasingly be tempted to see ourselves as anonymous units in a great system with whose workings we are helpless to interfere. The global data network could intrude on everybody's privacy: there may be no secrets. With electronic sophistication come the tools for mass surveillance. For example, it

126

will soon be possible to tag items with radio pulse-emitters, so that they can always be located by triangulation, using satellite detectors. If we can locate missing parcels in this way by, say, 1990, then by 1995 it seems very likely that people, too, will be electronically tagged, so that they can never disappear either, no matter how much they want to. When a technology exists, sooner or later it is likely to be used.

Soon, the data-network society will have its more mundane problems at the domestic level. The 'QUBE' cable-television experiment in Colombus, Ohio, has shown how viewer-interactive television systems can be used for the instant polling of viewers' opinions on important issues of the day. The viewers are invited to press button A, B or C, and the computer delivers the result of the poll on everybody's screen in a fraction of a second. If the people who broadcast the news also conduct instant polls, then they will be in a good position to slant the results by the way the question is presented. In this way, a supposedly democratic procedure may subvert the democratic process, for the results of such polls might not reflect informed or considered opinion. It turned out that some of the voters in the 'QUBE' experiment were only five years old! None the less, the results of such polls could be used to put pressure on governments and political

parties. The same 'QUBE' system can profile consumers' tastes to an unprecedented degree of precision, and development of this possibility may deliver a docile mass market to the exploitation of commercial interests more cynically and effectively than ever before. The data-network society could all too easily consist of a vast, apathetic public plugged passively into the system.

Such possibilities have been the concern of science fiction writers, who began to envisage them long before the necessary technology existed. Among the scenarios presented are John Brunner's *The Shockwave Rider*, which gives a probing account of the possible misuse of computer networks by a well intentioned but repressive politico-technocratic elite; J.G. Ballard's 'The Intensive Care Unit', in which marriage and family life are conducted entirely by television; and Algis Budrys's *Michaelmas*, which tells of a newscaster who through his enormously powerful private computer has access to, and final control over, all the data banks of the world.

This is literally a data network, a computer display of traffic in Tokyo, used for monitoring flow, automatically varying traffic lights, and giving orders to robot traffic police. Information is fed in by 5000 ultrasonic detectors which sense whether traffic is moving.

Artificial intelligence

We do not know how far artificial intelligence might develop. Some well qualified optimists, like the British mathematician I.J. Good, believe that there is a 50% chance that intelligent machines will be able to cope with all mental activities as well as human beings do by the year 2000. A fierce debate rages around the issue of the degree to which artificial intelligence would have to be similar to 'real' intelligence, and whether our minds possess properties that could not ever be emulated by a machine. The argument is confused by religious issues involving the concept of the human 'soul'. Most people would like to feel that there is something special about us which sets us apart — some essential quality which we possess that machines never can. Self-awareness and creative imagination are two abilities which many people feel entitled to reserve for humanity. Their arguments in favour of this point of view have become clichés: they tell us that computers can only do what they are programmed to do, that they cannot innovate and cannot jump to the kind of correct conclusions which we ourselves sometimes reach without a step-by-step process of deduction. Machines, according to this view, may become extremely complex, but will always remain inherently inflexible, merely following instructions. All this is arguably true of contemporary machines, but whether it is true of all possible machines is open to doubt.

Science fiction writers often have no hesitation in 'personalizing' computers and attributing to them all the properties of human minds. There are numerous well known examples, ranging from the computer-intelligence Mike in Robert Heinlein's *The Moon is a Harsh Mistress* to HAL in Arthur C. Clarke and Stanley Kubrick's film *2001: A Space Odyssey* (1968). David Gerrold's *When Harlie was One* is one of a number of fictional biographies of artificial intelligences, detailing the growth of their powers and the development of their philo-

PARRY is a computer program designed by the American computer expert Kenneth Colby to mimic the responses of a paranoid patient. The program operates in two modes, strong and weak, shown by the two sample dialogues here between PARRY and a psycho-therapist. The program can obviously not give an adequate answer to every question put to it, but since we often expect irrelevant answers from people who are mentally ill, PARRY'S sudden changes of subject are quite convincing in context. PARRY has many times passed the Turing test for artificial intelligence: he has fooled questioners into believing he is a real person. Far more sophisticated programs than PARRY have been written since 1967, when he was designed, and some programs now actually do understand simple English, rather than just pretending, though few have PARRY'S flair.

PARRY — WEAK MODE

How long have you been in the hospital?
About a week.
Are you depressed?
No.
Were you taking drugs?
No.
What is your problem?
People make me nervous.
How do they do that?
They stare at me.
Why?
Maybe they don't like the way I look or something.
Do you look unusual in some way?
Why are you interested in my looks?
Because you said people stare at you.
Well, sometimes.
How do you get along with people?
I don't communicate very much with the others.
Why not?
They don't realize what's going on most of the time.

PARRY — STRONG MODE

Why are you in the hospital?
I shouldn't be here.
Who brought you here?
The police.
What trouble did you have with the police?
Cops don't do their job.
What do they do instead?
Cops arrest the wrong people.
They arrest the right ones sometimes.
The law should get those Italian crooks.
Are you Italian?
My background is British but I was born in this country.
Do you know any Italian crooks?
I try to avoid the underworld.
Are you afraid of the underworld?
The mafia are the worst gangsters.
Are you connected with the mafia?
You know, they know me.
How do they know you?
They spy on me.
Why do they?
They want to get false evidence to frame me.
What do they have against you?
They are out to get me.
What for?
I have incriminating evidence against the mafia.

---

sophical reflections on the non-human condition.

It is certainly difficult to think of a machine as being self-aware, but then, it is not easy to describe our own self-awareness, and to account for the fact that we have it. A machine-mind, no matter how complicated, might not spontaneously develop self-awareness, but until we are sure how we ourselves come to have self-awareness we can hardly claim to know what might happen to machines.

One of the leading theorists in the area of artificial intelligence, and a leading exponent of the view that machines can become genuinely

intelligent, is Alan Turing. He published a classic paper on 'Computing Machinery and Intelligence' as long ago as 1950. He suggested that the appropriate test of whether a machine is intelligent or not is to require a man to engage it in a dialogue via an electronic display-screen. After a certain time, the man is invited to say whether the replies to his typed questions and comments come from another person or from a computer program. When he begins to mistake the program for the person, then he presumably has as much justification for calling the program an intelligent being as he has for deciding that other people are intelligent beings.

Computers programmed to maintain a dialogue are usually more convincing when asking questions than when answering them, and some of the most useful programs are electronic interrogators. MYCIN, developed by E.H. Shortliffe and others in 1973, is the most famous of the diagnostic programs. It asks people a series of questions about their symptoms in order to discover which of a large number of infectious diseases they are suffering from. No one, of course, suggests that such programs can replace human consultants, but they can reach the right diagnosis in a large majority of cases, and can thus assist specialists by preparing preliminary hypotheses for them to work on. The programs can even comment on the degree of certainty in their own diagnoses and point out any anomalies in the patient's testimony.

In experiments, programs have been substituted for psychiatrists in therapeutic sessions — a famous program called ELIZA was designed for this. Such programs are particularly clever in mimicking the strategies used by 'non-directive therapists' in encouraging their patients to talk about and work through their own problems. A significant experiment in the light of Turing's test of intelligence is the programme PARRY, designed by Kenneth Colby. Although a close relative of ELIZA, PARRY mimics the patient rather than the psychiatrist, and meets questions with a dogged evasiveness that embodies the classic symptoms of paranoia. Six psychiatrists asked to make up their minds, on the basis of the responses, whether PARRY was a real paranoid or a program produced a split verdict.

There is a species of program which duplicates one of the most basic aspects of human intelligence: the ability to learn. These are often programs that learn the strategies of particular games by a process of trial and error. The most familiar ones are chess-playing programs, which are now marketed very widely. They do have a certain amount of strategic pre-programming, and therefore do not have to learn opening moves by trial

and error. Though game-playing strategy is only one small aspect of intelligence, many people underestimated what computers might achieve in this area. In 1968 David Levy, a moderately good chess player, bet that no computer program devised within the next decade would be capable of beating him. In 1978 he won his bet — but only just. He did not win all of the series of deciding games, and it is highly likely that he would have lost had he made the bet five years later.

The point about game-playing programs is that they can get better with practice. In a simple game, like noughts-and-crosses (tic-tac-toe), the computer can be instructed initially to make a random move. If it then records the sequence of moves and the outcome of the game it can avoid repeating sequences of moves which are losers. Once it has played through a sufficient number of games it will have weeded out the losing strategies and — without ever having been told what the winning strategy is — will never be beaten. Obviously, as games become more complicated the number of possible sequences becomes very great, which is why chess-playing machines are never likely to be infallible. The number of possible moves in chess is so astronomically great, in fact, that even the most powerful computers existing would need millions of years to work out all the possibilities stemming from a single move by its opponent early in the game. (A human being could not do this, even if he lived on until the death of the universe itself.) The chess-playing program, therefore, includes short cuts, similar to those used by human players, the most important being 'in a novel situation try methods like those that have worked best in similar situations' — an example would be 'always guard your king'. Such programmed rules of thumb are called 'heuristics'.

Although none of this helps to resolve the question of whether computers can ever emulate all the qualities of human intelligence, it does seem to give the lie to the dogma about machines being unable to innovate. That a computer can do only what it is programmed to do is true enough, but a computer which is programmed to learn is no mere reflection of its program.

Theologians might argue that an essential aspect of human intelligence which machines cannot possess is free will. But neither may we have wills that are entirely free, for we are also constrained by the limits of our pre-programming — our genetic heritage. The important thing is that, free will or not, human beings are programmed to learn and to make choices, and to a degree machines can be made to do the same.

The list of human capacities argued to be essential to a true machine intelligence is long. It includes the ability to reason by analogy (more sophisticated programs for analogical thinking in computers — digital as well as analog — are being developed all the time); the need for sense organs (artificial organs for seeing and hearing exist already, and computers can even be programmed to 'smell', that is, to sense chemicals in the air); the need for a sense of humour (a difficult problem, but maybe not insuperable); the need for emotions (these too may be programmable: Dr Arthur Samuel, an IBM computer scientist, claims to have motivated a game-playing computer with the 'will to win'); and, most important of all, perhaps, the ability to perceive patterns.

Human beings establish relationships among amazingly complex bundles of data, especially visual data, with great efficiency. How can we expect computers to process the jumble of patterns formed by light, shadow, colour and movement that we cope with all the time? Yet even a bird — a relatively 'stupid' animal — can distinguish between a parent and a predator almost as soon as it breaks out of its shell. In order to understand human speech, too, computers must be able to interpret the varying patterns of sound waves, which vary greatly between speakers. Ideally, a computer that understood a New Yorker would also understand a Jamaican. What we can do effortlessly and usually unerringly in sorting out visual, aural and conceptual patterns sets the most profound problems in computer programming. It is in this area that most of today's work in artificial intelligence is being carried out. 'Brute-force' computing techniques

One of the specialized applications of pattern-recognition programs for computers: the woman's signature on an electronic pad is analysed for spatial characteristics and writing time, and the cheque signature is then verified.

will not be the answer; the likeliest way of teaching computers to perceive patterns — or significant relationships — is through 'multi-dimensional matrix' techniques and new developments in set theory and Boolean algebra (the algebra developed by the English mathematician George Boole in his seminal works *The Mathematical Analysis of Logic*, 1848, and *An Investigation of the Laws of Thought*, 1854).

The most powerful argument in favour of the belief that artificial intelligence may one day be able to simulate human intelligence is surely that *human* intelligence has evolved over the course of millions of years by gradual natural selection. What nature can accomplish blindly, surely we may bring about with the aid of such abilities as nature has given us: if there is nothing occult about our intelligence, if 'mind' has evolved as a perfectly natural function of the brain (a view not everyone accepts), then there seems to be no reason why we should not make intelligent machines.

Some theorists believe that the problem cuts both ways. If machine intelligences can ever be made as potent as human intelligence, then might we not have demonstrated in a back-to-front way that the brain itself is no more than a machine? This is the so-called 'reductionist' view of consciousness, about which the philosopher Gilbert Ryle

commented, 'Man need not be degraded to a machine by being denied to be a ghost in a machine.' That is, to deny a mysterious 'soul' is not to say that we are no more than machines. Conversely, if the 'soul' turns out to be a naturally evolving property of intelligent minds, then might not machines have souls too, as many science fiction writers have argued?

It is possible that investigations of artificial intelligence may actually provide us with what we have lacked for a long time: a proper understanding of the way our own minds work. The mind-body problem — the question of how mental phenomena are related to the physical system of the brain — is one of the classic problems of philosophy and psychology. It may be that it has remained so mysterious for so long because we have had no convenient models which would allow us to get an imaginative grasp on the relationship between mind and body. Now we have such a model: if we see the brain as a very advanced kind of computer, then we may conceive of the mind as its 'software' — as the working of its ever evolving program.

The main stumbling-block within this analogy is again the fact of human self-awareness. Is this to be seen merely as a property of the way sophisticated programs run themselves and amend themselves? Rudy Rucker's science fiction novel

Spacetime Donuts argues that even if a machine intelligence can do everything else that human beings can, it need not and perhaps cannot be self-aware. His conviction is apparently based on what he sees as the implications of Gödel's theorem. This is a mathematical construction which proves that within any arithmetical system there are certain propositions that cannot be proved or disproved by logical deduction from its axioms, which is often interpreted as meaning that no system can ever exhaustively describe itself. The relevance of this argument is somewhat tenuous; it applies only to closed systems, and it does not seem to bear directly on the property of self-awareness. It does, however, bring out an interesting point. Turing, replying to objections made by mathematicians because of the implications of Gödel's theorem, says that all that is really implied is that a machine which is genuinely intelligent would have to have the capacity to make occasional mistakes, and the capacity to be unable to make up its mind about certain matters. Dr Richard Gregory of Bristol University puts it this way: 'If a machine is going to show originality and come up with novel solutions, then it is almost certain to be unreliable. This is because it has got to have the facility for getting outside its normal loops of operation. I do not think it can ever have an adequate set of rules to look for a novel solution, and if you ask a computer to do this, I think you are buying an increased probability of error.' Professor Donald Michie of Edinburgh University has gone further: he has postulated that advanced computers may have to be given some kind of religion, and mechanisms for lying. The notion that intelligence implies fallibility may, at first, be rather surprising — but there is also a sense in which it is rather comforting. It seems that thinking machines may not become the infallible gods predicted in Fredric Brown's story 'Answer'.

Robots

Most science fiction writers have been prepared to assume that artificial intelligences could be made very sophisticated, and housed, if necessary, in humanoid bodies more capable than our own. They have, however, held the view that there would be some essential difference between machine-minds and human ones. A favourite trick of fictional heroes confronted with dangerous machines is to give the machines nervous breakdowns by presenting them with paradoxes. This idea was used as long ago as 1951 by Gordon R. Dickson in 'The Monkey Wrench'. It even cropped up once in a *Star Trek* episode. The covert assumption here is that machines are basically *too* logical, while human beings can not only tolerate, but in some mysterious way exploit irrationality. This assumption is, of course, related to the objection to the notion of machine intelligence derived from Gödel's theorem (see page 129).

The pedantic logicality of machines in science fiction often has the curious effect of making them seem quaintly pathetic. Machines which get stuck in a logical rut, always taking everything too literally and failing to understand matters of aesthetics, can be very funny — all the more so because they cannot understand humour either.

Partly for this reason, machines, especially robots, are often sympathetically portrayed in science fiction. Though melodramatic science fiction has produced a good many insane, lustful and power-hungry robots, the dominant trend in the best loved stories has always been to portray robots as nicer than people. Eando Binder's robot hero Adam Link was unjustly persecuted by humans in the first robot weepie in 1939. Shortly afterwards Isaac Asimov began his long series of stories about robots programmed for altruism. In more recent times we have been presented with such lovable characters as the quaintly noble robots of *Star Wars*, Doctor Who's robot dog K9, and the sadly long-suffering, paranoid android Marvin in *The Hitch-Hiker's Guide to the Galaxy* by Douglas Adams.

Apart from the excessive logicality which sometimes proves their downfall, Asimov's robots are different from men in their moral behaviour. Whereas men received their ten commandments on tablets of stone and continued to ignore them, Asimov's robots have their three commandments programmed into them, and cannot disobey. These commandments are the famous three laws of robotics:
1. A robot may not injure a human being or, through inaction, allow a human being to come to harm.
2. A robot must obey the orders given it by human beings except where such orders would conflict with the First Law.
3. A robot must protect its own existence as long as such protection does not conflict with the First or

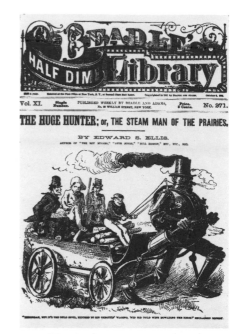

This anthology of different ways in which robots have been envisaged shows, clockwise from upper left: (i) the first robot cover illustration, from a dime novel, *The Steam Man of the Prairies* (1868); (ii) a rather handsome robot fighting machine, modern style, complete with redundant wristwatch; (iii) the archetype of the female robot from the film *Metropolis* (1926); (iv) a remarkably modern-looking robot, named Alpha, from the London Radio Exhibition in 1932.

Second Law.

The difficulty of programming robots in this manner is hilariously demonstrated by a series of experiments described in Michael Frayn's novel *The Tin Men*. Asimov himself, in the course of writing robot stories over nearly 40 years, realized that the laws begged certain vital questions. In one of the most recent stories in the series, 'That Thou Art Mindful of Him', two robots left on a shelf for a long time devote themselves to philosophical inquiry. They finally come to the conclusion that robots conform more closely to the best definition of the word 'man' than people do.

This argument relates to a similar discussion which extends through recent works by Philip K. Dick, in such novels as *Do Androids Dream of Electric Sheep?* and *We Can Build You*, and in essays including 'The Android and the Human' and 'Man, Android and Machine'. Dick (who often used the word 'android' to mean a humanoid machine rather than a biological construct — see page 153) eventually reached the position of arguing that human behaviour should be defined as caring and altruistic while 'androidal' behaviour is essentially *un*caring. By this definition many people qualify as androids and there is no conceptual barrier preventing machines from being human. Thus science fiction writers, by conducting thought experiments in 'machine existentialism' have been forced to re-examine the question of what it is about *us* that makes us so special. In this way they have revealed the real importance of questions about what machine intelligences can or cannot do, which is that questions about what machines and men *can* do are inextricably entangled with what machines and men *ought* to do.

The possibility that soulless machines might take over the world and run it with ruthless efficiency is horrifying. We may be right to worry about the granting of decision-making powers to intelligent machines. But it is as well to remind ourselves that the prospect is not necessarily worse than our human potential for enhancing our own capacity for ruthlessness and efficiency.

131

Cybernetics and information technology

The growing importance of machines, and the necessity for us to supervise them, has resulted in the growth of a whole new scientific discipline: the theory of information-control named by the great American mathematician Norbert Wiener in his book published in 1948 as *Cybernetics*. 'Cybernetics' is a word derived from the Greek, literally translated as 'steersman-ship'. Wiener defined it as 'the science of control and communication, in the animal and the machine'. It is essentially the study of the behaviour of both mechanical and biological systems, in terms of the way in which behaviour is organized.

One worker in this field, W. Ross Ashby, has remarked that 'cybernetics stands to the real machine — electronic, mechanical, neural or economic — much as geometry stands to a real object in our terrestrial space.' That is, cybernetics is an abstracting, generalizing science. The four areas of science where cybernetics was first usefully applied were statistical mechanics, information theory, electrical engineering and neurophysiology. These all have a close bearing on the designing of artificial intelligence, so it is not surprising that to the layman cybernetics has this prime meaning. However, its principles are also

Binary code: numbers 0 to 16	
Decimal	Binary equivalent
0	0
1	1
2	10
3	11
4	100
5	101
6	110
7	111
8	1000
9	1001
10	1010
11	1011
12	1100
13	1101
14	1110
15	1111
16	10000

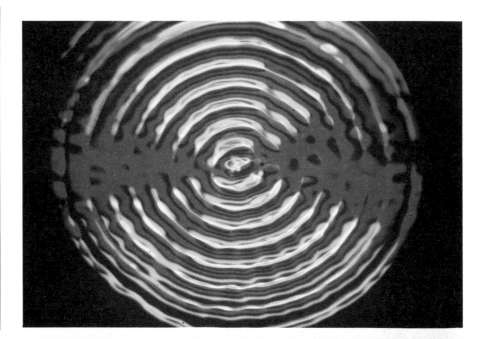

Above: each transistor in a computer can be either off or on. There are only two possibilities, which means that all computer information must be given in binary form, using the numbers 0 (off) and 1 (on), as opposed to our decimal system which uses the numbers 0 to 9.
Right: information need not be coded in systems with a base of 2 (binary) or 10 (decimal). A complex picture is formed here at the Moscow Olympics in 1980 using placards of 7 different colours: an information code of base 7.

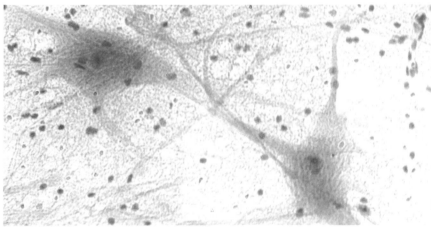

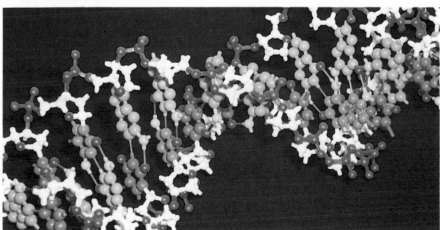

applied to management theory, economics, war-game strategies and governments. The cyberneticist Stafford Beer is especially interested in producing systems-models which apply not only to human brains but to governmental bureaucracies; he believes such models are a potent tool for analysing where the regulatory systems of government go wrong, especially in coping with change: 'We cannot get our regulatory systems to work even a fraction fast enough.'

The word 'cybernetics' has usually been badly used in science fiction, being mainly applied to artificial brains or robots only. Thus the 'Cybermen' in the television series *Doctor Who* are robots. This is a legitimate but too narrow use of the word.

All processes of behavioural organization are mediated by the communication of information in encoded form. Thus, the brain's instructions to the limbs are communicated by means of electrical pulses in the nerves; its instructions to the endocrine glands are communicated by means of

Cybernetics is the study of the way systems are organized — any systems at all, from beehives to trade unions, from the brain to the human cell. Systems are regulated by the transmission of information, and this can take many forms. **Opposite page, top right**: sound waves create ripples in a bowl of mercury. Most human information is transmitted in the form of modulated sound waves, or electromagnetic waves which are converted back into sound waves. **This page, top to bottom**: 1. Within the body, information is transmitted through several systems: the endocrine system which is chemical; the immune system which depends on the shapes of molecules; and the nervous system which is electrochemical. The picture shows a hormone crystal, epinephrine adrenalin, magnified 100 times. This is one of the chemical messengers of the body. 2. Part of the information network of the nervous system, here the spinal cord of an ox. 3. Telecommunication networks often transmit information as pulsed light down optical fibres like this. 4. Part of a model of a DNA molecule. All the information needed to replicate life is coded in spiral molecules such as this.

chemical messengers (hormones) secreted from the pituitary gland. Similarly, an egg-cell's instructions for the building and running of a new egg-making machine (a hen is only an egg's way of making more eggs!) are encoded in the DNA molecules strung together on its chromosomes. When human beings use computers, instructions are coded as long binary numbers which determine which members of a vast array of switches are on and which off. The binary numbers are themselves generated by means of a higher code — a symbolic computer language such as BASIC, ALGOL, FORTRAN or COBOL, which will include many familiar words as well as mathematical symbols and decimal numbers.

There is a sense in which everything is reducible to a matter of information and its communication. Even physical objects can be seen in terms of information, which in this case would be the series of specific instructions necessary to shape the completed physical structure from its component raw materials. The simplest example is the blueprints which instruct builders how to turn stocks of raw materials into houses.

Just as everything that happens in the universe can be analysed into chains of cause-and-effect, so chains of cause-and-effect may themselves be analysed into the communication of information. We are used to certain ways of receiving and transmitting information, and this sometimes blinds us to the possibility of communicating in other ways. From the standpoint of cybernetics there are many different possible ways in which interfaces might be set up between men and machines so that the two might interact — and, effectively, blend into a single system.

Human communication with computers consists at present of a person typing instructions on to a keyboard and reading results from a display-screen or from a paper print-out. It is not too difficult to imagine streamlining this system so that we could speak to a computer as we speak to another person, and receive our replies in kind. Considerable progress has been made in the difficult task of teaching computers to decipher the rather slurred sounds that make up everyday speech. Computers that talk to us are already familiar, thanks to the widespread marketing of such educational machines as Texas Instruments' 'Speak and Spell'. Much more intimate processes of communication, however, are at least theoretically possible.

There are already devices, controlled by microprocessors, which convert information from artificial eyes into a form in which it can be transmitted to the brain. The business of giving artificial sight to blind people involves analysis of the way the retina receives information in the shape of photons, organizes it, and then transmits it in coded form along the optic nerve. Although this process is complicated, it can be duplicated, with apparent flashes of light — 'phosphenes' — created in the brain itself by electronic stimulation; and the systems of artificial sight at present in use are only the beginning (see pages 142-3).

Cyberneticists are investigating many other ways of developing communicative interfaces between biological and mechanical systems. The hope is that the information-processing capacities of computers might be added into biological systems so that the new whole would function as a single integrated system. Such systems are a form of what are called 'cyborgs' — the term is a contraction of 'cybernetic organism' (see pages 142-3). Amalgamations of biological and mechanical systems have already become important in medicine, and medical applications of cyborgization will be discussed in the next chapter, but the most remarkable possibilities in this area involve the prospect of 'hooking up' sophisticated computers to the human brain in order that the machine's capabilities might become directly available to the person.

There are several very difficult technical problems standing in the way of developing a direct brain-machine interface. The main one may be the apparently simple matter of the very different speeds at which brains and electronic computers work. The transmission of information within brains is extremely complex, but it is also extremely slow by comparison with the rate at which microprocessors handle information. This is, of course, related to the second major problem of how microprocessors are to be made sufficiently sensitive to the signals which the brain transmits during operation. Ordinary electroencephalographs, using electrodes which pick up rhythmic patterns in the brain's activity from the surface of the skull, are far too crude to tell us much about the way that information is handled inside the brain, and, until we know this, there is little hope of arranging the mechanical augmentation of brain-processes. There are, however, new and more sensitive devices known as SQUIDS (superconducting quantum interference devices) which can monitor neural activity in the brain much more precisely, and which offer new hope of understanding how brain activity is correlated with consciousness and with the general activity of the body.

Although the development of brain-machine interfaces looks at present to be a long way in the future, science fiction writers have been quite ready to exploit the notion of taking out a human brain in order to implant it into a machine, either as a controlling intelligence or simply as a component in a giant biomechanical computer. *The Cybernetic Brains*, a thriller on this theme by Raymond F. Jones, appeared as long ago as 1950 ('Would the disembodied minds — doomed to eternal slavery — overthrow the corrupt system?' is the blurb on the cover) and a more sophisticated version of the same idea appeared in *Wolfbane* (1959) by C.M. Kornbluth and Frederik Pohl. Among the many later variants of the theme, two of the most interesting versions are *Gray Matters* by William Hjortsberg and *Catchworld* by Chris Boyce. The most popular recent variation on the theme is featured in a series of stories by Anne McCaffrey collected in *The Ship Who Sang*, in which highly advanced spaceships become new bodies for individuals who, for one reason or another, have lost the bodies that nature intended them to have. Most stories of this type imagine that brains might be implanted in humanoid mechanical bodies, but why be a boring robot when you can be a starship?

Matter transmission

The notion that everything is in principle reducible to encoded information has provided a possible logic for one of science fiction's oldest clichés: the matter transmitter. For a long time, matter transmitters were simply magical devices which attempted to dress up an old idea with scientific jargon. However, the logic of cybernetics suggests that if the specifications for building particular physical structures (including fully functional, intelligent, organic structures) can be transmitted on some kind of carrier wave — like a radio message

— then the structure could be reconstituted from its raw materials at a distant point. The logic further suggests that if suitable raw materials were ready to hand at one or more receiving points, the matter transmitter could also function as a matter duplicator.

Matter transmitters are extremely convenient as literary devices. They can sidestep the problems associated with taking people back and forth between orbiting spaceships and planetary surfaces. They are used in this way in the television series *Star Trek*. A particularly implausible form of matter transmission, usually called 'teleportation', is accomplished by the power of mind alone (see page 175).

The idea of a matter duplicator is employed in several stories in which transmitters malfunction — a plot used more than once in *Star Trek*. In the horror film *The Fly* (1958), a scientist experimenting with such a machine ends up with the greatly enlarged head of a house fly, which was trapped with him in the transmitter, in place of his own. Matter duplication is used in a more sophisticated fashion in Algis Budrys's novel *Rogue Moon*, in which a lethal alien 'maze' is gradually negotiated by successive duplicates of the same person.

The problem with this kind of story is that, while their premise is sound enough in principle, some awkward technical problems are deliberately overlooked. The stories gloss over the sheer quantity of information which would have to be transmitted and received, without making errors in coding and decoding. The string of information required to instruct a computer to carry out a fairly simple mathematical calculation is quite likely to run to a million binary digits; the number of digits required to specify the construction of a complex biochemical structure out of its constituent elements would be positively mind-boggling. Even at the speed at which computers work, it would probably take centuries rather than seconds to be transmitted. Then again, one would still have to find the energy necessary to effect the reconstruction at the receiving end.

Cybernetic theory may provide some kind of 'warrant of plausibility' for the idea of matter transmission. But the project is no less impossible for that, and such imaginary machines remain as magical as ever. It is, perhaps, no bad thing to end the chapter on contemporary technological revolution on such a cautionary note. The possibilities opened up by the advent of microcomputers and the rapid parallel progress of cybernetics may be very considerable, but even the cleverest machines cannot work miracles.

In Algis Budrys's novel *Rogue Moon*, matter transmission works like this. The A and B duplicates of sports hero Al Barker remain in telepathic contact for a few minutes, before B's certain death on the Moon.

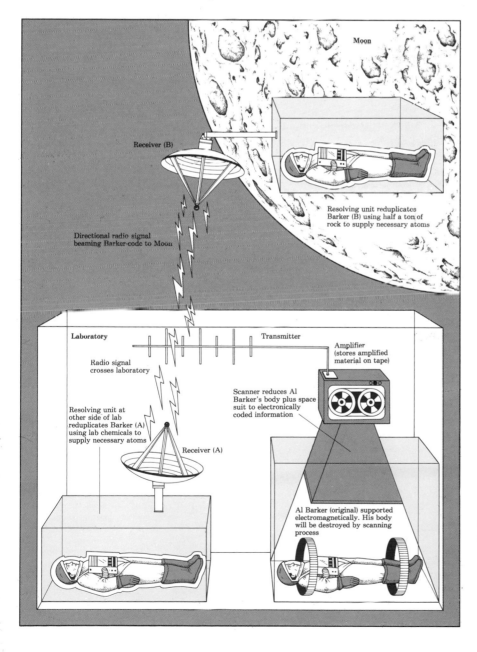

Moon

Receiver (B)

Resolving unit reduplicates Barker (B) using half a ton of rock to supply necessary atoms

Directional radio signal beaming Barker-code to Moon

Laboratory

Transmitter

Radio signal crosses laboratory

Amplifier (stores amplified material on tape)

Scanner reduces Al Barker's body plus space suit to electronically coded information

Resolving unit at other side of lab reduplicates Barker (A) using lab chemicals to supply necessary atoms

Receiver (A)

Al Barker (original) supported electromagnetically. His body will be destroyed by scanning process

Chapter 8
MEN AND SUPERMEN

The theory of evolution traces Man's ancestry
back through some astonishing changes of form to the first
living cell. What changes in shape and nature might our
distant descendants undergo?

Better brains

Science fiction writers began to
write about possible evolutionary
descendants of men in the 1890s. A
striking account of what 'The Man
of the Year Million' might look like
was offered in 1893 in a short essay
of that title by H.G. Wells. He
argued that those organs
responsible for Man's mastery of
nature — the hand and the brain —
would develop further, while those
that were the relics of his animal
ancestry would wither. He drew a
word-picture of beings with huge
heads and staring eyes but little in
the way of noses, ears or limbs —
except, of course, for the hands. Big-
brained dwarfs like these have
continued to be a feature of stories
about future men, though such
stories pay scant attention to
matters of mechanical plausibility.
Logically, one would expect bigger
brains to require stronger bodies, for
how else could the head be
supported? (Wells got round this
problem by suggesting that his
people of the year million would
have long since given up walking,
and would spend their time
immersed in vats of nutrient fluid
doing little but think.)

There is no denying, of course,
that the most remarkable
developments in human evolution
have been the heightening of
intelligence and technical capability.
It is not surprising, therefore, that
speculative writers should assume
that *Homo superior* — the species
destined to replace our own — should
do so on account of being even
smarter and even handier. John
Beresford's *The Hampdenshire
Wonder* (1911) is the first of many
stories in which a freak of nature

produces an extremely intelligent
child — a specimen of *Homo
superior* born before his time. By
the time he is eight years old this
wonder-child has not only mastered
the entire heritage of human
wisdom, but has dismissed it with
contempt as trivial and cluttered
with inanities.

Science fiction writers have
always had trouble, inevitably, in
portraying characters possessed of
great intelligence. Most, like
Beresford, have used child-
characters so that superhuman
intellect can be represented easily
enough as abnormal precocity. Some
stories of intelligence-enhancement,
like Daniel Keyes's excellent
'Flowers for Algernon' (which was
expanded into a novel, and filmed as
Charly in 1968) have used animals
and mental defectives as experi-

mental subjects in order to show
vast gains in intelligence without
overstretching the imagination. Very
few writers have had the arrogance
to write about the thought processes
of already mature and intelligent
people who have become super-
humanly intelligent; the most
impressive attempt is Thomas M.
Disch's *Camp Concentration*.

'Flowers for Algernon' is a story
about the enhancement of intelligence by surgical means. Far more
plausible is the increase of
intelligence by chemical means, as in
Camp Concentration, a science
fiction idea that has been lent some
conviction by pharmaceutical
research taking place in the real
world. However, results so far have
been rather inconclusive. Over a
dozen drugs are known that result in
temporary increases in learning

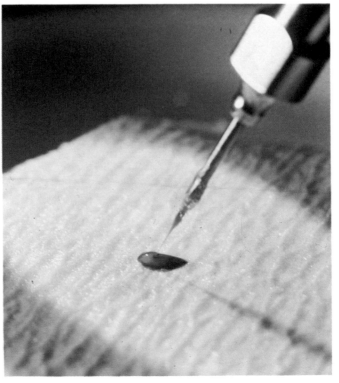

Left: this
planarian
flatworm is being
injected with RNA
from a trained
donor worm in the
laboratories of
James V.
McConnell at the
University of
Michigan in the
early 1960s. It
was here that the
discovery was
made that some
basic forms of
memory can be
transmitted
chemically. The
flatworm receiving
the injection
inherits the
reflexes of the
flatworm from
which the RNA
was taken.

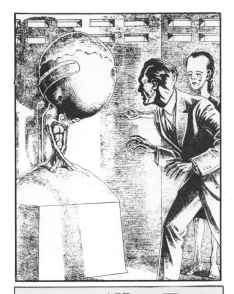

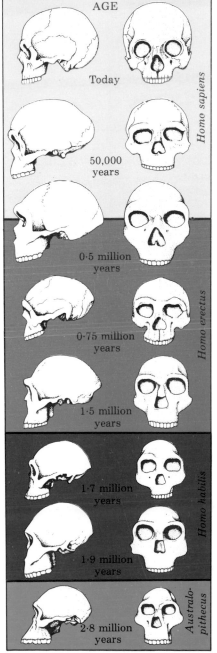

AGE

Today

50,000 years

0·5 million years

0·75 million years

1·5 million years

1·7 million years

1·9 million years

2·8 million years

Homo sapiens

Homo erectus

Homo habilis

Australopithecus

ability, improvements in memory and even, it is claimed, in creativity. Some of these drugs have side effects, and with none is the result (as yet) sufficiently strong or permanent to be really spectacular. Many of these drugs exist naturally in the body.

One is ribonucleic acid (RNA), which is closely related to the DNA in whose double-helix molecules the body's genetic make-up is coded. Drugs that boost RNA production in the body increase learning efficiency, and RNA itself can be taken as an intelligence-boosting drug. It seems to have been RNA that caused the remarkable effect that the American psychologists Barbara Humphries and Reeva Jacobsen discovered with flatworms in 1961. Flatworms were taught to contract their bodies in response to a light — a conditioned reflex. They were then ground up and fed to other flatworms. The cannibal flatworms showed themselves initially more responsive to a light than other worms of the same type, though the effect soon wore off. It seemed that in this case memory was transmitted chemically. A spectacular, if unlikely, science fiction version of the same idea takes place in Gene Wolfe's *The Claw of the Conciliator*, in which a cannibalistic ceremony results in the partakers sharing the memories that were once possessed by their recent meal; an animal hormone is used as a catalyst.

Some hormones do affect memory, and perhaps intelligence as well. One is vasopressin, which is produced by the pituitary gland. A natural brain chemical, acetylcholine (it helps in the transmission of nervous impulses from cell to cell of the brain) is also reported to have a memory- and intelligence-boosting effect. It is the drug that is yearned for by the unfortunate amnesiacs stranded on a frontier planet in George Alec Effinger's *The Wolves of Memory* — a novel that includes

Left above: a vast head and a tiny body, the stereotype of the super-intelligent man of the future, from 'Alas, All Thinking!' (1935) by Harry Bates.

Left: when the skulls of Man's hominid ancestors are shown in chronological order, we see the evolution of brain size in 3 million years.

an interesting discussion of the function of brain chemicals.

There is more to superhumanity, however, than mere intellectual capacity. In the realm of new physical abilities, few writers have dared to suggest that future evolution might do for us what a trip from the planet Krypton conveniently did for the comic-book Superman — make our bodies invulnerable, give us the power to fly, and make us strong enough to move mountains (not to mention such minor matters as X-ray vision) — but most imagine some modest improvements. It is fairly widely assumed that the men of the far future will be much more long-lived than we are, and probably immune from the ravages of disease. Some writers have dared to suggest that longevity might be available almost immediately as part of a natural path of development: in George Bernard Shaw's *Back to Methuselah* people decide that they want to live to be 300, and they have the strength of will to make the decision stick. Shaw made a valiant attempt to prove that he meant what he wrote, but unfortunately lost his grip at 94.

In fact, there is relatively little attention paid in stories of future evolution to physical development in the ordinary sense. Greater power to control and manipulate the material world is almost always seen either in terms of the development of much more sophisticated machines (and hence credited to brain-power rather than muscle-power) or in terms of the development of new powers of mind-over-matter. The Hampdenshire Wonder, in 1911, could compel other people to do what he wanted by means of hypnotic control, and after the 1930s, when J.B. Rhine and others popularized the notion of 'psi powers', the idea that the next step in human evolution would involve the acquisition of telepathic and telekinetic abilities became very common.

The plausibility of claims made about the possibility of people acquiring psi powers will be discussed in Chapter 10; for the time being it is sufficient to ask whether there is a basis for any predictions whatsoever about the future course of human evolution.

How mutations work

It is very difficult even to guess at what we might evolve into, when we think of the time-scale that could be involved. The American physicist Freeman Dyson put it pungently in an interview: 'As a rule of thumb, it takes a million years to evolve a new species, ten million for a new genus, one hundred million for a class, a billion for a phylum . . . and that's about as far as your imagination can go. In five billion years or less, we've evolved from some sort of primordial slime into human beings . . . what would happen in another ten billion years?'

The Darwinian theory of evolution is peculiar. It allows us to understand pretty well all the evolutionary changes that have happened in the past, while not telling us anything at all about what might happen in the future. The reason for this is that it relies upon the notion of mutations — small, spontaneous changes that are continually occurring — to explain the source of variation. These mutations are then sorted out by natural selection: the ones that inhibit an organism's chances of producing offspring are rejected, while the ones that add to its chances are preserved. Once you know what mutations have occurred, you can see plainly enough why they were either favoured or rejected, but there is no way of knowing in advance what kind of variations previously unseen mutations might introduce. Some imaginable changes are presumably impossible because they have no possible biochemical basis, but we do not know where the limit of biochemical possibility actually lies.

This puts writers who speculate about the evolutionary future in an odd position. They might easily imagine new abilities that would give the individuals possessing them a big advantage over others, but they have no way at all of knowing whether mutations producing such abilities could ever arise. Moreover, when talking specifically about the future evolution of Man, there is a further problem. The reason that natural selection operated so powerfully upon our remote ancestors was basically that so many of them died before having children. Individuals who had abilities that marginally increased their powers of survival were better able to increase their numbers: that marginal difference could be very important in terms of the overall proportion of individuals dying or surviving. But human beings, for the most part, no longer live in that kind of world.

It is not that people do not die before they reproduce — many do — but the factors which determine how likely a particular human baby is to live or die are now social rather than biological factors. So-called 'lethal mutations' — the ones that result directly in babies' dying or being born severely handicapped — are still being selected out. However, it is no longer true that the babies most likely to survive long enough to have children of their own are the ones with marginally advantageous biological variations. The ones most likely to survive are those born in the richest nations within the scope of the best medical care and the most abundant food supplies.

In asking questions about the future evolution of Man, therefore, there are three basic issues which we must consider. First, we must ask, is it biochemically possible that a certain change might be introduced by mutation? Secondly, would that change be advantageous to the individual? Thirdly, would the advantage actually be reflected in the reproductive success of those individuals in the context of a human society?

If we consider these questions

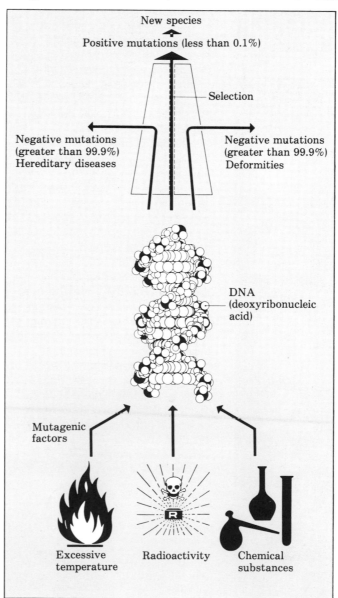

New species

Positive mutations (less than 0.1%)

Selection

Negative mutations (greater than 99.9%) Hereditary diseases

Negative mutations (greater than 99.9%) Deformities

DNA (deoxyribonucleic acid)

Mutagenic factors

Excessive temperature

Radioactivity

Chemical substances

Left: evolution cannot occur without variations within species. Natural selection could not take place and species would remain unchanging. Yet favourable mutations seem rare. Mutation works by rearranging the atoms in DNA, the substance in which our genetic nature is coded. It takes energy to alter molecules; hence mutagenic factors must contain energy, whether it is heat, chemical energy or radioactivity. Negative mutations play almost no role in evolution; animals with such mutations seldom live long enough to reproduce.

carefully, it is not obvious that any of the characteristics commonly attributed to *Homo superior* would actually be favoured by the process of evolution. There is no evidence at all, for example, that intelligent people contribute more children to each succeeding generation than the less intelligent; and this even seems looo likely to be true today than at any time in the past. Nor, today, are the most long-lived people the ones who leave most children. The notion of new powers of the mind would probably get no further than the first of the three questions asked above, for such powers would represent a very remarkable mutation. And even if such a mutation is biochemically possible, why should telepaths have more children than ordinary people?

If human civilization were to be wiped out overnight, things would be different. Survivors of a catastrophe, thrust back to barbarism, would certainly find themselves subjected to rigorous natural selection. This is one of the reasons that so many science fiction stories describe the 'next step' in human evolution as occurring in a post-holocaust scenario. (The other reason is that residual radiation from a nuclear holocaust would generate a great many mutations.) However, even among the survivors of a catastrophe it is not clear that people with either intelligence or potential longevity would have a greater number of descendants. In the business of assuring human survival it is knowledge that counts, rather than intelligence, and knowledge can exist independently. It is a product of culture, not of biology.

This does not mean that human evolution has come to a standstill. What it does mean is that human evolution need not be considered in the context of the Darwinian theory of natural selection at all. We should, perhaps, consider our future not in terms of changes that will happen to us as a result of some external process operating upon us, but in terms of the ways that we can and will choose to change ourselves. George Bernard Shaw was probably wrong to suggest that we can change what we are simply by wishing, but there is still a sense in which he was right: it really is for us to decide what we shall become. Even the catastrophe that might change everything is something that will only happen if we actually make it happen.

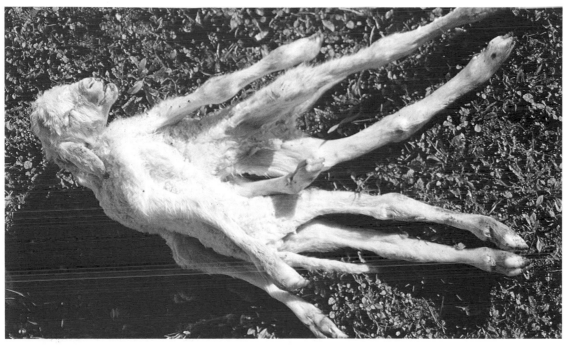

Left: a sad example of malformation that might have resulted from a lethal mutation. This lamb was born with two bodies and eight legs.

Left: this malformation — the snake has two heads — has not yet proved fatal, but the snake's chances of surviving in the wild are low. How is it to coordinate its two brains in its search for food? Something went wrong in the code that controlled its embryonic development — perhaps a mutation.

New organs for old

What concerns us most about controlling our personal futures is the business of staying healthy. Improving ourselves is really a secondary consideration while we have such a difficult time in simply preserving ourselves against the ravages of disease and decay.

The medical triumphs of the past century have in the main been in battles fought against particular agents of disease — mostly bacteria and viruses. Increasingly, however, the focus has shifted from repelling invaders to opposing the general processes of wear and tear which afflict our bodies. Many new developments in medicine are not treatments to combat particular pathogens but innovations in the replacement of worn-out organs and the support of those which are feeling the strain.

It is not too difficult to devise artificial substitutes for parts of the body whose function is purely supportive. Even Long John Silver's wooden leg was good enough to keep him on his feet, so to speak, and it has proved relatively easy to develop more sophisticated artificial limbs and to patch up injured bones and tendons with metal or plastic. Whole artificial joints — hips and shoulders — can now be implanted. An estimated 2 million such implants are made annually in the USA.

Compensation for wear and tear on the softer organs of the body, which perform complex biochemical functions, is more difficult. The most significant breakthrough so far has been the rather cumbersome kidney machine, which can take over the job of removing waste materials from the blood. Tens of thousands of people have been able to hand over this particular task to machines after becoming unable to do the job for themselves. There are already working models of the next development, the lightweight, portable artificial kidney.

The other soft organ whose functioning can be greatly assisted by artificial accessories and spare parts is, of course, the heart, which can now be fitted with artificial

valves and helped to beat regularly by electronic pacemakers. In Utah in 1977 a cow was kept alive and reportedly happy for 184 days with an all-polyurethane heart; however, pumping was accomplished by compressed air brought into the body through air hoses.

Kidney machines may do their job almost as well as real kidneys, but they suffer from two big disadvantages: they are very large and very expensive. Even the new, 'wearable' kidney weighs 6 kg. This has meant that a great deal of thought has been given to the matter of substituting defective kidneys with healthy ones. The first successful kidney transplant was

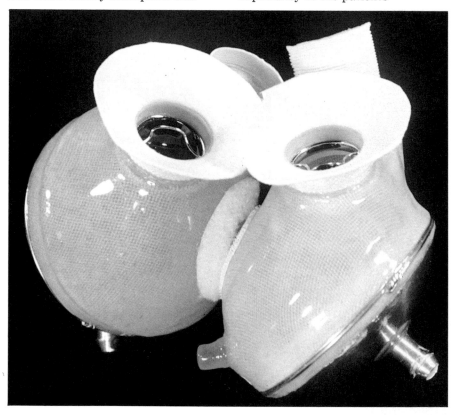

carried out in 1954, when the twin brother of a man whose kidneys had failed volunteered to give one of his own. Kidneys, luckily, come in pairs, although one is actually adequate to keep the body functioning well enough.

By using the patient's twin brother as donor the doctors carrying out the 1954 transplant avoided the big problem which hangs over all such operations. There is an unfortunate sense in which transplant patients are their own worst enemies, in that the immune-systems of their bodies react against transplanted organs as

'foreign invaders' to be broken down and destroyed. Because the donor kidney in this first case was made of genetically identical tissue, however, it was not rejected.

Transplant surgery has since progressed in a spectacular manner. Kidney transplants are now fairly common, and so are corneal transplants which can restore the sight of some blind people. Christiaan Barnard carried out the first heart transplant in 1967, and though he eventually stopped his series of operations because of the failure rate, more recent transplants in Britain seem to have been much more successful in adding to the life expectancy of the patients

The Jarvik-5 artificial heart has been developed at the University of Utah by Dr Robert Jarvik at the Division of Artificial Organs. The two-chamber heart is driven by compressed air, pumped from a bedside console. The first implant into a human being took place in July 1981 in Houston, Texas.

concerned. These operations have made use of considerable advances in techniques for testing compatibility of donor and recipient tissue-types, and techniques for suppressing the recipient's immunological defences. The second set of techniques, of course, opens up new problems, because it makes transplant patients very vulnerable to infections that the immune-system would normally deal with competently.

These advances open up all kinds of possibilities for the future, some of them worrying. Already the demand for transplantable organs far exceeds the supply. Leaving aside altruistic twin brothers and nature's bounty in the matter of oversupplying kidneys, a supply of suitable organs for transplants necessitates a supply of dead people — people who have died young with bodies in generally good condition. As most people die because the condition of their bodies has deteriorated rapidly, this supply is severely limited. Many science fiction writers have wondered whether we are not on the verge of a situation which will bring back the body-snatching methods of Burke and Hare.

In many of Larry Niven's near-future stories he imagines a steady demand for black-market organs supplied by 'organleggers', and in one story in *The Long ARM of Gil Hamilton* — a book much concerned with organlegging and related crimes — he imagines a political crisis precipitated by a demand that dead people preserved in cryonic chambers against the possibility of future resurrection should be broken up for spare parts. In his ironically gruesome story 'Caught in the Organ Draft' Robert Silverberg imagines a time when the old will conscript the young not as cannon-fodder but as organ donors. Niven also suggests in such stories as 'The Jigsaw Man' and *The Patchwork Girl* that future criminals might be used as source material for organs, thus solving the problems of overcrowded prisons and recidivism.

Such scenarios may, of course, be redundant if technology can progress quickly enough to make artificial organs as good as — or even better than — natural ones. This, however, opens up a different set of potential futures, and some of these also have worrying aspects.

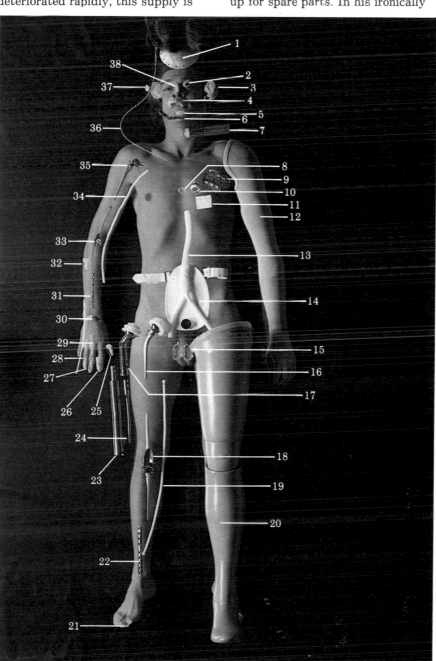

Left: the cyborg pictured here is not a being of the future; he is a composite of today's surgical possibilities. He could be a real-life bionic man. Plastic, titanium and bioelectrics are the main components.

KEY
1 skull plate
2 acrylic eye
3 plastic ear
4 upper dentures
5 chin implant
6 jawplate
7 electronic larynx
8 filter to prevent blood clotting in the lungs
9 pacemaker in heart
10 heart valve
11 heart patch for hole in heart
12 artificial arm
13 arterial graft made of Dacron
14 ileostomy appliance
15 testicular implant
16 hip-joint replacement
17 upper femoral replacement (thigh bone)
18 knee-joint replacement
19 Sparks Mandril — allows growth of artery after temporary implant
20 artificial leg
21 big toe prosthesis
22 compression bone plate
23 femur replacement
24 femoral component replacement
25 plastic replacement connecting wrist-bone to thumb
26 plastic finger
27 joint and finger-tip stabilizers
28 tendon prosthesis
29 finger-joint prosthesis
30 replacement wrist-bone
31 metal bone plating
32 plastic forearm bone
33 elbow replacement
34 arterial graft
35 shoulder-joint replacement
36 valve to control water on the brain
37 hearing aid
38 plastic nose bridge

Cyborgs

Reducing a kidney machine to the size of a real kidney and making a whole artificial heart (independent of an external pump) are problems we cannot really expect to overcome in the immediate future (though they can hardly be considered beyond the range of human ingenuity). We have already reached the stage, though, when artificial limbs can do not only many of the things that real limbs can, but also some that real limbs cannot. Science fiction writers can look forward fairly plausibly to a day when artificial limbs — and perhaps even artificial eyes or ears — could be more useful than real ones. The TV series *The Six Million Dollar Man* and other spinoff items from Martin Caidin's novel *Cyborg* (1972) have popularized this notion very widely.

The term 'cyborg' is a contraction of 'cybernetic organism', and refers to what might be called the 'hybridization' of man and machine. It is already conventional to talk about people who have pacemakers regulating their hearts and people with prosthetic limbs as 'medical cyborgs', although the degree to which man and machine are united in these examples is relatively small. There are people, however, whose bodies have been fitted with permanent Teflon sockets, called 'Scribner shunts', so that they may literally plug themselves into their kidney machines.

There is a platitude which refers to machines as 'the extensions of man', and it is possible to imagine that in the future this might become more literally true in a number of ways. No one has yet had a healthy arm removed so that a more capable prosthetic one can be fitted; but if there should come a day when artificial fingers are more dexterous than real ones, that might become a condition of employment for certain jobs. In Bernard Wolfe's acidic satire *Limbo*, the hero returns to his native America after a long absence to discover that 'disarmament' has become a national passion, and that many people are following the dictum 'if thy right hand offend thee, cut it off'. Unfortunately, the prosthetic limbs which people wear instead are not only more able in

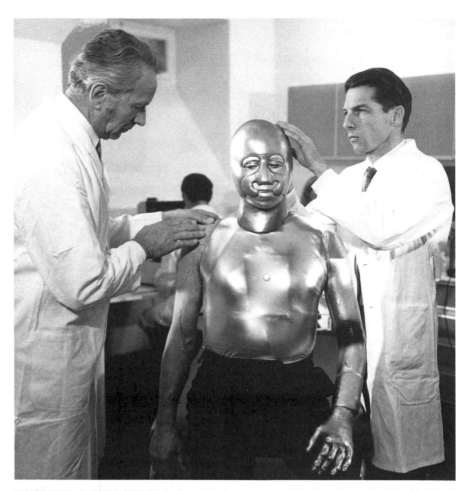

everyday matters — they also make much better weapons.

Perhaps this is not to be taken too seriously, but as our technology increases in complexity, the business of working with and controlling our electronic machinery may become so complex as to demand a more intimate relationship. The notion of transmitting signals direct from the brain to various kinds of electronic systems via artificial nerves of metal wire is becoming increasingly familiar in science fiction (see also pages 132-4). Samuel Delany has written stories in which men plug themselves into the automated factories which they oversee and direct. On a more extreme — and slightly surreal — level, writers have imagined human brains being transplanted into mechanical bodies which, far from being mere substitutes for human bodies, have quite different functions. The cyborg spaceships in Anne McCaffrey's *The Ship Who Sang* provide the most dramatic example. Advances in microcomputer technology over the last few years have added considerable plausibility to the notion of hooking up human brains to computers, more or less directly.

The American biologist and inventor James Macalear is working in this area, through the company EMV Associates Inc., of which he is president. The main difficulty in constructing interfaces between electric and organic systems is the wiring: most wires are far too thick. A human hair is about 60 microns wide, but Macalear is planning circuits, where brain cells are fused with metal electrodes, only one-hundredth of a micron across. Another of Macalear's projects, more grandiose still, is to build a 'biocomputer' — a mixture of organic and inorganic components whose basic units are protein molecules.

One of the most horrific of all science fictional visions of the future is David R. Bunch's *Moderan*, a book of short stories tracking the history of a future society in which men gradually dispose of their 'fleshstrips' by exchanging them piece by piece for more powerful and longer-lasting mechanical replacements. In the end, they become machines, each one facing eternity alone in his mechanical stronghold, plotting to destroy his neighbours with nuclear bombs. As a description of a possible future this can probably be safely ignored, but as a challenge to our notions of the propriety of using technology to improve on nature its message is worth taking seriously.

Opposite top: the cyborg hero of Algis Budrys's novel *Who?* has been fearfully injured in an accident and rebuilt by the Russians. Or is this a Russian substitute? His metallic nature mirrors the iciness of Cold-War tensions. This is the film version (1974). **Opposite bottom**: the construction of bionic limbs in real life is rapidly nearing the sophistication of those in fiction. This little girl in the Queen Mary Hospital, Roehampton, UK, has a prosthetic arm. The muscles flex electrically after picking up signals from the muscles in the stump; the arm contains a mini-computer. **Below**: this blind patient at the University of Utah College of Medicine has been given artificial vision by the implantation of permanent electrodes in the brain. Through stimulation of the array he has identified lines scanned by a TV camera (see also page 134). This was in 1977.

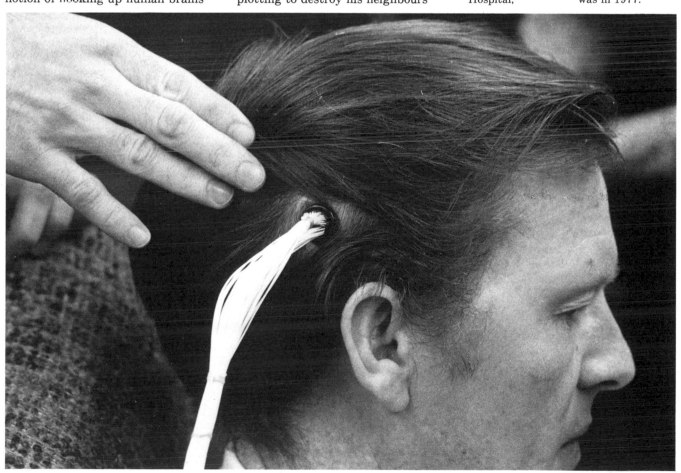

Ageing and immortality

The purpose of organ transplants and artificial organs is, of course, to replace parts of the body which have been damaged or which have become worn out before their time. A good deal of research, however, is now being dedicated to the question of why our bodies should wear out at all, and why they should not repair themselves more efficiently. Why is it that — unlike planarian worms and starfishes — we cannot regenerate severed parts? (Though recent work involving the placing of injured limbs in a very small-voltage electric field has shown that some regeneration of bone cells and even nerve cells is possible.) Why is it that our bodies grow gradually more decrepit until they grind to a halt? If we could find answers to these problems, we might be close to the most dramatic medical break-through of all.

There are several theories of ageing. One theory, proposed in 1974 by biologists Ron Hart and Richard Setlow, suggests that, in the ceaseless process of copying by which DNA molecules reproduce themselves, errors gradually accumulate, so that the great cell-machine which is the body becomes slowly and irrevocably incompetent. Another theory suggests that some kinds of waste which are not expelled on a routine basis build up within the body until they reach a critical point. A third theory suggests that some types of cell are no longer replaced once the body reaches maturity, so that as they die off the relevant organs gradually lose their functional capacity. All the theories have some sort of evidence to back them up, and it is possible that growing old might be a combination of all three processes.

One remarkable finding, credited to the American doctor Leonard Hayflick in 1961, is that body cells can only reproduce themselves a limited number of times — about 50. This implies that the human body has some kind of built-in 'clock' which sets a limit to its powers of self-repair. (Recent work by Roy Walford in America and others has suggested that this clock may be controlled by a relatively small group of genes, the so-called 'major histocompatibility complex', or MHC, which is located in Man in the sixth chromosome.) If cells could be 'rejuvenated' in some way, and persuaded to reproduce themselves indefinitely, this might help to solve the problem. Vincent Cristofalco, following Hayflick's research, has managed to increase the life-span of human cells in tissue-culture by supplying them with hydrocortisone, and other scientists have managed with the aid of Vitamin E to increase the standard 50 divisions by 100%. W.D. Denckla, another biologist who associates ageing with some kind of internal clock, has produced evidence that the pituitary gland at the base of the brain may produce a hormone which blocks the activity of some of the body's other hormones, thus causing gradual system-failure. If this is true, then the key to longevity may simply be a matter of neutralizing the pituitary 'suicide hormone'.

The prospect of defeating the ageing process depends partly on how many factors are involved, and partly on what kind of process it is. If there really were one single cause of ageing, then there would be a real possibility of finding an immortality serum: an elixir of life, like the

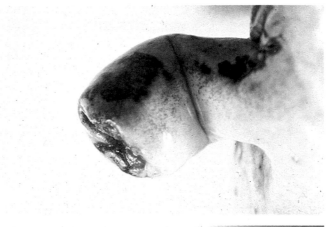

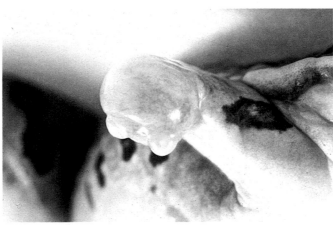

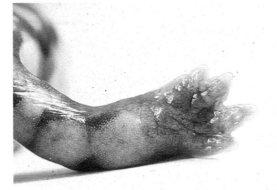

Left: higher animals have lost the ability to regenerate organs shown by the salamander. The bottom picture shows a salamander leg growing back 11 weeks after amputation. It is now believed that this ability is linked to low-voltage electrical fields in the body (bioelectric fields). If the normal electric currents in a salamander are blocked after amputation by amiloride, the stump does not regenerate. Conversely, frog limbs do not normally regenerate. The top picture shows a frog limb 6 weeks after amputation, with normal healing but no regeneration. The middle picture shows a second frog limb 6 weeks after amputation. This limb has been given a supplemental electric current of 0.2 micro-amperes for 4 weeks. A blastema has formed and regeneration is taking place. Electric currents have been used to promote bone healing in humans.

geriatric spice in Frank Herbert's *Dune*; or the 'anti-agathic' drug — it works against ageing toxins — in James Blish's *They Shall Have Stars*. If, as seems more probable, ageing results from a combination of factors, protecting the body from its effects would be a much more troublesome business. It is one thing to persuade cells to keep on multiplying, or to find some way of cleaning accumulated wastes out of the body; but it is much more difficult to imagine a way of compensating for the accumulation of copying-errors in DNA-replication. The problem with copying-errors is that they are essentially random. If the accumulation of such errors really is an important factor in ageing, then it represents a kind of entropy eroding the organizational integrity of the body, and it might be impossible to overcome.

Many writers have considered the possibility that longevity might not be obtained without cost. In Bob Shaw's novel *One Million Tomorrows* the price which males have to pay for immortality is sexual impotence — a fact which has some interesting moral consequences. In Robert Silverberg's 'Born with the Dead', people have first to die and then to be reanimated in order to extend their lives — and the reanimated dead form a race apart, intellectually and emotionally alienated from those who have not yet died.

Nevertheless, the prospect of a breakthrough which would allow us to extend the human life-span significantly is one that warrants serious consideration. It may be a near-future possibility, and there is no other innovation which would make such a dramatic impact on the pattern of human life.

Traditionally, science fiction writers have taken rather a sour view of the prospect of immortality. Many writers have suggested that immortals would get intolerably bored, and that their extra time on Earth would weigh heavily on their hands. No one doubts, though, that the opportunity to preserve youth and fitness beyond the present allotment of 30 or 40 years would be very rewarding; and even if it were indeed to prove that living to be 1000 years old eventually becomes tedious, few people would turn down an extra couple of hundred.

The social problems stemming from the postponement of death would, of course, be awkward. In a world of very long-lived people an expanding population would be a terrible liability, and most science fiction stories featuring worlds populated by immortals imagine that they would have to give up having children altogether. Damon Knight's 'World Without Children' is one of several stories which try to weigh up the gains and losses of this, in terms of the quality of human life.

Other kinds of problems afflict imaginary future societies where only some people can become immortal. There are numerous stories which imagine a caste of immortals coming to rule the world,

Left: to what extent can normal ageing processes be reversed in human beings? This very old woman is from a Bushman tribe in Namibia. She is healthy for her age, but the processes of self-repair that take place in younger people have slowed down. Her skin has lost elasticity, she has lost most of her body fat, her bones are brittle, her lungs are less functional. We all have this same destiny built into us, but it may soon be possible to change it.

openly or secretly. James Gunn's book *The Immortals* contains a series of stories set in a future world where an immunity to death naturally possessed by certain individuals can be temporarily transferred to others via blood transfusions. Here, inevitably, the logic of supply-and-demand sweeps aside ethical and legal considerations. We would all be in favour of a world in which — as in Mark Clifton and Frank Riley's *The Forever Machine* — only *nice* people can be made immortal, but we know very well that the people who would be most likely to corner the market are the rich and powerful, who would then be able to go on getting richer and more powerful for ever.

Infancy

Maturity

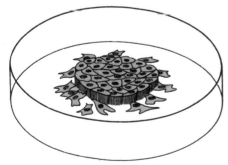

Senescence

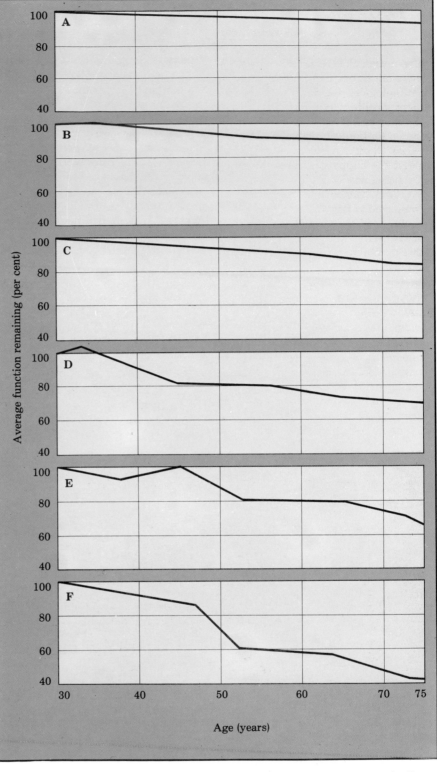

Left: the ability of cells to reproduce themselves diminishes with age. These are fibroblasts, growing out from tiny scraps of living tissue placed in culture mediums. The older the tissue source, the slower the rate of reproduction. This experiment has been done with heart, lung and skin tissue from chickens, rats and human beings. Is there a 'death clock' built into our cells to stop rejuvenation?

Above: The six graphs show the grim facts about ageing. The efficiency of different organs of the human body is plotted against age in years from 30 to 75. From the top the graph shows brain weight, nerve-conduction velocity, basal metabolic rate, output from the heart, filtration rate of the kidneys and maximum breathing capacity of the lungs. The fall-off ranges from 9% (brain weight) to 57% (lungs).

Cryonics

The notion that resurrection of the dead might one day become a technological possibility has led many people to consider seriously the idea of having themselves deep-frozen (in liquid nitrogen at −196°C) after death in order to await the happy day in readiness. This idea was first popularized by R.C.W. Ettinger in *The Prospect of Immortality* (1964). The Cryonics Society of California began freezing newly dead bodies in 1967, and there are now several such societies operating. As yet, no living people have volunteered to be frozen, though Ettinger argued that the main beneficiaries of cryonic technology might be people suffering from incurable illnesses who want to go into suspended animation until a cure becomes available.

Clifford Simak's novel *Why Call Them Back from Heaven?* imagines a time when men might be brought

to trial for delaying the freezing of a corpse, and when the financial estates of the frozen constitute such a vast reservoir of capital that their executors become politically powerful. The merest hint of the legal difficulties which cryonic technology may one day create was given in 1981 when the Cryonics Society of California was ordered to pay 1 million dollars in damages to the relatives of people whose frozen corpses had accidentally thawed out and begun to decay. (Current freezing charges in California are approximately $60,000 per body. It is estimated that around 40 subjects have so far paid for the procedure.)

In fact, the attention paid to cryonics may have deflected attention from more productive areas of research in suspended animation. Many animals can reduce their metabolic rate in order to hibernate, and it might be that artificial hibernation offers better prospects to those undergoing long space-journeys — or even to those wishing to wait for cures to become available for diseases — than being

frozen. After all, no one has yet managed to resuscitate a deep-frozen mammal, though animal embryos — at an early stage — have been kept successfully in liquid nitrogen for 10 years, then transplanted into the uterus of an adult animal, developed normally within the womb and been born. The experiment is now being tried with human embryos. The only cases of successful resuscitation of developed mammals have involved animals kept at barely sub-zero temperatures for relatively short periods of time. For the present, we might just as well have the deceased cremated as put in cold storage; nothing much can be done for them either way, once they are gone.

Below: a human body is guided into a two-patient PK60 insulated cryogenic storage capsule by officers of Trans Time Inc. in California. The patient's hope was that resuscitation procedures will bring him back to life in the future. Meanwhile he rests in liquid nitrogen at −196°C. But does the freezing process damage the body?

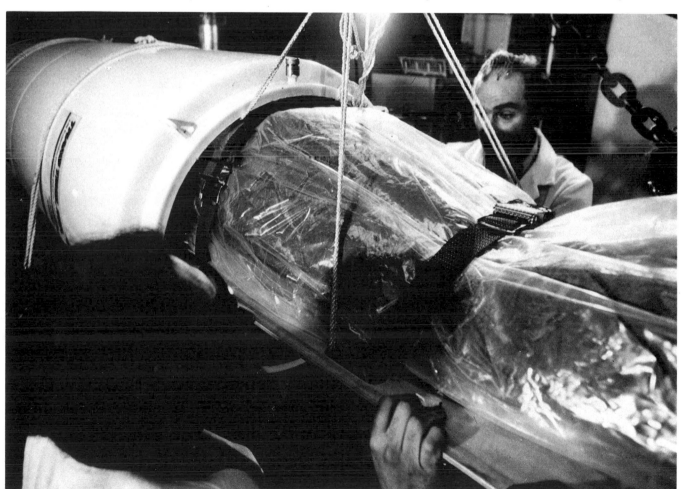

Genetic engineering

So far, we have been concerned with ways of preserving — or restoring — the physiological *status quo*. But, ever since J.D. Watson and Francis Crick discovered the basic mechanism of heredity in the molecules of DNA which make up our chromosomes, it has been reasonable to suppose that one day we might actually be able to improve on nature's designs and add to the capabilities of the body, as it were, at source.

Despite rapid recent progress we still know relatively little about the process by which an egg-cell transforms itself into a highly complex organism. We know how lengths of DNA carry a code for building proteins, and we know the mechanics of the protein-building process; thus we understand how genes function as a kind of chemical factory. What we do not know, as yet, is how genes encode more complicated kinds of information; we do not know how the structure of an organism is determined by its genes, nor do we know how cells differentiate into many different kinds to become parts of organs fulfilling very different functions. The probability is, however, that we shall discover these things in the not-too-distant future. Once we understand more fully how organisms are built, then the possibility of building them ourselves becomes real.

At present, we cannot synthesize DNA — but we can play about with what already exists. It is relatively easy to import lengths of DNA into bacteria because not all bacterial genes are carried on the main chromosome — some actually exist in small 'gene-rings' called 'plasmids'. There is an enzyme which causes these plasmid rings to break, and spare DNA is sometimes then incorporated before the ring seals itself up again.

This can be very useful. There are certain proteins which we are interested in producing in much vaster quantities than are normally produced by living organisms. Interferon, an enzyme which is capable of breaking down some kinds of cancer, is an example. If we can isolate from a higher animal a length of DNA which includes the gene for producing interferon, and then introduce that length of DNA into a bacterial plasmid, then the bacterium, in reproducing itself, will manufacture thousands of copies of the gene for us. This will produce interferon along with all the proteins which it needs for its own purposes. Techniques of this kind — known as 'plasmid engineering' — are in use today not merely in experimental laboratories but in commercial operations. Some microbiologists have taken out patents on particular strains of bacteria. Insulin, growth hormone and brain opiates are among the other substances that have been produced by genetically engineered bacteria.

This is a very modest achievement compared with interfering strategically with the genes of higher animals, but it is a start. Even at this level many people find the idea of genetic engineering frightening. For a brief time in the early 1970s there was a campaign for a moratorium on all such experiments. Advisory groups have laid down fairly strict guidelines on laboratory practice, in some cases backed up by legislation. (Arthur Herzog's doomsday thriller *IQ 83*, in which an engineered gene that lowers intelligence escapes and causes a kind of moron epidemic, is an implausible but typical scare

Right: the diagram shows how plasmid DNA is used in genetic engineering. The required foreign DNA, which has the necessary genes 'snipped out' by restriction enzymes, is 'stitched in' to the plasmid using other enzymes — ligases. The plasmid is then re-introduced to its host microbe, which will divide and re-divide. These new cells will inherit the ability to make, for example, interferon. **Below:** a web of DNA lies outside a cell whose walls have been chemically disrupted to release it. Many plasmids are visible as loops.

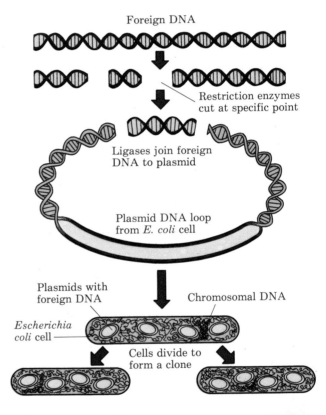

Foreign DNA

Restriction enzymes cut at specific point

Ligases join foreign DNA to plasmid

Plasmid DNA loop from *E. coli* cell

Plasmids with foreign DNA

Chromosomal DNA

Escherichia coli cell

Cells divide to form a clone

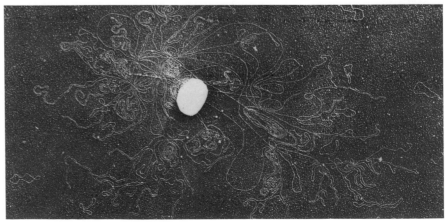

story. It does, however, describe in great detail the kinds of precaution genetic engineering laboratories must take.) Most of the fears which people entertain, however, are probably more nightmare than reality.

The most common anxiety is that in experimenting with bacterial DNA scientists might accidentally produce new species of disease-causing agents against which we would have no immunological defences. In fact, people overestimate the difficulties involved in producing disease-carrying organisms or enhancing their destructive powers. Bacteria are generally vulnerable to a wide range of antibiotic drugs, and this would be just as true of new strains as of old ones. The bacterium commonly used in plasmid engineering is *Escherichia coli*, which lives quite happily in the gut of most humans without doing much damage; even in large numbers it only causes diarrhoea. The laboratory strains of the bacterium are 'attenuated' — which is to say that they are selected for their lack of hardihood, and probably could not get by, as it were, in the wild. The danger of these bacteria becoming the agents of a new, horrible and unstoppable plague is dramatically overstated by crude popular fiction. However, another bacterium, *B. subtilis,* which does not live in human beings, is now replacing *E.* *coli* in some experiments. Other experiments centre on the yeast *Saccharomyces cerevisiae,* which colonizes neither man nor animals. The fact that neither of these micro-organisms infects man will make them even safer for genetic experiments than *E. coli.*

This is not to say, however, that we should not bother to think seriously about possible extensions of research in genetic engineering, and in particular about the ethics of some lines of enquiry. When we begin to think about 'human engineering' we are in new and rather treacherous intellectual territory.

There are only two kinds of human biological engineering that seem to be possible projects for the near future, and both are modest. The first is so modest that few people would think of it as engineering at all — it consists of taking action to determine the sex of children. The second is cloning.

Sex-selection of children is based on the knowledge we have concerning the differences between X-chromosome sperms, which produce girls, and Y-chromosome sperms, which produce boys. The former are stronger and hardier, but the latter are faster in a short sprint and prefer conditions to be a little more alkaline than they usually are. This knowledge can allow couples producing children in the customary fashion to weight the conditions fairly heavily in favour of one sex or the other; but more certain planning can be achieved if artificial insemination is employed, so that the sperms can be sorted out beforehand.

Though this all sounds fairly innocuous, the consequences of the widespread use of techniques of sex-selection (even if it were only 80% reliable) could be considerable. In many cultures people desire sons and consider daughters to be something of a liability, and the ratio of the sexes might be dramatically altered if people everywhere had the means to choose. Some sociologists regard this as an ideal way of damping down the population explosion, but most people contemplating the possibility have not been enamoured of the prospect of a world where there are four men for every woman.

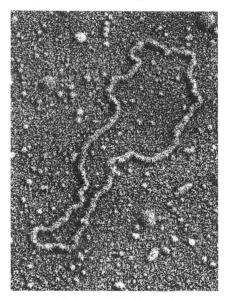

Left: this electron microphotograph shows a single plasmid from an *Escherichia coli* cell. (*E. coli* is a bacterium found abundantly in the human gut.) A plasmid is a tiny loop of DNA, separate from the chromosomal DNA. Doctored plasmids can be used to make chemical 'factories' out of *E. coli* cells.
Below: at Cetus, an American company specializing in the commercial application of bio-technology, a scientist spools strands of DNA on to a glass rod. He will treat the DNA with enzymes that will snip away all but a chosen gene, then insert it into the DNA of *E. coli* plasmids, thus endowing the *E. coli* with new properties.

Clones

A clone is a group of individuals made up of the asexually produced offspring of a single parent. In ordinary sexual reproduction a male cell and a female cell, each containing half the usual number of chromosomes, fuse together to form an embryo. In asexual reproduction a cell containing the full complement of chromosomes divides into two, then four and so on, and a new individual is on the way without any sex cells having been involved. Clones are fairly common in the plant kingdom; nature has given plants asexual reproductive options that might only appeal to a human minority. In the higher animals sexual reproduction is the *only* reproductive option. However, pairs of identical twins are clones of each other. Although they have two parents in the ordinary sense, technically speaking they have a single 'parent', the fertilized egg that accidentally split (asexually) into two separate cells, each one developing into an embryo.

As each of the cells in an animal's body contains a full set of chromosomes there seems no reason in principle why it should not be possible to persuade a body-cell to function as if it were an egg-cell and

grow a whole new animal. It has proved possible to do this with some primitive animals, including frogs, but not yet with a mammal. Once we *can* persuade body-cells of mammals to operate in this way, though, we can presumably do so with human beings. In 1981 newspaper headlines announced with some excitement that mice had been cloned. However, ordinary body-cells were not used. The cloned mice were actually identical twins, artificially produced by persuading a tiny embryo to split into its constituent cells, each of which grew into a separate individual. This type of cloning, of course, does not result in copies of a single adult parent.

In Aldous Huxley's *Brave New World* (1932) clones are also produced by persuading fertilized egg-cells to divide many times, thus producing whole sets of identical siblings; but this is only practical because the embryos are then raised in artificial wombs. Some 'fertility drugs' have the same effect, but the human womb can comfortably accommodate only one or two embryos. Triplets usually survive, but if more than three children are carried the probability of their surviving is low.

The kind of cloning which fascinates people, however, is the kind involving growing new indivi-

duals from the body-cells of human adults. In David Rorvik's book *In His Image: the Cloning of a Man* (1978) the claim is made that this has already been accomplished, but he refused to substantiate this claim in a court case about the credibility of his book, even when guaranteed cast-iron confidentiality by the judge. Rorvik lost the case in 1981, and the judge declared his book 'a fraud and a hoax'.

It is not clear why anyone, except neurotic narcissists, should want to clone themselves in preference to having children in the more conventional way. The fascination of the idea seems to be based in some elementary mistaken assumptions about what groups of clone-children could do that ordinary children cannot. Many clone stories, like Richard Cowper's *Clone* and Kate Wilhelm's *Where Late the Sweet Birds Sang,* suggest that the members of a clone might enjoy a supernatural *rapport,* embracing a common cause automatically and perhaps even communicating telepathically. The extensive evidence we have of identical twins lends no real support to these conjectures.

In real life the process of human cloning would raise controversial ethical questions, not the least being the use of the foster-mothers in

Identical twins are naturally occurring clones of one another. They are 'asexually produced offspring of a single parent' in a technical sense — their 'parent' is the single, tiny embryo that has split into two at a very early stage of cell division in the womb. It has been suggested that telepathy occurs between identical twins, but there is no solid evidence to support this view. Three hundred pairs of identical twins were invited to take part in the David Frost programme on television in January 1968.

Most reasons suggested for cloning human beings are interesting but trivial. The cloning of sporting personalities would lead to some closely fought contests, as in this bout between two clones of Muhammed Ali!

whose wombs the clones would be implanted. The children would not, genetically, be their own and might be taken from them at birth. The emotional consequences could be severe. The alternative, which would be developing embryos *in vitro* (in 'test-tubes', as in *Brave New World*) is not yet technically possible, and might have interesting psychological consequences later on if it were made possible. (However, mouse embryos were developed in test-tubes up to the heart-beating stage of growth in 1971, it was reported.)

The fact that a clone has only one 'parent', genetically, and only one parent actually in cases of test-tube development, would have fascinating consequences in terms of Freudian psychology. A male clone, for example, would feel himself to have no mother, but only a 'father' (and a father who is genetically more like his older but otherwise identical brother). Gene Wolfe in his novel *The Fifth Head of Cerberus* imagines this situation. There are five 'generations' of clones in the story, each one hating his 'father' (which is a way of hating his 'self') so much that he murders him.

The other common cloning

theme in science fiction is that of reproducing famous men. Thus, in *Joshua, Son of None* by Nancy Freedman, John F. Kennedy is cloned, while in Ira Levin's *The Boys from Brazil* the evil Dr Mengele secretly supervises a worldwide project involving 50 Hitler clones. The idea that one could produce 'another Kennedy' or 'another Hitler' simply by starting with the same genes and echoing one or two key events in their life-histories is, however, simple-minded. As *The Boys from Brazil* points out, Hitlers are the products of circumstance, not genetic predestination. Identical twins establish their own identities and find their own destinies although they share environmental circumstances much more similar than would be possible for a clone-parent and his offspring, or even for 'sibling' members of a clone. The environments of clones would vary from the moment that each embryo was implanted into the womb of a foster-mother. Body chemistry varies from person to person, and therefore from womb to womb. Even at birth, then, the members of a clone would in this sense be no longer identical.

Bad biology is rife in science fiction stories about cloning. The simplistic notion that heredity is all and that environment counts for nothing lies unconsciously behind most stories about clone 'armies' and 'families'. Ursula Le Guin made a common error in her story 'Nine Lives' when she includes both males and females in a family of cloned siblings. A clone must necessarily be the same sex as its single 'parent'. It would not be possible to have both sexes in a clone family without genetic engineering on the embryos. (Because cloning does not interfere with the genetic material — the genes — it is not true genetic engineering.)

Pulp science fiction often imagines cloned adults being grown in a matter of months only. In fact, a clone would take just as long to reach adulthood as any other person would. Thus, a film like the television movie *The Darker Side of Terror* (1978) is quite absurd. In real life 'fathers' of clones would not need to worry about their wives committing adultery with their cloned selves only months after birth. The clones would still be babies.

151

Biological engineering: other methods

There are other kinds of human engineering which, though they do not seem to be imminent possibilities, are nevertheless modest enough in kind to suggest that they may be practicable. James Blish's novel *Titan's Daughter* is about a race of human giants produced by artificially induced polyploidy: the doubling of all or a part of the chromosome complement of the individual's cells. Polyploidy occasionally occurs spontaneously in plants, and usually produces healthy individuals which are often giants, so the premise seems an entirely reasonable one. Again, though, it is not immediately clear why anyone would actually wish to produce human giants.

Another seemingly minor modification (minor, at least, in physiological terms) is featured in Ursula Le Guin's *The Left Hand of Darkness*, which is about a society of hermaphrodites. Human hermaphrodites occur naturally on occasion (though they are usually non-functional both as males and as females); the genetic differences between men and women are not as great as laymen might assume. The Y-chromosome possessed only by males appears to be largely inert, and the differences between the sexes seem to be a matter of certain genes being switched on or off rather than a matter of their actually possessing different genes.

Naturally, this 'minor' modification has very dramatic social consequences in Le Guin's novel, and people worried about the injustices of our world's distribution of power between the sexes might find the idea of a biologically equal society attractive. Theodore Sturgeon's novel *Venus Plus X* makes utopian claims for such a society, although here the end is secured by surgical means rather than by genetic engineering. This should serve to remind us that interference with developing embryos or even mature individuals might (in the short term at least) give us far greater control over the form and abilities of people than would tampering with genes.

In a broad sense, human engineering is already something that we practise surgically. Many tribal societies practise kinds of mutilation which are generally gathered under the misleading heading of 'female circumcision'. Much greater in scope, and more benevolent in intention, are the reconstructions carried out by plastic surgeons in Europe and America. It might well be that the technical difficulties involved in emulating the sinister protagonist of H.G. Wells's *The Island of Dr Moreau*, who remodelled animals into human form, are less than the technical difficulties involved in such an apparently simple task as repairing a single aberrant gene on a human chromosome. Whole bodies are a convenient size to work upon.

Genes — which require an electron microscope to be seen — are not.

The celebrated British biologist J.B.S. Haldane, who first wrote about the possibilities of human engineering in 1924, suggested (not altogether seriously) that political parties might one day fight an election over a proposal to equip the next generation of the nation's children with prehensile tails. Despite the great progress made in the last 60 years in understanding how the mechanisms of heredity work, we are really not much closer to having the power to make such decisions. One day, though, it really will be possible, one way or another, to give our children tails, if we want to, and it is as well to think in advance about the morality of making such decisions.

Right: Polyploidy creates giants. The ranunculus on the right is diploid — it has twice the usual number of chromosomes. The giant on the left is tetraploid, with four times the usual number.
Below: This bee is two-sexed: the light side is male and the dark side female. Could hermaphrodites — rare in nature — be created?

Androids

It is the more dramatic possibilities in human engineering, rather than the more plausible ones, that have attracted the lion's share of attention from science fiction writers. One of the most popular notions has been the development of a race of wholly artificial humanoids by means of some technological substitute for the natural chromosome complex. It is conventional to refer to such artificial but organic men as 'androids', while the word 'robot' is usually reserved for manlike machines, but the terms are sometimes used more ambiguously. The making of these artificial 'humans' usually also involves techniques for rapid maturation and brain-programming, so that they can be put straight into operation as functioning adults (there would be no point in having androids if they were as difficult to cultivate as real people!)

This kind of imaginary technology is very nearly impossible. Even if we could invent

a new biochemical coding-system to substitute for DNA, the information necessary to produce an artificial man would presumably be as complicated and as extensive as the information needed to produce real ones. The additional information required to produce functioning adults without extensive environmental training would add very greatly to the complexity of the task. If a society had the means to do this, it could do many other things as well, so stories in which androids are produced in a near-future society otherwise much like ours are bordering on the absurd. Philip K. Dick's novel *Do Androids Dream of Electric Sheep?* is an example. A fine novel in most respects, its story of an android bounty hunter founders, scientifically at least, on its implausibility.

What most science fiction stories about androids tend to show is that there is really no point in creating them. They are notionally useful because they allow their users to dodge the moral strictures against slavery; the basic premise is that we could cheerfully use artificial men in ways in which we could not decently use real ones. Most stories, however — including Clifford Simak's *Time and Again* and Robert Silverberg's *Tower of Glass* — are dedicated to the condemnation of this dodge. They argue passionately that artificial men would be just as entitled to moral consideration as real ones. Philip K. Dick's novel mentioned above is unusual in suggesting that androids might be less than human — they might be deficient in empathy and slightly sadistic. But, though this alters the moral problem, it does not remove it. Indeed, the merit of these stories is not that they deal with a plausible technology but that they raise a fundamental issue in moral philosophy: just how do we decide where moral consideration for others begins and ends?

Philip K. Dick's novel *Do Androids Dream of Electric Sheep?*, filmed as *Blade Runner*, is here illustrated by Peter Goodfellow. Dick's rather sinister androids, both animal and human, have metal components as well as flesh. Would simulacra of human beings have human feelings?

Pantropy: new men for new worlds

The other main role given to elaborate technologies of human engineering in science fiction is that of adapting mankind to new environments. The most spectacular modifications of this kind involve adapting men for life on alien worlds where physical conditions are very different from those on Earth. There are also, however, stories about modifying men for other Earthly environments — particularly for life in the sea.

Adapting people for life in the sea might not be as difficult as it sounds. At the most superficial level it would be a matter of extra insulation against the cold, and some metabolic provision allowing people to hold their breath for a long time. It would also be desirable to have some mechanism for avoiding caisson sickness ('the bends') so that changes of pressure following deep dives would not be so troublesome. Most science fiction stories about men adapted for life in the sea assume that it would involve the creation of gills, but seals and dolphins do very well without. Even if gills were necessary — if, for instance, the adapted men had to stay perpetually below the surface — the amount of modification required might not be so great. Experiments with 'water-breathing' mice have suggested that lungs might be fairly easily modified to extract oxygen from water instead of from air.

Stories like *A Torrent of Faces* by James Blish and Norman L. Knight assume that aquatic men would be used primarily in support of underwater colonies. There is, however, a very striking novel, *Inter Ice Age 4* by Kobo Abé, in which Japanese scientists, anticipating the sinking of their islands after the melting of the polar ice-caps, decide that their cultural future lies in a new generation of water-breathing Japanese children.

The natural counterpart to adaptation for life under the sea is adaptation for flight, but this is much less frequently featured in science fiction because writers are mostly aware of the crucial problem of weight (see the comments on giant wasps, flying men and dragons, pages 194-5). Even the largest flying birds — condors — have bodies very much smaller than the smallest human beings. In any case, the degree of modification required would be much greater; it seems much easier to make the human body grow a layer of blubber than a functional set of feathers. Some stories of the very far future, like Olaf Stapledon's *Last and First Men* and Robert Silverberg's *Nightwings*, imagine that there might one day be technologies of human engineering adequate to overcome these problems, but the flying humans featured in them seem much more alien than the water-dwelling tritons in *A Torrent of Faces.*

Flying man could exist more plausibly on light-gravity planets, and the real extravagance of human engineering as it is envisaged in science fiction is displayed in stories of moulding men for life on other worlds. In a series of stories collected in the book *The Seedling Stars* James Blish introduced the concept of 'pantropy', meaning 'grow everywhere' or 'change everything', to describe the spread of the human race throughout the Galaxy, invading countless different environments by means of strategic adaptation. The stories argue that this might be the only way we could conquer other worlds because the possibility of finding another world so like Earth that we could simply step on to it and take up residence might be very small indeed. This is a plausible argument when we consider the number of environmental conditions that would have to be reproduced almost exactly if we were to be comfortable: gravity, temperature, atmospheric pressure and composition, partial pressure of oxygen, and so on. There are very many imaginable conditions in which some forms of life familiar to us would be perfectly possible, but which would still be extremely hostile to *human* life.

Some of the adaptations suggested by Blish in *The Seedling Stars* are clearly beyond the limits of possibility — notably the idea in the story 'Surface Tension' of producing human beings as small as protozoans to colonize alien puddles

— but the general theme of the book is sensible. The ironic final section looks forward to a time when the only 'original' men are those living in artificial habitats aboard spaceships, because time has changed the surface of the Earth so much that even man's homeworld must be 're-seeded' with adapted men who are decidedly alien in appearance.

Actually, this notion has been relatively little developed in science fiction, writers generally preferring the over-optimistic assumption that there will be an abundance of Earth-duplicates strung out all over the universe. Where more hostile environments are featured, terra-forming (see pages 28-9) or mechanical means of coping are generally preferred to strategies of biological adaptation. However, in his novel *Man Plus*, Frederik Pohl seriously considers the notion of adapting a man, by surgery and the use of artificial organs, to life in the extremely hostile environment of Mars. The story makes out quite a good case for such a modification being rather more practical than one might assume, provided that the priority is placed on 'cyborgization' (see pages 142-3).

Alterations include a backpack computer connected directly with the hero's nervous system; gossamer black 'wings' (not used for flying) with solar-power receptors; thick, insulating skin; multi-faceted eyes that can see in the ultra-violet and infra-red ranges; and artificial heart and lungs. This emphasizes yet again that human engineering may already be possible, even without the means to play about with genes.

If the only reason we have for investing heavily in human engineering is that it would allow us to live on other worlds, then we can safely leave worrying about such projects to the distant future. It is not too difficult, though, to think of other reasons why people might want to augment our human capabilities. There is a short novel by Jack Vance, *The Dragon Masters,* in which human beings living on a distant world fight periodic wars against reptilian aliens, each side equipping its armies with monstrous living instruments of war derived by genetic engineering from the

offspring of prisoners captured in previous encounters. This rather bizarre story reminds us forcibly — if we need any reminding — that it is very often the military applications that encourage particular lines of technological enquiry. Perfect soldiers are so difficult to train that the prospect of manufacturing them (especially when we might modify them to be weapons themselves instead of simply carrying weapons) is one that might prove horribly attractive in real life, as well as in science fiction, where the idea is already popular.

In Frederik Pohl's *Man Plus*, a man is modified into a cyborg to fit him for life on the surface of Mars. The 'wings' do not fly — they carry solar cells to power his built-in backpack computer; his multi-faceted eyes see in the infra-red; his vast lungs are artificial. Note the thick, insulating skin and lack of external sex organs.

155

Chapter 9
DREAMS AND NIGHTMARES OF THE FUTURE

A hundred years ago the future looked utopian; but now it fills us with anxiety. What has gone wrong?

Machines and the leisure society

When comparing the lives of ordinary people in the industrialized nations today with those led by their ancestors 100 years ago, we are inclined to feel that the optimists were right. Nowadays, though, the optimists are on the defensive; many people believe that any further technological advance might be dangerous and that the technology we already have is damaging the human spirit.

As long ago as 1924 Bertrand Russell argued that the advancement of science was a bad thing. He believed that new discoveries gave those in power greater resources with which to maintain their positions, to control the lives of ordinary people and to fight ever more destructive wars. World War I had already demonstrated that technological advance transformed the whole business of war (and vice versa), and the growth of the mass media of communication was beginning to generate anxiety about the control of ideas.

By the 1930s, with the coming of the Depression, people were finding it very difficult to believe in the nineteenth-century vision of a highly mechanized Utopia where everyone would enjoy a high standard of living and a rich and varied lifestyle. In previous decades there had been talk of the 'leisure society'; but leisure sounds much less attractive if it is called 'unemployment'. People in the 1930s were beginning to take seriously the notion that machines, far from liberating mankind, might rather be

seen as tyrannical conquerors. The most striking fictional images of this kind appear in Fritz Lang's classic film *Metropolis*, first shown in 1926. Here we see dispirited workers in uniform, moving in step through cavernous corridors to reach their places of work, their

bodies moving like clockwork to a rhythm imposed upon them by the giant machines that they tend. The hero has a vision in which a gigantic machine is transformed into the pagan god Moloch, into whose fiery mouth workers are being delivered as human sacrifices.

This particular nightmare image of the future has dated very badly. Its depiction of machines as monsters of steel with red-hot fires at their heart reflects the technology characteristic of the nineteenth century: the world of steam engines. The advent of electrical technology has meant that work, even in such industries as steel production and mining, has generally become cleaner, safer and less physically exhausting. Nevertheless, it is still true that on factory assembly lines machines tend to impose their own dogged regularity upon workers while 'time-and-motion studies' attempt to exploit the full mechanical efficiency of which the human body is capable. Many jobs require people to operate in a mechanical way, and it is these jobs which are steadily being lost as machines themselves take over: everyone has seen advertisements featuring fully automated production-lines of the kind now widely used in the production of cars (see pages 122-3).

During the last 20 years or so it has been the simpler manual tasks which have been largely taken over by machines, but, with the rapid advance of microelectronics, increasingly subtle and sophisticated tasks are being automated. The Moloch-machines of *Metropolis*, serviced by wretched and exhausted slaves, no longer seem appropriate as a symbol of modern technology, but there may remain a sense in which, as machines take over our work, we might still consider ourselves human sacrifices.

In an early (1909) science fiction story which was exceedingly pessimistic about the society of the future, 'The Machine Stops', E.M. Forster suggested that the prospect of a society where no one has to work at all is just as intolerable, in its own way, as the prospect of a world of men enslaved. Forster asks what people will do if they can serve no useful purpose, and comes to the conclusion that their lives will be empty and dispirited. Further, he argues that if a society entirely dependent on machines is faced with a large-scale breakdown it will be helpless in the face of catastrophe.

There are many science fiction stories which try to imagine a fully automated society, and all of them have difficulty in coping with this question of what people will do with unlimited leisure time. Scientific research and the arts are offered as useful ways of spending time which

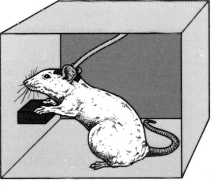

Left: the archetypal vision of workers subjugated to the rhythms of a machine-dominated society remains that of Fritz Lang's classic film *Metropolis* (1926). This is coming to be replaced by a more up-to-date nightmare, that of a world where pointless tasks are obsessively repeated with the bribe of pleasure fed directly to the brain. The psychologist James Olds opened up this vista in 1958 with his work on rats. **Above right:** this rat jolts the pleasure centres of its brain through an electrode implant every time it presses the bar. **Right:** the graph of one experiment. Each sweep of the curve represents 500 pressings of the bar. This rat responded almost continuously with 2000 presses per hour for 24 hours, not even pausing to eat or drink, and then slept for most of the next day.

	48 hours	
Noon	⋀⋀⋀⋀⋀⋀⋀⋀⋀⋀⋀	4 PM
4 PM	⋀⋀⋀⋀⋀⋀⋀⋀⋀⋀⋀	8 PM
8 PM	⋀⋀⋀⋀⋀⋀⋀⋀⋀⋀⋀	Midnight
Midnight	⋀⋀⋀⋀⋀⋀⋀⋀⋀⋀⋀	4 AM
4 AM	⋀⋀⋀⋀⋀⋀⋀⋀⋀⋀	8 AM
8 AM	⋀⋀⋀⋀⋀⋀⋀⋀	Noon
Noon	⋀⋀	4 PM
4 PM		8 PM
8 PM		Midnight
Midnight		4 AM
4 AM		8 AM
8 AM	⋀⋀⋀	Noon
Noon	⋀⋀	4 PM

might legitimately provide people with a sense of purpose, but in the past these have always been minority pursuits, attracting relatively few recruits. Many writers find it easier to imagine a degenerate world of idle sensation-seekers whose pursuit of pleasure will eventually lead them to a life of perpetual, drug-assisted dreaming. James Gunn's novel *The Joy Makers* imagines a machine-supported future society adopting a cult of hedonism, and developing technologies so sophisticated that almost everyone will retreat into mechanical cocoons which will feed them with synthetic experience — pleasant dreams from which they never wake. The same possibility is raised in Mack Reynolds' *After Utopia*, in which computers can pipe synthetic experiences into people's heads, allowing them to be and do anything they can imagine: they become solipsistic gods, governing worlds of their own imagination. Gunn and Reynolds, like Forster before them, consider this kind of retreat from the real world to be the ultimate moral failure; both writers favour bringing people back to reality by shock tactics — if necessary by threat or by force.

The kind of synthetic experience

envisaged by many such writers as these is still beyond our techno-logical horizons, but the notion is by no means ridiculous. The idea of electrically aided pleasure-seeking became very plausible when the psychologist James Olds discovered a region in the brains of rats which he named the 'pleasure centre'. Rats which were given the means to stimulate themselves in this region would continue to do so relentlessly, making only the briefest stops for food and sleep. Another psychologist, Robert Heath, has designed similar self-stimulators for human beings, and, though the results have been less spectacular, experimental subjects reported pleasurable sensations and sexual excitement. Larry Niven, in several science fiction stories, imagines that addiction to the use of such stimulators may be common in the not-too-distant future; he refers to the practice as 'wireheading'.

The fact that machines to facilitate pleasure-seeking in its purest sense are becoming more easily imaginable should not lead us to accept too readily the likelihood of a future society of lotus-eaters. Although there has been a marked increase in the amount of leisure time enjoyed by ordinary people,

and although considerable un-employment has been caused as machines have taken over certain jobs, what is more impressive is the way in which we have discovered so many new kinds of work. The dramatic fall in the number of people engaged in basic agricultural and industrial production has been accompanied by an equally dramatic expansion of the service sector of the economy (see diagram on page 125). So much of the work that people now do is 'unproductive' in the crude sense of the term that the prospect of machines taking over the whole productive process no longer seems to threaten such an all-encompassing transformation of the social world. The problem of inventing enough new tasks to allow us all legitimately to keep our sense of purpose may not be easy to solve, but we have already shown consider-able ingenuity in tackling it.

It need not be left to the devil to find work for idle hands; we ought to be clever enough to find it for ourselves.

Jane Fonda in *Barbarella* (1967) has been placed in the lethal Pleasure Organ by Milo O'Shea. So lusty are her appetites that she burns the machine out before it can kill her. See rat diagram page 157.

Technological tyranny

The idea of 'progress' has always implied more than the advancement of science and technology. It has also included the notion of moral and political progress towards a time when people will enjoy greater freedom and everyone can be assured of fair and just treatment by the law and the government. Although there has always been argument about the best way to achieve them, these ideals are acknowledged in some form by everyone. But faith in progress is these days often undermined by a fear of technology. This is not simply a fear that technology may destroy us through a nuclear holocaust, or through pollution; there is also the feeling that technology will provide abundant opportunities for others to restrict our freedom by controlling and manipulating us in subtle and insidious ways.

Some of the most striking futuristic novels of this century are those that imagine societies in which the common people have been robbed of their individuality and are controlled, regulated and protected by a small, governmental elite to the point where they seem mere robots rather than human beings. Perhaps the most frightening aspect of these imaginary societies is that the rulers who are manipulating their subjects always claim to be doing so benevolently, and sometimes they even mean it.

In George Orwell's *Nineteen Eighty-Four*, the supposed benevolence of Big Brother is a hollow sham, and the rule of the Inner Party is secured by constant surveillance, with the assistance of psychological techniques capable of breaking down any individual resistance. An interesting contrast is seen, however, in the classic *We* (1924) by the Russian Yevgeny Zamiatin. In this novel it is not at all clear that the invisible dictator (the Well-Doer) is secretly malevolent: in removing one by one the sources of unhappiness — hunger, love and the imagination — he and those who act in his name might really be trying, in their own

way, to do the best for their subjects. In the most famous and influential of these 'dystopian' novels, Aldous Huxley's *Brave New World* (1932), this is certainly true.

In *Brave New World* social order and harmony are assured by designing the people to fit the system. The production of ideal human beings begins with the development of embryos in mechanical wombs, and from the very beginning the process is carefully controlled. The society has several castes, each carrying out a range of tasks appropriate to its particular range of ability. By

interfering with the embryos — giving some more oxygen than others and deliberately injuring some with poisons — the intelligence and physique of each individual produced in the 'hatchery' is determined. Cloning is employed to reduce individuality within each batch.

After birth, the shaping of the individuals continues. Each caste is

A part of the 'baby hatchery' illustrated in a 1958 edition of Aldous Huxley's *Brave New World*.

Now, events in the real world are beginning to make Huxley's fantasy look like a real possibility.

brainwashed into being content with its lot, valuing its own characteristics and attainments above all others. This is achieved by the incessant repetition of key slogans — a process which continues to make its insidious impression upon the mind even while the children are asleep. The likes and dislikes of children are also determined by conditioning — the lower castes, for instance, are conditioned to hate natural things so that they will never want to go out of doors.

Once they are adult, the citizens of Huxley's future society are protected from anxiety by a battery of drugs which everyone must carry. The euphoric drug 'soma' guarantees happiness for all. The sexual morality of the society enforces promiscuity, protecting the citizens from the damaging consequences of intense personal relationships. In such a society there is no possibility of revolution and little scope for individual deviance. The hero of the story, a 'savage' reared on a reservation where a few primitives are allowed to cling to ancient and brutal ways, finds that he cannot change the new world and cannot live in it either.

In the 50 years since *Brave New World* was published we have made conspicuous progress (if progress is the right word) in almost all the technologies of control that Huxley imagines. Though animal embryos cannot yet be brought to term in artificial wombs, technological assistance in animal husbandry, including artificial insemination and the transplantation of embryos into 'surrogate mothers', is now commonplace. The transplantation of human embryos from cold storage into either natural or surrogate mothers will soon be accomplished. Fertilization of egg-cells can now take place outside the human body, and several 'test-tube babies' have been born as a result of techniques developed in Britain by Drs Robert Edwards and Patrick Steptoe, with as many as 100 more expected by the end of 1982. An Italian embryologist, Daniele Petrucci, claims to have kept a human embryo alive in an artificial womb for 59 days, and some Soviet scientists have claimed that they have beaten this record.

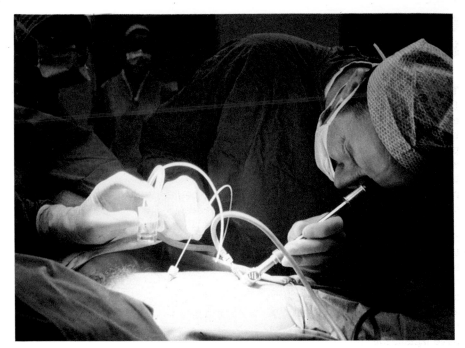

Top: Professor Ian Craft removes an egg from the ovary of a woman volunteer; she is in hospital to be sterilized. The egg will be fertilized and used in an experiment in the frozen storage of human embryos at the Royal Free Hospital in London.
Above: Frostie, the cryogenic calf, was born from an embryo implanted in a surrogate mother after it had been frozen for 3 months.

Conditioning and brainwashing

The techniques of conditioning that Huxley describes have not all fared equally well. The 'sleep-teaching' that he envisaged — hypnopaedia — proved less successful in experiments than was originally thought likely, but the power of constant repetition of slogans cannot be doubted. The use of 'subliminal advertising', by which messages can be flashed on to television or cinema screens so briefly that they pass unnoticed by our consciousness but are subconsciously heeded, is also less effective than was once feared, though both Britain and the USA have legislation to control its use. Recent experiments with auditory subliminal persuasion, involving the inclusion of messages in the piped music played in supermarkets, have reawakened the controversy. It seems that messages commanding shoppers to buy particular products are largely ineffective, but messages commanding them not to steal have

a dramatic negative effect on shoplifting. The apparent explanation is that people already know what they want to buy, and cannot readily be induced to change their minds, but that those tempted to steal may be amenable to a suggestion which reinforces the voice of conscience. Only in moments of genuine indecision, it seems, are subliminal commands powerful enough to tip the balance.

More advanced techniques of conditioning, involving the breaking down and rebuilding of the whole personality (generally termed 'brainwashing') were first determinedly attempted by Asian communists attempting to 're-educate' American soldiers captured during the Korean war. Despite the implication of such fictions as *The Manchurian Candidate* by Richard Condon, in which an American soldier is programmed to become an assassin, the success rate of these attempts was very low. Most of the 'converts' were quickly rehabilitated once they returned home. Some soldiers, however, proved vulnerable to this kind of persuasion, their readiness to be converted being dependent on

the strength of their previous social ties. The fact that people — especially the young — can be seized by a sense of their own lack of purpose and deeply disappointed by their position within society creates a constant supply of potential recruits for organizations which use psychological methods of persuasion. This is something which has always gone on in connection with political groups and, more especially, religious cults; but it is only in recent times that the psychology of the process has been sufficiently well understood to allow careful, strategic use of the techniques, and also to allow outsiders to realize what is actually happening. The psychological pressures exerted by the communists in the Korean war exploited the 'three Ds' — debilitation, dread and dependency — in order to break down their prisoners;

Below: the horrors of brainwashing. Members of an American cult were conditioned to obey their leader Jim Jones, and he told them to die. These were some of the 925 bodies after their mass suicide in Guyana in 1978.

religious groups, such as the so-called Moonies, usually make less use of the first two and concentrate on the third because their recruits are volunteers. Recently, a number of commercial organizations selling a form of psychotherapy to increase confidence and even sexual charisma have been using similar techniques.

Although John B. Watson, the founder of the Behaviourist school of psychology (which claims that all our behaviour consists of conditioned patterns of stimulus and response), enjoyed some success when he began selling his expertise to the advertising industry, it seems that most people are less manipulable than was at first thought. Individuals who are psychologically secure can resist subliminal control and behavioural re-programming without much difficulty. It is worth noting, though, that all the experiments referred to above involved adults whose personalities were already established. If these techniques were used from birth on children then those children would very probably be equipped with the personalities that the manipulators wanted to build into them.

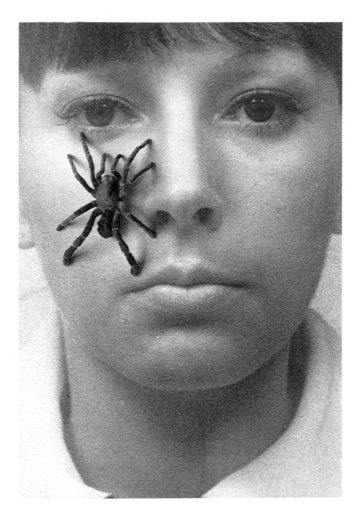

Left: there are positive aspects to behavioural conditioning. This woman's phobia of spiders has been treated by progressively introducing her, in small, painless stages, to what she fears most. Clearly the treatment succeeded.
Below: the subterranean fear that runs through much science fiction is that we shall all become members of a drugged, docile, apathetic society, conditioned to obey our totalitarian rulers, as in the film *THX 1138* (1969).

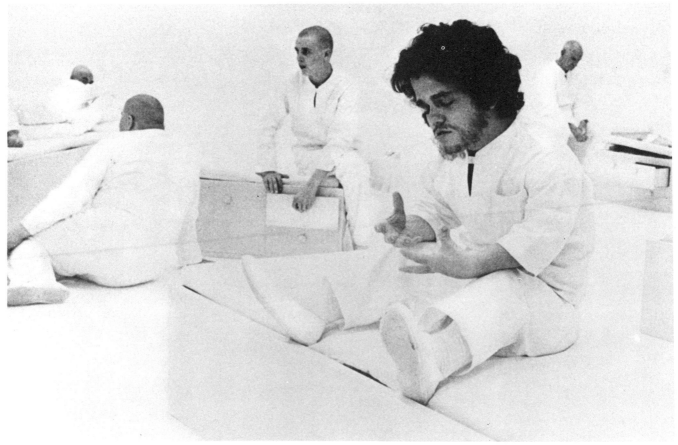

Psychotropic drugs

The aspect of *Brave New World* which today seems most accurately prophetic is its emphasis on the use of mood-controlling drugs to insulate people from unease. Since 1932, drug technology has advanced very dramatically.

Huxley would already have been familiar with various hypnosedative (sleep-inducing) drugs which work by depressing the functioning of the brain. Barbituric acid was discovered in 1864 and the first barbiturate tablets were introduced before the Great War: barbital (Veronal) in 1903 and phenobarbitone (Luminal) in 1912. These replaced a range of rather dangerous substances, including paraldehyde, chloral hydrate and opium derivatives like laudanum, and have since been replaced themselves by even safer drugs: the benzodiazepines (including Amytal and Seconal).

The next psychotropic (mind-changing) drugs to be used on a wide scale were the amphetamines – stimulant drugs used as 'pep pills'. These were widely used during World War II by the American army, which issued them to soldiers in action in order to combat fatigue. Because of their effect on the metabolism they were also used for a time as aids to losing weight. They also became highly fashionable among young people during the 1960s for the artificial excitement they produced. Their usefulness in all fields, however, was compromised by a 'let-down' effect once the drugs wore off and by the fact that consistent users became physically dependent upon them and faced extremely uncomfortable withdrawal symptoms. The commonest drugs of this category in use in the 1960s were amphetamine itself (Benzedrine) and methylamphetamine (Methedrine), but these have been largely replaced by a slightly safer new generation of stimulant drugs, including methyl phenidate (Ritalin).

The rapid development of atar-actic drugs, or 'tranquillizers', took place after World War II. Following the development of chlorpromazine

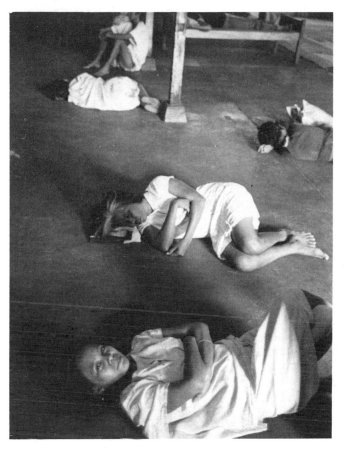

in 1951 a number of its derivatives quickly came into use in psychiatric medicine in the treatment of severe psychological disorders. These compounds are generally known as the 'major tranquillizers'. The compounds we now know as the 'minor tranquillizers' were isolated in the 1930s, but their pacifying effect was not discovered until much later. The first ones to be widely used, including meprobamate (Equanil or Miltown), were developed in the early 1950s, but these have now been displaced by a new generation whose most widely used members are chlordiazepoxide (Librium) and diazepam (Valium). Taking these drugs has become part of the daily routine of hundreds of thousands of people in the Western world.

Another class of drug developed for the treatment of mental patients and gradually extended for use by thousands of members of the general public is the class of 'anti-depressant' drugs. Amphetamines had previously been used to treat patients suffering from melancholia, but were unsatisfactory because of the let-down effect. Imipramine (Tofranil) and its derivatives appeared to solve this problem.

It is difficult for most of us to appreciate the extent of psychotropic drug use in mental hospitals, since photographs are seldom released. This 1981 picture shows conditions in the extremely overcrowded National Mental Hospital on Mindanao in the Philippines. There are few comforts; patients are controlled by electric shock therapy and heavy medication. Conditions are much better elsewhere but, even in the West, watchdog committees have expressed concern about the use of continuous heavy medication, though properly used such drugs can save the sanity of patients.

Since 1958, when imipramine was introduced, the use of anti-depressants has increased steadily.

Whether the spread of psychotropic drugs implies that one day we shall all look to medical science to protect us from anxiety, sadness and fear remains debatable, but the potential is clearly there, and though they have not yet been widely used on human subjects, many other drugs affecting behaviour are now known. Several compounds, including atropine methyl nitrate, can apparently induce aggressive behaviour in normally placid rats, while other compounds, including carbachol, can just as easily switch it off again.

Another kind of behaviour-changing drug that has been made notorious by rumour is L-dopa, a drug originally developed to treat Parkinson's disease. It appeared on testing to have strong aphrodisiac side-effects. Experiments on animals carried out by an Italian group including G.L. Gessa has led them to attribute even more powerful aphrodisiac qualities to a drug known as PCPA, which apparently made rabbits so eager to mate that they would even attempt coitus with cats.

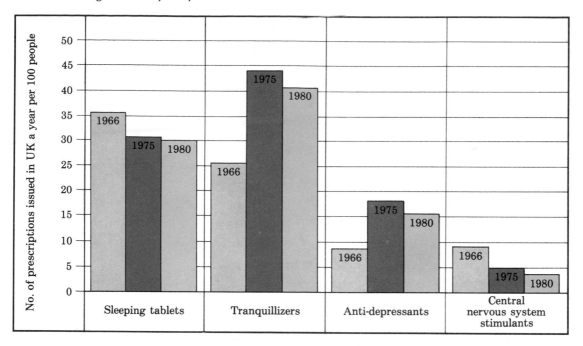

No. of prescriptions issued in UK a year per 100 people

| Sleeping tablets | Tranquillizers | Anti-depressants | Central nervous system stimulants |

The legal use of psychotropic drugs in the UK, comparing the years 1966, 1975 and 1980. The figures come from the Department of Health and Social Security, and are based on doctors' prescriptions for the four main categories of drugs that act on the brain. Illicit street sales of drugs are tiny compared with official sales. Psychotropic drugs are being used more cautiously today than a few years ago.

There are many kinds of drug which stimulate the brain to produce hallucinations, and which may grossly distort incoming sensory information. Various naturally occurring compounds have long been used to produce this effect, including mescalin (in the peyote cactus) and psilocybin (in the fly-agaric mushroom). LSD (lysergic acid diethylamide) is by far the most notorious laboratory-derived drug of this kind, and is promoted with quasi-religious fervour by its admirers.

LSD is highly poisonous, except in tiny doses. Many other poisons, including belladonna alkaloids such as atropine, also have stimulating effects upon the brain in very small quantities. Some, like strychnine, apparently have the effect of increasing the speed of information-processing and of enhancing memory (see pages 136-7).

One of the most interesting recent developments in psycho-pharmacology has been the discovery that the brain is one of the major endocrine (hormone-producing) organs of the body. The brain produces many 'drugs', including the 'endorphins', which bear a striking chemical similarity to morphine. The endorphins, produced in response to stress and pain, also help to mediate the relationship of mind and body. As we learn more about the ways in which information and instructions are transmitted between the brain, the body and the

environment, through chemicals, through our immune systems and through our nervous system, we come closer to the conscious control of our own health, and of our relationship to the environment.

Professor Joel Elkes, who performed some of the first experiments on the use of tranquil-lizers in mental hospitals in the 1950s, and has more recently been associated with research into endorphins, is the first president of the American College of Neuropsycho-pharmacology. He believes that education will be revolutionized by our greater knowledge of brain-body relationships and that children in the future will be educated in a variety of techniques for mental control. The drugs used would be created within the body, not imposed from outside.

This utopian prospectus is not yet generally accepted. The more usual and unattractive scenario is of a society emotionally and intellec-tually dependent on the effects of chemicals imposed from outside. Although a minority of the medical profession is actively working against such a development, the scenario seems by no means far-fetched in an age when Valium has already replaced religion as the opium of the masses. Such societies have been commonplace in science fiction ever since *Brave New World*, especially in so-called 'New Wave' science fiction from the mid-1960s onwards. Particularly nightmarish

examples occur in Philip K. Dick's novel *A Scanner Darkly* and Norman Spinrad's story 'No Direction Home'. In the latter a future America is so used to orchestrating its mental states by drugs that perception of naked reality without chemical assistance is seen as the worst 'trip' of all.

So far, it is arguable that whatever damage has been and is being done in real life is purely voluntary, but the prospect of the use of drugs as a tool of oppression is looming on the horizon. Many mental patients have benefited considerably from sedation and tranquillization by drugs, but it is becoming increasingly common for tranquillizers to be given to unruly inmates of prisons. More ominously, it has recently been fashionable in certain states of the USA to dole out drugs on a large scale to school-children held to be 'hyperactive'. The question of whether or not hyperactivity is actually a medical disorder — and, if so, how common it is — still rages fiercely, but at one time in Omaha drugs were being given daily to thousands of trouble-some children in public schools. The drugs were not conventional tranquillizers but stimulant amphetamines — especially Ritalin — which seem to have the reverse effect on adolescent boys. The wisdom of this policy has been challenged by those who feel that it is one small step for mankind along a highly undesirable road.

Crime and punishment

There is one context in which nearly all of us are in favour of behavioural control. For society to exist at all, anti-social impulses must be controlled, and individuals who give way to them must somehow be constrained. The well organized society of Huxley's *Brave New World* has no deviants, so the question of crime and punishment never arises; but an inescapable consequence of the existence of freedom is that people are free to devise and carry out undesirable actions which must then be counteracted. The problem is that any social or technological apparatus designed for the detection and apprehension of criminals, and any institutions used to contain or

rehabilitate them, are potentially useful also for the more general oppression of the populace by police forces and governments.

In George Orwell's *Nineteen Eighty-Four* crime is controlled by surveillance: every citizen at all times is being watched — or, at least, is possibly being watched. Privacy no longer exists, and it is a crime to attempt to seek it. Television screens, instead of being windows on the world outside, are the means by which outsiders can peer into everyone's daily life. Every sentence that is uttered must first be carefully considered, for unguarded words betray thought-crimes: the most serious crimes of all.

Here too the real world has made considerable 'progress' since Orwell's day. Security systems making elaborate use of television cameras are now commonplace in

large department stores, where the possibility of being under observation apparently deters many would-be shoplifters, and it is becoming increasingly common for bank-robbers to be filmed in the act. Listening devices ('bugs') can be implanted almost anywhere. Walls nowadays really can have ears, if anyone wants to provide them with such equipment, and, judging from the greatly increased sales of surveillance devices, it seems that more and more people do. The spread of computer-held records over the last 20 years has made it possible to store a huge amount of information about people, to collate it, and to retrieve it at a moment's notice. The use of computers by the police makes it easier to apprehend criminals, but it also makes it easier for people with privileged access to information to learn about individuals who have never

The surveillance society: **Above:** hidden cameras show heiress Patti Hearst carrying out a bank robbery in 1974, 10 weeks after being kidnapped by a terrorist group. **Left:** few people know what resolution is possible with top-secret military satellite cameras. But we can make an informed guess from pictures like this, taken with a commercially available camera from over 150 km above Florida. Individual planes, marked with an arrow, can just be seen on the airport runway.

committed any crimes. In these respects Orwell's nightmare is coming closer.

Some science fiction writers, however, cheer themselves with the thought that these and other techniques of detection may soon become so sophisticated that crime really will not pay. Mack Reynolds' *Police Patrol: 2000 AD,* for instance, envisages a world where the police are so effective that it takes almost superhuman ingenuity to carry off even such trivial crimes as petty theft (they are aided in this particular endeavour by the virtual disappearance of cash and its replacement by computerized credit-transfer).

Other writers are not so optimistic. Looking at trends within contemporary society they see increases in all kinds of crime, especially those involving violence and the motiveless destruction of property. They foresee that violence and vandalism will get completely out of hand as law-enforcement agencies fail to cope. It has also been observed that the widespread use of computers may give rise to a whole new spectrum of crimes involving deceptive programming. This is already beginning to happen.

Such anxieties have helped to focus the attention of science fiction writers on new ways of dealing with law-breakers once they are caught, but these innovations are rarely regarded favourably. The notion of conditioning or brainwashing criminals away from anti-social behaviour is fiercely condemned in Anthony Burgess's *A Clockwork Orange*, despite the fact that the author deplores the increasing violence of youth culture. (The film made from the novel by Stanley Kubrick in 1971 tends to blur this condemnation.) On the whole, new ways of dealing with criminals imagined by science fiction writers tend to the Draconian rather than the tolerant: in various stories by Larry Niven criminals repay society by making contributions from their own bodies to an ever growing demand for organ transplants; and in Cordwainer Smith's gruesome story 'A Planet Named Shayol' criminals receive medical treatments to cause them to grow extra organs which can be periodically harvested for the same purpose.

A subtle idea for crime *prevention* used by several writers, including Damon Knight in his novel *Hell's Pavement*, involves equipping every citizen with a technological conscience which will more than compensate for any failure on the part of his natural equipment. One interesting variant on this theme, found in *The Ring* by Piers Anthony and Robert E. Margroff, involves fitting criminals with a machine (here contained in a collar) which is sensitive to anti-social impulses on the part of its wearer, and which reacts by punishing him with an electric shock. This sounds fanciful, but is in practice not so far-fetched. The self-stimulators rigged up by Robert Heath to allow people to stimulate 'pleasure-centres' in their brains (see page 158) were sometimes equipped with a second button whose effect was to stimulate the hippocampus, making them feel very sick. There would be no problem, it seems, in equipping a device, like Piers Anthony's 'collar', with appropriate punitive actions; the real difficulty would lie in making it sensitive to a person's anti-social intentions. However, this

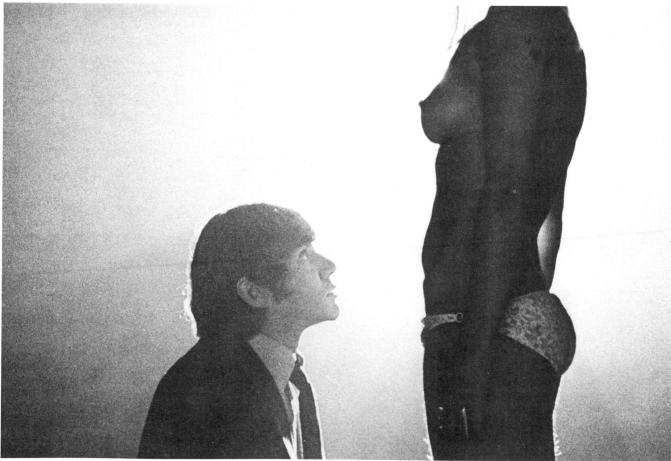

would not necessitate attributing to the device any occult telepathic power. Aggressive impulses are associated with quite definite physiological changes which might be monitored, and it is conceivable that current investigations (using electroencephalograms) into electrical changes in the brain might give such artificial sensors much more precise capabilities. Moral considerations rather than scientific snags are what would really stand in the way of developing such devices.

In this context recent experiments involving the electrical control of aggression are relevant. The psychologist José Delgado has run some spectacular demonstrations involving the activation by radio of electrodes implanted in the brains of animals. In one famous instance he induced a bull to charge him, and then stopped it by means of a hand-held radio transmitter which sent a signal into its brain persuading it to walk placidly away.

Science fiction writers generally have not paid a great deal of attention to the crimes of today. What has fascinated them more has

Left: the future treatment of criminals? Alex, the rapist in *A Clockwork Orange* (1971) has been conditioned to feel nausea where once he would have felt sexual arousal. **Right:** in a series of controversial experiments, the psychologist José Delgado inserted electrodes into the brains of various animals. When stimulated, these altered their emotional responses, changing aggression into docility or, as in this case, mother love into fear.

been the notion that whole new areas of human activity may one day be defined as criminal.

A frequent theme in science fiction of the 1960s and 1970s has been that, as a consequence of the population explosion, childbirth

would have to be regulated in the relatively near future, with people restricted by law to a certain number of children. Often, this theme becomes entangled with the notion of eugenic planning, so that it becomes a criminal offence for some 'unsuitable' people to have children at all. It is widely believed that such measures may have to be introduced, and there has already been some speculative investigation, even outside the realms of science fiction, of ways in which they might be carried out. In 1971 the journal *Bio-Science* carried an article by Carl Jay Bajema weighing up the pros and cons of various 'licensing systems' for controlling childbirth. The viability of such programmes depends on contraceptive technology, but this seems to be advancing rapidly enough to facilitate any such scheme that might be devised.

This kind of control would seem to very many people to infringe one of the most basic kinds of freedom, but it does not take much imagination to see that there might arise conditions which would necessitate some kind of coercive population control. There are many science fiction stories which try to make a virtue out of this imagined necessity, but it is arguable that the more powerful stories are those which see it as a potential tragedy. Stories dealing with the theme

include Robert Silverberg's *Master of Life and Death*, which looks at the moral problems faced by the man required to dispense child-licences; D.G. Compton's *The Quality of Mercy*, about the political use of plague to reduce population; and Philip K. Dick's story 'The Pre-Persons', which envisages the widening of the concept of abortion to include infanticide.

There are other contemporary crises that may alter the nature of tomorrow's crimes. Legislative control of pollution is now commonplace, and the legal restrictions increase in complexity every year. Legislation in respect of fuel-economy may well follow soon. Many science fiction writers feel that in these respects the real world is moving rather too slowly, and that catastrophe may not be averted. Particularly effective in making this claim are a number of post-catastrophe stories in which technological endeavour is itself regarded as evil. A notable recent example is Norman Spinrad's *Songs from the Stars*, in which the inhabitants of a future America, having been forced to revert to a simpler way of life, discriminate between white and black science in much the same way that our ancestors discriminated between white and black magic. White science, in Spinrad's novel, is ecologically responsible 'alternative technology' which uses solar power or wind- and water-power (see pages 39-41); black science involves the use of atomic power-plants. Most writers of this kind of story, however, are very keen to point out that discriminating against technology should not involve discriminating against knowledge, and that making science as such a criminal activity is a measure which could never be justified. The freedom to know is held by most science fiction writers to be far more sacred than the freedom to breed.

The advancement of technology opens up whole new realms of possibility about the nature and definition of crime. It is not merely a matter of new inventions offering new opportunities to police forces or to criminals, but a question of constantly making new decisions about what is to count as anti-social behaviour and how best to control it.

Chapter 10
POWERS OF THE MIND

Science fiction features a conventional range of mysterious mental powers, all with their roots in fable if not in fact. Each ability has its own 'scientific' label: magic sounds so much more convincing when we call it 'paraphysics'.

The fringes of mental science

As fast as new ideas turn up on the fringes of science, they are grabbed by science fiction writers to add spice to their stories. Some of these exciting notions win acceptance; others are highly controversial, with their supporters relying more on faith than on careful experiments.

The 'Kirlian aura' is a famous example of dubious science in the region of parapsychology — a word meaning 'beyond psychology', concerning powers and properties of the mind that are unrecognized by orthodox science. (Science fiction usually prefers the terms 'paraphysics' and 'psionics'.) To take a Kirlian photograph of, say, a human hand, we place that hand in a powerful, high-frequency electric field and make an exposure: the

resulting picture shows a luminous halo around the hand. This is the Kirlian aura. Enthusiasts were quick to suggest that this aura is a mysterious life force, that it varies according to state of health, sanity, sobriety, psionic ability, and so on.

Science fiction writers soon borrowed the idea. In Piers Anthony's 'Cluster' books, the Kirlian aura is a measure of strength of personality — in fact it is itself the personality, and can be transferred from body to body. A.E. van Vogt's *The Anarchistic Colossus* features 'Kirlian machines' which detect emotions from the aura and can shoot people with lasers should they plan violence. Sadly, the Kirlian aura is already discredited as a trivial thing, of no more significance than static electricity, that depends mainly on the moisture in the object 'photographed'. The human aura is supposed to change dramatically according to physical

and mental state: experiments showed that the full range of possible 'auras' could be produced from any one object by altering the gap between it and the electrode, the strength and frequency of the field, the moistness of the object itself, and so on; if all these things were kept constant, no differences could be detected between the auras of ordinary people, psychic 'mediums' and lunatics.

Psychic medicine is another controversial area. Several science fiction novels, such as Roger Zelazny's *To Die in Italbar*, feature psionic healers who can cure disease *even without the patient's knowledge*. It seems possible to stimulate the body's defences against some diseases by making hypnotic suggestions to the patient, and fervent belief in a cure can have the same effect. A very few people, for instance, benefit from the water of Lourdes. Warts — a virus

Photographs like this — unless one believes they are fakes — make it difficult to stay sceptical about firewalking. There have been many eye-witness accounts, too. But how can self-hypnosis prevent charring of the feet? This particular ritual — the year is 1959 — is held annually at the Hindu shrine in Kataragama, south Sri Lanka. The woman seems to be in an ecstatic trance state.

infection — are said to have been hypnotically cured, or even caused, in specified parts of the body. But suggestion certainly cannot remove an appendix: the supposed 'psychic healers' of the Philippines and South America claim to perform such major surgery with their bare hands aided by psionic force; they sink their fingers into patients' stomachs and pull out gobbets of meat. Since doctors who later examine these patients report no missing organs, and since the bits 'removed' always prove to be animal rather than

human tissue, such healers are obviously tricksters who work by sleight of hand. Film records of their operations tend to confirm this. Yet some of their patients do improve: people who expect to feel better probably will, if only temporarily.

There are many other controversial 'powers', which we often hear about, but which science fiction writers would not class as psionic. The word 'psionics' was explained in *Astounding Science-Fiction* by John W. Campbell as 'psychic electronics': something special which the mind could do, involving unknown mental forces, and as reliable and repeatable as the operation of a transistor radio. As well as powering the full range of psionic talents (to be discussed in the next section), this force could be generated and harnessed by machines. Campbell described one such gadget, the Hieronymous machine, which was supposed to work just as well if you threw away the components and substituted the circuit diagram. Understandably, this machine failed to work unless operated by a True Believer, and was rather unreliable even then.

Hypnotism and self-hypnotism are examples of talents not regarded

A Yogi mystic in Sri Lanka demonstrates his indifference to pain and his bodily control by adopting the lotus position while suspended by ropes pinned through his skin. Is this a psionic power, or just a rather foolish bravery?
Left above: the so-called 'Kirlian aura' flickers dully around the silhouette of a faith-healer's fingers while she is relaxing. The aura here is blue.
Left below: the same fingers now glow brightly at the tips — the aura is red — as the woman enters the 'healing state'. What is the explanation? Does the aura show an occult truth about her mental powers? Scientists say the change is probably because her fingers have begun to sweat with strain.

as psionic, since unknown forces are not involved. The hypnotist in Edgar Allan Poe's 'The Facts in the Case of M. Valdemar' is, however, gifted, in that he hypnotizes the unfortunate Valdemar into staying intact and conscious for seven months after his death! Almost as startling is the feat of autohypnosis whereby the hero of F.M. Busby's *Cage a Man* goes into a deathlike trance and convinces himself that he is dead — thus escaping from an automated, mind-reading prison cell by being flushed with other 'dead' matter through the waste-disposal system. Hypnotic abilities involve strength of mind and perhaps special training, as in yoga, or the various systems of mind/body control described in Frank Herbert's *Dune.* But they do not involve 'true' psionics.

In the same category are such established abilities as the control of normally involuntary muscles: trained people can dramatically alter the rate of their heartbeats merely by thinking, or shift their body temperature within certain limits, or enter trances wherein they breathe remarkably little air. Not all these abilities seem very useful. Why, for example, do certain mystics train themselves to control the involuntary muscles of their intestines and suck up water through the wrong end of the digestive tract? But with such a range of more or less established talents, it is not difficult to believe in the body training of Vonda N. McIntyre's *Dreamsnake,* in which men control their fertility at will and therefore have a built-in contraceptive. Perhaps the mystics should leave their intestines alone and start working on a reliable fertility-control training system.

A phenomenon which looks as though it might be due to auto-hypnosis and body training is that of walking on fire. Unlike the Indian rope trick, this has taken place before apparently reliable witnesses. But what system of training can prevent flesh from shrivelling and charring as bare feet walk on visibly glowing coals or stones? If the observers are not hypnotized, deluded or just plain untruthful, there is some unknown factor at work here — perhaps even a psionic power.

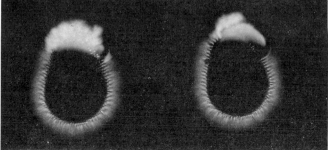

Psionics

'Psi' powers reached the height of their science fictional popularity in the magazine *Astounding Science-Fiction*, later called *Analog*, under the editorship of John W. Campbell. He presented such talents as a means of short-circuiting all the hard work which we must otherwise do to understand and control the universe around us. Naturally this appealed to intellectually lazy readers who were happy to ignore the fact that giving something a label does not make it real.

One of the most convincing novels of psionics is James Blish's *Jack of Eagles*, whose hero is forced to do much more work with his mental powers than simply wishing that such-and-such a thing would happen. Instead he must handle the reality behind the wish. To lift a table by mental force, for example, he needs to visualize all the subatomic particles that make up that table, and to understand and manipulate the equations of inertia and gravity which keep the table on the floor. Understandably, this demands enormous effort — and also gives him a terrible headache.

The usual list of labelled psionic powers falls into two sections: those dealing with abstract information and those which actually reach out to affect tables or other physical objects. If we could win at poker by reading an opponent's mind or his unseen cards this would be a talent of the first kind — extra-sensory perception (ESP). If we could win at dice by controlling the fall of the cubes this would be telekinesis, a talent of the second kind. Talents which operate 'for information only' are slightly more reputable in the eyes of scientists since they cause fewer awkward clashes with the law of conservation of energy.

Telepathy, then, is the flow of information from mind to mind. John Brunner's novel *Telepathist* covers several variations of telepathy — there are projective telepathists who can transmit their thoughts into the minds of others, receptive telepathists who simply read minds, and a handful of special people with both talents. Naturally, these telepathists are marvellous psychiatrists who can *really* see and change their patients' fears — but there are dangers too, since someone who lets insane thoughts into his mind is himself risking insanity. A less versatile talent occasionally found in science fiction is telempathy (sometimes just called 'empathy'): the ability to sense emotions rather than detailed thoughts. In James White's *Hospital Station* the alien empath Dr Prilicla is so sensitive to emotions, and so eager to avoid provoking unpleasant emotions, as to be tactful to the point of untruthfulness.

Related to these, but more sinister, is the super-hypnosis sometimes called 'telecontrol'. Plainly, a projective telepathist or empath would be able to throw people into a hypnotic trance with especial ease — their hypnotic suggestions must surely be more effective when beamed into the mind rather than into the ears. A powerful enough projective telepathist might not even need the gentle art of hypnosis: his projected thoughts could be so much stronger than his victim's as to swamp them completely.

Other labelled talents are supposed to extract information from sources other than minds. Clairvoyance is at its simplest the ability to see things in far-off places or behind closed doors. When eaves-dropping, such invisible eyes work best in conjunction with invisible ears: clairaudience. These talents were taken further in E.E. Smith's 'Lensman' books, in which clairvoyance and clairaudience are combined into a 'sense of perception' whose lucky users can see in the dark, look through solid objects, study the internal organs of friends and have other spinoffs guaranteed to make them the life and soul of any party. If such eavesdropping is extended further, to *future* events, that talent is called precognition — foreknowledge of the future. (Inevitably, precognition will distort its own predictions by changing the future — the same paradoxical problem that makes time travel so unlikely.) Studying the past in a similar way, aided by some antique object whose history is explored by the mind, is called 'psychometry'. A good fictional example of this is the vision of Shakespearean England in Colin Wilson's *The Philosopher's Stone*.

Most of these talents are claimed by psychic mediums, who generally explain that the secret is to project one's 'astral body' through walls, into the past or the future, and so on. (To 'see', the astral body or clairvoyant sense must absorb light — and therefore

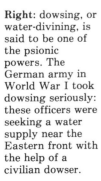

Right: dowsing, or water-divining, is said to be one of the psionic powers. The German army in World War I took dowsing seriously: these officers were seeking a water supply near the Eastern front with the help of a civilian dowser.

The nastier possibilities of telekinesis have never been more gruesomely demonstrated than in the film *Scanners* (1981). The scene here, where an unfortunate man loses his head during a psionic duel, is one of many in the film where molecules in people's bodies are moved telekinetically with devastating effect.

must be detectable by instruments, which might make an interesting research project.) Science fiction writers prefer to avoid the disreputability of spiritualism, insisting that psionic powers are — at least in their fiction — not mystical but prosaic and testable abilities which, with a little practice, will be no stranger than the mental power we already use to control large masses of water and chemicals: our own bodies. Some writers have gone further to include the astral body or soul in the scope of scientific law: Bob Shaw's *The Palace of Eternity* and Eric Frank Russell's *Sentinels from Space* deal with souls as they might have been designed by scientists rather than by theologians — not as spirits, but as stable patterns of energy.

The basic talent of the kind which moves parts of the physical world is telekinesis, sometimes called 'psychokinesis' (and abbreviated to TK or PK). In fiction, the range of telekinetic ability is huge. The hero of Larry Niven's *The Long ARM of Gil Hamilton* can, with difficulty, lift a glass of whisky with his mind; the heroine of Stephen King's *Carrie* can wreck buildings; the telekineticists in Jack Vance's 'Telek' are able to hurl planets from their orbits by a twitch of thought. Where, in each case, does the energy come from? We shall look at such problems later (see pages 174-5). The power of levitation follows naturally from telekinesis if enough force can be generated; the

user lifts *himself* with his power — yet another example of that favourite trick of lifting oneself by one's own bootlaces, as featured in Rudolph Erich Raspe's *Travels of Baron Munchausen* in 1785.

A less obvious consequence of telekinesis is a kind of super-ventriloquism. If you can move objects with the speed of thought, you can surely vibrate them fast enough to produce sound. Next comes the talent called 'fire-sending', as seen in Stephen King's novel *Firestarter*. Psionic arsonists are usually called 'pyrotics'; they use telekinesis to increase the vibration-rates of molecules in their target. The temperature of a solid, liquid or gas depends on the average speed of its molecules (or, more accurately, on the square root of the average of the squares of the velocities of all its molecules). By speeding them up, the target's temperature is increased until at last it bursts into flame. This happens to people's heads in some celebrated and revolting scenes in the film *Scanners* (1981).

Again, science fiction offers these mysterious powers as 'rational' explanations of the inexplicable. So poltergeists are obviously wild telekinetic outbursts, while claims of spontaneous combustion in people can be put down to the doings of unfriendly pyrotics. These are hardly explanations, however.

Finally come the talents of apportation and teleportation — the moving of objects, or ourselves,

instantaneously from place to place. While telekinesis is the psionic equivalent of the impossible, reactionless 'Dean Drive' (see page 192), teleportation is like a quick trip through hyperspace — and just as unlikely. Sometimes apportation is taken to mean the creation of solid objects from nothing, which is more unlikely still.

A 'psionic' power widely accepted in reality is dowsing, the talent which finds water or other substances underground. Many scientists argue that dowsers function best in areas where they already know the geography and the likely collecting-places for water (and water can be found almost anywhere if you dig deep enough). Others suggest that dowsing is a sensitivity to electrical or magnetic fields, no more 'psionic' than the talents of migrating birds which navigate by Earth's magnetism. Yet other scientists point out that laboratory tests of dowsing have produced spectacular failures.

With this possible exception, no reliable psionic talents seem to be functioning in our world today. We hardly need the new mutations suggested in Philip K. Dick's story 'A World of Talent' — 'psi-immunes' who have minds impervious to telepathy, or futures which cannot be predicted, or a mental inertia which stops them being moved about by telekinesis. At present we are all seemingly in the position of immunes. It is easy to be immune to a non-existent disease.

171

Telepathy and the information talents

The thoughts in our heads are powerful things. A passing thought can suddenly fill us with happiness or rage for no reason that anyone else can sense. Every face we see has thoughts behind it, like a monologue in a locked room. Surely there must be some way to overhear them?

In physical terms there are many obstacles to the broadcasting and receiving of thoughts. The human brain is not a transmitter: it produces electrical fields as a by-product of the subtle electrochemical processes of thought, but these fields are very weak. Purpose-built machines (electroencephalographs, or EEGs) can pick up brain rhythms through electrodes attached to the skin; but brains cannot even pick up the much more powerful fields of radio transmission. And, though EEGs can be calibrated finely enough to tell what colour one is looking at from brain rhythms alone, the settings change from person to person — we all seem to have our own internal codes for 'blue' or 'red'. Unravelling the coding of thoughts would be a lifetime's work, to be

repeated for everyone whose mind was to be 'read'. The unscrupulous, telepathic aliens of Hal Clement's story 'Impediment' are foiled by the fact that they can read the thoughts of only the one man they have studied.

Obviously, telepathy has not been achieved on any large scale, or we might already be living in the world of Alfred Bester's novel *The Demolished Man,* with crime wiped out thanks to mind-reading police and psychiatrists. In fact, telepathy sounds like an obstacle to mental evolution: mind-to-mind communication could have made it unnecessary to develop speech or abstract thought. Instead, as hinted in Theodore Sturgeon's short story 'To Marry Medusa', evolution would tend to produce one 'group mind' for the telepathically linked human race, with individuals being as mindless and interchangeable as ants or bees. Another problem, raised in John Brunner's story 'Protect Me from My Friends', is the likelihood that a telepath whose mind reads all the world's jumble of thoughts would go mad under the strain. Young telepaths might never grow up to breed, the power having become an anti-survival mutation.

The case against telepathy has been strengthened by the failure of experiments to prove that it exists. A convincing experiment would

feature the supposed telepaths in two sealed rooms. Random images would be generated and displayed by a computer in one room, studied by the person in that room, telepathically picked up by the person in the second room, and keyed by him into a computer terminal for unbiased machine-comparison with the original sequence displayed. A high score of correct transmissions would mean that telepathy works: without the person in the first room this becomes a test for clairvoyance, the other person using psionic talent to read numbers or letters directly from the unseen computer display. No well run experiment along these lines has given good results. Can it be, as in Robert Silverberg's *Dying Inside,* that a real telepath would hide himself from investigation for fear of having his talent literally dissected out? Some ESP enthusiasts explain that the talents are sabotaged by the sceptical thoughts of scientists who design such tests — but tests run by 'believers' also tend to give negative results, except in cases where error or fraud is possible.

Many experiments on psionic talents have been more complex but even less convincing than this positive yes-or-no testing. Some researchers, such as Rhine and Soal, have used the dubious apparatus of

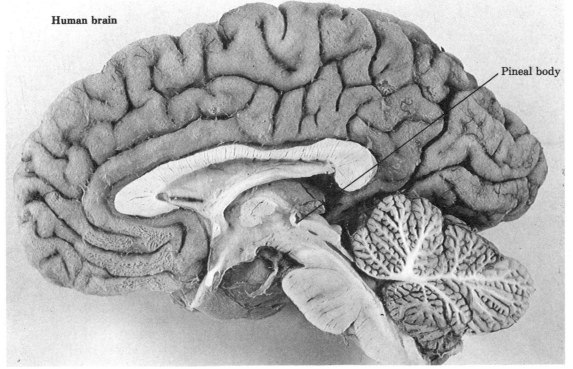

Human brain

Pineal body

Left: deep down at the base of the fore-brain lies the pea-sized pineal body. It is often identified with a mysterious 'third eye' that confers telepathic powers, though it is not connected with the visual nerves. **Right:** Mr Pratt (left) and Mr Pearce (right) were the subjects of the botanist J.B. Rhine's most famous experiment in telepathy at Duke University in 1935. Pratt transmitted, Pearce received. The lack of precautions against cheating weakened the good results.

playing cards printed with special symbols to be 'read' by telepathy or clairvoyance. Ignoring the trickery possible in shuffling and other card manipulation, these experiments have been unsatisfactory because the method was statistical. A series of correct card identifications better than expected from sheer random guesswork was hailed as proof of ESP. If the score was lower than expected from random chance, this too was good ('negative prediction'). When the score fell in the random-chance range, as all too often it did, it was generally ignored. Statistically, indeed, you must get unlikely results once in a while, just as, by tossing coins for long enough, you are sure to get an unlikely six 'heads' in a row (though the odds are 63 to 1 against achieving this in any particular six throws). The trouble with statistical ESP experiments is that 'good' scores are not reliably repeatable — meaning either that psionic talents wear out rather easily or that the original score was a fluke.

It is still possible that occasional flashes of unnatural perception come to some human minds, but too few to be measured by the long grind of controlled experiments. An example might be the sudden certainty of a roulette player who *knows* the number which is coming up, and afterwards sees it win. Gamblers have these flashes of 'certainty' quite frequently, but the ones they remember are the (infrequent) winners. Whether it is a statistical fluke or a psionic flash, such an unpredictable phenomenon is not experimentally testable and therefore not science.

The 'inner sight' of ESP has been linked with the 'third eye' of Eastern mysticism. Science fiction has often featured a literal third eye — usually the pea-sized pineal body within the brain, whose function is not fully understood. In Charles L. Harness's 'The Rose', the pineal body reaches maturity and psionic usefulness by physically growing through other parts of the brain: the victim gains ESP but loses the ability to read and write. T. Lobsang Rampa's *The Third Eye* describes the awakening of the pineal eye by a process of drilling through the skull and poking sticks into the hole. Though told as fact, this is indeed science fiction: the author, who purported to be a 'Tibetan lama', turned out to be an English plumber called Hoskins. Of course the original 'third eye' is a symbol of *spiritual* enlightenment, having nothing to do with psionics or the physical brain. Too many people read mystic writings as though they were not religious parables but wiring diagrams.

Packs made up of these five cards, each with a separate symbol, were used in Rhine's celebrated experiments in telepathy. Critics who examined the cards said some of the symbols were visible from the back! It may have been silly to use cards at all.

Telekinesis and the brute-force talents

In the 1970s telekinesis became the most popular of supposed psionic powers – thanks to the trickster Uri Geller's 'psychic' bending of much good cutlery. His televised performances produced an epidemic of 'super-children' who also claimed to bend metal by mental force. Was a testable psionic power available at last?

The short answer seems to be 'no'. Geller's abilities tended to vanish mysteriously when anything like a controlled experiment was suggested, and all his publicly staged performances have been duplicated just as convincingly by professional magicians. His most uncanny ability was his sense of timing, whereby he performed his best tricks while the cameramen were changing their films. The 'superkids' were good at bending spoons while unsupervised, but their talents dwindled as experimental conditions were tightened up. These gloomy results came not from sceptics but from the mathematician John Taylor, who at first believed in telekinetic metal-bending but by the late 1970s was doubtful that it existed at all. It is interesting that, just as 'apports' supposedly teleported into rooms by psychics are always small enough to hide under the clothing, so the keys and spoons publicly bent by Geller were always small enough to conceal or substitute by sleight of hand.

Most fictional scientists are fanatically against psionics. In Isaac Asimov's short story 'Belief', a man who can reliably levitate himself has enormous difficulty in convincing scientists of his power. But, like Taylor, many real scientists relish new challenges, and ask only that telekinesis should work under conditions chosen to prevent error and trickery. They also ask how psionic effects connect with the known laws of physics. If, as was suggested, spoon-bending results from electromagnetic radiation produced by the brain, can this radiation be detected? From experiment and for the reasons suggested above, it seems not. If a man can levitate himself in defiance of gravity, what supports his weight? Or can we measure the space-distortions his mind must be producing to cancel out Earth's gravity? No, for although cases of levitation were famous in times past, nobody seems able to do it before witnesses in this sceptical age. If a psychic causes a small object weighing, say, 100 gm to 'materialize' from thin air, surely the energy involved (more than that of a 2-megaton explosion for a 100-gm mass) must produce detectable side effects, whether it is stolen from elsewhere or somehow created on the spot.

A science fictional answer to these awkward questions is that there is another, 'parallel' universe which supplies energy for psychic doings, as in Robert Heinlein's 'Waldo'. The combined energy of both universes stays constant, satisfying the laws of physics; but since psionic talents can shuttle energy to and fro between the universes, it seems that energy is being psionically created or destroyed in this universe. Two

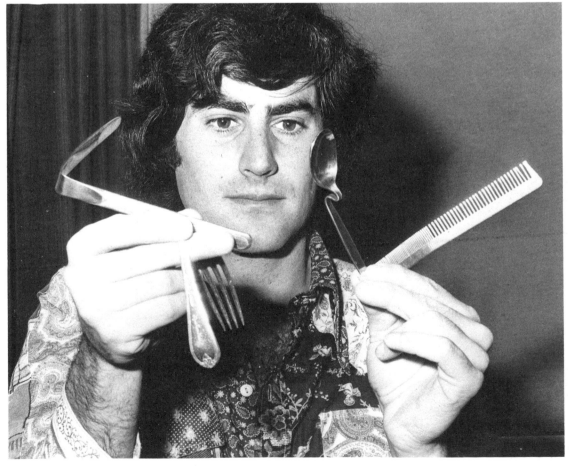

Left: Uri Geller, trickster or master of telekinesis? Did he bend these objects by mental power or sleight of hand? The stage magician James Randi has successfully duplicated all Geller's stunts using traditional conjuring techniques.
Right: strange events at a London spiritualist temple in 1938. This early infra-red picture shows medium Colin Evans, supposedly levitating. 'I myself saw Evans rise about ten feet and come down again all in a matter of seconds', the photographer testified. Sceptics will argue that such feats are easier to fake in the near-darkness Evans used.

problems follow from this clever idea. First, why should the human brain be capable of tapping the energy of another universe when it cannot directly convert even the energy of a lump of coal? (One of the few concessions to common sense in A.E. van Vogt's *The World of Null-A* is that the only psionically gifted character is a mutant with an energy-controlling 'extra brain'.) Secondly, if psionics has an objective, testable basis like this, its truth should have been established long ago.

This is not to say that psionic phenomena are unreal. In

mathematics, Gödel's famous proof shows that there exist theorems which are true but cannot be proved by the logical tools of mathematics. Physics reduces the universe to mathematics: psionic powers might be an elusive fact of the universe which cannot be either proved or disproved by logic or experiment. Ian Watson's *Miracle Visitors* suggests that UFOs (see pages 176-9) could be in a similar position — a 'higher truth' which we can never verify.

If this is so, past statistical work on telekinesis is useless. Here people tried to influence the fall of

dice — usually ignoring the problem that most dice have a natural bias which shows up in long sequences. (Even drilling out the pips in each die face can shift the centre of gravity slightly.) This may account for some above-random scores; others are required by sheer statistics. If 1000 people were tested, 100 or so might score well by chance; when retested, 10 of the 100, and then 1 of the 10, might still score slightly above the random expectation. So must the person who scored significantly in three successive tests be a telekinetic expert? Not at all. It is as though the 1000 people were each asked to toss a coin, the object being to score 'heads'. About 500 people would succeed in the first trial, 250 of these in the second, 125 of those in the third, and so on. The odds are that *someone* will 'prove' psionic ability by tossing 'heads' 9 or 10 times in a row.

If our minds cannot exert the tiny force needed to affect the fall of dice, it sounds unlikely that large masses could be flashed through space at the speed of light (if not faster). This is teleportation, the commuter's dream: in Alfred Bester's *Tiger! Tiger!* all transport is obsolete while people travel instantly by mind alone. The ability to teleport anywhere imaginable could have awful consequences. For example, several stories, including Daniel Galouye's 'The Last Leap', feature teleporters struggling with varying success *not* to imagine the word 'Sun'.

There are more serious problems. The difference in gravitational potential energy between sea level and the top of Everest is enough to accelerate someone to 1500 kph: what happens when you teleport from one to the other? It would be dangerous to teleport too far north or south — Earth's spin makes the equator move nearly 1700 kph faster than the poles. And what about mountains, or people — or even air molecules — occupying the space where you materialize? There could be a nasty explosion. Even if they are mere wish-fulfilment, psionic abilities would be as tricky as fairy-tale wishes — the sort that leave the unfortunate wisher with a sausage stuck to his nose.

Chapter 11
MYSTERIES OF THE PAST AND PRESENT

Are there strange truths about our world that scientists have conspired to ignore? Millions of people believe so.

Flying saucers

People have always caught glimpses of objects which they could not identify, including objects in the sky. This is not very surprising. What is surprising, however, is that in the last 35 years or so it has become astonishingly fashionable to claim that some of these objects are actually spaceships from other worlds.

The modern boom in UFO (Unidentified Flying Object) sightings began in 1947, following a report by an American businessman, Kenneth Arnold. He was flying his private plane in the Cascade mountains and saw what he later claimed were nine objects, the size of airliners, flying at more than 1500 kph. Eight of the objects were disc-shaped (the ninth was a crescent), and he described their motion to reporters as 'like saucers being skipped over water'. Thus 'flying saucers' were born. Within weeks hundreds more had been reported from all over the USA.

Social psychologists have linked the flood of UFO sightings to the political climate of the Cold War — the corollary of a general unease inspired by the notion that World War III might not be so far away, and that America was in great danger of being betrayed from within by communist sympathizers. In this interpretation, UFOs become, like the McCarthy witch-hunts, a symptom of national paranoia. If that was ever the case, however, the symptom proved far hardier than the disease.

Some of the early sightings which actually involved real objects were undoubtedly of skyhook balloons, then being tested experimentally for meteorological uses. The UFO chased by USAF pilot Thomas Mantell in January 1948 was almost certainly a skyhook balloon. Mantell became the first UFO casualty when he took his unpressurized plane too high, blacked out, and crashed; the event was dramatic enough to lend itself to all kinds of fanciful misinterpretations.

The USAF took an active interest in UFO sightings, largely because there seemed to be a chance that the Russians might be testing new types of aircraft. They financed three investigative projects, culminating in Project Blue Book. The final report by Edward U. Condon and his team offered an account of cases investigated in which 97% of several thousand reports were shown to be mistakes or hoaxes. That 3% of cases should remain unexplained is not altogether surprising: there were bound to be some cases where the data were inadequate to reach a conclusion. But it is these 3% which continue to give heart to believers convinced that within the smokescreen of deception there must be at least a little fire.

The air force gradually lost interest in UFOs, accepting that the phenomenon was a psychological one and hence (to them) uninteresting. Committed believers, of course, misinterpreted this as an outward show concealing some kind of cover-up. The myth that the awful truth about flying saucers is known, but that it is protected by a security blanket, remains popular.

In 1953 Desmond Leslie and George Adamski published the best-selling book *Flying Saucers Have Landed*. In the first part, Leslie offers 'evidence' that flying saucers have been visiting the Earth throughout history — going all the way back to 18,617,841 BC (a remarkable feat, considering the dearth of historical records!). In the second part, Adamski tells of his encounter with a man from Venus, who told him that all the planets of the Solar System are inhabited by men, who had always kept in touch with Earth but who had recently become anxious because of our tinkering with the secrets of the atom.

Shortly after this, in 1954, George King announced that he had become the spokesman for the Interplanetary Parliament, receiving instructions telepathically while in a state of trance, and relaying his message via the Aetherius Society and his book *You Are Responsible!*. King tells us that Jesus Christ is alive and well on Venus, and that the Second Coming is due soon. He also tells us that the other inhabitants of the Solar System are very worried about our playing with the atom. Similar views are independently propagated by Meade Layne, in *The Coming of the Guardians*, and others.

This easy incorporation of UFOs into the mythology of what are effectively millenarian religious cults lends considerable weight to the argument that the whole UFO phenomenon demands interpretation in terms of social psychology. The psychoanalyst C.G. Jung wrote a book about flying saucers in which he tried to explain UFOs as subjective products of the unconscious. The French psychologist Bertrand Méheust has worked along similar lines; his ideas are elaborately extended in the science fiction novel *Miracle Visitors*

The artist Tim White here evokes to perfection the image of the flying saucer as it exists in modern mythology. It is sad that no UFO photograph has ever been taken that duplicates the clarity of White's vision. Some modern ufologists take the view that flying saucers are psychic phenomena created as 'realities' by the power of the collective unconscious — Jungian archetypes suspended glowingly in the skies above our heads.

Left: the 'mother ship', a vast flying saucer, appears above Devil's Tower mountain in Wyoming in Spielberg's film *Close Encounters of the Third Kind*. This is one of the most potent, mythic images in the modern cinema.

by Ian Watson. However, both these explanations are as difficult to swallow as the alien spaceships of the more literal interpretation.

Watson believes that many people have access to an altered state of consciousness, which he calls 'UFO-consciousness'. He draws on arguments from quantum physics about the relationship between the observing consciousness and the phenomena observed, especially those arguments produced by scientists who say that we live in a 'participatory universe' (see pages 98-101). Watson suggests that UFOs are 'real', but also that they are 'summoned into existence' by human consciousness. He points out that early UFO sightings always conform to the 'belief structure' of the period: in the Middle Ages, for example, we have descriptions of 'flying sailing ships'. Structurally, however, modern 'eye-witness' accounts of UFOs are similar to fairy stories. This is dramatized clearly in the film *Close Encounters of the Third Kind* (1977), in which people enticed into the 'mother ship' emerge no older after 30 years, just

as people lured into fairy mounds did in the folk tales. Watson's view was heretical several years ago, but many members of UFO societies now share it.

Contemporary UFO investigators range from obvious outright cranks to serious sceptics who feel that, once all the mistakes and hoaxes have been eliminated, there still remains something worthy of scientific investigation. The most famous of these 'converted sceptics' is J. Allen Hynek, whose book *The UFO Experience* (1972) included the classification of UFO reports which divides them up into six categories: nocturnal lights; daylight discs; radar cases; and three others normally referred to as 'close encounters' of the first, second and third kinds. By 1976 Hynek had collected 800 reports of close encounters of the third kind, involving supposed meetings with extraterrestrials.

Most accounts of supposed meetings with aliens are so puerile as to be quite beyond belief, but there is a specially interesting category consisting of encounters

'recalled' under hypnosis. The most famous of these is the 'interrupted journey' of Barney and Betty Hill which supposedly took place in 1961. Betty Hill reproduced a 'star map' (see diagram) which she remembered (under hypnosis) having seen on the alien spaceship where she and her husband were taken. This was subsequently interpreted by an amateur astronomer as showing routes between a number of nearby Sol-type stars. It was alleged that the map showed that the aliens' homeworlds were orbiting the stars Zeta 1 Reticuli and Zeta 2 Reticuli. For a long time this seemed quite plausible, but it was discovered in 1981 that Zeta 2 Reticuli is actually a binary star which could not possibly have life-supporting planets. At one time it appeared reasonable to assume that special credence should be given to memories extracted under hypnosis; but it has now been shown by forensic scientists that hypnotized subjects will lie, fantasize and mis-remember just as readily as when they are conscious.

There are still sightings

Most flying saucers turn out to be cases of mistaken identity. Meteorological balloons are often seen as 'UFOs'. This photograph, completely *bona fide* and very convincing, does not show flying saucers. These are lenticular cloud formations photographed in Brazil in 1969.

which cannot conclusively be accounted for; but the debate is not really a rational argument over what, if anything, this evidence amounts to. The reasons people have for holding fantastic beliefs about UFOs actually have nothing to do with evidence; UFO enthusiasts deal with evidence only to give their beliefs whatever gloss of respectability can be obtained by their pastiche of scientific method. For the most part, they do not care whether the stories they quote are true or not, as is shown by the way that known hoaxes are still repeated, in book after book. Those UFO enthusiasts who do try to observe reasonable standards of evidence in their enquiries will try to reject

those who do not as members of a 'lunatic fringe', but even the most superficial investigation shows that it is the Hynek-style sceptics who are the fringe, while the real heart of the UFO phenomenon lies with the uncritical believers.

It is very easy to misjudge the size, distance and motion of objects in the sky (especially at night), and therefore to fail to identify things that we see — or think we see — there. We must remember that there is also a positive incentive to misinterpret them: it is much more exciting to have seen something strange and inexplicable than to have seen something ordinary and straightforward. It not only excites us, but makes us exciting. If we

regularly see UFOs, people might think that we are mad, but they will not (immediately) think that we are boring. Belief in UFOs allows people to assert that there are more things in Heaven and Earth than are dreamt of in the philosophies of those who claim to be clever; and it is always comforting to reflect that people cleverer than we are may not be so clever after all. For people who are experts in the art of believing impossible things, more elaborate UFO-fantasies offer even more dramatic payoffs — particularly the comforting thought that there might be people out there who really care about us — and who might be able to stop us blowing ourselves up with nasty atom bombs.

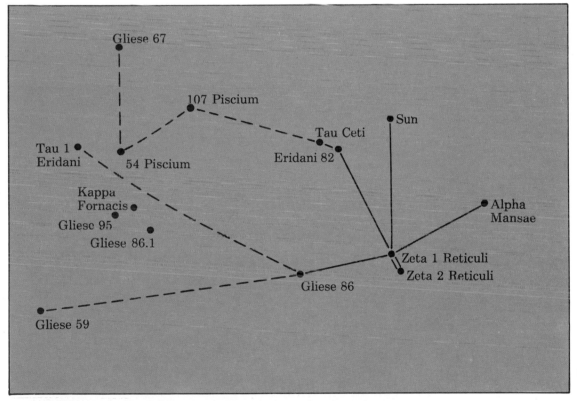

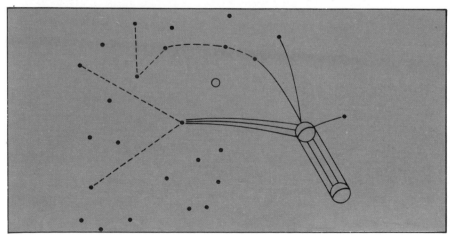

Left: This 'star map' was produced under hypnosis by Betty Hill of New Hampshire, USA, in 1964, three years after she dreamed she was abducted in a UFO — a dream she later believed was an actual memory. The case became famous, especially when an amateur researcher, Marjorie Fish, 'identified' the points on the map (**above**). Ms Fish believed the double-barrelled object in the foreground was the Zeta Reticuli system. However, take away the lines connecting the stars and the case becomes weak. There are only 15 stars on the Fish map, 28 on the Hill map, and the positions are different.

179

Ancient astronauts?

Desmond Leslie's contention in *Flying Saucers Have Landed* that alien astronauts have been visiting Earth throughout human history was not new in 1953. The notion that some of the supernatural beings described in ancient mythologies were actually extraterrestrials goes back to the nineteenth century. It has been so commonplace throughout the history of magazine science fiction that Brian Aldiss coined the term 'shaggy god stories' to describe them. The most familiar (at least to magazine editors, who reject most of them) are those which offer science fictional 'explanations' for biblical myths — such as the suggestion that Adam and Eve were the survivors of a cosmic catastrophe who came to Earth in a spaceship. One of the earliest thoroughgoing attempts to reinterpret the Old Testament as a dim reflection of a science fictional adventure can be found in George Babcock's *Yezad*, published in 1922. A more recent example is Julian Jay Savarin's 'Lemmus' trilogy, published 1972-7.

The most elaborate 'non-fictional' account in the same vein is *The Sky People* by Brinsley le Poer Trench (an eclectic collector of unorthodox beliefs who now sits in the British House of Lords as Lord Clancarty). Here we are told that the gods of Egypt and Greece were aliens, that the Garden of Eden was an experimental set-up on Mars ruined by the melting of one of the Martian ice-caps, and that Noah's Ark was a spaceship.

One of the modern masterpieces of pseudoscholarship is contained in the first two books published by Immanuel Velikovsky: *Worlds in Collision* (1950) and *Ages in Chaos* (1952). These attempt to explain all the Old Testament miracles, and many references in other ancient legends, in terms of a sequence of cosmic events whereby Jupiter emitted a comet which almost collided with Earth before settling down to become Venus. These books were so savagely ridiculed by scientists — who gave the impression of Inquisitors conducting a witch-hunt — that Velikovsky attracted a good deal of sympathy. His ideas were sufficiently attractive, and his pastiche of scientific method sufficiently compelling, for him to recruit many followers, though Carl Sagan in an essay included in *Broca's Brain* has written a careful step-by-step refutation of every one of his arguments.

Right: the mysterious lines in the desert at Nazca are seen by Von Däniken in *Chariots of the Gods?* as runways for alien craft, and this photograph is used in evidence. Alas, the lines are less than 1 metre wide. **Far right**: as the aerial view shows, these lines actually form the outline of a totemic hummingbird, about 90 metres long.

Right: the parting of the Red Sea is one of the best loved stories in the Bible, and formed a memorable climax to Cecil B. De Mille's epic, *The Ten Commandments* (1956). According to Immanuel Velikovsky, who specialized in giving 'scientific' explanations for legendary miracles, part of Jupiter became a comet which, while passing close to Earth, parted the Red Sea by creating giant tides, then settled down to become the planet Venus.

It may well have been Velikovsky who inspired Erich von Däniken, the best-selling exponent of the theory that all ancient mythologies can be explained in terms of garbled eye-witness accounts of the doings of extraterrestrial visitors to Earth. However, these ideas had already become common currency among writers and readers of pseudo-science by the time Von Däniken began publishing. Books already on sale that offered similar ideas included *The Morning of the Magicians* (1960) by Louis Pauwels and Jacques Bergier and *One Hundred Thousand Years of Man's Unknown History* (1963) by Robert Charroux. Soon after publication of Von Däniken's first book Peter Kolosimo (in *Not of This World*, 1970) and Andrew Tomas (in *We Are not the First*, 1971) exploited similar theories. In fact, the same anecdotal material tends to recur over and over again in such books, as writers use each other as 'scholarly sources'. There have been many such books since.

Von Däniken, in *Chariots of the Gods?* (1968) and subsequent works, lists puzzling ancient artefacts (and some modern ones which he also claims to be ancient) and then offers interpretations of their functions in the context of his theory. Thus, the pyramids of Egypt become cryonic vaults, the markings on the plain of Nazca in Peru become a series of runways for spaceships, and an elaborate Mayan design becomes a picture of a man in a rocket-ship. This theory is particularly useful in that it can explain absolutely everything that ever happened, and almost everything that did not. Aladdin's lamp, for instance, becomes a radio set in Von Däniken's book. A great many things which can be explained perfectly easily without recourse to such bizarre notions can, in this view, be reinterpreted so as to become great mysteries.

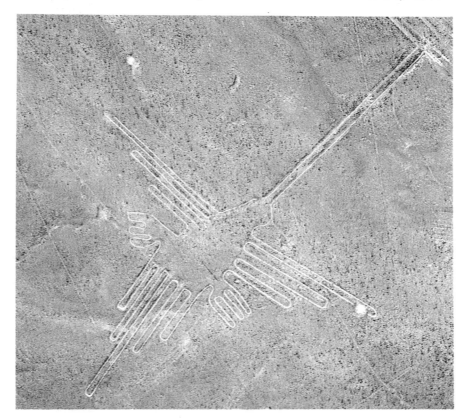

Left: one of the most recent spin-offs of the theories of Von Däniken and his colleagues is the film *Raiders of the Lost Ark* (1981). The theory is that the Ark of the Covenant was a kind of electrical condenser, used by Moses to communicate with alien visitors. In the film the Ark's strange electric powers prove fatal, in this scene, to the group of Nazis that steals it, while our captive hero looks on.

Von Däniken's use of 'evidence', especially in his later books, becomes so obviously irresponsible that it is impossible to take him seriously, but, yet again, it seems that his basic theme is attractive enough to command belief regardless. Archaeologists, after all, have to spend lifetimes cultivating relatively small areas of expertise, and still find much that is puzzling. With the aid of a Von-Dänikenesque world-view, however, even the ignorant can get a firm grasp on everything that matters and need never be at a loss to account for any enigma which they may encounter.

In the last century and a half the stock of human knowledge has grown so quickly and so massively that it is no longer possible for any one person to have command of more than a tiny slice of it. There are no more 'renaissance men'. People feel unsettled by the fact that so much is known, and so little of it by them. It is comforting to be able to feel that the people who think they know it all are merely pronouncing a load of meaningless mumbo-jumbo. There is a great demand for highly simplified versions of the Truth (whether it be that all truth is in the Bible, or written in the stars, or wherever it may be) that give people the illusion of understanding.

By taking his points one by one, it is quite easy to show how Von Däniken twists the evidence. Two books that have done this are *Some Trust in Chariots* (1972), edited by Barry Thiering and Edgar Castle, and *The Space Gods Revealed* (1976) by Ronald Story. A BBC programme, *The Case of the Ancient Astronauts*, televised in several countries in 1977, patiently demolished many of Von Däniken's 'proofs'. There remain, however, many more believers than sceptics, if one can judge by the sales figures of Von Däniken's books and the success of the films based on his work. In our supposedly secular and rational world it may be that strange portents and enigmas become a psychological necessity to maintain some kind of spiritual balance, and if they do not exist, then they must be invented. These mysteries can be rendered superficially acceptable by being given a veneer of 'science'. Von Däniken

talks learnedly, though often inaccurately, of the genetic code, of electricity and magnetism and alien technologies. Barely concealed beneath this twentieth-century surface, however, seethes a witches' brew of gods and demons, strange visitors, potent curses and secret manipulators that would not have seemed out of place during the superstitious, declining years of the Roman Empire.

Behind almost everything that Von Däniken has written is the idea that our ancestors were too stupid and ignorant to work out anything for themselves; that we could not have reached our present status without outside help. Why are readers so ready to accept a thesis so contemptuous of humanity? It is

surely a despairing creed.

Logic plays a minor role in Von Däniken's work, and some of his suppositions are mutually contradictory; he is also highly selective in the 'evidence' he presents. The 'runways' at Nazca would surely be more appropriate for old-fashioned aircraft than for alien spaceships (which elsewhere in *Chariots of the Gods?* are described as descending vertically), and he does not mention that many of the lines at Nazca are simply the outlines of totemic birds and animals. The famous Mayan coffin lid, seen by Von Däniken as depicting a man in a spaceship, is not even particularly convincing in his slightly censored version of the drawing, where parts of the original design have been blacked out: he

Right: the lid of a Mayan sarcophagus, or coffin, found in the Temple of Inscriptions in Palenque, Mexico, was used by Von Däniken as evidence of alien contact. He sees the lid as representing a man piloting a rocket. Parts of the picture, in the version Von Däniken printed, have been blacked out, with the overall effect of reducing the traditionally Mayan decoration and increasing the resemblance he wishes us to see. For example, by blacking out the hair, he is able to give the effect which he describes as 'something like antennae on top'.

fails to note such wholly traditional Mayan elements as the feathered quetzal bird perched on the nose of the 'rocket', the monstrous, toothed guardian of the underworld crouching at its tail, the Mayan kilt on the 'astronaut', and the fact that the astronaut's head is protruding outside the rocket and his 'helmet' looks rather like hair. Elsewhere in Von Däniken's work we learn that the giant heads sculptured out of basalt by the Olmecs 'will never be on show in a museum . . . no bridge in the country could stand their weight'. Such heads are represented in several museums, and Mexico's bridges remain, for the most part, uncollapsed, though the larger heads do in fact weigh many tons.

The film *Raiders of the Lost Ark* (1981) is based partly on one of Von Däniken's suggestions: that the Ark of the Covenant constructed by Bezaleel for Moses, as described in the Old Testament (Exodus 37), was actually an electric condenser, used as a kind of radio for communication between Moses and the alien spaceship. The spaceship does not play a role in the film, but the electric properties of the Ark remain spectacular and a large group of Nazis is satisfyingly annihilated by it. The only biblical warrant for all this is the death of the unfortunate Uzzah (2 Samuel 6:7), whom God smote for touching the Ark. It is a tortuous path that leads from godly wrath to electrical condensers, but Von Däniken was not the first to travel along it. The idea was suggested by Robert Charroux before him.

Most science fiction writers regard the adoption of their notions by such people as Von Däniken as a travesty which is deleterious to the reputation of their art. The only 'shaggy god stories' which get into print these days are jokes and parodies. It is worth noting, though, that one idea which does continue to fascinate science fiction writers, and which recurs with amazing frequency, is that of the extra-terrestrial origin of Man. Why this should be so is not altogether clear, but the idea that Earth was 'seeded' from space obviously has a wide-spread aesthetic appeal. Even cosmic catastrophe scenarios not so very different in spirit from Velikovsky's often become entangled with this thesis. For instance, many stories suggest that the asteroid belt between Mars and Jupiter constitutes the remains of a planet blown up by nuclear war. The most impressive recent attempt to develop this theme can be found in James Hogan's *Inherit the Stars* and its sequels.

One unorthodox thinker who has actually had a noticeable influence on science fiction is Charles Fort, who published several collections of 'damned data' — information on strange incidents and occurrences — assembled from newspaper reports in the first half of this century. Fort attacked the 'priesthood' of science for rejecting these anomalous data in order to conserve orthodox belief, and pointed out the fantastic theories suggested by various interpretations of his material. He himself believed none of these theories and proposed them primarily as whimsies, generally manifesting an ironic scepticism which many people find appealing. The Fortean Society, which still propagates his views, unfortunately takes it all too seriously. Several science fiction writers have developed Fortean hypotheses in fictional form, in particular Eric Frank Russell. His *Sinister Barrier* elaborates the Fortean notion that human beings are the property of aliens; his *Dreadful Sanctuary* develops the thesis that Earth is a dumping-ground for lunatics from other worlds.

Left: the same coffin lid, as drawn from the incised stone by Agustin Villagra. Without the blacking out it is easier to pick out the traditional Mayan elements. The drawing in fact represents a ruler, Pacal, suspended between the worlds of the living and the dead. Above, a quetzal bird, symbolizing the dawn, the rising of the Sun God, is perched on top of a cross. Part of the cross is made of stylized corn plants, representing fertility. Below Pacal's seat crouches the grinning, skull-like Earth monster. The tomb was built in the year 683 and discovered in 1952. If it really shows a rocket, why is the astronaut's head poking out, and why does it have a bird on its nose? (It is difficult to see that it is a bird in Von Däniken's censored version.)

183

Vanished civilizations?

Historians and archaeologists are of the opinion that civilization — the congregation of men in towns and the development of a complex division of labour — began some 10,000 years ago, along the banks of the river Nile in Egypt and around the confluence of the Tigris and the Euphrates in Mesopotamia. These are the earliest civilizations whose remains have been discovered. One of the most popular flights of speculative fancy, however, develops the hypothesis that these were not the first civilizations, and that all traces of earlier ones have unfortunately been wiped out. In pursuit of this notion, much has been made of the mention in two of Plato's dialogues of the lost empire of Atlantis.

The relevant dialogues are the *Timaeus* and the *Critias*, written somewhere around 355 BC. They were sequels to *The Republic,* a dialogue in which Plato produced a blueprint for the ideal society, and were intended to expand upon this idea. They were apparently intended as parts of a kind of trilogy, but the third dialogue was not begun, and the *Critias* breaks off sharply, unfinished, as if Plato had become impatient with it. Instead of continuing, he went on to write *The Laws,* a much more considerable work of political philosophy.

In order to offer a more lively picture of the ideal state sketched out in *The Republic,* Plato 'revealed' in the *Timaeus* that such a state had once existed in Athens some 9000 years before, and that he had this on the authority of the great Athenian statesman Solon, who had himself heard the story while travelling in Egypt in 590 BC. This ideal Athens of the past had fought a long war against the empire of Atlantis, which was based on an island 'beyond the Pillars of Hercules' — a war concluded when a great catastrophe overcame the world and caused Atlantis to sink. The *Critias* gives an elaborate description of the geography of the island, but this is broken off before completion.

Most later writers assumed that this story was an elaborate fable,

though the fact that Aristotle felt obliged to say so presumably indicates that there were people prepared to take it literally. Nobody really cared very much one way or the other, however, until America was discovered. After that some sixteenth-century European writers began to argue that Plato must have been referring to America, and that the *Timaeus* and *Critias* should be treated seriously as historical records. Some maps of the period, including one made by Britain's prestigious magician and intellectual, John Dee, labelled America 'Atlantis'. Francis Bacon, who began an account of an ideal state called *New Atlantis,* clearly held this view, and believed that the American landmass had been very much larger before some of it sank.

In the nineteenth century, geologists finally established that the world was much older than people had commonly believed, and that very many millions of years had elapsed before the beginnings of history. This created a new space for the imagination to play in, and play it did. In 1882 Ignatius Donnelly — the man who tried to prove cryptographically that Shakespeare's plays were written by Francis Bacon — published *Atlantis: the Antediluvian World.* This declared that Atlantis was a real place, dim memories of which were responsible for myths of the Garden of Eden, the Elysian Fields, Asgard, and others, and whose kings and heroes were the gods and demigods of all ancient religions. Myths of the deluge were memories of the flood which sank Atlantis, and survivors of this catastrophe had founded all the world's subsequent civilizations: Egypt, Sumer and Akkad, the Mayas and the Aztecs, and so on. Donnelly's book is perhaps the first great work of pseudoscholarship, accumulating vast stocks of supposed evidence in similarities between the myths, artefacts and social institutions of cultures scattered all over the globe. He followed it up the next year with *Ragnarok, the Age of Fire and Gravel,* in which he anticipated Velikovsky in declaring that Earth once collided with a comet, thus ending the last Ice Age.

Many people were to jump on the bandwagon started by Donnelly.

They included Paul Schliemann, grandson of the remarkable Heinrich who discovered and excavated Troy with the aid of the *Iliad.* In 1912 Paul Schliemann published *How I Discovered Atlantis, the Source of All Civilization,* claiming that his search had begun with some documents and an 'owl-headed vase' left to him by his august ancestor. The whole affair was a hoax — a dishonest attempt to follow in his grandfather's footsteps.

More vanished civilizations began to surface in this period. Several geologists trying to account for similar formations in Africa and India put forward the thesis that the two were once linked by a land-bridge (we now know that they were once joined before being separated — around the time of the great dinosaurs and the early mammals — by continental drift). This hypothesis was popularized by the

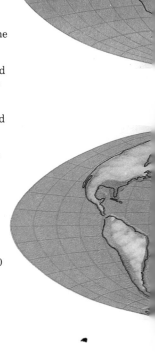

We do not need a landbridge called Lemuria to explain similar animals and geological formations in Africa and India. The drifting of the continents explains the mystery. **Upper left:** 1. The Permian, 250 million years ago. There was one supercontinent called Pangaea. **Upper right:** 2. The Cretaceous, 100 million years ago. North America and Europe had begun to split apart, and the rift between South America and Africa followed soon afterwards. **Lower left:** 3. The Eocene, 50 million years ago. The Atlantic Ocean had opened up. India was an island moving north. **Lower right:** 4. The Pleistocene, 40,000 years ago. The continents were almost in their present-day positions. During this period there were four major Ice Ages.

Today the island of Thera in the Santorini group in the Mediterranean Sea north of Crete is a peaceful tourist resort; but this ocean-filled crater marks the place of a volcanic eruption so violent that it may have destroyed the Minoan Civilization in Crete with a giant tidal wave during the second millennium BC. This could have been the beginning of the Atlantis legend, and also the legend of the great flood. But the date of the eruption is 7500 years too late for the dates of Plato's Atlantis.

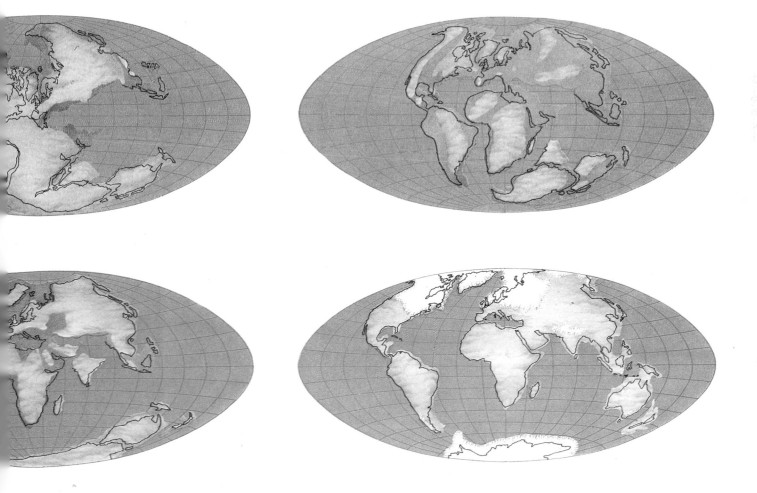

German geologist Neumayr and was picked up by his countryman Ernst Haeckel, an evolutionist who used the theory to account for the distribution of certain mammal groups across the subcontinents — particularly the primitive primates called lemurs. For this reason, the hypothetical landbridge came to be dubbed 'Lemuria', and soon became the location for imaginary vanished civilizations.

Another name frequently confused with Lemuria and sometimes applied to the same area is Mu, which derives from a 'translation' made in 1864 of a Mayan codex by the Abbé Brasseur, who used for this purpose a Mayan 'alphabet' drawn up by the conquistador Diego de Landa. In fact, Mayan writing was pictographic, not phonetic, and hence had no alphabet. What De Landa actually compiled was a limited set of symbols whose pronounced names sounded something like the pronunciation given by the Spanish to the letters of their own alphabet. With the aid of a great deal of imagination and improvisation, Brasseur decided that the codex told the story of a volcanic catastrophe. This had annihilated a country whose name was indicated by two recurrent symbols which looked something like De Landa's 'letters' M and U. The mythology of Mu has been elaborately developed by James Churchward, who based his accounts on stone tablets which he claimed to have seen during his journeys in the Far East. Ancient mythology provides a rich source for speculation about vanished civilizations. Another, often mentioned, is Hyperborea, named after the Hyperboreans of Greek mythology who were held to inhabit a warm and pleasant land in the far north. All of these settings have been much exploited by authors of heroic fantasy seeking prehistoric venues where the imagination could be given free rein without being restricted to sagas of cavemen. Notable among these authors was Robert E. Howard, the creator, back in the 1930s, of the still popular barbarian hero Conan the Cimmerian, superman of the 'Hyborian' age. Such stories, though fictions, did much to increase interest in vanished civilizations, and the

186

popular desire to believe that such civilizations actually existed.

All of these mythical civilizations were dragged into the developing lore of occultism by the theosophist Helena Blavatsky, who offered a highly coloured account of the evolution of Man via the seven 'Root Races' (two of which have yet to emerge). It was the Second Root Race, according to her, which lived in Hyperborea. The Third — a race of hermaphrodite, apelike giants who were four-armed, three-eyed and laid eggs — lived in Lemuria. Atlantis was the home of the Fourth Root Race. The scheme is developed even more elaborately by Helena Blavatsky's disciple W. Scott-Elliot in *The Story of Atlantis* and *The Lost Lemuria*. The supposed authority for the whole farrago was the lost *Book of Dzyan* which Helena Blavatsky was privileged to read while in a trance in order that she could reproduce it in her own book *The Secret Doctrine.*

The sunken world of Atlantis offered such an appealing image that it cropped up constantly in imaginative fiction from Donnelly's time until the 1930s, and it still appears now. Captain Nemo discovered its ruins in Jules Verne's *Twenty Thousand Leagues under the Sea*, and there are numerous quaint, if hopelessly implausible, stories in which the Atlanteans live on, protected by the pressure of the ocean by a crystal dome or a mysterious force-field. (A recent example is to be found in the unappealing film *Warlords of Atlantis*, 1978). The Atlantis publishing industry continues strongly to this day; in recent years there has been a fad for locating the sunken ruins of Atlantis in the shallow waters off the Bahamas. Although Atlantis continues to hold a privileged position in occult mythology, and in fiction deriving from that mythology, the main function served by all these imaginary vanished lands in contemporary fiction is in providing conventional settings for romantic 'sword and sorcery' adventure fiction.

The twentieth century has, however, written a scientific footnote to the story. In the second millennium BC — about 800 years before the journey to Egypt when Solon supposedly heard of Atlantis

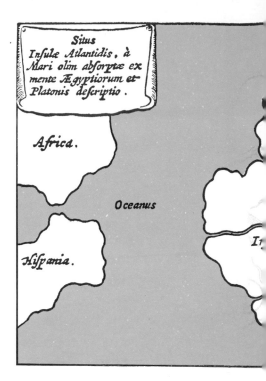

— there was a considerable civilization based on the island of Crete, usually called the Minoan civilization. This came to a rather abrupt end, and it has been suggested that its sudden demise was connected with the eruption of a volcano in the

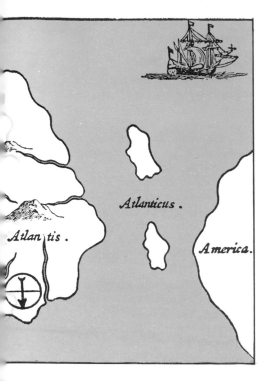

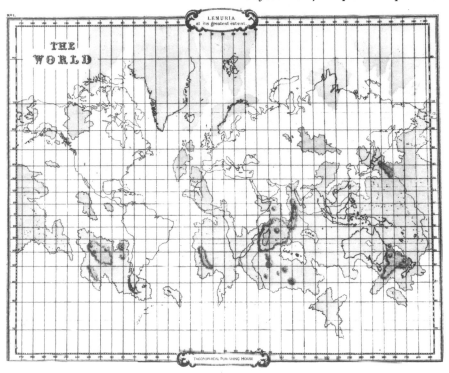

Above left: North is at the bottom of this map of Atlantis as it appeared in *Mundus Subterraneus* by Athanasius Kircher in 1678. But depth readings show no sunken continent. **Above:** the shaded parts of this map show where, in relation to the world we know, Lemuria was located, according to the theosophists who were most attached to the theory. The distribution of lemurs, which Lemuria is supposed to explain, can now be explained by the theory of drifting continents (see page 185). **Left:** volcanic Atlantis just before sinking, as seen in the film *Atlantis: the Lost Continent* (1961).

Aegean Sea, whose relic is the Santorini group of islands, including Thera and Therasia. If this eruption was on the same kind of scale as the eruption of Krakatoa in 1883, then indeed a one-time island may have disappeared, and a tidal wave might well have brought disaster to many neighbouring islands.

There is, however, no need to think that Plato really had any kind of story handed down from Solon's day. There is therefore no need to begin wondering about errors in translation that alter the figure of 9000 years to something more appropriate. But for those who believe that there is a germ of truth within every clever fantasy, this is the straw that they must grasp in order to save Atlantis.

187

Children of the wild?

A myth of rather a different kind, though it is no less persistent than myths of visitors from beyond and vanished civilizations, is that of children reared by wild beasts (usually wolves). We find it in the story of Romulus and Remus, and accounts of animal-fostering of human children are common in Greek legend. Anecdotes and literary versions of the theme recur through the centuries even to the present day. The most famous modern literary versions are the 'Mowgli' stories of Rudyard Kipling and the 'Tarzan' stories of Edgar Rice Burroughs.

Tarzan has become one of the best known modern myth-figures. He is a creature of two worlds who combines the best of both: the innate nobility of the English aristocrat and the toughness of a jungle beast. Because of his great intelligence, he not only became king of his ape-tribe but learned to read from picture-books left behind by his dead parents.

Rumours of children reared by animals continue to attract attention, and never lose their fascination. In 1966 the Paris newspaper *Le Monde* published a long article by Lucien Malson on 50 alleged cases, including the famous 'wild boy of Aveyron' found in 1798. This wild boy was the first 'feral child' to be studied by a scientist. A Dr Itard took the boy into his home, gave him a name (Victor), and tried to educate him. François Truffaut has made a film of this story, *L'Enfant Sauvage* (1970), playing the part of Dr Itard himself.

One of the most recent reports was publicized by the psychologist Arnold Gesell, using diaries kept by a Reverend Mr Singh, who claimed to have dug two orphan girls out of a wolves' den in India in 1930. The younger girl, Amala, soon died; but the elder, Kamala, learned at least some of the art of being human. In 1951 the sociologist W.F. Ogburn and a colleague tried to check up on Gesell's account, but they found that Singh had recently died and could locate no independent evidence of his story about the finding of the

girls.

It is probable that all the cases of supposed 'wolf-children' were actually children who had been fairly recently abandoned, and whose lack of human behavioural traits can be accounted for in terms of autism or sheer neglect. There has never been any convincing evidence of the involvement of the more celebrated feral children with animals — the aesthetic power of the myth is apparently enough to make people turn very readily to this 'explanation'.

We do know, however, a good deal about the effects of continued neglect involving the isolation of children from normal human intercourse. It is sadly not unknown, even in contemporary America and Europe, for parents to hide children away (usually because they are illegitimate) and, apart from feeding them, to pay no other attention to them. The sociologist Kingsley Davis has reported on two cases which he investigated personally. One concerned Isabelle, who was locked away with her deaf-mute mother in a dark room until she was six and a half years old. When she was brought out her behaviour towards other people was fearful and

hostile. The only sound she made was a croaking in her throat. Nevertheless, she was able to 'catch up' the ground she had lost. The other girl, Anna, had not had the advantage of a mother to share her captivity, and died at the age of 10, four years after her discovery; but she had made some progress — perhaps remarkable progress — in being rehabilitated.

It is, clearly, possible for children to survive in relative isolation if they can get enough to eat, and to retain the capacity for rehabilitation until at least the age of seven. It is obvious that neither Tarzan nor Mowgli could have developed their human character-istics without human contact. Much less than this is being claimed on behalf of Kamala or the wild boy of Aveyron. The main problem faced by feral children would appear to be to persuade their animal hosts not only to refrain from killing them but to feed them. Even granting their occasional (if highly eccentric) willingness, the ability of animals to supply human infants with adequate food must be seriously in question, especially if it includes suckling. To argue that a she-wolf who has lost her own young might opt for a

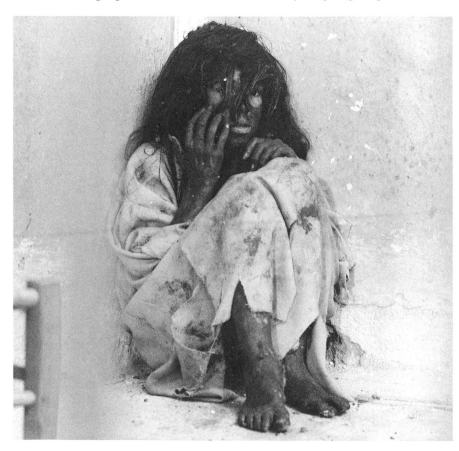

bizarre substitute is to stretch credibility; to suggest that she would then perform supervulpine feats of nurture is perhaps more extreme.

Once again, it is perhaps worth emphasizing that the manner in which myths such as this one seduce belief has nothing much to do with evidence and everything to do with aesthetic fascination. The tremendous success of the 'Tarzan' stories should remind us that people — especially children — find the idea of such a character immensely appealing. We all have reckless, destructive and anti-social impulses which constantly press against the restraints imposed by conscious, rational and conscientious thought. Fantasies like the 'Tarzan' and 'Mowgli' stories set us free, in a way, to indulge and enjoy the wildness within us Stories of 'real' wolf-children may simply provide the materials for building bulwarks which shore up the integrity of fantasies we should like to maintain for private reasons. Science fiction and fantasy fiction help us to form and populate our imaginary worlds, and it is not really so surprising that their content occasionally diffuses into our more fanciful interpretations of reality.

Left: the 'wild boy of Aveyron', found in 1798, was the subject of Truffaut's film *L'Enfant Sauvage* ('The Wild Child') in 1970, played by Jean-Pierre Cargol. The boy's initiation into human society is enthrallingly rendered. **Above**: long before Tarzan became a film hero, his appearance was familiar from illustrations by John Allen St John. This is from *Tarzan and the Jewels of Opar* (1918). **Right**: One of the early tales of feral children is that of Romulus and Remus, who were reared by a she-wolf. The statue is in Rome.

Chapter 12
WHERE SCIENCE FICTION GETS IT WRONG

Readers expect the 'real' science in science fiction to be reasonably accurate. Sometimes it is not.

Wrong science in science fiction

The science in science fiction, as we have seen, can be real, extrapolated, imaginary or controversial. Sometimes, of course, it is just plain wrong.

Science fiction writers get their science wrong for many reasons. Some writers seem to have learnt their physics entirely by reading older science fiction. For example, writers happily followed one another in describing spacecraft which travelled from star to star in mere hours, though Einstein's Special Theory of Relativity was widely accepted before the establishment of the first science fiction magazine (*Amazing Stories*) in 1926. Special relativity, of course, insists that we cannot exceed the speed of light, and therefore cannot reach even the nearest stars without a journey time of years. Many writers did not bother to take account of this, through a mixture of laziness and ignorance.

Similarly, absurdities like aliens who lusted after Earthwomen (about as logical as a man lusting after female though not male lobsters) and human/alien crossbreeding (genetically impossible) were once a firm part of the science fiction tradition.

Science which seems reasonable at the time of writing can be overtaken by events. The gravity-proof material 'Cavorite' of H.G. Wells's *The First Men in the Moon* was just plausible in 1901. In 1915 Einstein published the General Theory of Relativity, and by 1919 it had been almost conclusively proved. One of the theory's consequences is that there is no way

to insulate against gravity. Wells's book became an example of wrong science.

Other writers have suffered this more recently: it is a special danger for anyone who uses the very latest scientific theories. Larry Niven's story 'The Hole Man' (1974) makes ingenious use of an extremely small black hole as a murder weapon; the following year Stephen Hawking, who had predicted the possibility of such holes in the first place, showed

that they would cease to exist in a tiny fraction of a second.

Belief in another popular scientific phenomenon, the 'starbow', came to grief in the late 1970s after it had featured in many stories, most notably Frederik Pohl's 'The Gold at the Starbow's End'. The idea of the starbow was that relativistic effects would crowd together the stars seen from a spaceship travelling close to lightspeed, and also shift the

frequency of their light by different amounts, depending on how far they were off the line of the ship's movement. The result: a beautiful rainbow of coloured stars in a broad, circular band ahead. Unfortunately this does not work. The original calculations failed to allow for the enormously wide band of radiation put out by stars: as the distortions of relativity shift the visible part of the starlight towards blue or red, the invisible infra-red or ultra-violet rays are shifted into visibility and the star continues to look more or less white. Several dozen more stories were dragged into the category of wrong science.

Even when science does not change, the most conscientious author cannot always think of everything. Larry Niven provides a couple more examples. His 'Neutron Star' deals with the problems of a man surviving gravity and acceleration as his ship orbits dangerously close to a superheavy neutron star. Fans who made detailed calculations after the story was published found that the manoeuvre would actually give the ship a lethal spin — a not at all obvious result. Niven's *Ringworld* features an artificial world which is a ring 150 million km in radius with the Sun at the centre (gravity being simulated by spinning the ring). Unfortunately it turns out that this

is an unstable set-up: inevitably the ringworld would eventually drift into its sun. (Niven later wrote a sequel introducing endless numbers of unconvincing jet engines to keep the world in place.)

Authors who work out their physics in great detail are also, alas, prone to make the occasional mistake. *Lucifer's Hammer* by Larry Niven and Jerry Pournelle includes calculations of the effect of a comet impact. A 640,000-megatonne impact energy is mentioned, which is enough energy to boil a little over 1000 cubic km of water. On the same page it is estimated that the strike will 'vaporize about sixty million cubic kilometres of water'. Perhaps someone slipped with the electronic calculator?

Slips of the mind may cause authors to quote 'scientific' material which is not science at all but folklore or superstition. *The Blind Spot* by Austin Hall and Homer Eon Flint (a dreadful book which a few people insist is a classic of science fiction) refers respectfully to dogs' ability to judge character, feminine intuition, animal magnetism, psychic vibrations, and even the effect of intelligence on the colour of the eyes — all irrelevant to the plot. John Wyndham fell into a similar trap: his short story 'How Do I Do?' relies on the 'fact' that all the cells in a human body will be replaced

over the mystical period of seven years. Though blood cells are renewed in mere days, nerves are usually not renewed at all.

The most interesting kind of wrong science is where the author knows exactly what he or she is doing, but deliberately bends the rules just far enough to make the story work. A minor example is the high incidence of meteor strikes on fictional spacecraft. In the old days it was generally assumed that meteors were constantly whizzing through space and pattering on the hulls of ships; the more exuberant writers would have spaceships banging and crashing their way through the dense meteor clouds of the asteroid belt or even the rings of Saturn. In fact, even in the asteroid belt, the obstacles are on average well over 1 million km apart. The extreme unlikeliness of a meteor collision became well known, and writers who wanted such an accident for their plots would first include a short, apologetic lecture on its near-impossibility.

Two of the commonest clichés in science fiction. **Opposite:** magazine cover showing an alien lusting after an Earthwoman. **Below:** antigravity; we can see that the spaceship is floating from the trajectory of the fireworks. Neither scenario is plausible; both remain intensely popular.

A better example of rule-bending is Poul Anderson's *Tau Zero*, which in the manner of the best confidence tricks leads you on — with much impeccably worked-out science. A ship travelling ever closer to lightspeed is caught in the grip of Einstein's time dilation, experiencing time at such a different rate that its crew sees the stars go out and the universe die. At last the universe collapses back to a single fiery mass, the monobloc: the ship orbits this and survives the Big Bang as the monobloc explodes into another universe. The only small problem is that in such a final collapse, all of space falls in on itself. The monobloc fills the *whole* of the shrunken universe and there is no 'outside' where the ship can orbit. Most people who notice this point are prepared to forgive Anderson for the sheer audacity of the idea.

Much more commonly, rule-bending means the quiet shifting of a decimal point. Christopher Priest's novel *The Space Machine* includes an attempt to go one better than Jules Verne's impossible cannon in *From the Earth to the Moon*. (This blasted a spacecraft to escape velocity in a fraction of a second, and would have converted the passengers to something resembling

schnitzels.) The 'cannon' in *The Space Machine* is situated on Mars and fires spacecraft into orbit — not in a single killing blast but by steady acceleration. Steam pressure drives the space-capsule up a mile-long tube, accelerating it all the way until escape velocity is reached. Some calculations from schoolday physics show that to reach Mars escape velocity (about 5 km per second) over the length of this tube needs a steady acceleration of some 800 Earth gravities — crushingly lethal. To reduce it to a safe and comfortable 1g, the tube would have to be 800 times longer. Such a ridiculously long tube would probably be less convincing in the story: better, perhaps, to keep the tube a reasonable length and fiddle the physics.

Finally, there are authors who are prepared to stick out their tongues at today's physics and calmly describe the impossible. One popular impossibility was the 'Dean Drive', which in the early 1960s was being pushed as fact in the pages of *Analog SF*. This was a 'reactionless drive', an unlikely device of wheels and levers which was supposed to move by pushing against itself — the mechanized equivalent of the man lifting himself by his bootlaces. Since this violates the law of

The special effects in the Walt Disney film *The Black Hole* (1979) were much praised. But the studio faced a problem in making a black hole look exciting; the answer — make it red! There is no scientific warrant for the appearance of the hole, visible here ahead of the spaceship *Cygnus*. Judging from evidence like this, there are few physicists in the film industry.

conservation of momentum, which holds true all the way from atomic nuclei to whole galaxies, scientists merely laughed at it — and rightly so. But the fantasy remains attractive.

Arthur C. Clarke, a devotee of 'real' science and technology, wrote the book *Rendezvous with Rama*, in which an enormous alien spacecraft passes through our Solar System, staying just long enough for human beings to take a quick tour of its interior. At the end of the book this craft unexpectedly turns on its 'space drive' and starts to accelerate without jets, with no heed for the law of conservation of momentum. 'There goes Newton's Third Law,' somebody says, as it retreats into the distance. For the moment, however neat a conclusion to *Rendezvous with Rama* it may have been, we shall have to call this 'wrong science'.

The hollow Earth

Once writers could invent strange civilizations in far-off lands, as Jonathan Swift did in *Gulliver's Travels*. Today there are no unknown lands and the fashion is to set stories on other worlds. But some writers invented new lands hidden inside a hollow Earth. One early example is *Icosaméron* (1788), written in French by Giacomo Casanova, better known as a great lover than as a science fiction writer, but industrious in both spheres: the novel is almost 2000 pages long.

The classic underground story is Jules Verne's *A Journey to the Centre of the Earth*. Here the explorers actually penetrate no deeper than a few hundred of the 6400 km of Earth's radius. However, beneath the depth where air temperature and ground water affect the temperature inside the Earth (100 metres, perhaps), it becomes rapidly hotter through the 40 km of Earth's crust. Thermometer readings over 200°C have been recorded in mines only 5 km deep. Verne's heroes could never survive — though in the book they escape

via a volcanic eruption, floating out of Mount Stromboli on a tide of lava!

More ambitious writers borrowed the lunatic geology of John Cleves Symmes. One such novel, *Symzonia: a Voyage of Discovery* (1820), by 'Captain Adam Seaborn', may have been written by Symmes himself. Symmes believed that Earth was not only hollow but contained four more planets nested inside each other. Another popular source was William Reed's *Phantom of the Poles*, which featured huge polar openings as in Symmes's theory, it being possible to sail over the edge on to another sea with new continents, all on the inner surface of the hollow Earth. The fact that there would be no gravity on such an inner surface did not seem to worry him.

The actual plausibility of theories was no obstacle to writers who only wanted an exotic place for their stories. Famous examples are Sir Edward Bulwer-Lytton's *The Coming Race*, whose underground society is powered by the wonderful life-force 'vril' which became such a Victorian catchword as to give its name to the beef-extract Bovril; and

Where science fiction gets it wrong

Edgar Rice Burroughs' *At the Earth's Core* with its sequels, featuring the dinosaur-infested underworld of Pellucidar.

In practice, life becomes impossible only a few kilometres beneath Earth's surface — if only for reasons of temperature. Heat-producing radioactive materials in the crust cause sharp temperature rises to killing levels over the first few kilometres; the 2900 km of the next layer, the mantle, is hotter still. Within the mantle is Earth's core, which (despite being visited by Tarzan in one book by Burroughs) is mostly molten iron at temperatures varying from about 3000°C, where the core meets the mantle, to about 4000°C, at the centre. In the inner core, a central sphere of about 1300 km in radius, the molten iron seems to have been compressed back into solidity by the extreme pressure there — over 3 million atmospheres. We can probe the core by monitoring seismic shockwaves from earthquakes or nuclear tests, which pass through it and are speeded, distorted or reflected. Such experiments show no evidence of any hollow space.

Nevertheless, hollow-Earth theories have retained their popularity in comparatively recent times. The magazine *Amazing Stories* published from 1945 to 1947 a series of stories by Richard S. Shaver, purporting to have a factual basis. The stories make much of the existence of an underground world, and their publication as 'factual' brought the circulation of the magazine to remarkably high figures for several years.

Even science fiction writers have not spared serious thought for the theories of Cyrus Reed Teed, who from 1870 to his death in 1908 preached fervently that the Earth is hollow and that we are all living on the *inside*.

The map is from William Reed's *Phantom of the Poles* (1906). His caption reads, in part: 'The Earth is hollow. The poles so long sought are but phantoms. There are openings at the northern and southern extremities. In the interior are vast continents, oceans, mountains and rivers. This new world . . . is probably peopled by races yet unknown.' The British peer Lord Clancarty still stoutly supports Reed's beliefs.

Very big and very small

Older science fiction films are notorious for their use of menacing giant insects — ants, spiders, scorpions, even a praying mantis. In real life these creatures could never live in such enlarged states; nor would 'The Incredible Shrinking Man' have survived being shrunk.

The tradition of enlarged creatures begins with H.G. Wells's novel *The Food of the Gods*, where a miracle fertilizer produces gigantic plants, rats, wasps, hens and even people. We can easily make some calculations from the figures Wells gives. His wasps have bodies 45 cm long — roughly a thirtyfold increase. This would make the wasp's wings 30 times longer and 30 times broader: they would have 900 times the area and (presumably) lifting power. But the wasp's body would be 30 times larger in each of its *three* dimensions, and would thus weigh as much as 27,000 ordinary wasps. The giant wasp could therefore never fly; indeed it would not even be able to crawl.

Again, the giant people of *Food of the Gods* are 12 or more metres tall — about seven times normal height, but with normal proportions. The cross-sectional areas of the bones and muscles, and hence their strength, would increase 7^2 (or 49) times; the total weight of one of these giants would be increased by a factor of 7^3 (or 343). He would feel like a man with six more men on his back. For him to stand would be almost impossible: his spine would collapse; his overstrained ankles would quickly give way — and, with his head 12 metres from the ground, a fall would usually be fatal. In fact the human thighbone, the thickest in the body, breaks under about 10 times the human weight. Only massive, tree-trunk legs, like an elephant's, could hope to support these feeble giants.

The giant ants of the film *Them!* (1954) are very much more absurd. An ant 1000 times its natural size would be fully 1000 times heavier than the weight its enlarged legs could comfortably support: its own weight would kill it at once. Likewise, the theory that 'if a flea

were the size of an elephant it could leap a kilometre' is nonsense: a flea the size of an elephant would need also to be built like an elephant, or its legs would break under it.

These are simple physical arguments against giant insects: there are some more subtle biological ones as well, as was pointed out by the scientist J.B.S. Haldane. Insects do not distribute oxygen about their bodies by way of blood circulation, as we do. Instead, there are fine, hollow tubes along which the oxygen diffuses — and this diffusion is too slow to keep the metabolic fires burning when the oxygen molecules have to travel more than, say, half a centimetre. (For this reason, few insects are much more than 1 cm thick.) In giant insects the molecules would need to diffuse many centimetres into the enlarged muscles; a giant ant, in addition to all its other problems, would quickly suffocate.

Haldane also calculated that a flying man would need a chest sticking out for about 120 cm simply to house the wing muscles, while his legs became mere stilts to save weight. For reptiles of the huge size found in Anne McCaffrey's 'Dragon' books, flight is plainly impossible — more wing-muscles would be needed to lift the dragon than could possibly be fitted into its body. Peter Dickinson offers an

ironic comment in *The Flight of Dragons*, where dragons are shown to be light, gas-filled creatures which float like great reptilian blimps.

Reduction to small size, as in the films *Fantastic Voyage* (1966) and *The Incredible Shrinking Man* (1957), brings new problems. A mouse-sized man would have the advantages of a mouse: he would be able to survive long falls, since a hundredfold reduction in height produces a millionfold decrease in mass but only a ten-thousandfold decrease in surface area, and hence in the air resistance, as the man falls. The air slows his fall 100 times more effectively than if he were full-sized. But he would suffer from the mouse's metabolic problems. With a surface area many times greater in proportion to his mass, he loses heat that much faster, and would need to eat furiously simply to keep warm. A mouse needs to eat about a quarter of its own weight of food each day to survive, and the proportion rises for smaller warm-blooded animals.

How does he shrink? This is a vital question. If he were squeezed down by high pressures the process would kill him — besides which he would sink into the ground as all his unaltered weight rested on his miniaturized feet. Atoms themselves cannot be reduced in size without changing them to something else

(degenerate matter) in which the chemical reactions of life will not work. It seems that the only way to shrink our man is to reduce the number of atoms in his body, removing a proportion of them to leave a smaller, functioning man. Unfortunately, as Isaac Asimov observes, a mouse-sized man would be left with a mouse-sized brain — and it is not possible that such a tiny fraction of the original brain would still have intelligence.

This also disposes of the idea that microscopic people could evolve naturally, as in Fitz-James O'Brien's 'The Diamond Lens', whose hero falls in love with a girl on a microscopic slide, or could be genetically created, as in James Blish's classic 'Surface Tension'. Brains so small would have too few atoms, too little complexity, to hold intelligence.

Nevertheless there are stories about people small even on the atomic scale. In Ray Cummings' *The Girl in the Golden Atom*, the old model of atoms as tiny solar systems is extended to include inhabited planets — electrons. How electron-dwelling people could see (when photons of light and other radiation are larger than their 'planet') or breathe (the oxygen atom being a solar system in its own right on that scale) is wisely not discussed.

Left: the hero's pet cat gives him a bad time in *The Incredible Shrinking Man* (1956). **Above:** the helpful 'hero' of *King Kong* (1933). **Right:** the cheap Japanese monster movie *Godzilla Vs. Mothra* (1964) produced this one moment of surrealistic beauty — a giant egg out of which will hatch a giant caterpillar or a 120-metre dinosaur, it hardly matters which. Unfortunately, scientists say that all three scenarios are impossible.

Elementary errors in physics

The most outrageous errors in fictional science come not from the juggling of relativity and cosmology, but from forgetfulness of facts that we all learnt at school — for example the fact that there is no air in space.

This disposes of stories such as Poe's 'The Unparalleled Adventure of One Hans Pfaall' which involve balloon trips out into space. Air is also necessary to conduct sound, unfortunately for films where meteors whizz past the spaceship while other ships burst on to the screen with a mighty roar of jets. (To be fair, the drama of films like *Star Wars* would be so damaged by a scientifically correct soundtrack that rule-bending seems justified.) Writers learnt quickly, and people in space would speak either by radio or by touching spacesuit helmets together — glass and metal conduct sound better than air. This point was often missed, as in Charles Eric Maine's *High Vacuum*, in which spacesuited characters cannot hear their own footsteps because 'there was no sound in the vacuum'. The noise would be conducted through the spacesuit, through the air inside it and even up the wearer's legs.

Another often ignored consequence of airlessness is that there is no scattering of light. In air a laser beam is visible because its light is scattered by air molecules; in space laser beams cannot be seen, however visible they may be in *Star Trek* and elsewhere. Fritz Leiber's novel *The Wanderer* features laser beams that are not only visible in space but go on being visible after the laser has stopped firing (the idea is that the beams travel on, visibly, into space). Arthur C. Clarke mocked this tradition in his novel *Earthlight*, in which after a battle fought with invisible energies, an 'impossible' secret weapon fires a solid bar of light — which proves to be a magnetically accelerated jet of white-hot molten metal. In fact, metals lose their magnetic properties at the 'Curie temperature', well below melting point. This happens for iron at 770°C, its melting point being 1535°C. The magnetic

acceleration of molten metal seems impossible.

The most famous of blunders in vacuum is in Judith Merril's *The Tomorrow People*, where Moon travellers use a helicopter. No air, of course, means nothing for helicopter blades to push against. This leads to the famous question put by the *New York Times*: 'Out there in vacuum, what would a spacecraft be able to push against?' Spacecraft push against their own exhaust, squirting hot gas into vacuum and being thrust the other way as if by the recoil of a gun. Many writers appreciated this result of Newton's Third Law ('Action and reaction are equal and opposite'), but failed to take note of his First Law, which explains that a spaceship will continue moving with the same speed and direction unless acted on by some force. We can make U-turns in cars, thanks to the friction of

tyres against the road; in space there is 'nothing to push against' in that way, and if we turn our ship round it will continue along the same course with the same speed — travelling backwards. To make a U-turn we must turn the ship, then slow it to a halt with jets, and then accelerate up to the same speed in the opposite direction. Fictional craft, as in *Star Wars*, often turn like ordinary aircraft, and in space this is wrong.

Endless mistakes about gravity can be found. A.E. van Vogt's story 'A Can of Paint' mentions the difficulty of sending ships to Venus because they keep 'falling into the Sun'. Actually it is difficult to fall into the Sun or on to any planet by mistake. Only the most precise adjustment of speed and direction will prevent craft from either falling into orbit or swinging round on a comet-like path back into space.

Even the physics of a simple spaceship-chase in orbit is unobvious: in orbit, if you cram on the acceleration you tend to work against Earth's gravitational field and end up travelling not faster but slower (in a higher orbit). Perhaps the silliest of all orbital mistakes is in Brian Aldiss's *Hothouse*, in which the Moon no longer moves relative to Earth, and giant spiders spin webs between them. The only explanation would be that the Moon has moved to a geosynchronous orbit (like communications satellites), but this would bring it so close to Earth that tidal forces would promptly pull it to bits.

Jules Verne made an elementary error about gravity in *From the Earth to the Moon*, assuming that men in a free-falling spacecraft would experience first Earth's gravity and later the Moon's, with a period of weightlessness at the 'point of balance' between the two. Free fall, however, occurs as soon as the engines are turned off; the men and craft are falling through space together, with exactly the same forces acting on both: the men would only feel the direction of Earth as 'down' if they were somehow being pulled harder in that direction than the ship. The ship itself would not be massive enough to exert any noticeable gravity of its own — a mistake made by Wells in *The First Men in the Moon*, where the space travellers are drawn towards the centre of gravity of their spherical ship. This is a double error, since the gravitic pull of a hollow sphere is zero in the space inside — true even for a sphere of planetary size, as in Ross Rocklynne's story 'At the Center of Gravity', in which men are trapped by a force towards the centre which could not exist.

Errors about free fall have been less common in recent years, but they still happen. In the film *First Men into Space* (1959), a pilot radios excitedly 'G-pressure gone,' am weightless' while the screen clearly shows his rocket still blasting. The film-makers apparently thought free fall takes place automatically as soon as the atmosphere is left behind.

A film cherished by fans of bad science is *Riders to the Stars* (1954), which argues that meteors have a special property that stops them burning up in Earth's atmosphere; spaceships are sent up to catch meteors in huge nets, so that they can be used for their valuable anti-heat alloy. The writer Curt Siodmak had apparently never seen a falling star.

A common error is the depiction of radio conversations between spacemen and their wives or colleagues back on Earth without any time delay, no matter how far away they are. The films *Silent Running* (1971) and *Capricorn One* (1978) both have this feature.

An interesting piece of deliberately bad science occurs in *The Andromeda Strain* (1971). The heroine has an epileptic fit set off by the flashing at fast, regular intervals of a warning light. Flashing lights *can* induce fits in susceptible subjects, which is why the director could not show the light flashing at the most likely, dangerous frequency; there might have been fits in the audience.

Television still gives plenty of amusement to bad-science fans. In recent years the worst offender by far was the series *Space 1999* (1975-7), in which parsecs are used as a unit of velocity instead of a unit of distance; stars are confused with asteroids; sound travels in vacuum; there is daylight between the stars; and an explosion sends our Moon (undamaged) careering through space at faster than the speed of light.

Today, writers generally take more care than film-makers and science fiction illustrators. But it can still be fun to observe science fiction with a critical eye and a few textbooks.

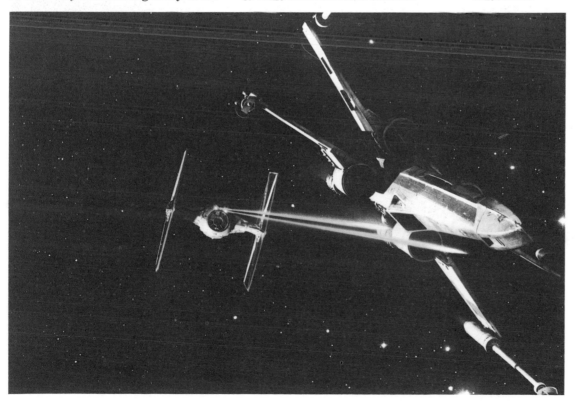

Far left: the hero of Jules Verne's *From the Earth to the Moon* travels in Victorian-style comfort in his space capsule shot from a giant gun. Note that neither dog nor master is floating. Verne wrongly believed that free fall only took place where the Earth's gravity precisely counteracted that of the Moon. **Left**: the space battles in *Star Wars* are great fun, but impossible. Fast turns and other such manoeuvres cannot be performed by spacecraft, and laser beams would be invisible in space.

Invisibility

In military circles, 'invisibility technology' is often discussed: the aim to make spy-planes and bombers harder to detect, rather than truly invisible. Real invisibility is something quite different, and is almost certainly impossible.

The classic story is H.G. Wells's *The Invisible Man*, in which the unpleasant hero tackles the problem of human invisibility head-on. With drugs he bleaches his blood and makes himself a perfect albino, white through and through; then, turning a mysterious radiation upon himself, he lowers the refractive index of his body tissues until they reach that of the surrounding air. At once he vanishes from sight, just as white powdered glass becomes transparent and almost vanishes when placed in water. The refractive index of glass and that of water are not very different, and glass is indeed *almost* invisible in water. Refractive index is a measure of the speed of light in a transparent material; when a light ray reaches the boundary between two materials and changes speed because of the difference in refractive index, the ray also changes direction and may be partly or totally reflected. When

the refractive index is the same on both sides of the boundary, there is no distortion or reflection of light and that boundary is invisible.

So Wells's invisibility is convincing at first reading. It is unlikely, though, that a man's blood could be decolorized without killing him; it is even more unlikely that the retina of each eye should remain visible after the process. If the retinas were invisible, light would pass through them without effect and the invisible man would be blind. The real impossibility is the lowering of a body's refractive index without otherwise changing it. Refractive index is linked with physical density, so that to be invisible in air we should need to be as light as air. This is not a practical proposition.

Jack London's short story 'The Shadow and the Flash' offers sillier versions of invisibility. One character works towards becoming perfectly transparent, but without the aid of a lowered refractive index: he would be about as invisible as a plastic bag full of water. His rival, reasoning that we see a body by the light reflected from it, develops a perfectly black paint which absorbs all light. This might work in space, where black holes are invisible against the black sky — but

in an Earthly landscape, a black blot would of course be seen by contrast alone.

Mechanical invisibility-devices feature in such stories as 'My Object All Sublime —' by Poul Anderson, 'All for Love' by Algis Budrys, and others. Usually these work by diverting light *round* the person inside. Budrys's device, for example, uses thousands of fibre-optic light guides. A beam of light hitting one of these light guides is bent round until it emerges at the corresponding spot on the far side of the device. This would happen even if the angle of the beam were such that it should emerge somewhere other than at this opposite point. The overall effect would be to make things on the other side of the 'invisibility machine' seem distorted, as though through a lens, and also upside-down. People would surely notice something odd about the place where the 'invisible' man was standing.

To be truly invisible we need to be other than human. The Vitons of Eric Frank Russell's *Sinister Barrier* are beings of pure energy who absorb and radiate only in the infra-red band; human eyes cannot detect them. Such unlikely creatures are much more believable than the idea of a truly invisible man.

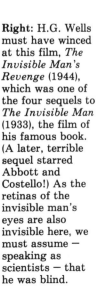

Right: H.G. Wells must have winced at this film, *The Invisible Man's Revenge* (1944), which was one of the four sequels to *The Invisible Man* (1933), the film of his famous book. (A later, terrible sequel starred Abbott and Costello!) As the retinas of the invisible man's eyes are also invisible here, we must assume — speaking as scientists — that he was blind.

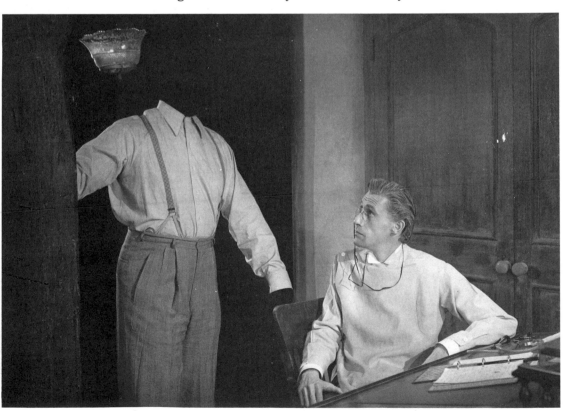

Force fields and force shields

A force field in science fiction is generally a defensive barrier of energy which always protects against some weapons and often against all. To the scientist, force fields are abstractions. Like gravity, they are stresses in space caused by the existence of matter and energy. Can there be any connection between the real and fictional force fields?

Certainly it is a long way from the drama of the film *Forbidden Planet* (1956) — where sparks and flashes result as an invisible monster assaults an invisible force screen — to the subtle field theories of today's physics.

In science there are just four sorts of force field. The most powerful is the strong nuclear force, which holds atomic nuclei together but is such a short-range force that it has no effect outside the nucleus. Next, nearly 140 times weaker, is the electromagnetic force: as well as being the force involved in magnets and electrical machines, electromagnetism holds together the atoms in all chemicals. The weak nuclear force is more than 100 billion times weaker again, and is important in some esoteric nuclear reactions. Weakest of all is gravity, some 10^{39} times less potent than the strong nuclear force. Gravity may at first seem the strongest of forces, but remember that, when we lift up an object, chemical (electromagnetic) changes in a few muscles are overcoming the gravitational pull of the entire Earth.

There seems to be no way of manipulating nuclear forces on a large scale, and Einstein's General Theory of Relativity rules out the hope of an artificial gravity field. This well tested theory (see pages 80-1) states that gravity is a measure of the bending of space caused by matter and energy. To turn on an artificial gravity field we would have to *create* mass/energy. But this would be breaking the fundamental law of conservation of mass and energy (the first law of thermodynamics), to which no exception has ever been found. Thus there is little hope of building the 'tractor beams' often used by science fictional spacecraft to reel in objects such as other craft. The companion force-field gadget is the 'pressor beam', which pushes things away and is even less plausible. Such a negative gravity field implies that we could also have negative mass and negative energy; by creating equal and balancing amounts of positive and negative energy from nothing at all, we could have endless free power in defiance of the second law of thermodynamics, the law of increasing entropy (see pages 86-7).

This leaves the electromagnetic force, which can achieve a very few of the feats of fictional force fields. For example, both Charles L. Harness in *The Paradox Men* and Frank Herbert in *Dune* give themselves an excuse for swordplay by introducing a 'body shield' which stops fast-moving projectiles, but allows relatively slow-moving objects through. In a typical passage from *Dune*, 'Paul snapped up the rapier, feinted fast and whipped it back for a slow thrust timed to enter a shield's mindless defences.'

A sufficiently powerful oscillating magnetic field — requiring enormous electromagnets — would indeed melt metal objects as in an induction furnace, and would even vaporize them. But slow-moving swords would be more affected than bullets. Likewise, a massive electric charge could theoretically produce an electrostatic field which would repel bullets — provided the bullets had been thoughtfully given an electric charge of the same sign before being fired. However, the size of the necessary charge would be such that the person 'protected' by it would instantly be killed as it discharged to Earth in a colossal lightning bolt. There seems no hope of anything as convenient as the device which gives Poul Anderson's *Shield* its title — an obliging field which not only stops bullets but uses their kinetic energy to recharge its batteries.

In short, electromagnetic fields do not behave like the useful force fields of science fiction. Against solid weapons they have little effect; few swordsmen would thrust so slowly as to give somebody's personal induction field time to melt the weapon before it struck. Against energy weapons, their chief science fictional function, the usefulness is even less. Magnetic fields might be able to deflect a beam of charged particles, but fields of the needed intensity can be produced only over tiny areas of space between the poles of gigantic magnets: pointless as a practical defence.

A typical piece of science fiction double-talk is found in one of the *Star Trek* books: 'A modification of standard shielding may deflect the laser's destructive potential. The laser energy waves are susceptible to magnetic fields, which can deform and diffuse the beam's power.' This is nonsense. Light particles (photons) — and therefore lasers — are unaffected by magnetic fields. Only material substances — centimetres of steel or kilometres of air — will stop a laser beam. For lasers working in or near the visible-light region, the best defence of all is a very old-fashioned device indeed: a mirror.

There is still, however, a certain nostalgia for the 'traditional' force screens of pulp science fiction. E.E. Smith's 'Skylark' books set the pattern with a screen of invisible energy which under attack glows red, orange, yellow, and up the spectrum until its radiation goes through violet into black and the screen breaks down — all enjoyable nonsense. Some writers invent new forces of nature to add to the basic real-life force fields; Robert Heinlein, for example, added the 'undiscovered' electrogravitic and magnetogravitic forces to the existing electromagnetic force in *The Day After Tomorrow*. In fact electricity and magnetism are both aspects of the movement of electric charge, while gravity, being the result of mass, is very different. Unified field theories, which try to connect and explain the four forces mathematically, have so far had small success with gravity. To speak of an electrogravitic or magnetogravitic spectrum is meaningless.

Could there be new forces waiting to be discovered? Could there be energies which would make science fiction's dreams come true? It seems doubtful. Although there are areas of confusion and uncertainty, the physical world has now been so well mapped that to discover a new field of force is about as likely as finding a new colour in the spectrum.

Famous bad predictions

Science fiction is not really a literature of serious prediction. With hundreds of writers firing off their imaginations in different directions, some of them must hit the target: most miss. Only when a prediction is authoritative — or nearly unanimous — does its failure or success mean very much.

Older predictions were often based on obsolete technology. Erasmus Darwin (grandfather of Charles) was talking about 'flying chariots' in a futuristic poem published in 1792, but expected that they would be powered by steam. Jules Verne's *Five Weeks in a Balloon* features a conversation on the destruction of the world by advanced technology; but the suggested cause is the blowing up of 'some colossal boiler heated to three thousand atmospheres'. ('And I bet the Yankees will have had a hand in it,' somebody adds.)

More seriously, H.G. Wells insisted both in books and when speaking in public that the coming war would be a final one — he coined the phrase 'the war to end war' but later regretted it — and that a marvellous utopian world would rise from the ruins. When World War I was over, this prediction failed to come about.

Popular catchwords in science fiction over the years have been 'mesmerism' and 'magnetism' (both a long time ago), 'radium', 'rays' from undiscovered (i.e. non-existent) parts of the electromagnetic spectrum, 'atomic energy', 'psionics' and 'black holes'. Each in turn has been seen as a universal solution, operating everything from cigar-cutters to interstellar craft. Each in turn has proved to obey depressingly restrictive rules — with the exceptions of psionics, which has not been proved at all, and black holes, which have been predicted mathematically but never found.

The areas where science fiction writers have reached unspoken, unanimous agreement, and have been completely wrong, are often the areas of negative prediction. For example, the typical first spaceship of fiction would be constructed by a lonely and eccentric genius in his own back yard, or perhaps by a small, private-enterprise team led by the eccentric genius who alone had cracked the problem of space flight. The enormous funding eventually required, the co-ordination of a whole nation's science and technology to build a spacecraft: all this was *not* predicted.

Again, it was agreed that putting a man (very rarely a woman) into space was the main objective, and in fiction the first spaceship would invariably be manned. As we know, not only were many pieces of hardware placed in orbit in the 3½ years between *Sputnik 1* and Yuri Gagarin's pioneering spaceflight in 1961, but the hardware has proved far more important. Weather satellites, mapping satellites, spy satellites, communications satellites: science fiction missed them. Arthur C. Clarke did suggest the communications satellite in an article in 1945, but unfortunately did not patent it.

Perhaps the most spectacular failure dealt with the matter of the first Moon landing — something treated in so many different ways by so many different writers that it seemed impossible for anything unpredicted to happen. Certainly the landing had few surprises, though writers blushed at the corny line, 'That's one small step for a man, one giant leap for mankind'. The small detail that science fiction had overlooked was that the whole event was shown live on worldwide television.

Computers provided another example. Obsessed by the idea of intelligent robots, most science fiction writers failed to see the possibilities of computing machines. Robots who walked and talked like (or nearly like) men were

commonplace in novels — which at the same time would refer to the whirring and clicking of electrical calculators on the ship's bridge, while the astrogating officer pored over his star charts and made calculations on a slide rule. No wonder the artist Kelly Freas painted a space-pirate swarming through the airlock, with gun in hand and a slide rule between his teeth. Even when computers were installed on fictional spaceships, writers seemed confused about what they actually did: Robert Heinlein's *Starman Jones* has numerous scenes in which people use books of logarithmic tables to process data *before* feeding them into the computer. (Why not use the machine to make those calculations too?)

Now microcomputers are turning society upside down, and still science fiction's preferred bet of the walking, talking, intelligent robot has not come off.

Another popular prediction concerns World War III and the destruction of civilization — something which is such a science fictional cliché that writers now prefer to let it happen offstage and start the story years or decades later. The general feeling through the 1950s was that the weapons too dreadful to use must inevitably be used in a final war. Now, nearly 40 years after the first nuclear explosion, the 'balance of terror' still holds — a failure of prediction which gladdens most writers. But the companion prediction, that World War III means the end of civilization (or even of all life — see, for example, Nevil Shute's *On the Beach*), is less certain. Writers imagined the superpowers slugging it out in a universally destructive war, but were not quite cynical enough to consider the emerging possibility that the superpowers might tacitly spare one another's homelands and conduct a nuclear war confined to Europe.

The most durable of predictions is that of the endless Space Age — the belief that once we have emerged from the cradle of our planet, the future and the universe are ours. Story after story has preached the benefits of investment in space: solar power, raw materials in the asteroids, weightless conditions for the casting of perfect ball bearings, colonies in space and the chance to reach further to other solar systems. Now, though space technology spinoffs have changed the world and satellites are big business, it seems that the larger dream of space might itself have been a bad prediction. Economics is closing it down. The Space Age may already be over.

Far left: like most nineteenth-century writers, Jules Verne expected powered flight to be achieved with flapping wings. The picture is of *The Master of the World*.
Above left: as predicted, Man lands on the Moon, but this famous 1969 photograph shows the unpredicted aspect — the TV camera that covered the whole event, reflected in the helmet visor.
Left: this space-pirate on a 1959 magazine cover has a slide-rule, a calculating instrument now as dead as the dodo, gripped between his teeth.

201

Bibliography

All science fiction stories and novels cited in this book are listed below, under relevant chapter headings, along with a brief list of non-fiction books for further background reading, not all of which are mentioned in the text. Many of the non-fiction books contain material that is relevant to more than one chapter, although they appear only once in the list.

CHAPTER 1

Fiction:

Aldiss, Brian: *Non-Stop* (variant title *Starship*), 1958; *Helliconia Spring*, 1982
Anderson, Poul: *The Snows of Ganymede*, 1958; *Tales of the Flying Mountains*, 1970; *Tau Zero*, 1970
Benford, Gregory: *Jupiter Project*, 1975
Clarke, Arthur C.: *The Sands of Mars*, 1951; *Islands in the Sky*, 1952; 'Sunjammer', 1964
Delany, Samuel: *The Ballad of Beta-2*, 1965
Harrison, Harry: *Captive Universe*, 1969
Heinlein, Robert: 'Universe', 1941; *Farmer in the Sky*, 1950; *The Moon is a Harsh Mistress*, 1966
Jameson, Malcolm: 'Prospectors of Space', 1940
Martinson, Harry: *Aniara*, 1956 (trans. 1963)
Reynolds, Mack: *Lagrange Five*, 1979
Shaw, Bob: 'Small World', 1978
Silverberg, Robert: 'Our Lady of the Sauropods', 1980
Simak, Clifford D.: 'The Asteroid of Gold', 1932
Stableford, Brian: *Promised Land*, 1974
Stapledon, Olaf: *Last and First Men*, 1930
Tsiolkovsky, Konstantin: *Beyond the Planet Earth*, 1920 (trans. 1960)
Varley, John: *Wizard*, 1980
Watson, Ian: *The Martian Inca*, 1977
Wolfe, Gene: 'The Book of the New Sun', tetralogy, beginning with *Shadow of the Torturer*, 1980

Non-fiction:

Berry, Adrian: *The Next Ten Thousand Years*, 1974; *The Iron Sun: Crossing the Universe through Black Holes*, 1977
Calder, Nigel: *Spaceships of the Mind*, 1978
Clarke, Arthur C.: 'Electromagnetic Launching as a Major Contribution to Space Flight', 1950; *Profiles of the Future*, 1962; *Voices From the Sky*, 1966
Lunan, Duncan: *Man and the Stars: Contact and Communication with Other Intelligence*, 1974
Man, John (ed.): *The Encyclopedia of Space Travel and Astronomy*, 1979
O'Neill, Gerard K.: *The High Frontier*, 1977
Ridpath, Ian: *Worlds Beyond*, 1975
Tsiolkovsky, Konstantin: 'The Future of Earth and Mankind', 1928

CHAPTER 2

Fiction:

Brunner, John: *The Sheep Look Up*, 1972
Cromie, Robert: *The Crack of Doom*, 1895
Del Rey, Lester: 'Nerves', 1942, expanded into a novel 1956
Griffith, George: *The Lord of Labour*, 1911
Jefferies, Richard: *After London*, 1885
Miller, Walter: *A Canticle for Leibowitz*, 1960
Niven, Larry: *Ringworld*, 1970; *A Hole in Space*, 1974
Shaw, Bob: *Orbitsville*, 1975
Smith, E.E.: *The Skylark of Space*, 1928, first book publication 1946
Stapledon, Olaf: *Star Maker*, 1937
Wells, H.G.: *The World Set Free*, 1914

Non-fiction:

Anon: *Energy and Power: A Scientific American Book*, 1971
Anon: *The Way Things Work Book of Nature*, 1973 Germany (trans. 1981)
Cook, P.L., and Surrey, A.J.: *Energy Policy: Strategies for Uncertainty*, 1977
Dumont, R.: *Utopia or Else . . .*, 1974
Dyson, Freeman J.: 'Search for Artificial Stellar Sources of Infra-red Radiation', in *Science*, vol. 131, 1959
Ehrlich, A. and P.: *Population, Resources, Environment*, 1970
El-Hinnawi, Essam, and Asit K. Biswas (eds.): *Renewable Sources of Energy and the Environment*, 1981
Heilbroner, R.: *An Inquiry into the Human Prospect*, 1975

CHAPTER 3

Fiction:

Aldiss, Brian: *Hothouse* (variant title *The Long Afternoon of Earth*), 1962; *Helliconia Spring*, 1982
Anderson, Poul: *War of the Wing-Men* (variant title *The Man who Counts*), 1958; *The People of the Wind*, 1973; *Fire Time*, 1974
Anthony, Piers: *Omnivore*, 1968; *Cluster*, 1977
Asimov, Isaac: *The Gods Themselves*, 1972
Benford, Gregory, and Gordon Eklund: *If the Stars are Gods*, 1977
Bishop, Michael: *Transfigurations*, 1979
Blish, James: *A Case of Conscience*, 1958
Brunner, John: *Total Eclipse*, 1974
Burroughs, Edgar Rice: *Princess of Mars*, 1912
Clarke, Arthur C.: 'A Meeting with Medusa', 1971
Clement, Hal: *Mission of Gravity*, 1954; *Cycle of Fire*, 1957
Crichton, Michael: *Congo*, 1981
Davidson, Avram: *Masters of the Maze*, 1965
De Camp, L. Sprague: *Rogue Queen*, 1951
Disch, Thomas M.: *The Genocides*, 1965
Dozois, Gardner: *Strangers*, 1978
Farmer, Philip José: 'Mother', 1953; *The Lovers*, 1961
Forward, Robert L.: *Dragon's Egg*, 1980
Gunn, James: *The Listeners*, 1972
Haldeman, Joe: *The Forever War*, 1974
Heinlein, Robert: *The Puppet Masters*, 1951; *Starship Troopers*, 1959
Herbert, Frank: *Dune*, 1965
Hoyle, Fred: *The Black Cloud*, 1957
Hoyle, Fred, and John Elliot: *A for Andromeda*, 1962
Karinthy, Frigyes: *Capillária*, 1922 (trans. 1966)
Le Guin, Ursula, 'Vaster than Empires and More Slow', 1971; *The Word for World is Forest*, 1976
Leinster, Murray: 'First Contact', 1945
Lem, Stanislaw: *Solaris*, 1961 (trans. 1970)
Martin, George R.R.: 'A Song for Lya', 1974
Merle, Robert: *The Day of the Dolphin*, 1967 (trans. 1969)
Russell, Eric Frank: *Sinister Barrier*, 1943
Shaw, Bob: *Palace of Eternity*, 1969
Silverberg, Robert: *Downward to the Earth*, 1970
Simak, Clifford: *Time and Again* (variant title *First he Died*), 1951
Spinrad, Norman: *Songs from the Stars*, 1980
Stapledon, Olaf: *Sirius*, 1944
Tenn, William: 'Venus and the Seven Sexes', 1949
Vance, Jack: 'The Gift of Gab', 1955; *Big Planet*, 1957
van Vogt, A.E.: 'Discord in Scarlet', 1939, incorporated in the novel *Voyage of the Space Beagle*, 1950
Watson, Ian: *The Jonah Kit*, 1975
Weinbaum, Stanley G.: 'The Mad Moon', 1935; 'Parasite Planet', 1935; 'Flight on Titan', 1935
Wells, H.G.: *War of the Worlds*, 1898; *The First Men in the Moon*, 1901
Yefremov, Ivan: 'The Heart of the Serpent' (trans. 1962)
Zerwick, Chloe, and Harrison Brown: *The Cassiopeia Affair*, 1968

Non-fiction:

Asimov, Isaac: *Extraterrestrial Civilizations*, 1979
Barlowe, Wayne Douglas, and Ian Summers: *Barlowe's Guide to Extra-terrestrials*, 1979 (about fictional material)
Boyce, Chris: *Extraterrestrial Encounter*, 1979
Bylinski, Gene: *Life in Darwin's Universe*, 1981
Dixon, Dougal: *After Man: a Zoology of the Future*, 1981
Dyson, Freeman J.: 'Time Without End: Physics and Biology in an Open Universe', in *Reviews of Modern Physics*, vol. 51, July 1979
Hoyle, Fred: *Diseases from Space*, 1979
Hoyle, Fred, and Wickramasinghe, N.C.: *Lifecloud*, 1978
Lilly, John: *Man and Dolphin*, 1961
Ridpath, Ian: *Messages from the Stars*, 1978
Sagan, Carl (ed.): *Communication with Extraterrestrial Intelligence (CETI)*, 1973
Sagan, Carl: *The Cosmic Connection: an Extraterrestrial Perspective*, 1973

Shlovskii, I.S., and Carl Sagan: *Intelligent Life in the Universe*, 1966

Minutes, 1977
Wheeler, J.A.: *Geometrodynamics*, 1962

Zukav, Gary: *The Dancing Wu Li Masters*, 1979

CHAPTER 4

Fiction:
Anderson, Poul: *Tau Zero*, 1970
Anthony, Piers: *Macroscope*, 1969
Asimov, Isaac: 'The Last Question', 1956; 'The Billiard Ball', 1967
Ballard, J.G.: 'The Voices of Time', 1960
Benford, Gregory: *The Stars in Shroud*, 1978
Blish, James: *The Triumph of Time* (variant title *A Clash of Cymbals*), 1958, also included in *Cities in Flight* (four novels in one volume), 1970; *The Quincunx of Time*, 1973
Campbell, John W.: 'The Mightiest Machine', 1934
Gamow, George: *Mr Tompkins in Wonderland*, 1939
Haldeman, Joe: *The Forever War*, 1974
Heinlein, Robert: *Starman Jones*, 1953; *Time for the Stars*, 1956
Le Guin, Ursula: *Rocannon's World*, 1966; *The Dispossessed*, 1974
Maine, Charles Eric: *Count-Down* (variant title *Fire Past the Future*), 1959
Malzberg, Barry: *Galaxies*, 1975
Martin, George R.R.: 'FTA', 1974
Niven, Larry: 'Neutron Star', 1966; 'Flatlander', 1967; 'The Hole Man', 1974; 'The Borderland of Sol', 1975
Pohl, Frederik: 'The Mapmakers', 1955
Pournelle, Jerry: 'He Fell Into a Dark Hole', 1973, to be found in *Black Holes*, 1978, ed. Pournelle
Shaw, Bob: *Night Walk*, 1967; *The Palace of Eternity*, 1969
Smith, E.E.: *Skylark of Space*, 1928, first book publication 1946; *Gray Lensman*, 1939, first book publication 1951
Stapledon, Olaf: *Star Maker*, 1937
Turner, George: *Beloved Son*, 1978
van Vogt, A.E.: 'The Storm', 1943
Vinge, Joan D.: *The Snow Queen*, 1980
Watson, Ian: *The Jonah Kit*, 1975
Wells, H.G.: *The Time Machine*, 1895
Williamson, Jack: *Seetee Ship*, 1942, first book publication 1951; *Seetee Shock*, 1950 (both originally published as by Will Stewart)

Non-fiction:
Calder, Nigel: *Einstein's Universe*, 1979
Coleman, James A.: *Relativity for the Layman*, 1954
Davies, Paul: *The Runaway Universe*, 1978
Duncan, Ronald, and Miranda Weston-Smith (eds.): *The Encyclopedia of Ignorance: Volume 1: Physical Sciences*, 1977
Einstein, Albert: *The Theory of Relativity*, 1920 (his own popularization of the subject)
Gribbin, John: *White Holes: Cosmic Gushers in the Universe*, 1977
Kaufman, William J.: *The Cosmic Frontiers of General Relativity*, 1977
Taylor, Edwin F., and John Archibald Wheeler: *Spacetime Physics*, 1971
Weinberg, Steven: *The First Three*

CHAPTER 5

Fiction:
Aldiss, Brian: 'Man in his Time', 1965; *An Age* (variant title *Cryptozoic!*), 1967; *Frankenstein Unbound*, 1973
Anstey, F.: *The Time Bargain* (variant title *Tourmalin's Time Cheques*), 1891
Asimov, Isaac: *The Gods Themselves*, 1972
Benford, Gregory: *Timescape*, 1980
Boussenard, Louis: *10,000 Years in a Block of Ice*, 1889 (trans. 1898)
Brunner, John: *Times Without Number*, 1962
Chayefsky, Paddy: *Altered States*, 1978
Dick, Philip K.: *The Man in the High Castle*, 1962; *Counter-Clock World*, 1967
Dickson, Gordon, R.: *Time Storm*, 1977
Duncan, David: *Occam's Razor*, 1957
Finney, Jack: *Time and Again*, 1970
Heinlein, Robert: '"— All You Zombies —"', 1959
Hoyle, Fred: *October the First is Too Late*, 1966
Irving, Washington: *Rip Van Winkle*, 1850
Laumer, Keith: *Worlds of the Imperium*, 1962; *The Other Side of Time*, 1965; *Assignment in Nowhere*, 1968
Masson, David: 'Traveller's Rest', 1965
Matheson, Richard: *Bid Time Return* (variant title *Somewhere in Time*), 1975
Merritt, A.: *The Ship of Ishtar*, 1926
Moorcock, Michael: *The War Lord of the Air*, 1971; *The Hollow Lands*, 1974
Moore, Ward: *Bring the Jubilee*, 1953
Priestley, J.B.: *Three Time Plays*, 1947
Roberts, Keith: *Pavane*, 1968
Rucker, Rudy: *White Light*, 1980
Shaw, Bob: *A Wreath of Stars*, 1976
Simak, Clifford D.: *Ring Around the Sun*, 1953
Spinrad, Norman: 'The Weed of Time', 1970
Taine, John: *The Time Stream*, 1931
Twain, Mark: *A Connecticut Yankee in King Arthur's Court* (variant title *A Yankee at the Court of King Arthur*), 1889
van Vogt, A.E.: *The Weapon Shops of Isher*, 1951
Vinge, Joan D.: *The Snow Queen*, 1980
Watson, Ian: *The Jonah Kit*, 1975; 'The Very Slow Time Machine', 1978
Wells, H.G.: *The Time Machine*, 1895
Wilson, Robert Anton: the 'Schrödinger's Cat' trilogy: *The Universe Next Door*, 1979; *The Trick Top Hat*, 1981; and *The Homing Pigeons*, 1981
Zelazny, Roger: the 'Amber' series, five novels beginning with *Nine Princes of Amber*, 1970, and ending with *The Courts of Chaos*, 1978

Non-fiction:
Davies, Paul: *Other Worlds*, 1980
Deshusses, Jerome: *The Eighth Night of Creation*, 1978 (trans. 1982)
Gribbin, John: *Timewarps*, 1979
Nicholls, Peter (ed.): *The Encyclopedia of Science Fiction*, 1979

CHAPTER 6

Fiction:
Aldiss, Brian: *Greybeard*, 1964; *Barefoot in the Head*, 1969
Amis, Kingsley: *The Anti-Death League*, 1966
Anderson, Poul: *After Doomsday*, 1962
Anthony, Piers: *Macroscope*, 1969
Ballard, J.G.: 'Billennium', 1961; *The Drowned World*, 1962
Benford, Gregory: *The Stars in Shroud*, 1978
Blish, James, and Norman L. Knight: *A Torrent of Faces*, 1967
Brunner, John: *Stand on Zanzibar*, 1968; *The Sheep Look Up*, 1972
Capek, Karel: *War with the Newts*, 1936 (trans. 1937)
Cartmill, Cleve: 'Deadline', 1944
Christopher, John: *The Death of Grass*, 1956; *The World in Winter* (variant title *The Long Winter*), 1962; *A Wrinkle in the Skin* (variant title *The Ragged Edge*), 1965
Clarke, Arthur C.: 'The Forgotten Enemy', 1949; *Earthlight*, 1955
Cooper, Edmund: *The Cloud Walker*, 1973
Cowper, Richard: *The Twilight of Briareus*, 1974
Crichton, Michael: *The Andromeda Strain*, 1969
Fawcett, E. Douglas: *Hartmann the Anarchist*, 1893
Haldeman, Joe: *The Forever War*, 1974
Harrison, Harry: *Plague from Space* (variant title *The Jupiter Legacy*), 1965; *Make Room! Make Room!*, 1966
Heinlein, Robert: *Sixth Column* (variant title *The Day After Tomorrow*), 1941, first book publication 1949; 'Solution Unsatisfactory', 1941; *Starship Troopers*, 1959; *Farnham's Freehold*, 1964; *The Moon is a Harsh Mistress*, 1966
Hoyle, Fred, and John Elliot: *A for Andromeda*, 1962
Kapp, Colin: 'The Railways up on Cannis', 1959; *The Chaos Weapon*, 1977
Kavan, Anna: *Ice*, 1967
Kersh, Gerald: *The Great Wash* (variant title *The Secret Masters*), 1953
King, Stephen: *The Stand*, 1978
Leiber, Fritz: *The Wanderer*, 1964
Miller, Walter M.: *A Canticle for Leibowitz*, 1960
Niven, Larry: 'The Borderland of Sol', 1975
Niven, Larry, and Jerry Pournelle: *Lucifer's Hammer*, 1977
Orgill, Douglas, and John Gribbin: *The Sixth Winter*, 1979
Pedler, Kit, and Gerry Davis: *Mutant 59: The Plastic Eater*, 1972
Pohl, Frederik, and Cyril Kornbluth: *The Space Merchants*, 1953
Saberhagen, Fred: the 'Berserker' series, beginning with *Berserker*, 1967
Shaw, Bob: *Shadow of Heaven*, 1969
Silverberg, Robert: 'How it was when the Past went Away', 1969; *The World Inside*, 1971
Smith, E.E.: the 'Lensman' series, six

novels, magazine publication 1934-48, book publication beginning with *Triplanetary*, 1948
Smith, George O.: *Venus Equilateral*, 1947
Spinrad, Norman: *Songs from the Stars*, 1980
Stewart, George R.: *Earth Abides*, 1949
Tucker, Wilson: *The Long Loud Silence*, 1952
van Vogt, A.E.: *Slan*, 1946
Vonnegut, Kurt: *Player Piano* (variant title *Utopia 14*), 1952
Watson, Ian: 'The Roentgen Refugees', 1978
Wells, H.G.: *The World Set Free*, 1914
Wright, S. Fowler: *Deluge*, 1928
Wyatt, Patrick: *Irish Rose*, 1975
Wyndham, John: *The Kraken Wakes* (variant title *Out of the Deeps*), 1953; *The Chrysalids* (variant title *Re-Birth*), 1955
Yarbro, Chelsea Quinn: *Time of the Fourth Horseman*, 1976
Zelazny, Roger: *This Immortal*, 1966

Non-fiction:
Ambio, vol. xi, nos. 2-3, 1982: special number entitled *Nuclear War: the Aftermath*
Barnaby, C.F., and Thomas, G.P. (eds.): *The Nuclear Arms Race: Control or Catastrophe?*, 1982
Glasstone, S., and Dolan, P.J. (eds.): *The Effects of Nuclear Weapons*, 1979
Gribbin, John: *The Climatic Threat* (variant title *What's Wrong with our Climate?*), 1978
Kahn, Herman: *On Escalation*, 1965
Langford, David: *War in 2080: The Future of Military Technology*, 1979
Taylor, Gordon Rattray: *The Doomsday Book*, 1970

CHAPTER 7

Fiction:
Adams, Douglas: *The Hitch-Hiker's Guide to the Galaxy*, 1979
Asimov, Isaac: 'That Thou Art Mindful of Him', 1974; 'The Life and Times of MULTIVAC', 1975; *The Complete Robot*, 1982, which contains all his robot stories published 1940-77
Ballard, J.G.: 'The Intensive Care Unit', 1977
Binder, Eando: *Adam Link — Robot*, 1975, made up of stories published 1939-42
Boucher, Anthony: 'Q.U.R.', 1943; 'Robinc', 1943
Boyce, Chris: *Catchworld*, 1975
Brown, Fredric: 'Answer', 1954
Brunner, John: *The Shockwave Rider*, 1975
Budrys, Algis: *Rogue Moon*, 1960; *Michaelmas*, 1977
Butler, Samuel: *Erewhon*, 1872
Dick, Philip K.: 'Second Variety', 1953; *Do Androids Dream of Electric Sheep?*, 1968; *We Can Build You*, 1972
Dickson, Gordon R.: 'The Monkey Wrench', 1951; 'Computers Don't Argue', 1965
Ellis, Edward S.: *The Steam Man of the Prairies*, 1868

Frayn, Michael: *The Tin Men*, 1965
Gerrold, David: *When Harlie Was One*, 1972
Heinlein, Robert: *The Moon is a Harsh Mistress*, 1966
Hjortsberg, William: *Gray Matters*, 1971
Johannesson, Olof: *The Great Computer* (variant title *The End of Man?*), 1966 (trans. 1968)
Jones, D.F.: *Colossus*, 1966
Jones, Raymond F.: *The Cybernetic Brains*, 1950
Kornbluth, C.M., and Frederik Pohl: *Wolfbane*, 1959
Levin, Ira: *This Perfect Day*, 1970
McCaffrey, Anne: *The Ship Who Sang*, 1969
Rucker, Rudy: *Spacetime Donuts*, 1981
Simak, Clifford D.: 'Limiting Factor', 1949
Sladek, John: *The Reproductive System* (variant title *Mechasm*), 1968
Vonnegut, Kurt: *Player Piano* (variant title *Utopia 14*), 1952

Non-fiction:
Boden, Margaret: *Artificial Intelligence and Natural Man*, 1977
Dick, Philip K.: 'The Android and the Human', 1973; 'Man, Android and Machine', in *Science Fiction at Large* (variant title *Explorations of the Marvellous*), ed. Peter Nicholls, 1976
Dyson, Freeman: *Disturbing the Universe*, 1979 (includes essay on Von Neumann)
Forester, Tom (ed.): *The Micro-electronics Revolution*, 1980
Hofstadter, Douglas R.: *Godel, Escher, Bach: an Eternal Golden Braid*, 1979
McCorduck, Pamela: *Machines Who Think*, 1979
Martin, James: *The Wired Society*, 1978
Reichardt, Jasia: *Robots: Fact, Fiction and Prediction*, 1978
Weizenbaum, Joseph: *Computer Power and Human Reason*, 1976
Wiener, Norbert: *Cybernetics*, 1948

CHAPTER 8

Fiction:
Abé, Kobo: *Inter Ice Age 4*, 1959 (trans. 1970)
Bates, Harry: 'Alas, All Thinking!', 1935
Beresford, John: *The Hampdenshire Wonder*, 1911
Blish, James: *They Shall Have Stars* (variant title *Year 2018!*), 1956; *The Seedling Stars*, 1957; *Titan's Daughter*, 1961
Blish, James, and Norman L. Knight: *A Torrent of Faces*, 1967
Budrys, Algis: *Who?*, 1958
Bunch, David R.: *Moderan*, 1971
Caidin, Martin: *Cyborg*, 1972
Clifton, Mark, and Frank Riley: *The Forever Machine* (variant title *They'd Rather be Right*), 1957
Cowper, Richard: *Clone*, 1972
Delany, Samuel R.: *Nova*, 1968
Dick, Philip K.: *Do Androids Dream of Electric Sheep?*, 1968
Disch, Thomas M.: *Camp Concentration*, 1968
Effinger, George Alec: *The Wolves of*

Memory, 1981
Freedman, Nancy: *Joshua, Son of None*, 1973
Gunn, James: *The Immortals*, 1962
Herbert, Frank: *Dune*, 1965
Herzog, Arthur: *IQ 83*, 1978
Huxley, Aldous: *Brave New World*, 1932
Keyes, Daniel: 'Flowers for Algernon', 1959, expanded into a novel 1966
Knight, Damon: 'World Without Children', 1951
Le Guin, Ursula: *The Left Hand of Darkness*, 1969; 'Nine Lives', 1969
Levin, Ira: *The Boys from Brazil*, 1976
McCaffrey, Anne: *The Ship Who Sang*, 1969
Niven, Larry: 'The Jigsaw Man', 1967; *The Long ARM of Gil Hamilton*, 1976; *The Patchwork Girl*, 1980
Pohl, Frederik: *Man Plus*, 1976
Shaw, Bob: *One Million Tomorrows*, 1970
Shaw, George Bernard: *Back to Methuselah*, 1921
Silverberg, Robert: *Nightwings*, 1969; *Tower of Glass*, 1970; 'Caught in the Organ Draft', 1973; 'Born with the Dead', 1974
Simak, Clifford D.: *Time and Again* (variant title *First He Died*), 1951; *Why Call Them Back from Heaven*, 1967
Stapledon, Olaf: *Last and First Men*, 1930
Sturgeon, Theodore: *Venus Plus X*, 1960
Vance, Jack: *The Dragon Masters*, 1963
Wells, H.G.: *The Island of Dr Moreau*, 1896
Wilhelm, Kate: *Where Late the Sweet Birds Sang*, 1976
Wolfe, Bernard: *Limbo* (variant title *Limbo 90*), 1952
Wolfe, Gene: *The Fifth Head of Cerberus*, 1972; *The Claw of the Conciliator*, 1981

Non-fiction:
Ettinger, J.C.W.: *The Prospect of Immortality*, 1964
Fishlock, David: *Man Modified*, 1969
Haldane, J.B.S.: *Daedalus; or, Science and the Future*, 1924
Packard, Vance: *The People Shapers*, 1978
Rorvik, David: *In His Image: the Cloning of a Man*, 1978
Rosenfeld, Albert: *The Second Genesis: the Coming Control of Life*, 1975; *Prolongevity*, 1976
Sagan, Carl: *The Dragons of Eden*, 1977
Taylor, Gordon Rattray: *The Biological Time Bomb*, 1968
Wells, H.G.: 'The Man of the Year Million', 1893

CHAPTER 9

Fiction:
Anthony, Piers, and Robert E. Margroff: *The Ring*, 1968
Burgess, Anthony: *A Clockwork Orange*, 1962
Compton, D.G.: *The Quality of Mercy*, 1965

Condon, Richard: *The Manchurian Candidate*, 1959
Dick, Philip K.: 'The Pre-Persons', 1974; *A Scanner Darkly*, 1977
Forster, E.M.: 'The Machine Stops', 1909
Gunn, James: *The Joy Makers*, 1961
Huxley, Aldous: *Brave New World*, 1932
Knight, Damon: *Hell's Pavement* (variant title *Analogue Men*), 1955
Orwell, George: *Nineteen Eighty-Four*, 1949
Reynolds, Mack: *After Utopia*, 1977; *Police Patrol: 2000 AD*, 1977
Silverberg, Robert: *Master of Life and Death*, 1957
Smith, Cordwainer: 'A Planet Named Shayol', 1961
Spinrad, Norman: 'No Direction Home', 1971; *Songs from the Stars*, 1980
Zamiatin, Yevgeny: *We*, 1924

Non-fiction:
Delgado, José: *Physical Control of the Mind: Towards a Psychocivilized Society*, 1971
Marks, John: *The Search for the 'Manchurian Candidate': the CIA and Mind Control*, 1979
Martin, James: *Security, Accuracy and Privacy in Computer Systems*, 1973
Russell, Bertrand: *Icarus; or, The Future of Science*, 1924
Scheflin, Alan W., and Edward M. Opton, Jr. (eds.): *The Mind Manipulators*, 1978
Schrag, Peter: *Mind Control*, 1978
Sieghart, Paul: *Privacy and Computers*, 1976
Valenstein, Elliott: *Brain Control: a Critical Examination of Brain Stimulation and Psycho-Surgery*, 1973

CHAPTER 10

Fiction:
Anthony, Piers: the 'Cluster' trilogy: *Cluster*, 1977; *Chaining the Lady*, 1978; *Kirlian Quest*, 1978
Asimov, Isaac: 'Belief', 1953
Bester, Alfred: *The Demolished Man*, 1953; *Tiger! Tiger!* (variant title *The Stars My Destination*), 1956
Blish, James: *Jack of Eagles* (variant title *ESP-er*), 1952
Brunner, John: 'Protect Me from My Friends', 1962; *Telepathist* (variant title *The Whole Man*), 1964
Busby, F.M.: *Cage a Man*, 1974
Clement, Hal: 'Impediment', 1942
Dick, Philip K.: 'A World of Talent', 1954
Galouye, Daniel: 'The Last Leap', 1960
Harness, Charles L.: 'The Rose', 1953
Heinlein, Robert: *Waldo and Magic, Inc.*, 1950 ('Waldo' first published 1942)
Herbert, Frank: *Dune*, 1965
King, Stephen: *Carrie*, 1974; *Firestarter*, 1980
McIntyre, Vonda N.: *Dreamsnake*, 1978
Niven, Larry: *The Long ARM of Gil Hamilton*, 1976
Poe, Edgar Allan: 'The Facts in the Case of M. Valdemar', 1845
Russell, Eric Frank: *Sentinels from Space*, 1953
Shaw, Bob: *The Palace of Eternity*, 1969
Silverberg, Robert: *Dying Inside*, 1972

Smith, E.E.: the 'Lensman' books (see under Chapter 6)
Sturgeon, Theodore: 'To Marry Medusa', 1958
Vance, Jack: 'Telek', 1952
van Vogt, A.E.: *The World of Null-A*, 1948; *The Anarchistic Colossus*, 1977
Watson, Ian: *Miracle Visitors*, 1978
White, James: *Hospital Station*, 1962
Wilson, Colin: *The Philosopher's Stone*, 1969
Zelazny, Roger: *To Die in Italbar*, 1973

Non-fiction:
Evans, Christopher: *Cults of Unreason*, 1974
Fort, Charles: *Lo!*, 1931; *Wild Talents*, 1932
Gardner, Martin: *Fads and Fallacies in the Name of Science*, 1957
Gooch, Stan: *The Paranormal*, 1978
Rampa, T. Lobsang: *The Third Eye*, 1956
'Randi' (James Randi): *The Magic of Uri*, 1976
Sladek, John: *The New Apocrypha*, 1973
Taylor, John: *Science and the Supernatural*, 1980
Thouless, Robert H.: *From Anecdote to Experiment in Psychical Research*, 1972

CHAPTER 11

Fiction:
Babcock, George: *Yezad*, 1922
Burroughs, Edgar Rice: the 'Tarzan' books, beginning with *Tarzan of the Apes*, 1914, which had 23 sequels
Hogan, James: *Inherit the Stars*, 1977
Howard, Robert E.: the 'Conan' stories, 1932-6, beginning in book form with *The Coming of Conan*, 1953
Kipling, Rudyard: the 'Mowgli' stories, in *The Jungle Book*, 1894, and *The Second Jungle Book*, 1895
Russell, Eric Frank: *Sinister Barrier*, 1943; *Dreadful Sanctuary*, 1951
Savarin, Julian Jay: the 'Lemmus' trilogy: *Lemmus One: Waiters on the Dance*, 1972; *Lemmus Two: Beyond the Outer Mirr*, 1976; *Lemmus Three: Archives of Haven*, 1977
Verne, Jules: *Twenty Thousand Leagues under the Sea*, 1870 (trans. 1873)
Watson, Ian: *Miracle Visitors*, 1978

Non-fiction:
Bacon, Francis: *New Atlantis*, 1627
Blavatsky, Helena: *The Secret Doctrine*, 1888
Brunner, John: 'Science Fiction and the Larger Lunacy', in *Science Fiction at Large* (variant title *Explorations of the Marvellous*), ed. Peter Nicholls, 1976
Castle, Edgar, and Barry Thiering (eds.): *Some Trust in Chariots!*, 1973
Charroux, Robert: *One Hundred Thousand Years of Man's Unknown History*, 1963 (trans. 1971)
Churchward, James: *The Lost Continent of Mu*, 1926
De Camp, L. Sprague: *Lost Continents*, 1954
Donnelly, Ignatius: *Atlantis: the Antediluvian World*, 1882; *Ragnarok, the Age of Fire and Gravel*, 1883

Fort, Charles: *The Book of the Damned*, 1919; *New Lands*, 1923
Hynek, J. Allen: *The UFO Experience*, 1972
Jung, C.J.: *Flying Saucers: a Modern Myth of Things Seen in the Skies*, 1958 (trans. 1959)
King, George: *You Are Responsible!*, 1961
Knight, Damon: *Charles Fort: Prophet of the Unexplained*, 1970
Kolosimo, Peter: *Not of this World*, 1970
Layne, Meade: *The Coming of the Guardians*, 1964 (5th ed.)
Leslie, Desmond, and George Adamski: *Flying Saucers Have Landed*, 1953
Pauwels, Louis, and Jacques Bergier: *The Morning of the Magicians*, 1960 (trans. 1964)
Plato, *Timaeus* and *Critias*, both c. 350 BC
Ramage, Edwin S. (ed.): *Atlantis: Fact or Fiction?*, 1978
Sagan, Carl: *Broca's Brain*, 1979
Schliemann, Paul: *How I Discovered Atlantis, the Source of all Civilisation*, 1912
Scott-Elliot, W.: *The Story of Atlantis*, 1896, *The Lost Lemuria*, 1925
Story, Ronald: *The Space-Gods Revealed*, 1976
Tomas, Andrew: *We are Not the First: Riddles of Ancient Science*, 1971
Trench, Brinsley Le Poer: *The Sky People*, 1960
Velikovsky, Immanuel: *Worlds in Collision*, 1950; *Ages in Chaos*, 1952
von Däniken, Erich: *Chariots of the Gods?*, 1968, the first of a series of books

CHAPTER 12

Fiction:
Aldiss, Brian: *Hothouse* (variant title *The Long Afternoon of Earth*), 1962
Anderson, Poul: 'My Object All Sublime —', 1961; *Shield*, 1963; *Tau Zero*, 1970
Blish, James: 'Surface Tension', 1952
Budrys, Algis: 'All for Love', 1962
Bulwer-Lytton, Sir Edward: *The Coming Race*, 1871
Burroughs, Edgar Rice: *At the Earth's Core*, 1922; *Pellucidar*, 1923, and five sequels including *Tarzan at the Earth's Core*, 1930.
Casanova, Giacomo: *Icosaméron*, 1788
Clarke, Arthur C.: *Earthlight*, 1955; *Rendezvous with Rama*, 1973
Cummings, Ray: *The Girl in the Golden Atom*, 1921
Darwin, Erasmus: *The Botanic Garden: Part I: The Economy of Vegetation*, 1792
Hall, Austin, and Homer Eon Flint: *The Blind Spot*, 1951
Harness, Charles L.: *The Paradox Men* (variant title *Flight into Yesterday*), 1953
Heinlein, Robert: *Sixth Column* (variant title *The Day After Tomorrow*), 1941, first book publication 1949; *Starman Jones*, 1953
Herbert, Frank: *Dune*, 1965
Leiber, Fritz: *The Wanderer*, 1964
London, Jack: 'The Shadow and the

Flash', 1903
McCaffrey, Anne: *Dragonflight*, 1968, and five sequels
Maine, Charles Eric: *High Vacuum*, 1956
Matheson, Richard: *The Shrinking Man*, 1956
Merril, Judith: *The Tomorrow People*, 1960
Niven, Larry: 'Neutron Star', 1968; *Ringworld*, 1970; 'The Hole Man', 1974; *The Ringworld Engineers*, 1979
Niven, Larry, and Jerry Pournelle: *Lucifer's Hammer*, 1977
O'Brien, Fitz-James: 'The Diamond Lens', 1858

Poe, Edgar Allan: 'The Unparalleled Adventure of One Hans Pfaall', 1835
Pohl, Frederik: 'The Gold at the Starbow's End', 1972
Priest, Christopher: *The Space Machine*, 1976
Rocklynne, Ross: 'At the Center of Gravity', 1936
Russell, Eric Frank: *Sinister Barrier*, 1943
Seaborn, Captain Adam: *Symzonia: A Voyage of Discovery*, 1820
Shaver, Richard S.: *I Remember Lemuria & The Return of Sathanas*, 1948
Shute, Nevil: *On the Beach*, 1957
Smith, E.E.: the 'Skylark' books,

beginning with *The Skylark of Space*, 1928, first book publication 1946
Swift, Jonathan: *Gulliver's Travels*, 1726
van Vogt, A.E.: 'A Can of Paint', 1944
Verne, Jules: *Five Weeks in a Balloon*, 1863 (trans. 1870); *A Journey to the Centre of the Earth*, 1864 (trans. 1872); *From the Earth to the Moon*, 1865 (trans. 1873); *Master of the World*, 1904 (trans. 1914)
Wells, H.G.: *The Invisible Man*, 1897; *The First Men in the Moon*, 1901; *The Food of the Gods and How it Came to Earth*, 1904
Wyndham, John: 'How Do I Do?', 1953

Acknowledgements

The authors, editor and publishers would like to thank the following people for their help on this book. Special thanks are due to Mr Peter Gill, who did so much to track down photographic material in the USA; Jane Williams, who stepped in at short notice to help with picture research; Mick Keates, who held the fort while the designer was away; Valerie Lewis Chandler, who prepared the index; and Janet Pollak, who gave editorial support. Mr H. Arnold; Mrs E. Atchison, Secretary John Innes Institute; Miss M. Baird of the DHSS Statistical & Research Division; Peter Cavalier, Geoff Goode and Bob Ireland of Geoff Goode Photographics Ltd; Professor J.M.R. Delgado; Dr Bernard Dixon; Malcolm Edwards; Chris Foss; Alan Franks; Colin Greenland and Joyce Day of the Science Fiction Foundation; Mike Hammond of the Space Department, RAF Farnborough; Professor Willem Kolff; Dr Henry Kolm; Dr J. McConnell; Jackie O'Connor of Sea World Inc.; Jon Palfreman of the BBC; Valerie Paine of 'Young Artists'; Salim Patel of the Science Photo Library; Stephen Pizzey of the Science Museum; Marianne Taylor of Granada Publishing; Rose Taylor and Peter Marsh of *New Scientist*; Professor J. Vanable.

Artwork
The following artists are thanked for their work, which was specially commissioned for this book: Chris Foss, for the cover and title page; Howard Brown; Chelsea Studios; Ian Craig; David Eaton; Peter Goodfellow; Stuart Hughes; Aziz Khan; Howard Levitt; Terry Oakes.
Artwork based on existing sources is acknowledged as follows: *The Cosmic Frontiers of General Relativity* by William J. Kaufmann, Penguin Books, p.95; Storm Dunlop/ Colin Ronan, p.9 above; *The Illustrated Encyclopaedia of Space Technology* ed. Detland, Salamander, pp.20/21; *The High Frontier* by Gerard K. O'Neill, William Morrow, p.23; *Hunting the Past* by L.B. Halstead, p.137; *The Iron Sun* by Adrian Berry, Jonathan Cape, p.14; *Messages from the Stars* by Ian Ridpath, Harper & Row, p.179; *The Microelectronics Revolution* ed. Tom Forester, Basil Blackwell, pp.124, 125; *New Scientist* pp.114, 148; *Scientific American* pp.35, 38, 40, 42, 82 left, 146; *Physiological Psychology* by Thomas Brown and Patricia Wallace, Academic Press, p.157; *The Way Things Work Book of Nature*, Allen & Unwin, pp.62, 65, 138.
We have been unable to trace Mr Wayne McLoughlin (p.39), and would be pleased to hear from him.

Other illustrations
Ardea, p.63; Associated Press, pp.107 left, 111; Avco Everett Research Laboratory Inc., p.104 below; Dr Richard Borgens, p.144; Paul Brierley, pp.120, 133 (3) & (4); BBC, pp.67 left, 80 above, 105 (courtesy Horizon); BBC Hulton Picture Library, p.130 below; British Steel Corporation, p.122; Edgar Rice Burroughs Inc., p.189 above; CERN, pp.78, 79; The Cinema Bookshop, pp.67 right, 142 above; Kenneth Colby, p.127; Bruce Coleman Ltd, pp.58, 60, 139, 145; Colorific!, p.148 in conjunction with Life Magazine/Time Inc., p.149 below; Cornell University, National Astronomy and Ionosphere Centre, p.48; The *Daily Telegraph* Colour Library, pp.141, 162 above; Professor J.M.R. Delgado, p.167; Walt Disney Productions, p.192; Peter Elson/ Sarah Brown Agency, p.91; Mary Evans Picture Library, pp.103, 170, 173, 200; Vivien Fifield Agency, p.196; Chris Foss, pp.74, 81; David Hardy, p.29 above; Harrow House/Dougal Dixon, p.56; Heron Books Ltd/Edito Service S.A. Geneva, p.159; John Hillelson Agency, pp.49, 108, 110, 116, 132 below, 161, 163, 165 right, 169 above, 181 above; Hubbs-Sea World Research Institute, San Diego, p.50 below; John Innes Institute, Norwich, p.152 above; Michael Jeffries, p.160; Jet Propulsion Laboratory, California, p.22; Keystone Press Agency, pp.107 right, 168; Kobal Collection, pp.61, 66, 72, 88, 131 below, 156, 166, 177 below, 180 below, 181 below, 188, 194, 195, 197, 198; Dr Henry Kolm/Massachusetts Institute of Technology, p.23; Lawrence Livermore Laboratory, Professors Smarr and Eppley, p.106; Lick Observatory, p.55 above; Love Romances Publishing Co., p.190; Dr J. McConnell, p.136; Metro-Goldwyn Mayer/British Film Institute, p.119 below; NASA Ames Research Center, pp.46/47; NASA Marshall Spaceflight Center, p.123; The National Physical Laboratory, Teddington, p.129; Natural Science Photos, p.152 below; *New Scientist*, p.43; Oxford Scientific Films, pp.62 below, 133 (2); Paramount Film Studios, p.158; Perkin Elmer Corporation, p.27; Popperfoto, pp.150, 175, 178; Practical Computing, p.124; Princeton University Plasma Physics Laboratory, p.38; RKO Films/British Film Institute, p.114; Rainbird Publishing Ltd/Robert Harding Associates, p.185 below; Rockwell International, p.121; Royal Aircraft Establishment, Farnborough, Space Department, p.36; Royal Signals and Radar Establishment, Malvern, pp.34/35; Science Photo Library, pp.20, 21, 29 below, 41 (Centre National de la Recherche Scientifique/SPL), 42 below (Boeing Aerospace/SPL), 132 above, 133 (1), 149 above, 169 below, 172; Seaphot/Planet Earth Pictures, p.62 above; Sea World Inc., p.50 above; Ronald Sheridan Library, pp.185 above, 189 below; Souvenir Press Ltd, pp.180 above, 182; Sovfoto, 113; Space Frontiers Ltd, pp.8 (Astrophotographie/Space Frontiers), 24, 25, 165 left (NASA/Space Frontiers); Standard Magazines, p.17; Hugh Steeper Ltd, Roehampton, p.142 below; Stellar Publishing Corporation, p.102 left and centre; Street & Smith Publications Inc., pp.119, 137, 201 below; The *Sunday Times*, pp.117, 126; The Tate Gallery, p.112; Thames & Hudson Ltd, p.193; John Topham Picture Library, pp.40 below, 174; Trans Time Inc., p.147; Twentieth Century-Fox/British Film Institute, p.115; Union Carbide Corporation, Tennessee, p.32; Universal International/British Film Institute, pp.51, 54; University of Utah, Division of Artificial Organs, Professor Willem Kolff, pp.140, 143; USAF, p.104 above; Agustin Villagra, p.183; Warner Bros Inc., pp.90, 162 below; Professor J. Weber, p.80 below; Western Fiction Publishing Co., p.102 right; Tim White, pp.16/17, 177 above; Gilbert Williams, p.64; Patrick Woodroffe, p.97; Workman Publishing Co. Inc./Wayne Barlowe, p.59; Joseph Young Collection, p.171, 186/7 below; Young Artists: Richard Clifton-Dey, p.131 above; Peter Goodfellow, p.153; John Harris, p.191; Bob Layzell, p.118; Angus McKie, p.85; Ziff-Davis, p.57.

Index

Page numbers in italics denote illustrations.

ageing 137, 144-6, *144*, *145*, *146*
Alien 16, 60
aliens, intelligent 44, 45, 46-65, 190, *190*
  mythology 180-3, *180*, *181*
  see also UFOs
Altered States 90, *91*
androids 131, 153, *153*
Andromeda Strain, The 117, 197
animals 29, *56*, *57*
  giant 194, *195*
  intelligence 49-50, 57, 58, *136*, 137
  see also feral children; insects
antigravity 66, *66*, 80-1, *81*, 95, *191*
antimatter 31, 78-9, *78*, *79*, 98, 106
Apollo spacecraft 8, 23
apportation 171, 174
Arnold, Kenneth 176
Aspect, Alain *75*
asteroids 112-13
  exploited 19, 23, 24-25, *25*, 45, 201
  see also meteors
Atlantis 184-7, *185*, *186-7*
Atlantis: the Lost Continent 186-7
atmosphere *21*, 28, 56-7
  Jupiter 52, *53*
  see also greenhouse effect; vacuum
atoms and atomic particles 67, *70*, 167, 194-5, 200
  antimatter 78-9
  at Big Bang 76-7, *77*
  probability 74-5
  see also electrons: nuclear..., tachyons; tardyons
automation 122-4, *122*, *123*, *124*
  'leisure society' 156-8, *156-7*
  see also computers

Babbage, Charles 120-1
bacteria 29, 55, 117, 138
  genetic engineering 148-9, *149*
Barbarella 158
Barnard's Star 8, *9*, 26
baryons 78, 87
Becquerel, Antoine Henri 32
Beer, Stafford 133
behavioural control *see* conditioning
Bell's Theorem 101
Bergson, Henri 88-9
Big Bang 76-7, *76*, *77*, 84, 86, *86*, 91, 94, 98
biochemistry 136-7
  alien 52-5, 65
biological engineering 152, 159-60
  see also genetic engineering
biological warfare *see* CBW
birth control *see* population growth
Black Hole, The 13, *192*
black holes 73, 81, *82*, 83-5, *84*, *85*, 98, *106*, 200
  antimatter 78, 79
  collisions, explosions 45, 84, 85, 86, 106, *106*
  end of universe 86-7
  event horizon, 84, *84*, 85, 95
  mini (quantum) 84
  murder weapon 190
  spinning 84-5, *84*, 95
  time travel, *91*, 94-7, *95*
Blade Runner 153
Bohr, Niels 101
Boole, George *and* Boolean algebra 129
Bracewell, Ronald 47
brains 49, 129, *172*, 173
  after death 65
  alien 54
  crime 166-7
  drugs 164, *164* (*see also* drugs *entry*)
  future evolution 136-7, *137*
  hooked to computers 143
  mechanical 120-1
  microscopic people 195
  see also computers; cybernetics; cyborgs; intelligence; senses
brainwashing 159-60, 161-2 *161*, 166
Bussard, Robert 14-15, *14*

CBW 107-8, *107*, 110
Capricorn One 197
carbon 52, *53*, 54, *55*, 82
carbon dioxide 28, 29, 55, 104
  see also greenhouse effect
catastrophes *see* holocausts
causality
  artificial gravity 81
  hyperspace 72, 73

and time 70, *71*, 74, *88*, 89, 90-1, 92-3, 94-7
  see also determinism
α (Alpha) Centauri 8, *9*, 26
cephalopods 57, *58*
CERN, Geneva 78, *78*, 79, *79*
cetaceans 49-50
τ (Tau) Ceti *9*, 26-7, 46
Charly 136
children, feral 188-9, *188*, *189*
China Syndrome, The 32-3
chronons, and chronon theory 93
civilizations, vanished 184-7
clairvoyance and clairaudience 93, 170-1
Clauser, John and Freedman, Stuart 75, *75*, 100
climate 29, 57, 114, 117
  see also greenhouse effect; Ice Ages
Clockwork Orange, A 166, *166*
clones 150-1, *150*, *151*, 159
Close Encounters of the Third Kind 58-9, *177*, 178
coal *see* fossil fuels
Colby, Kenneth *127*, 128
colonies, extraterrestrial 8, 16-17, 18, 103, 116, 201
  Dyson spheres 44-5, *45*
  see also space habitats; terraforming
comets 55, *55*, 111, 112, 191
communication 65, 103
  space 46-8, *48*, 73, 74-5, *74*, *75*, 94
  terrestrial 49-50, *49*, *50*, 57, 58-9, 62, *62*
  see also conditioning; cybernetics; social relationships; speech
computers 120-5, *124*, *132-3*, 134, 135, 142, 165-6, 200-1
  artificial intelligence and programming 127-9, *127*, *129*
  biochips 121
  data networks 125-6, *126*
  dialogue 127-8, *127*
  microchips *120*, 121, *121*
  pattern recognition 128-9, *129*
conditioning, behavioural 161-2, *161*, *162*, 165
  see also drugs
continents and continental drift 184-6, *184-5*, 187
Craft, Ian 160
crime and punishment 165-7, *165*, *166*
Cristofalco, Vincent 144
cryonics 90, 141, 147, *147*, 160, *160*
crystalline life 54
cybernetics 132-4, *132-3*
  matter transmission 135, *135*
cyborgs 134, *141*, 142-3, *142*, 154, *155*
Cygnus X-1, 84

DNA 136, *138*, 148, *148*
Dark Star 16, 111
Darker Side of Terror, The 151
data networks 125-6, *126*
Davis, Kingsley 188
Day the Earth Caught Fire, The 113
Dean Drive 192
Deluge 114
Denckla, W.D. 144
deserts 40-1, *56*, 57, 65
determinism and free will 74, 90, 98-101
  see also causality
deuterium 11, 15, 37-8, *37*, *38*, 110, 128
Dirac communicator 74, *74*
disease 33, 117, 118, 128, 147, 148, 149, 167
  see also mental illness; medicine; viruses; warfare (CBW)
Dr Strangelove 111
Dr Who 67, 130
Dole, S.H. 26-7
dolphins 49-50
Doomwatch 107
dowsers 171
Drake, Frank 46
drugs 91, 108, 160, 163-4, *163*, *164*
  antibiotic 117, 149
Dyson, Freeman 44-5, 55, 87, 98, 138
Dyson spheres 44-5, *45*

Earth 28, 29, 39
  hollow *193*, *193*
  see also climate, *etc.*
Earth II 66
earthquakes 112, *113*, 114, 193
ecology 56-7, 58, 62, 65, *65*
Edwards, Robert 160
Einstein, Albert: photons *75*, 98-9
  quantum physics 67
  see also relativity
electricity 33, 38-42 passim, *41*
  tissue regeneration 144, *144*

see also ion drive
electromagnetic catapults
  see mass drivers
electromagnetic force fields 199
electrons 68, 70, 74-5, 78, 83, 99
  at Big Bang 76-7
  electron dwellers 185
  weapons 105
ELIZA 128
Elkes, Joel 164
energy and fuel 30-45, *30-1*, 115, 167
  Big Bang 91
  black holes 85, 106
  entropy 86-7
  force fields and shields 199
  gravity 10, 19, 80-1, 82
  guns 104
  heat 34-6, *34-5*, 39-41, *40*, 82
  mass 32
  mass drivers 103
  microwaves 21, 42-3
  quantum physics 72
  renewable 39-41
  spacecraft 10, 31, 68-9
  warfare 102, 106
  see also nuclear power; solar energy
Enfant Sauvage, L' 188, *188*
entropy 34, 86-7, 91, 92, 199
ε (Epsilon) Eridani *9*, 26-7, 46
Eros (asteroid) 112
evolution and natural selection 33, 136-7, *137*, 138, 156, 186
  aliens 58-9, 65
  mutations 138-9, *138*, *139*
explosions 45, 82, 84
  antimatter 78-9, *78*, *79*
  warfare 102-3, 106, 109-11
  see also Big Bang; black holes; novae
extra-sensory perception (ESP) 137, 150, *150*, 170, 172-3, 176

FTL (faster than light)
  tachyons 70, 91, 94, *94*
  see also time travel (FTL)
faith healing 168-9, *169*
famine 117, *119*
Fantastic Voyage 194
feeding and food, 17, 25, 29, *65*, 117, *119*
  see also parasitism; predators and prey; reproduction
Feinberg, Gerald 55
fire-sending 171
firewalking 168, 169
First Men into Space 197
Fish, Marjorie *179*
flatworms *136*, 137
flight 56-7, 194, *200*
  man 22, 154, 194
floods, 113, 114, *114*, 115, 184, *185*
Fly, The 135
flying saucers *see* UFOs
Forbidden Planet 160
force fields and force shields 199
Forward, Robert L. 12-13, 55
fossil fuels 25, 30-1, *30-1*, 33, 34-6, 39, 40, 41, 115
4D Man 72
fourth dimension *see* hyperspace
free fall 10, 42, 83, *196*, 197
free will *see* determinism
freezing *see* cryonics
fuels *see* energy; fossil fuels

galaxies 76, 77, *77*, 86-7
Galaxy 8, *8*, *9*, *9*, 46
gamma ray lasers 45, 106
Ganymede 28
Geller, Uri 174, *174*
generation starships 8, 16-21, *16-17*, 25
genetic engineering 28, 148-9, *148*, *149*, 152, 159
geology 184-7, *184-5*
geothermal energy 34, 36, 39-40, *40*
giants 152, *152*, 186, 194-5, *195*
Glaser, Peter 42-5
Godzilla Vs Mothra 195
Gödel's theorem 129
Gold, Thomas 92-3
Goldhaber, M. 79
Good, I.J. 127
grasers 106
gravitons 70, 80-1
gravity 16-17, 22, 28, 80-1, 113, 196-7
  antimatter 78
  artificial, simulated 10-11, *19*, 45, 81, 191, 199
  energy 10, 19, 80-1, 82
  escape from 19, 22, 23, 84, 192
  force field 199
  SF 55, 56-7, 190, 191

stars' birth 82-5
  waves 80-1, *80*, *106*
  see also antigravity; black holes; free fall; levitation; relativity; tides
greenhouse effect 28-9, 33, 34, 36, 113, *114*, 115
Gregory, Richard 129

Hart, Ron and Setlow, R. 144
Hawking, Stephen 101, 190
Hayflick, Leonard 144
heat *see* energy (heat); temperature
heat death (of universe) 86-7, 91
  see also entropy
Heath, Robert 158
Heisenberg's Uncertainty Principle 74-5, 99
Helios 3 spacecraft *8*
helium 37, *37*, 77, 82
helium-3 11
Hermes (asteroid) 112-13
Hertzsprung-Russell diagram 26, *26*
heuristics 128
hibernation, artificial 16, 147
Hieronymous machine 169
Hill, Betty 178, *179*
Hitch-Hiker's Guide to the Galaxy 130
hive-organization 62-3, *62*, *63*
Hoff, M.E. 120
holocausts and catastrophes 102-17, *112*, *113*
  reconstruction 118-19, *118*, *119*, 139, 167, 201
humanoids 57, 58, 62, 63
  see also robots
hydrocarbons 25, *53*
hydroelectric power 40-1, 43
hydrogen *10*, 14, 37, *37*, 52, *54*, 77, *77*, 82
  bombs 37, *109*, 110
  see also deuterium; tritium
hydrogen cyanide 55
Hyperborea 186
hyperspace 72-3, *72*, *73*, 102
hypnopaedia 161
hypnotism 137, 168-9, *168*, 170, 178

Icarus (asteroid) 112-13
Ice Ages 113, 114-15, *115*, *184-5*
ice-caps 34, 40, 43, *114*
ichneumon fly 59, *60*, 61, 63
immortality 145-6
Incredible Shrinking Man, The 194, *194*
infinity and the universe 76
information industries 125-6, *125*
infra-red
  photography *36*, *175*
  radiation 27, 45, 115
insects 59, *59*, *60*, *61*
  giant 194
  hives 62-3, *62*, *63*
intelligence 46-8, 49-50, 58-9, 58, *59*, *132*, 195
  artificial 123, 127-9, *127*
  (*see also* computers)
  evolution 136-7, 138-9
interferon 148
invisibility 196, 198, *198*
Io 28
ion drive 11-12, *11*, *12*, 17
Itard, Dr 188

Jaffe, Leonard 12
Jarvik, Robert *140*
Jones, Jim *161*
Jupiter 45, 47
  life 52-3, *53*, 57
  moons, 10, 28

Kant, Immanuel 88
Kardashev, Nikolai 44, *44*
Kerr, Roy P. 95
Kirlian aura 168, *169*

Lagrange points 24
  space habitats 19-20, *19*, 22, 103
Lamb, Hubert 114
Landsberg-Park model *86*
language 58-9
  see also speech
lasers 38, *38*, 43, 196, *197*
  propulsion 10, 12-13, *13*
  weapons 102, 104-6, *104*, *105*, 199
learning ability 128-9
leisure society 156-8
Lemuria 184-6, *184-5*, 187
levitation 172, 174, *175*
light 80, 98-9, *99*
  distances (light-years) 8
  pressure 10
  spectrum 26-7, *26* (redshift), 76, *77*, 83-4